AFRICAN CONTRIBUTIONS IN SHAPING THE WORLDWIDE INTELLECTUAL PROPERTY SYSTEM

About the Author

Tshimanga Kongolo is an intellectual property researcher. He was formerly Assistant Professor, Osaka University, Osaka, Japan. His key areas of interest are International Intellectual Property Law and global IP challenges. He has published widely on these areas in books and articles in renowned international IP journals.

This well-written volume puts forward African initiatives on intellectual property matters which affect their development. The nicety of this book is that it displays in an accurate manner, present intellectual property negotiations taking place at several international organizations where the African Group is an active actor through its revolutionary initiatives in the areas of traditional knowledge, public health, and access to genetic resources. It will enable readers to well perceive the role played by Africa in this new area of international trade—trade of ideas.

Luanga Mukela Faustin, World Trade Organization, Switzerland

African Contributions in Shaping the Worldwide Intellectual Property System

TSHIMANGA KONGOLO

ASHGATE

Published by

Ashgate Publishing Limited
Wey Court East
Union Road
Farnham
Surrey, GU9 7PT
England

Ashgate Publishing Company
110 Cherry Street
Suite 3–1
Burlington
VT 05401-3818
USA

www.ashgate.com

British Library Cataloguing in Publication Data

Kongolo, Tshimanga.
African contributions in shaping the worldwide intellectual property system.
1. Intellectual property (International law)
2. Intellectual property--Africa.
I. Title

The Library of Congress has cataloged the printed edition as follows

Kongolo, Tshimanga.
African contributions in shaping the worldwide intellectual property system / by Tshimanga Kongolo.
pages cm
Includes bibliographical references and index.
ISBN 978-0-7546-7740-6 (hardback) -- ISBN 978-0-7546-9471-7 (ebook) 1. Intellectual property--Africa. I. Title.
KQC370.K66 2013
346.04'8096--dc23

2012034191

ISBN 978-0-7546-7740-6 (hbk)
ISBN 978-0-7546-9471-7 (ebk – PDF)
ISBN 978-1-4724-0425-1 (ebk – ePUB)

MIX
Paper from responsible sources
FSC www.fsc.org FSC® C018575

Printed and bound in Great Britain by the MPG Books Group, UK

Dedication
To my wife Mieko, my son Kazadi, and my daughter Awoi

Contents

Preface

Since I embarked on intellectual property research 21 years ago, my geographical boundaries of research have been defined within three realms: *international–developing countries–Africa*. My own interest in the issues related to these spheres grew when I started questioning the *raison d'être* of the current IP system for developing countries in general and African countries in particular. After several years of research, I came to the understanding that the best IP system is the one which is beneficial to all stakeholders, takes into consideration all their interests and concerns, and, in the end, is well balanced.

At the international level, this means that the outcomes of any negotiations leading to the adoption of international IP laws must be the result of this approach. This is not, however, easy to achieve.

Subsequent to the publication of my earlier book, *Unsettled International Intellectual Property Issues*, where I discussed IP issues in the international context without a particular focus on African countries, a question came to my mind about how African countries were contributing to efforts to achieve a balanced international IP system. So I decided to deepen my research and examine initiatives taken by African countries, mainly as a Group, in the negotiations of international norms. The results of that work are presented in this book.

Up until recently, the standards of most international IP norms were proposed by developed countries and were based on their own IP environment and needs. At the negotiating table, there was a clear divide between developed and developing countries. The latter were considered to be essentially powerless or, at best, to possess a limited bargaining power. Nowadays, the international IP environment has changed dramatically. In the last 15 years, the African Group has emerged as a dynamic Group on the international scene with its breakthrough proposals on many IP issues, most importantly including traditional knowledge, traditional cultural expressions, access to genetic resources, biodiversity, public health, and exceptions and limitations to copyright. Twenty years ago, no one could have imagined that Africa would become an active participant in the international consideration of IP rights, introducing influential initiatives in respect of the subject matters mentioned above.

Questions to be asked, and answered, in this book are, *inter alia*, the following: Why did the African Group take the lead in IP and public health issues? What made Africa appear at the forefront of debates and negotiations on traditional knowledge, traditional expressions of culture, and access to genetic resources and biodiversity? Why is the African Group supportive of exceptions and limitations to copyright for visually impaired persons/persons with print disabilities, for archives and libraries, and for educational and research institutions? What is the position of the African countries on the protection of life forms, the research exemption/exception to the exercise of patent rights, or genetically modified organisms? This book will provide an indispensable insight into the essential considerations of these subject matters.

This book discusses not only the African contributions in the ongoing international negotiations on these controversial and unsettled IP issues. It also puts forward African regional initiatives taken within the framework of the African Union, the African Regional Intellectual Property Organization, and the Organisation Africaine de la Propriété Intellectuelle on the subject matters mentioned above.

This book will not only assist scholars and academics concerned with international IP issues in understanding how the African nations have most recently not only contributed to but also significantly influenced the contemporary direction of discussions on IP law. It is also expected to provide both context and guidance to policy-makers from Africa or elsewhere who are interested in IP issues that are of concern to African countries.

This book is a complex work that addresses several IP issues. With the exceptions of the Introduction and the General Conclusion, each chapter/section deals with a very specific issue. The table of contents may be a useful guide to lead readers to the chapter(s)/section(s) that may address their particular interest.

One thing this author has learned in his 21 years of research, however, is that every 'single issue' or 'particular interest' about IP is inextricably linked to all the others. If this is true, then it becomes even more essential that whatever regime for the protection of IP rights is adopted by the international community, it incorporates those criteria mentioned earlier: that it is beneficial to all stakeholders, takes into consideration all their interests and concerns, and, in the end, is well balanced.

Finally, I faced a lot of challenges while writing this book. I knew exactly what to write about and how to write. But I did not know *when* to write. I am thankful to my family for allowing me to use the living room as part of my virtual office (instead of using my existing separate office at home). My children were an important part of my inspiration. I could write for an hour, play with them for 30 minutes, and then do research for another 30 minutes before writing again. I enjoyed very much this family atmosphere while doing such serious work.

Acknowledgments

The author is grateful to his wife Mieko for her support and understanding, and to his son Kazadi and daughter Awoi for their patience and for being part of the scenario with their noises while writing this manuscript, which sounded like Congolese music to him, the source of his inspiration.

The author is thankful to Mr. James Boyce, who devoted his time to edit this book and for his valuable advice.

Disclaimer

The views expressed in this book are solely those of the author and should not be interpreted otherwise.

Acronyms and Short Forms

ARIPO	African Regional Intellectual Property Organization
AU	African Union
Bangui Agreement	Agreement Relating to the Creation of an African Intellectual Property Organization of March 2, 1977 (also known as the OAPI Agreement)
Banjul Protocol	Banjul Protocol on Marks of November 19, 1993 (ARIPO)
Berne Convention	Berne Convention for the Protection of Literary and Artistic Works of September 9, 1886
CBD	Convention on Biological Diversity of June 5, 1992
EoF	Expression of folklore
ESARIPO	English-Speaking Africa Regional Industrial Property Organization (predecessor to ARIPO)
EU	European Union
GI	Geographical indication
GMO	Genetically modified organism
GRs	Genetic resources
Harare Protocol	Protocol on Patents and Industrial Designs within the Framework of the ARIPO of December 10, 1982
HIV/AIDS	Human immunodeficiency virus/acquired immunodeficiency syndrome
IGC	Intergovernmental Committee on Intellectual Property and Genetic Resources, Traditional Knowledge and Folklore (WIPO)
IP	Intellectual property
IPRs	Intellectual property rights
IRCC	Internationally Recognized Certificate of Compliance
IWG	Inter-sessional Working Group (IGC)
LDCs	Least developed countries
MAT	Mutually agreed terms
Nagoya Protocol	Nagoya Protocol on Access to Genetic Resources and the Fair and Equitable Sharing of Benefits Arising from their Utilization of October 29, 2010 (CBD)

OAPI	Organisation Africaine de la Propriété Intellectuelle (also known as the African Intellectual Property Organization)
OAU	Organization for African Unity (predecessor to the AU)
PAIPO	Pan-African Intellectual Property Organization (proposed)
Paris Convention	Paris Convention for the Protection of Industrial Property of March 20, 1883, as revised
Paris Union	States Signatories to the Paris Convention
PCT	Patent Cooperation Treaty of June 19, 1970
PIC	Prior informed consent
R&D	Research and development
SCCR	Standing Committee on Copyright and Related Rights (WIPO)
SCP	Standing Committee on the Law of Patents (WIPO)
STRC	Scientific, Technical and Research Commission (AU)
Swakopmund Protocol	Protocol on the Protection of Traditional Knowledge and Expressions of Folklore of August 9, 2010 (ARIPO)
TCEs	Traditional cultural expressions
TK	Traditional knowledge
TRIPs Agreement	Agreement on Trade-Related Aspects of Intellectual Property Rights (WTO)
TWN	Third World Network
UN	United Nations
UNDP	United Nations Development Programme
UNEP	United Nations Environment Programme
UNESCO	United Nations Educational, Scientific and Cultural Organization
UNICEF	United Nations Children's Fund
UNO	United Nations Organization
UPOV	International Union for the Protection of New Varieties of Plants
WHO	World Health Organization
WIPO	World Intellectual Property Organization
WTO	World Trade Organization

Chapter 1
Introduction

The world has changed. Africa must change and is changing. The contribution of African nations, as a group, in the setting of international intellectual property (IP) norms is more and more significant nowadays. This may be evidenced by those initiatives taken in this field by the African Group[1] that have been recently adopted as international norms or guiding principles.

Intellectual property in the sense it is widely understood today was traditionally a foreign concept to most African countries. Consequently, Africa had no say in most of the early norm-setting negotiations on IP at the international level. It largely accepted those arrangements that were based on the interests of the former colonial powers. Up until recently, most of the IP laws of African countries were based on the legal systems they had inherited during the colonial era. These laws were just the reflection of European-based IP laws without any adjustments having been made to accommodate their national conditions, needs, or interests. Most of the African countries belonging to the common law system, for instance, did not have their own IP laws during the colonial era. This was true even up until the 1990s for a number of countries. The registration of intellectual property rights (IPRs) was carried out in the United Kingdom, and that protection was extended to its colonies. At the same time, African civil law countries were very active in 'cutting and pasting' the French IP-related laws without any adjustments to their national needs and priorities.

It was obvious that these IP laws did not serve their national interests. Intellectual property rights had a very bad reputation in the developing world in general and African countries in particular. The IP system was not considered to be a development tool by those countries. Not long ago, not only was the importance of IP questioned, but so was the appropriate level of IPR protection in developing countries. There was a division of interests between the developed and developing countries.

However, circumstances changed with the globalization of the world economy and the adoption of the Agreement Establishing the World Trade Organization

1 The Member States of the United Nations (UN) are unofficially divided into five geopolitical regional groupings. The African Group, comprising 54 Members, is the largest regional group both in membership and in percentage of Members (28 percent of all UN Members). Each specialized UN agency (International Organization) is comprised of these regional groupings. This is sometimes also the case in some intergovernmental organizations, such as the World Trade Organization (WTO), which is not part of the UN family.

(WTO), including the Agreement on Trade-Related Aspects of Intellectual Property Rights (the TRIPs Agreement), which provides the so-called minimum standards of protection of IPRs applicable to all WTO Members. Before and during the negotiations that led to the adoption of this Agreement, a large number of African countries' trade negotiators were not knowledgeable about IP. Consequently, it was extremely difficult for them to perceive the implications that IP norms could have, particularly in connection with such other fields as agriculture, public health, and biotechnology. As a result, the overall 'deal' that was reached in regard to IPRs was accepted under this circumstance of ignorance.

Nowadays, the situation has improved considerably and the importance of IP is accepted worldwide, even though the conflict of interests is yet unsettled. Why have African expectations toward IP been raised in the last 15 years? Some external factors contributed to the change in perception of IP in the late 1990s, the main ones being the conflict between patent rights and public health, the need to provide adequate protection to traditional knowledge (TK), and the necessity of safeguarding genetic resources from widespread misappropriation through controlled access.

Public health-related cases challenged the *raison d'être* of the patent system by bringing to light new issues pertaining to the interface between patents and public health. The aftermath of the South African case,[2] to cite just one example, required the international community to tackle public health issues in a different manner and to increasingly consider the human face of the IP system. Africa played a very important role in the shift in perception of the relationship between IP and public health. The African Group within the WTO initiated the discussions about IP and public health in 2001 and took the lead in determining their direction. This can be perceived through the first Draft Doha Declaration on the TRIPs Agreement and Public Health, which was submitted by the African Group to the WTO and subsequently endorsed by most developing countries. As a result, it was adopted with a few amendments as the Declaration on the TRIPs Agreement and Public Health on November 14, 2001. The Decision of the General Council of WTO implementing Paragraph 6 of the Doha Declaration on the TRIPs Agreement and Public Health of August 30, 2003 attempted to respond to the concerns of African countries that lacked manufacturing capacity to produce the needed drugs to save human lives. To render this Decision permanent, the Protocol amending the TRIPs Agreement was adopted in 2005 and remains open for acceptance by WTO Members. Discussions on the relationship between public health and IP have also taken place under the auspices of the World Health Organization (WHO) through a variety of forums, and Africa's voice has been loudly heard therein. Africa expressed its views, for example, in the context of the adopted Global Strategy

2 *Pharmaceutical Company Lawsuit against the Government of South Africa*, Case number: 4183/98 of February 18, 1998, reprinted at http://www.cptech.org/ip/health/sa/pharmasuit.html (last accessed on November 26, 2012).

and Plan of Action.[3] Recently, within the World Intellectual Property Organization (WIPO), discussions on patents and health were initiated by the African Group, which requested that the Standing Committee on the Law of Patents debate this issue, among others.

The need to protect traditional knowledge (TK) and prevent its widespread misappropriation pushed the international community to debate the issue and to seek ways to resolve it. For three decades, the issue of the protection of folklore has been heavily discussed on the international scene under the auspices of WIPO and the United Nations Educational, Scientific and Cultural Organization (UNESCO) with no satisfactory outcome. The amendment of the Berne Convention for the Protection of Literary and Artistic Works in 1967 to include the international protection of unpublished and anonymous works did not provide an adequate solution. Other attempts through Model Laws in 1976 and 1982 did not bring the expected results even though they influenced a great number of laws of developing countries in general and African countries in particular. A new approach was required.

Unlike traditional cultural expressions (TCEs) or expressions of folklore (EoF), which have quite a long history of seeking appropriate systems of protection, TK is a relative newcomer in this field. The issue of the protection of TK came to light when persons who did not belong to the communities which were the traditional owners of such knowledge used it for commercial purposes without rewarding the community owners. WIPO undertook a Fact Finding Mission between 1998 and 1999 to examine the importance attached to the protection of TK. The Fact Finding Mission on TK was carried out worldwide, covering some selected countries from North to South and from East to West. Its objective was to identify and explore the IPR needs and expectations of new beneficiaries, including the holders of indigenous knowledge and innovations, in order to promote the contribution of the IP system to their social, cultural, and economic development.[4] The findings of the Fact Finding Mission revealed the urgent need to protect TK. They also demonstrated that the conventional IP system was not adequate to protect TK and to meet the expectations of TK holders. The Intergovernmental Committee on Intellectual Property and Genetic Resources, and Traditional Knowledge and Folklore (IGC) was established by the WIPO General Assembly in 2000 to deal with issues relating to IP, genetic resources, TK, and TCEs or EoF.[5] The IGC became operational in 2001.

---

3 In May 2008, the Sixty-first World Health Assembly adopted Resolution WHA 61.21: 'The Global Strategy and Plan of Action on Public Health, Innovation and Intellectual Property'.

4 See, 'Intellectual Property Needs and Expectations of Traditional Knowledge Holders' on the WIPO website at: http://www.wipo.int/tk/en/tk/ffm/report (last accessed on November 26, 2012).

5 See, *Matters Concerning Intellectual Property and Genetic Resources, Traditional Knowledge and Folklore*, WIPO Doc. WO/GA/26/6, August 25, 2000, para. 14.

The misappropriation of TK and uncontrolled access to their huge biological resources, including genetic resources (GRs), prompted African countries to take the lead at the international level on these issues. The world's dependence on biological resources puts Africa in a better position than in the past as its natural resources could serve as a bargaining tool to offset the imbalance of power with the rest of the world. At WIPO, the African Group submitted the first document on the Objectives and Principles in respect of TK and TCEs that was discussed by the IGC. Under the IGC, the African Group has taken a number of initiatives that have both changed the direction of the debates and contributed to general understanding of TK. Within the WTO, the African Group has made tremendous contributions during the discussions of TK issues, revision of TRIPs Article 27.3(b), and the relationship between the TRIPs Agreement and the Convention on Biological Diversity (CBD). The African Group supports the revision of the TRIPs Agreement to include the proposed Article 29*bis*, which would establish a requirement to disclose the country of origin of GRs, including associated TK, in patent applications.

Finally, the relationship between TK and the public domain is not yet settled given that some still consider TK to comprise part of the public domain while owners of TK continue to explore ways to gain recognition of their positive rights over their knowledge. The African Group supports narrowing the scope of the public domain in the context of TK.

The African Group has been very dynamic in the course of the ongoing discussions on exceptions and limitations to copyright that are taking place in the WIPO Standing Committee on Copyright and Related Rights (SCCR). Exceptions and limitations to copyright were set out under the Berne Convention to balance the interests of authors with the interests of society as a whole. The content of such exceptions and limitations, as well as the accepted degree or levels of free access to copyright works, have been seriously questioned with the advent and growing importance of digital production, storage, and transmission of information. In addition, the terminologies used in this regard are not always the same and meanings may differ from one concept to another. The typical examples are the 'private use', 'fair use', and 'fair dealing' concepts. The issue of access to copyright works for the purposes of education, libraries, and disabled persons has been likewise discussed in the past in the framework of UNESCO. Under the SCCR, three possible international instruments on exceptions and limitations have now been negotiated, one covering exceptions and limitations for persons with print disabilities/visually impaired persons and those with other reading disabilities, one dealing with exceptions and limitations for libraries and archives, and the other covering exceptions and limitations for educational, teaching, and research institutions and persons with other disabilities. The African Group has made a significant contribution with its proposal on the Draft WIPO Treaty on Exceptions and Limitations for the Disabled, Educational and Research Institutions, Libraries and Archive Centers. Negotiations on the international instrument on exceptions and limitations to copyright for visually impaired persons/persons with print disabilities have progressed in the right direction.

Among other issues, the protection of life forms has been one where positions of countries have not yet fully evolved. From the beginning of the discussion, African countries were reluctant to provide any protection—mainly patent protection—to life forms. This has been reiterated by the African Group on many occasions and in many forums. The same goes for the patenting of micro-organisms and non-biological and microbiological processes for the production of plants and animals. Another area where African countries have not settled their positions is the suitability of genetically modified organisms (GMOs). Discussions are ongoing in several African countries as to whether to accept or refuse the use of GMOs. The AU Model Law may be a useful guide in this respect. On the other hand, the African Group is in favor of expanding the scope of the research exemption/exception. This is also acknowledged under the national IP laws of many African countries.

Is the dynamism of African countries present at the regional level? This question will be answered by looking at the work of the existing IP organizations, namely the African Regional Intellectual Property Organization (ARIPO) and the Organisation Africaine de la Propriété Intellectuelle (OAPI). In addition to an examination of the legal framework governing the two organizations, new initiatives taken within the regional level will be scrutinized. The newly adopted Protocol on the Protection of TK and Expressions of Folklore under ARIPO is one of these. In addition, a new initiative on the protection of plant varieties is on the table under ARIPO. OAPI is also in the process of revising its legal text.

The regional level is also marked by the ambitious initiative of the African Union (AU) to set up a Pan-African Intellectual Property Organization (PAIPO). The Final Draft Statute was adopted in mid-November 2012 at the Ministerial Conference which took place in Brazzaville in November 2012. Would the proposed PAIPO add value or bring new issues? The African Model Law for the Protection of the Rights of Local Communities, Farmers and Breeders, and for the Regulation of Access to Biological Resources, adopted in 2000, has been another important contribution of the African Union. It will be examined here whether or not the Model Law has been a good guide for African countries. In addition, to guide African countries concerned about the safety and regulation of GMOs, the African Union adopted a Model Law on Biosafety in 2001 which is again under review.

At the national level, many African countries have revised their laws to comply with the TRIPs Agreement. National perspectives on various IP issues will be scrutinized to see whether African countries are managing to strategically use IP for their own benefit and also to learn whether the international dynamism of the African Group is being reflected at the national level.

The aim of this book is to highlight most of the main African contributions in the enhancement of the current international intellectual property system. It is divided into five chapters, including the Introduction and the General Conclusion. Each chapter will be divided into three to four sections.

Chapter 2, entitled 'African Countries' National Perspectives on Various Intellectual Property Issues', will address selected subject matter related to scope of protection of patents; disclosure requirements; exclusions from patentability; exceptions to patent rights, including the research exemption/exception and exhaustion of patent rights; compulsory licensing; non-traditional marks; well-known marks protection; trademarks and the Internet; exceptions to breeders' rights; TK, TCEs, and GRs; and genetically modified organisms (GMOs), taking into consideration both the existing legal systems and ongoing discussions in Botswana, Burundi, Egypt, Ghana, Kenya, Mauritius, Morocco, South Africa, and Tunisia where appropriate. The choice of those countries is based on four parameters:

- geographical representations (East, West, North, South);
- legal systems (civil law and common law);
- memberships to regional systems (Botswana, Ghana, and Kenya are Member States of ARIPO, whereas Burundi, Mauritius, Morocco, South Africa, and Tunisia are Members of neither ARIPO nor OAPI);
- adoption of new IP laws (all of these countries have adopted new IP laws or revised their laws principally to comply with the TRIPs Agreement).

Chapter 3 will deal with the situation at the regional level. How well are ARIPO and OAPI playing their roles? ARIPO was originally composed of only English-speaking African countries and OAPI of French-speaking nations. The situation has evolved now, as some of the Member States in each of the two institutions are neither English- nor French-speaking countries. Are African Members of these organizations actively engaged at the regional level in creating regional IP systems that are suitable to their needs and priorities and adaptable to their interests? To respond to these questions, a study of these regional systems will be presented. An analysis of some regional initiatives such as the newly adopted Protocol on the Protection of TK and Expressions of Folklore under ARIPO and the Draft Protocol on Plant Variety Protection will be presented before highlighting the African Model Law for the Protection of the Rights of Local Communities, Farmers and Breeders, and for the Regulation of Access to Biological Resources as well as the AU Model on Biosafety and the discussions on the establishment of the Pan-African Intellectual Property Organization.

Chapter 4, entitled 'African Initiatives at the International Level', will mainly examine various proposals, initiatives, and positions of the African Group or individual African countries in connection with matters pertaining to TK, TCEs, or expressions of folklore (EoF), GRs, biodiversity, and patents and public health in WIPO, the WTO, and WHO, where appropriate. African contributions to the ongoing debates on exceptions and limitations to copyright within WIPO will also be examined. Other selected issues of particular importance to African countries, namely protection of life forms, the patenting of micro-organisms and non-biological and microbiological processes for the production of plants and animals, the research exemption/exception, and IP and GMOs, will also be highlighted.

Chapter 5, 'General Conclusions', will summarize different findings and propose the way forward.

Chapter 2
African Countries' National Perspectives on Various Intellectual Property Issues

Introduction

The IP laws in force in most of sub-Saharan Africa today are derived from colonial laws and legal systems. It was obvious that these IP laws did not serve their national interests. After the independence of the African countries in the early 1960s, the situation did not change dramatically because for the common-law countries the United Kingdom's IP Law continued generally to apply to its former African colonial territories. Most of the African countries belonging to the common-law system did not have their own IP laws up until the early 1990s. The registration of IP rights (IPRs) was carried out in the United Kingdom, and that protection was extended to Members of the Commonwealth through a re-registration procedure in those countries.

Most African civil law countries after their independence also continued to apply the IP laws that were adopted during the colonial period to serve the interests of the colonial powers. A few African countries belonging to the civil law system adopted new IP laws in the 1980s. However, these laws were heavily influenced by the old colonial IP laws with very few adjustments reflecting things other than national interests or priorities. Intellectual property was not considered by them to be a strategic tool for development.

Following the adoption of the TRIPs Agreement in 1994—which sets the so-called minimum standards of protection of IP rights for all WTO Members—the main question is how African countries have responded to this at the national level. Now that African countries are no longer in a situation of total ignorance of the value of IP, have they adopted new laws reflecting their interests and priorities by using the so-called flexibilities incorporated in a number of international conventions, including the TRIPs Agreement? Have African countries been able to 'Africanize' the IP system to prioritize protection of TK, TCEs, and other subject matters?

This chapter will highlight the similarities and differences among African countries' handling of the following subject matters: scope of patent protection; disclosure requirements; exclusions from patentability; exceptions to patent rights; compulsory licensing in the field of patents; protection of non-traditional marks; protection of well-known marks; trademarks and the Internet; exceptions and limitations to breeders' rights; TK, TCEs, and GRs; and GMOs.

These IP issues will be discussed with reference to the IP laws of the following African countries: Botswana; Burundi; Egypt; Ghana; Kenya; Mauritius; Morocco; South Africa; and Tunisia. The choice of these countries is based on four parameters:

- geographical representations (East, West, North, South);
- legal systems (civil law and common law);
- memberships to regional systems (Botswana, Ghana and Kenya are Member States of ARIPO, whereas Burundi, Mauritius, Morocco, South Africa, and Tunisia are not Members of either ARIPO or OAPI); and
- adoption of new IP laws (all of these countries have adopted new IP laws or revised their laws principally to comply with the TRIPs Agreement).

This study of national IP regimes will be complemented in the next chapter by an analysis of the regional systems which, taken as a whole, will reflect more or less the current IP situation of 43 African countries.

The aim of this chapter is not to assess the compliance with the TRIPs Agreement of the IP laws of the selected African countries. Rather, its purpose is to underscore convergences and divergences among African countries' handling of each selected subject matter, taking into consideration international IP norms where applicable.

Scope of Protection of Patents

The subject matter of patents is clearly set out in Article 27.1 of the TRIPs Agreement. Patents shall be available for any invention in all fields of technology, provided that the invention is new, involves an inventive step and is industrially applicable.[1] Thus, any invention that does not meet the three cumulative criteria of patentability cannot be protected.[2] The assessment of the novelty of an invention is carried out by a patent office principally through comparison with the prior art which reflects the status of the technology in that field. Unlike the Paris Convention, which provided a wide discretion to the Contracting Member States to decide on the scope of patents by choosing whether or not to grant patents for pharmaceutical products, under the TRIPs Agreement such a choice is not

1 Kongolo, T. (2002d), 'Towards a New Fashion of Protecting Pharmaceutical Patents in Africa', *International Industrial Property Review and Copyright Law (IIC)* 33, 185–211. See also, Kongolo, T. (2002c), 'Morocco's Patent System and Its International Connection', *IDEA: The Journal of Law and Technology* 42:1, 181–204; and Kongolo, T. (2004), 'Compulsory Licence Issues in African Arab Countries', *The Journal of World Intellectual Property* 7:2, 185–199.

2 The laws of some countries do provide for 'utility models', 'petty patents', or 'second-tier protection' for 'inventions' that may not meet these criteria.

allowed. Members of the WTO shall fully comply with TRIPs Article 27.1 by providing protection to both pharmaceutical processes and products.

The African countries dealt with in this study make available protection of inventions in all fields of technology and have established the same criteria of patentability, which are: novelty; inventive step; and industrial application.

Among those countries, Ghana, Kenya, and Mauritius have defined either a patent or an invention or both.

The Ghanaian Patent Act defines in Section 2 both patents and invention in the following terms:

> (1) Patent means the title granted to protect an invention.
> (2) Invention means an idea of an inventor which permits in practice the solution to a specific problem in the field of technology .

According to paragraph 1 of Section 21 of the Kenyan Industrial Property Act, an invention means a solution to a specific problem in the field of technology.

Pursuant to the Patent, Industrial Designs and Trademarks Act 2002 of Mauritius, a patent is a title granted to protect an invention. The Act goes on to define an invention as an idea of an inventor which provides the solution to a specific problem in the invention's field of technology (Section 11.1).

Although patent and invention are not defined under the laws of other African countries which are subjects of this study, it is understood that an invention relates to a solution to a technical problem.

Among the criteria of patentability, the main question concerns the scope of novelty of an invention as well as the prior art coverage. It is understood that the coverage of both novelty and prior art is worldwide. Burundi's Law No. 1/13 of July 28, 2009 relating to Industrial Property clearly states in Article 4 that the state of the art shall consist of everything that has been made available to the public, regardless of the place, means or manner, prior to the date of filing of the patent application. The Industrial Property Law of Botswana, Article 8(4), states that 'for the purposes of this Act, the state of the art in relation to an invention, means anything which has been disclosed to the public, whether in Botswana or outside Botswana, in a tangible form, orally, by use or in any other way, prior to the filing or priority date of the application claiming the invention'. The Ghanaian Patent Law, Section 3(3), prescribes that prior art shall consist of everything disclosed to the public, anywhere in the world, by publication in tangible form or by oral disclosure, by use or in any other way, prior to the filing or, where appropriate, the priority date, of the application claiming the invention. The Patent Law of Tunisia adopts the same approach for a worldwide coverage. Egypt also goes in the same direction by maintaining that the invention will not be deemed new if it was already disclosed in any part of the world prior to the filing date. Another question that can be raised is whether oral disclosure is also considered 'prior art' by countries where this is not clearly provided. This question is very relevant for countries where substantive examination is carried out before a patent is issued, enabling patent examiners to assess prior art.

Under the laws of all the countries covered under this study, an invention may relate to a process or a product. Prior to the enactment of the Egyptian Industrial Property Act of 2002, under the old Patent Law of 1949, patent protection was denied to chemical inventions relating to foods and medicines. Only pharmaceutical processes could qualify for protection, so no protection was offered to pharmaceutical products. The scope of patent protection in Egypt has been extended to cover inventions in all fields of technology, including both pharmaceutical processes and products.

With regard to the 'new use' concept, also known as the 'second pharmaceutical/ medical use' or 'Swiss type claim', the availability of patent protection is a matter of public policy in each country. Countries are divided into two schools, namely those adopting protection for new uses and those denying such protection on the assumption that the knowledge is not new but forms part of the public domain. It is also argued that without the benefit of patent protection, new research into further uses of known drugs will have no or lesser incentive. Practices also vary from one jurisdiction to another. It is clear under the Intellectual Property Law of Egypt that a new application of known industrial processes may be considered to constitute an invention and will therefore qualify for protection. In other words, a new application of a known process of producing drugs may meet the conditions of patentability.[3] Under the Kenyan Industrial Property Law, a new use of an existing process or product falls into the ambit of patentable inventions. Furthermore, Morocco's Industrial Property Law expressly prescribes that a new application or combination of known methods to obtain new results not available in the prior art may qualify as an invention and be eligible for patent. Burundi's Industrial Property Law adopts a different approach in Article 17(5), which lays down that known substances for which a new use has been discovered are not eligible for patent protection. Burundi's position is quite understandable; being a least developed country, it has explicitly excluded pharmaceutical products from the scope of patent protection up until January 1, 2016. Tunisia, Ghana, Botswana, Mauritius, and South Africa are silent as to the patentability of second or new pharmaceutical/medical uses.

While the term of patent protection is set at 20 years from the filing date of a patent application, African countries have always been reluctant to extend the

3 Criteria of patentability are provided in Article 1 (Egypt) as follows: 'Patents shall be granted, in accordance with the provisions of this law, to any invention which is industrially applicable, novel and involves an inventive step, either concerning new industrial products, new industrial methods, or new application of known industrial methods. Patents shall be independently granted, for any modification, improvement or addition to a previously patented invention, provided that the conditions of novelty, inventive step and industrial application are met; in which case patents shall be granted to the owner of the amendment, modification or addition, pursuant to the provisions of the law herein.'

term for any reason. Morocco has been the pioneer among African countries to accord possible extension of the term of patents through its Industrial Property Amendment Act 2006. Accordingly, pursuant to Article 17.1, the duration of patent protection shall be extended if the patent is delivered after a period of four years from the filing date of the patent application with the Patent Office. The extension of the duration of a patent shall be equal to the number of days elapsed between the expiry date of the four years period and the actual date of grant of the patent. Such extension is registered in the National Patent Register. Further, extension of the term of protection for a patent for a pharmaceutical product has been also set out, provided that a drug license could not be obtained within the prescribed dates. Such extension will cover a period equal to the number of days elapsed between the expiry date of the deadline prescribed for granting the drug license and the actual date of its issuance. The patent holder or the representative is the one entitled to request this extension upon payment of an appropriate fee to the Patent Office (see Article 17.2). According to Article 17.3, the extension of the term of protection shall be effective upon expiry of the legal term of the patent protection without exceeding two and a half years. The main conditions for benefiting from such an extension are provided in Article 17.4. The subject matter of the extension must be:

a. the product inasmuch as it is a drug that is protected by an unexpired patent;
b. the product inasmuch as it is a drug that has been subject to an unexpired drug license in accordance with the relevant legislation and regulations in force;
c. the product has not already been subject to a certificate of extension; and that
d. the license referred to under b) is the first drug license.

Disclosure Requirements

The TRIPs Agreement recommends that WTO Members require an applicant for a patent to disclose the invention in a manner sufficiently clear and complete for it to be carried out by a person skilled in the art (TRIPs Article 29.1).

The disclosure requirement is at the core of the patent system. The applicant makes available to the public this knowledge, which then may be reproduced by another person skilled in the art. The objective of this principle is to safeguard the public interest. In other words, patent protection and the derivative exclusive rights are granted to the patentee for a period of 20 years to facilitate full disclosure of the invention. With regard to inventions related to biological resources, including GRs, another type of disclosure demanded by many developing countries is known as the disclosure of country of origin or source of the GRs or associated TK in patent applications.

While acknowledging the traditional requirement for disclosure of the invention, African countries are increasingly revising their laws to take into account the second type of disclosure, requesting a patent applicant to disclose in the patent application the country of origin of the GRs or associated TK used in the invention.

The Intellectual Property Law of Egypt sets out in Article 13 that a detailed description of the invention, including a full statement of the subject matter and of the best mode of execution of the invention by any person skilled in the art, must be furnished by the applicant. Where an invention involves biological, plant, or animal products, or traditional medicinal, agricultural, industrial, or handicraft knowledge, cultural or environmental heritage, the applicant must disclose the source. In the same manner, where the invention involves micro-organisms, the applicant shall disclose the identity of such organisms and deposit a live culture thereof with the competent authority.

Under the Kenyan Industrial Property Law, among the obligations of the applicant is the requirement to disclose the invention in a clear and complete manner, and in particular to indicate at least one mode for carrying it out (Section 53.2(a)). For inventions pertaining to living matter, Section 29 stipulates that, if an invention concerns a microbiological process or the product thereof and involves the use of a micro-organism which is not available to the public and cannot be described in the patent application in such a manner as to enable the invention to be carried out by a person skilled in the art, a culture of the micro-organism shall be deposited with a depository institution.

South Africa amended its Patent Act in 2005 to expressly include the second type of disclosure requirement. According to the Patents Amendment Act, 2005:

> (3A) Every applicant who lodges an application for a patent accompanied by a complete specification shall, before acceptance of the application, lodge with the registrar a statement in the prescribed manner stating whether or not the invention for which protection is claimed is based on or derived from an indigenous biological resource, genetic resource, or traditional knowledge or use.
>
> (3B) The registrar shall call upon the applicant to furnish proof in the prescribed manner as to his or her title or authority to make use of the indigenous biological resource, genetic resource, or of the traditional knowledge or use if an applicant lodges a statement that acknowledges that the invention for which protection is claimed is based on or derived from an indigenous biological resource, genetic resource, or traditional knowledge or use.

This requirement has been established to ascertain whether the applicant was allowed through prior informed consent to access the biological resources, including TK, and how the applicant is willing to share benefits arising from the use thereof.

Under Article 21 of Burundi's Industrial Property Act, the description of an invention must contain a clear indication of the origin of the genetic or biological resources collected in the territory of Burundi and used directly or indirectly in the making of the claimed invention as well as any element of the TK which may or may not be linked to these resources that is protected and that has been used directly or indirectly in the making of the claimed invention without the prior informed consent of its individual or joint creators.

Section 12 of the Industrial Property Law of Botswana lays down in paragraph 4 that the description set out in the application shall disclose the invention in a manner which is sufficiently clear and complete to enable a person having ordinary skill in the art to carry out the invention and shall indicate at least one mode known to the applicant by which the invention can be performed. Paragraph 5 of the same Section prescribes that where an invention refers to or involves the use of biological material that is not available to the public and cannot be described in the patent application in such a manner as to enable the invention to be reproduced by a person skilled in the art, the description shall be regarded as inadequate for the purposes of the Act unless the biological material has been deposited with a depositary institution recognized by the Minister no later than the date on which the patent application was filed at the Office or unless the application as filed contains relevant information available to the applicant on the characteristics of the biological material deposited.

According to the Ghanaian Patent Law, the description of the invention shall disclose it in a manner sufficiently clear and complete for the invention to be carried out by a person having ordinary skill in the art and shall, in particular, indicate at least one mode known to the applicant for carrying out the invention. Mauritius' Industrial Property Law has adopted an identical provision on the disclosure of the invention. Similar language is included in the Tunisian Patents Law.

Exclusions from Patentability

Article 27.2 and 3 of the TRIPs Agreement lays down exclusions from patentability and some exceptions to patent rights. The first set of exclusions aims to protect public order or morality, human, animal or plant life or health and the environment.[4] The second set deals with exclusions in the medical field and biotechnology. Each WTO Member has the discretion to define immoral behavior and acts contravening public order.

4 TRIPS Article 27.2 reads: 'Members may exclude from patentability inventions, the prevention within their territory of the commercial exploitation of which is necessary to protect *ordre public* or morality, including to protect human, animal or plant life or health or to avoid serious prejudice to the environment, provided that such exclusion is not made merely because the exploitation is prohibited by their law.'

Regarding the second set of exclusions, related to diagnostic, therapeutic, and surgical methods for the treatment of humans and animals and biotechnology, it is also up to each country whether to provide protection or to exclude these from patentability.

According to TRIPs Article 27.3, Members may also exclude from patentability:

> (a) diagnostic, therapeutic and surgical methods for the treatment of humans or animals;
>
> (b) plants and animals other than microorganisms, and essentially biological processes for the production of plants or animals other than non-biological and microbiological processes. However, Members shall provide for the protection of plant varieties either by patents or by an effective *sui generis* system or by any combination thereof. The provisions of this sub-paragraph shall be reviewed four years after the entry into force of the Agreement Establishing the WTO.

African countries covered in this study provide exclusions from patentability. The first set of exclusions protecting public order or morality, human, animal or plant life or health, and the environment is provided by most of those countries. With regard to exclusions in the medical field and biotechnology, although the common denominator is the same, the approach differs from one country to another. African countries have also included in the list of exclusions other commonly excluded subject matters not explicitly mentioned in the TRIPs Agreement.

Using the same language as the TRIPs Agreement, the laws of Egypt (Article 2.1), Tunisia (Article 9.3), and Botswana (Article 9.2.b)) exclude from the purview of protection inventions whose exploitation is likely to be contrary to public order or morality or prejudicial to the environment or human, animal or plant life or health. The Kenyan law is straightforward in disqualifying from the scope of patent any inventions deemed at the outset to be contrary to public order, morality, public health and safety, and principles of humanity and environmental conservation. Mauritius emphasizes that any commercial exploitation of an invention which is contrary to public order or morality shall not be patentable (Section 12.8). Under Morocco's Industrial Property Law (Article 24.1), inventions the publication or implementation of which would be contrary to public policy or morality are not patentable. In South Africa, a patent shall not be granted for an invention the publication or exploitation of which would be generally expected to encourage offensive or immoral behavior. Burundi likewise excludes from the ambit of patent any inventions whose exploitation would be contrary to public order or morality. Burundi, Morocco, Mauritius, and South Africa are silent on the environment-related exclusion. Is it right to conclude that in these countries any invention whose exploitation would cause prejudice to the environment may still be patentable?

All the countries dealt with provide for the exclusion related to diagnostic, therapeutic, and surgical methods for the treatment of humans or animals. The laws of Burundi, Botswana, Ghana, Kenya, Mauritius, Morocco, South Africa, and

Tunisia expressly set out that this exclusion shall not apply to preparations or in particular to products and compositions used for the purposes of the application of any such method, but Egypt does not prescribe such an exception to the exclusion. In addition, Morocco and South Africa consider these methods as not meeting the requirement of industrial application, which is one of the criteria of patentability. South Africa further maintains that in the case of an invention consisting of a substance or composition for use in a method of treatment of the human or animal body by surgery or therapy or of diagnosis practiced on the human or animal body, the fact that the substance or composition forms part of the state of the art immediately before the priority date of the invention shall not prevent a patent being granted for the invention if the use of the substance or composition in any such method does not form part of the state of the art at that date.

With regard to exclusions relating to plants and animals and essentially biological processes for the production of plants or animals, other than micro-organisms, non-biological and microbiological processes for the production of plants or animals, Egypt, Mauritius, Botswana, Burundi, South Africa, and Ghana have set out such exclusions in their laws, whereas Kenya and Morocco are silent on this matter. Unless otherwise provided elsewhere, it could be interpreted that in the latter two countries plants and animals may be subject matter of patents. If this is the case, this would be in contradiction to the general African position on patent protection of plants and animals or life forms, as will be discussed later. Tunisia includes in its law more or less the same provision provided by the larger group of countries, prescribing, however, that the provision shall not apply to biological processes used in medicine or to products obtained using such processes.

All African countries covered within this study exclude plant varieties from the purview of patent protection. Mauritius (where the draft Plant Varieties Act is still under discussion), Burundi and Ghana have not so far adopted laws on plant breeders' rights but have clearly set out in their patent laws that plant varieties are excluded from the ambit of patents. Egypt (Industrial Property Act), Kenya (Seeds and Plant Varieties Act), Morocco (provisions of Law 9-94 on the Protection of New Plant Varieties), South Africa (Plant Breeders' Rights Act No. 15 of 1976 as amended), Tunisia (Law No. 99-42 of May 10, 1999 on Seed, Seedlings and New Plant Varieties) and Botswana (Industrial Property Act) have adopted *sui generis* systems for the protection of plant varieties.[5]

Discoveries, scientific theories, mathematical methods, programs, and schemes are excluded from the purview of patents under the laws of Egypt, Kenya, Mauritius, Morocco, South Africa, Tunisia, Burundi, and Botswana. Similarly, methods for doing business, performing purely mental acts or playing games are considered non-patentable in all these countries, with the exception of Egypt which is silent on this. In addition, under the laws of Morocco, South

5 See, Kongolo T. (2006b), 'The International Intellectual Property System(s) and African Countries: Issues, Challenges and New Expectations', *African Yearbook of International Law* 12:2, 191–205.

Africa, Tunisia, and Botswana, computer programs are excluded from the scope of patent protection. There would be no question in these countries at all as to the patentability of computer programs encompassing some components that may be new, involve an inventive step and be industrially applicable.[6] As long as the operation is defined as a computer program, it is not patentable under the present Law. On the other hand, Burundi, as the only country allowing patent protection of computer programs, does so in the following terms:

> The provisions of Article 17 (which deals with exclusions) shall not apply:
>
> - to process inventions which consist in full or in part of procedures which are carried out by a computer and run by a computer program;
> - to product inventions consisting of elements of an invention implemented by computer, in particular, a machine-readable computer code stored on a material medium such as a diskette, a computer hard drive or a computer memory and a universal calculator, the novelty of which in relation to prior art primarily stems from its combination with a specific software.
>
> It is understood that persons filing patent applications concerning computer programs and inventions relating to computers covered by paragraph 1 have waived their right to any copyright protection.

In Burundi, computer programs may be protected under either patent or copyright. Article 4 of the Copyright and Related Rights Act lays down that literary and artistic works shall include: books, pamphlets and other writings, including computer programs.[7] However, a dual or cumulative protection is not permitted. The choice of the patent route will prevent the applicant from benefiting from copyright protection. This provision may in the future lead to some debate over the scope of protection and the interface between patent protection of computer programs and the copyright regime, which does not require any registration. The filing of a patent application does not guarantee the granting of a patent. Would one be denied copyright protection for a computer program by the sole fact of filing for a patent on it? What then would be the legal consequences if a patent were denied?

Mauritius, South Africa, and Botswana explicitly exclude literary, dramatic, musical, or artistic works or any other aesthetic creation from the purview of patent protection, whilst Morocco excludes only aesthetic creations. Egypt, Kenya, Burundi, Tunisia, and Ghana are silent on this subject. Such silence however does

6 See, Kongolo, T. (1999), 'Does the Congo's Copyright and Neighboring Rights Law Conflict with the TRIPs Agreement?' *The Journal of World Intellectual Property* 2:2, 311–327, at 314. See, also, Kongolo, T. (2003), 'Computer Programs Protection in Africa', *International Journal of Technology Transfer and Commercialisation* 2:2, 139–149.

7 Act No. 1/021 of December 30, 2005, on the Protection of Copyright and Related Rights in Burundi.

not imply that these types of creation, deemed as copyright works, qualify as protectable subject matter under the patent laws of these countries.

Among other exclusions, Egypt unequivocally rules out patent protection of living organisms, tissues, cells, natural biological materials, deoxyribonucleic acids (DNA), and genomes. In accordance with this provision, inventions pertaining to life forms are not patentable. Kenya excludes patent protection of public health-related methods of use or uses of any molecule or other substance whatsoever used for the prevention or treatment of any disease which the Minister responsible for matters relating to health may designate as a serious health hazard or as a life-threatening disease. Tunisia excludes all types of living substances existing in nature from patent protection. Accordingly, life forms are not subject to patent protection in Tunisia. Burundi excludes patent protection of natural substances, even if they had been purified, synthesized, or isolated in another manner. This provision does not apply to processes making it possible to isolate these natural substances from their original environment. In addition, known substances for which a new use has been discovered are excluded from the scope of patent protection.

Exceptions to Patent Rights

TRIPs Article 30 sets forth exceptions to patent rights as follows:

> Members may provide limited exceptions to the exclusive rights conferred by a patent, provided that such exceptions do not unreasonably conflict with a normal exploitation of the patent and do not unreasonably prejudice the legitimate interests of the patent owner, taking account of the legitimate interests of third parties.

Exceptions to patent rights are diverse. It is not the purpose of this section to review all exceptions provided under the laws of the African countries that are subjects of this study. Exceptions may encompass, *inter alia*, exhaustion of rights, research exemptions/exceptions, acts done only for experimental purposes, prior use, compulsory licenses, and farmers' exceptions/rights.

The 'first sale doctrine' would entail that patented rights be exhausted nationally, regionally, or internationally from the first distribution of the patented products. The choice of the regime of exhaustion is a matter of public policy. Most countries that may be considered producers of technology have opted for national exhaustion of rights, thereby prohibiting parallel imports. On the other hand, most technology importing countries have given preference to international exhaustion of rights, thereby allowing the parallel importation of patented products.

Most of the African countries covered in this study provide for exhaustion of patent rights, and most of them have adopted the regime of international exhaustion. Tunisia's Law on Patents has opted for an international exhaustion of patent rights and parallel imports by clearly stating that rights conferred to the patentee shall not extend to the advertising, import, stocking, or use of the patented product or the product obtained using a patented process done on Tunisian territory after the product has been lawfully brought onto the market in any country by the owner of the patent or with his express consent. Kenya, Burundi, and Ghana also go in the same direction by adopting an international exhaustion of patent rights and allowing parallel imports. Two provisions are provided under the law of Mauritius with regard to the international exhaustion of patent rights.[8] Through the second provision, parallel imports have been clearly acknowledged. Morocco has opted for a national exhaustion regime by applying it only to acts relating to goods covered by a Moroccan patent and performed on Moroccan territory after the good has been placed on sale in Morocco by the patent owner or with his express consent. The reason for adopting a regime of national exhaustion of patent rights in Morocco is unknown, but it may be the result of external pressures. South Africa has not elaborated much on exhaustion of patent rights. The only provision is Section 45(2) of the Industrial Property Law, which stipulates that the disposal of a patented article by or on behalf of a patentee or his licensee shall, subject to other patent rights, give the purchaser the right to use, offer to dispose of, and dispose of that article. The South African Law is silent as to the geographical limitation of rights or the extent of these rights. Botswana has provided for an international exhaustion regime of patent rights. The only particularity of Botswana's Industrial Property Law is that the rights of the patentee do not extend to acts in respect of articles which have been put on the market by another person acting with the patentee's consent or having an economic tie to the patentee. According to the law, a person having an economic tie with the patentee exists where one person may exercise, directly or indirectly, on the other a decisive influence with respect to the exploitation of the invention or where a third party may exercise such an influence on both persons. In practice, this provision may lead to confusion as 'having tie with' and 'acting on behalf of' are two different things. Egypt is silent on the exhaustion of patent rights.

Another important exception relates to the so-called research exemption/exception. African countries subjects of this study have all provided under their laws this type of exception, although terminologies may vary from one country to another. In Egypt, activities carried out for scientific research purposes are permitted and do not infringe the exclusive rights of the patentee. Another provision under the Intellectual Property Law of Egypt which may relate to the

8 Article 21(4) of the Patent, Industrial Designs and Trademarks Act 2002 of Mauritius reads (in relevant part): 'Any right under the patent shall not extend -

> *(a)* to acts in respect of articles which have been put on the market in Mauritius or in any other country by the owner of the patent or with his consent, or by any other authorised party;
>
> *(b)* in respect of articles which have been put on the market in Mauritius or in any other country or imported into Mauritius.'

research exemption/exception is the acknowledgment that any indirect uses of the production process, subject of the invention, undertaken in order to obtain other products shall not be deemed to infringe patent rights. Kenya underlines that the rights under a patent shall extend only to acts done for industrial or commercial purposes and, in particular, not to acts done for scientific research. Mauritius provides that acts done only for research and experimental purposes relating to a patented invention do not infringe patent rights. Tunisia, Ghana, and Morocco set out that acts performed experimentally that relate to the subject matter of the patented invention are not deemed to infringe patent rights. Furthermore, in Tunisia and Morocco, the individual preparation of medically prescribed drugs by dispensing chemists, or acts relating to drugs so prepared, are not considered to be infringing acts. In addition, where drugs are concerned, under the Tunisian Patent Law acts necessary for the manufacture of generic drugs are permitted, provided that the commercial exploitation of the product of those acts may not be engaged in until the term of patent protection for the original drug has expired. The main question involves the definition of 'acts necessary for the manufacture of generic drugs'. Are these preparatory acts limited to research only? In addition, what is the scope of commercial exploitation? Is it allowed to produce and stockpile these drugs before the expiry of the patent and commercialize them once the patent expires? Burundi includes experimental, scientific, and technical research as acts that do not infringe patent rights. Botswana has extensively covered exceptions pertaining to scientific purposes. The following are not deemed as infringing patent holders' rights: acts done only for experimental purposes relating to the subject-matter of the patented invention; acts done solely for academic, scientific research, educational, or teaching purposes; acts done in respect of the patented invention for purposes of compliance with regulatory marketing approval procedures for pharmaceutical, veterinary, agrochemical, or other products subjected to such procedures; and the extemporaneous preparation in a pharmacy of a medicine for an individual in accordance with a prescription given by a medical or dental practitioner and the use of a medicine so prepared. South Africa does provide an exception relating to scientific research and experimentation.

The prior use exception is provided under the laws of most of the countries covered, except Tunisia, South Africa, and Kenya where these laws are silent. The exception considers that acts performed by a person who in good faith, before the filing or, where priority is claimed, the priority date of the application on which the patent is granted in the country, was using the invention or was making effective and serious preparations for its use are not infringements of the patent rights.

With the exception of South Africa, under the laws of the countries dealt with in this study the rights under the patent shall not extend to the use of articles on aircraft, land vehicles, or vessels of other countries which temporarily or accidentally enter the airspace, territory, or waters of the country.

Morocco, Tunisia, and Botswana expressly provide that acts done for private non-commercial purposes are outside the scope of patent rights.

Botswana is the only country in this study that provides for the farmer's exception, doing so in the following terms: use by a farmer in the harvest of farm produce for propagation or multiplication by the farmer on the farmer's holding, where there has been a sale of plant propagating material to the farmer by the patentee or with the patentee's consent for agricultural use, shall not be considered to be an infringement of plant breeder's rights. In addition, use of an animal or animal reproductive material by a farmer for an agricultural purpose following a sale to the farmer, by the patentee or with the patentee's consent, of breeding stock or other animal reproductive material which constitutes or contains the patented invention shall not be deemed an infringing act.

Kenya sets out that patent rights shall not extend to variants or mutants of living forms or replicable living matter that is distinctively different from the original for which patents were obtained where such mutants or variants are deserving of separate patents (Section 58(6)).

According to the Industrial Property Law of Burundi, the acts of any person who makes, produces, uses, or sells a patented invention solely for purposes having a reasonable relationship with the gathering and transmission of the information required by a law of Burundi or another country regulating the manufacturing, use, or sale of any product do not infringe the rights of the patentee.

Compulsory Licensing in the Field of Patents

TRIPs Article 31 provides conditions that must be complied with when granting compulsory licenses. The actual term 'compulsory license' is not used in the TRIPs Agreement, which instead uses the phrase 'other use without authorization of the right holder'. Some of the conditions provided in the TRIPs Agreement are similar to those provided under the Paris Convention for the Protection of Industrial Property.[9] At the outset, what is required before applying for a compulsory license is that the third party wishing to exploit the patented invention must make efforts to enter into a license agreement with the holder of the patent under reasonable commercial terms but without being successful in doing so within a reasonable time. This requirement may be waived by a WTO Member in the case of a national emergency or other circumstances of extreme urgency or in cases of public non-commercial use. In other words, in case of a national emergency or circumstances of extreme urgency, a prior effort to conclude a normal voluntary license contract is not required. The compulsory license shall be non-exclusive and shall be granted

9 Paris Convention for the Protection of Industrial Property, of March 20, 1883, as revised at Brussels on December 14, 1900, at Washington on June 2, 1911, at The Hague on November 6, 1925, at London on June 2, 1934, at Lisbon on October 31, 1958 and at Stockholm on July 14, 1967, and as amended on September 28, 1979; available at: http://www.wipo.int/treaties/en/ip/paris/trtdocs_wo020.html (last accessed on November 26, 2012).

on the basis of the individual merit of a specific request. The right holder shall be paid adequate remuneration in the circumstances of each case, taking into account the economic value of the authorization. The need to correct anti-competitive practices may be taken into account in determining the amount of remuneration in certain cases.

Further, the compulsory license shall be authorized predominantly for the supply of the domestic market of the Member authorizing such use. Where the compulsory license is for a second patent that cannot be worked without infringing another patent, the license may be granted only if the second patent involves an important technical advance of considerable economic significance. In that case, the owner of the first patent shall be entitled to a cross-license on reasonable terms to use the invention covered by the second patent.

Generally speaking, the term of the compulsory license shall not be longer than the term of protection required for patent rights, and such license shall be terminated when the circumstances that led to its authorization cease to exist and are unlikely to recur.

Under the laws of all countries covered by this study, a compulsory license regime is set out. Situations and conditions for granting compulsory licenses may vary from one country to another. Some of the countries dealt with have covered the compulsory license regime more extensively than others. Given the degree of this disparity, this section will examine in some detail the compulsory license regime as provided in the laws of each country. A comparison will be provided in the conclusion of this section, taking into account the following elements: conditions for granting compulsory licenses; failure to work patents; failure to conclude a voluntary license; cases of national emergency or circumstances of extreme urgency; remuneration; supply of the domestic market; non-exclusivity; dependent patents; non-commercial uses; abuses of patent rights; and *ex officio* licenses.

Botswana

In Botswana, the Industrial Property Law prescribes compulsory licenses for the public interest, for competition, in case of importation of the patented products by the Government or a third party, for failure to exploit a patent and in respect of dependent patents.

Both the Minister and the High Court may grant compulsory licenses under certain circumstances. Section 31 sets out the situations and conditions under which compulsory licenses may be granted in the following terms:

> (1) The Minister may, without the consent or authority of the patentee and after giving a hearing to the patentee and any other interested party, authorise a Government agency, other person or body to exploit the patented invention on the payment of adequate remuneration to the patentee where —

(a) it is in the public interest to do so for purposes of national security, nutrition, health, development of other vital sectors of the national economy, social service; or

(b) a court or administrative body has determined that the manner of exploitation of the invention by the patentee is anti-competitive or constitutes an abuse of the patent.

(2) In the determination of adequate remuneration under subsection (1), the Minister shall take into account the economic value of the exploitation of the patented invention and the need for the elimination of anti-competitive practices.

(3) The exploitation of the patented invention under subsection (1) shall be for the supply of the domestic market in Botswana only, except where paragraph 1 or 3 of Article 31*bis* of the TRIPS Agreement applies.

(4) Upon request by the patentee, a Government agency, other person or body authorised to exploit a patented invention under subsection (1), the Minister may, after hearing the parties, vary the terms of the decision authorising the exploitation of the patented invention as circumstances may justify.

(5) The Minister may revoke a decision made under subsection (1) where, after hearing all the parties he or she is satisfied that the circumstances which led to his or her decision have ceased to exist and are not likely to recur, or that the agency, person or body has failed to comply with the terms of the decision.

(6) Notwithstanding the provisions of subsection (5), the Minister shall not terminate the authorisation to exploit the patent if he or she is satisfied that public interest as referred to in subsection (1) justifies the maintenance of his or her decision.

(7) Where a third party has been designated by the Minister to exploit a patent under this section, such exploitation may be transferred only with the enterprise or business within which the patented invention is being exploited.

(8) The authorisation to exploit a patent under this section shall not exclude —

(a) the right by the patentee to grant a licence to another person to exploit the patent; or

(b) the continued exercise, by the patentee, of his or her rights under section 24(2).

(9) A request to the Minister under subsection (4) by an agency, other person or body for an authorisation to exploit a patent under this section shall be accompanied by evidence that the patentee has received, from the person seeking the authorisation, a request for a contractual licence, and that such person has been unable, within

a reasonable time, to obtain the licence on reasonable commercial terms and conditions.

(10) Subsection (9) shall not apply in cases of national emergency or other circumstances of extreme urgency, nor in the cases mentioned in subsection (1)(*a*).

(11) Where a competition authority has determined that the manner of exploitation of a patent in the field of semi-conductor technology is anti-competitive, the Minister shall authorise the issuance of a compulsory licence if he or she is satisfied that the issuance of a compulsory licence would remedy such practice.

(12) Any person who is aggrieved by a decision of the Minister under this section may appeal to the High Court against that decision.

In Botswana, the Minister may grant compulsory licenses upon request of a third party or a Government entity without the consent of the owner of a patent under certain conditions. The evidence of failure to conclude a voluntary license with the holder of patent is required and, at the same time, the applicant's capacity to work the invention must be demonstrated. However, in case of national emergency, this is not required. The patentee is entitled to the payment of remuneration from the compulsory licensee, and the amount thereof is fixed by the Minister, taking into consideration the economic value of the invention in the market. The compulsory license is granted to predominately supply the domestic market. It is non-exclusive. It can be issued to correct an anti-competitive practice.

According to Section 32(1) of the Industrial Property Law and subject to Section 31, the Minister may issue a license to a Government agency or any authorized person for the importation of patented products (such as generic pharmaceutical products) from any legitimate alternative foreign source without the approval of the patentee in the following situations:

(a) For purposes of national security, nutrition, health, development of other vital sectors of the national economy, social service; or

(b) When the market for the patented product is not being supplied in sufficient quantities or on reasonable terms in relation to market demand.

(2) Where the importation of the patented product by a Government agency or any authorised person shall be solely for public non-commercial use within Botswana, except where paragraph 1 or 3 of Article 31*bis* of the TRIPS Agreement is applicable.

Under this provision, it is also required that the compulsory license must include the name of the pharmaceutical product and an estimate of the quantities of the pharmaceutical product to be imported during the term of the license, provided that the estimate shall not limit the quantity of the pharmaceutical product required to address the public health problem that the importation seeks to address. As for the remuneration to be paid to the patentee, the law clearly states that it should not be borne by the importer but by the exporting country in accordance with the proposed new Article 31*bis* of the TRIPs Agreement (which is not in force yet and which will be examined in Chapter 4). This acknowledgement of the proposed Article 31*bis*, which will make permanent the Decision of 30 August 2003 of the General Council relating to the 'waiver',[10] is something to follow.

In Botswana, according to Section 33(1) of the Industrial Property Law, a compulsory license may also be granted by the High Court on the request of a third party if after the expiration of three years from the date of the grant of a patent or four years from the filing date of the application, whichever occurs later, the market for the patented product is not being supplied, or is not being supplied on reasonable terms, in Botswana, unless the patentee satisfies the High Court that circumstances exist which justify the non-exploitation or insufficient exploitation of the patent.

Where the High Court grants an order for the issue of a compulsory license, it shall define the following:

- the scope and function of the license;
- the time limit for the exploitation of the patent; and
- the conditions and amount of remuneration to be paid to the patentee.

The High Court may issue a compulsory license also in the case of dependent patents. The Court will decide on the conditions, including that the invention claimed in the second patent involves an important technical advance of considerable economic importance in relation to the invention claimed in the earlier patent.

The Industrial Property Law further provides that the High Court may issue a compulsory license where a holder of a plant variety right cannot exploit his or her right without infringing a prior patent. The affected holder may apply for a compulsory license for the non-exclusive use of that prior patent, to the extent necessary to allow the exploitation of the plant variety right. This provision is quite misleading, given that in Botswana plant varieties are protected under plant breeder's rights and patents are not available for them.

Another innovation of this Law is that the High Court is empowered to grant compulsory licenses where a patentee of a biotechnological invention cannot exploit the patent without infringing a prior plant variety right. The patentee may apply for a compulsory license for the non-exclusive use of the plant variety right, to the extent necessary to allow the exploitation of such patent.

10 The Decision allows the countries in need (importing countries) to waive their obligations vis-à-vis two conditions provided under the compulsory licensing regime of the TRIPs Agreement: i.e. they are granted an exemption to the requirement to pay remuneration to the owner of the patent and are authorized to import the needed products to supply their domestic market.

Furthermore, the High Court may, on an application made to it by the patentee in respect of an earlier patent or plant breeder's right, as the case may be, grant an order for the issue of a license to use the invention claimed in the later patent or plant breeder's right. The compulsory license granted under this regime shall not be transferable except in conjunction with the transfer of the license in respect of the later patent.

In all cases, the payment of remuneration is required with regard to any compulsory license issued by the High Court.

According to Section 36(1), the Registrar or the High Court may, on the application of any interested party, invalidate a patent if it is found:

(a) that the patent is not an invention within the meaning of the term as defined under the Act;
(b) that the patentee is not a person entitled, under section 10, to apply for a patent;
(c) that the patent concerned is not patentable under section 8;
(d) that the invention is a matter which should have been excluded from patent protection;
(e) that the patentee's application did not satisfy the requirements of section 12(4), (5), (7) and (8) and corresponding regulations, or that the conditions under section 13(3) or 15 (1), where applicable, were not complied with;
(f) that the patentee failed to inform the Registrar about any corresponding foreign application filed or furnished information which in any material particular was false; or
(g) that the patent was obtained on a misrepresentation.

In accordance with Section 36(2), a claim arising from an invalidated patent shall be regarded as null and void from the date of the grant of the patent.

Burundi

The compulsory license regime is covered extensively in Burundi's Industrial Property Law. The following subjects have been provided under the law: compulsory licenses for failure to work; compulsory licenses for dependent patents; compulsory licenses granted by the Minister responsible for trade; grant of a compulsory license by the courts; appeals against decisions to grant a compulsory license; rights and obligations of compulsory license holders; limitations on compulsory licenses; and modification and withdrawal of the compulsory license.

At the request of any interested person or the Public Prosecutor's Office, submitted after the expiration of a period of four years from the date of filing of the patent application or three years as from the grant of the patent, a compulsory license or a non-voluntary license may be granted if one or more of the following conditions has been met (Article 78):

1. The public interest, in particular national security, nutrition, health or the development of other vital sectors of the national economy, so requires;
2. A judicial or administrative body has deemed that the way in which the patent holder or his licensee are exploiting the invention is abusive, anti-competitive or fails to meet reasonable conditions of demand for the protected product in sufficient quality and quantity;
3. The refusal of the patent holder to grant licenses on reasonable commercial conditions and terms;
4. The establishment or development of industrial or commercial activities suffers unfair or substantial damage.

Nevertheless, a compulsory license may not be granted if the patent holder gives legitimate grounds to justify his failure to work the invention.

According to Article 79 of the Industrial Property Law, in the event that an invention protected by a patent cannot be used without infringing the rights attached to a prior patent whose holder refuses to authorize use under reasonable commercial conditions and procedures, the holder of the subsequent patent may obtain a non-voluntary license from the court for such use, on the same conditions as those which apply to the non-voluntary licenses granted under Article 78 but also with the following additional conditions:

> The invention claimed in the subsequent patent represents significant technical progress of considerable economic interest in relation to the invention claimed in the prior patent;
> The holder of the prior patent is entitled to a reciprocal license on reasonable conditions to use the claimed invention;
> The use authorized in relation to the prior patent shall be non-transferable unless the subsequent patent is assigned as well.

The Law has empowered the Minister of Trade to issue compulsory licenses for the exploitation of the invention by the State or by a third party on its behalf without a prior consent of the patent holder. Every request for compulsory licensing shall be examined by the Minister on its own merits. Exploitation of the invention shall be limited to the purposes for which the license was granted and shall be subject to the payment, to the patent holder, of appropriate compensation according to the case at hand.

Burundi has expressly stated that decisions relating to remuneration in the case of pharmaceuticals must take into consideration procedures and conditions set out under the Decision of the General Council of the WTO of August 30, 2003 implementing Paragraph 6 of the Declaration on the TRIPs Agreement and Public Health (which will be dealt with in detail in Chapter 4).

The Minister may, at the patent holder's request and after hearing the parties, modify the terms of the decision authorizing the exploitation of the patented invention in so far as a change in circumstances warrants such modification.

The Minister of Trade may terminate a compulsory license, at the patent holder's request, if he is convinced that the circumstances which led him to take his decision have ceased to obtain and shall not reoccur or that the State service or third party appointed by him has failed to respect the terms of the decision.

The compulsory license shall always be non-exclusive and shall not prevent the exploitation of the invention by the patent holder himself by manufacturing in Burundi, by import or by both means.

When addressing a request to the Minister of Trade for the grant of a compulsory license, the applicant must always prove his failure to obtain a voluntary license on reasonable terms and conditions within a reasonable time frame. The law goes further by putting a maximum period of negotiation with the patent holder of six months from the date the patent holder was informed about the request for a voluntary license, except in exceptional circumstances. In case of a national emergency or situations of extreme urgency, or in cases of non-commercial public use or if the license is granted to remedy a practice that has been recognized as anti-competitive at the conclusion of judicial or administrative proceedings, evidence of failure to obtain a voluntary license is not required. However, in such a case, the patent holder must be informed of the decision taken.

Burundi's Law prescribes that the granting of a compulsory license for the exploitation of an invention must aim primary at the supply of the domestic market, unless the compulsory license in question relates to pharmaceutical products or processes granted in the context of the waiver established by the WTO General Council Decision of August 30, 2003,[11] in which case it should be issued in accordance with the procedures set out therein.

Compulsory licenses for the exploitation of inventions in the field of semi-conductor technology shall be granted only for non-commercial public use, unless the compulsory license has been granted to prevent anti-competitive conduct.

In the event of dependent patents, a cross license must be granted.

In Burundi, the commercial court is also entitled to grant compulsory licenses under certain conditions. The request must contain:

- the name and address of the applicant;
- the title of the patented invention and the patent number for which the compulsory license is sought;
- proof that the industrial exploitation of the patented invention does not meet reasonable conditions of demand for the protected product;
- proof that the applicant first wrote by registered letter to the patent holder asking him for a contractual license, but was not able to obtain such a license from him on commercial conditions and procedures within a reasonable time frame;
- proof that the applicant is capable of industrially exploiting the patented invention.

11 See, ibid.

Egypt

A compulsory or non-voluntary license regime is provided by Law No. 82/2002. The situations and conditions for granting compulsory licenses as set forth under the Paris Convention and the TRIPs Agreement are incorporated into this Law. Articles 23 and 24 deal with compulsory licenses, while Article 25 sets out conditions for the expropriation of patents by the competent authority.

According to Article 23, the Patent Office is empowered to issue compulsory licenses for exploitation of an invention by a third party upon the approval of a Ministerial Committee. The latter decides the financial rights (remuneration) of the patent owner.

A compulsory license may be issued in the following circumstances as provided in Article 23:

(1) Where the competent Minister finds that the exploitation of the patent is required in the following situations:
  (a) Public non-commercial use (including the preservation of national security, health, environment and food security)
  (b) Cases of emergency or circumstances of extreme urgency
  (c) Support of national efforts in vital sectors for economic, social and technological development, without unreasonable prejudice to the rights of the patent owner and taking into consideration the legitimate interests of third parties.

(2) Upon the request of the Minister of Health, when the quantity of patented medicines made available fail to adequately meet the national needs, due to their poor quality or if they are offered at a prohibitive price, or if the patent is related to medicines addressing critical cases, incurable or endemic diseases or products used in the prevention of these diseases, or where the invention is related to the medicines, their manufacturing process, the raw materials necessary for their preparation or the process of manufacturing of those materials.

(3) Where the patent owner refuses to grant [a] license to a third party seeking the exploitation of the invention, whatever the purpose of the exploitation, and despite the offer of suitable terms and the lapse of [a] reasonable negotiation time.

(4) If the owner of the patent fails to exploit the invention in Egypt, himself or through a third party with his consent; or if the patent was not sufficiently exploited after the lapse of four years from the filing date of the application or three years since the grant of the patent, whichever comes later; or if the patent owner suspended, without a valid reason, the exploitation of the patent for more than one year.
The exploitation of a patent may be carried out through the manufacturing of the patented product or the use of the patented process in Egypt.

Nevertheless, where the Patent Office finds that, despite the expiration of either of the above mentioned time limits, failure to exploit the invention was due to legal, technical or economic reasons out of [the] control of the owner of the patent, he may be granted another grace period to exploit the invention.

(5) If it is determined that the patent owner has abused or exercised the rights conferred by the patent in a manner that is contrary to fair competition, such as:

(a) Fixing exorbitant prices for the patented products or preferential treatment of agents with regards to prices and sales conditions.

(b) Failure to supply the local market with the patented product, or supplying it under prohibitive terms.

(c) Stopping the production of the patented item or its production in a disproportionate manner, given the production capacity and the market needs.

(d) Undertaking acts or practices which have adverse effect on the free competition, according to the prescribed legal norms.

(e) Exercising of the rights conferred by this Law in a manner that adversely affects the transfer of technology.

(6) Where the exploitation of an invention by the legitimate patent holder requires inevitably the use of another invention, underlying concrete technical advance as well as technical and economical significance compared to the other, he shall be entitled to obtain a non-voluntary license for the exploitation of the other invention, in which case the other patent holder shall equally have the same right.

Under the circumstances identified in Article 23(1)(a) and (b), a prior negotiation is not required. However, what is important is that the patent owner must be notified promptly in the three cases of public non-commercial use, emergency use and use for economic, social, or technological development reasons. This is also required in other cases, such as compulsory licenses granted for public health purposes. In other cases or situations, reasonable efforts to obtain voluntary licenses from the owner of the patent must be evidenced.

Another provision that may raise some concerns is the requirement that the patent must be worked in Egypt. Failure to exploit the patented invention in Egypt may oblige the Patent Office to grant to a third party a compulsory license after the lapse of a certain time, as prescribed in Article 23(4). Nevertheless, a grace period may be provided.

In the case of abuse of exclusive rights by means of dishonest commercial practices, a compulsory license may be granted to a third party without prior negotiations with the owner of the patent. Furthermore, the Patent Office may revoke the patent if, two years after the grant of a non-voluntary license for its exploitation, it becomes clear that the grant of that license was not adequate to remedy the adverse effects caused to the national economy by the patent owner's abuse of his rights or his unfair competition practices. Any concerned party may challenge the revocation of a patent before the Committee provided for in Article 36 and in accordance with the conditions and procedures prescribed in the Regulations (Article 23(5)(e)).

Article 24 sets out conditions that must be complied with prior to the grant of a compulsory license or after its issue. Pursuant to these provisions, where a compulsory license is to be issued, the following elements shall be taken into account:

(1) A request for the grant of the non-voluntary license shall be considered on the merits of each case. The license shall mainly seek to satisfy the needs of the domestic market.

(2) The requesting party shall prove that he has made serious attempts during a reasonable period of time to obtain a voluntary license from the patent holder against fair compensation, and that he failed.

(3) The patent owner may, within one month from his notification of the grant of the license, appeal to the Committee provided for in Article 36 and in accordance with the conditions and procedures stipulated by the Regulations, against the decision to grant the non-voluntary license to a third party.

(4) The party requesting the grant of a compulsory license, or the party to whom a compulsory license is granted, must be able to exploit the invention in a serious manner in Egypt.

(5) The licensee must abide by the scope, terms and period prescribed by the decision granting such a license. The Patent Office may extend the duration of the license if it expires without achieving its purpose.

(6) The use of [the] compulsory license shall be limited to the applicant; the Patent Office may however grant it to a third party.

(7) The beneficiary shall not assign the rights of a compulsory license to a third party except with the enterprise or the part [thereof] related to the exploitation of the patent.

(8) The patent owner shall be entitled to an adequate remuneration for the exploitation of his invention. The amount of the remuneration shall be fixed on the basis of the economic value of the invention. He shall have the right to appeal against the compensation assessment, within 30 days of being notified the decision, before the Committee provided for in Article 36, in accordance with the rules and procedures prescribed by the Regulations.

(9) The compulsory license shall lapse on the expiry date. Nonetheless, the Patent Office may decide to terminate the compulsory license if the reasons which led to its grant cease to exist and are unlikely to reoccur; in which case, the procedure prescribed by the Regulations shall apply.

(10) The patent owner may request the termination of the compulsory license before its expiry, if the reasons which led to its grant cease to exist and are unlikely to reoccur.

(11) Where a compulsory license is terminated before its term, the legitimate interests of the licensee shall be taken into account.

(12) The compulsory license may be terminated or its terms amended by the Patent Office or upon a request from any interested party, if within two years after the grant of the compulsory license, the licensee fails to exploit the subject matter of the license or to meet his obligations as prescribed by the license.

Ghana

The compulsory licensing regime provided in Ghana is *mutatis mutandis* very similar to that of Botswana in terms of both contents and structure. Compulsory licenses may be granted by the Minister or by the Court under certain conditions and situations, and these are the same as those stipulated in the Law of Botswana.

The only main difference between the compulsory licensing regimes set out by the laws of Ghana and Botswana is that the former does not contain any provisions relating to the proposed Article 31*bis* of the TRIPs Agreement nor for compulsory licenses issued in relation to patents and plant varieties or breeder's rights.

Kenya

Situations and preconditions for the grant of compulsory licenses are set forth under the Industrial Property Act. The Act also provides for the use of patented inventions by the Government or on its behalf by third parties (*ex officio* license).

Sections 72 and 73 lay down two situations that may entail a grant of a compulsory license: in cases of non-working; and in cases of dependent patents.

Section 72 provides as follows:

(1) At any time after four years from the filing date of an application or three years from the grant of a patent, whichever period last expires, any person may apply to the Tribunal for a licence to exploit the patented invention on the grounds that a market for the patented invention is not being supplied on reasonable terms in Kenya.

(2) Notwithstanding subsection (1), a non-voluntary licence shall not be granted if the owner of the patent satisfies the Tribunal that circumstances exist which justify the fact that the market for the patented invention is not being supplied, or is not being supplied on reasonable terms, in Kenya.

According to this provision, a patent which is not worked within the prescribed period and where the owner failed to justify the reasons of the failure to work the invention, may enable a third party to apply for a compulsory license,

Section 73 provides as follows:

> (1) Where a patented invention cannot be worked without infringing the rights derived from an earlier patent, the owner of the latter patent may request the Tribunal at any time for the grant of a compulsory licence with respect to the earlier patent to the extent necessary for the working of his invention, if the invention constitutes an important technical advance of considerable economic significance in relation to the invention claimed in the earlier patent.
> (2) The owner of the first patent shall be entitled to a cross-licence on reasonable terms to use the invention claimed in the second patent.
> (3) The use authorized in respect of the first patent shall be non-assignable except with the assignment of the second patent.
> (4) In this section, 'earlier patent' or 'first patent' means a patent granted on an earlier application or benefiting from an earlier validly claimed priority date, and 'latter patent' or 'second patent' shall be construed accordingly.

In case of dependent patents, a cross license between the two parties is always considered as the best approach.

Regarding preconditions for the grant of a compulsory license, the Act lays down two conditions and one exception in Section 74 as follows:

> (1) A compulsory licence shall not be granted unless the person requesting the licence—
> *(a)* satisfies the Tribunal that he has asked the owner of the patent for a contractual licence but has been unable to obtain the licence on reasonable commercial terms and within a reasonable time; and
> *(b)* offers guarantees satisfactory to the Tribunal to work the relevant invention sufficiently to remedy the deficiencies or to satisfy the requirements which gave rise to his request.
> (2) The requirement under subsection (1)*(a)* shall be waived in the case of a national emergency or other circumstances of extreme urgency, provided the owner of the patent shall be so notified as soon as is reasonably practicable.

An effort to secure a voluntary license from the owner of the patent is the prerequisite before any compulsory license is issued to a third party. This requirement is waived in case of a national emergency or other circumstances of extreme urgency.

Provisions for the grant and terms of compulsory licenses are set forth in Section 75, which provides as follows:

> (1) In considering a request for a compulsory licence, the Tribunal shall decide whether a compulsory licence may be granted and shall then, if

it decides in favour of the grant taking into account any terms agreed by the parties, proceed to fix the terms which shall be deemed to constitute a valid contract between the parties and shall be governed by the provisions of contractual licences.

(2) In fixing the terms under subsection (1), the Tribunal shall ensure that the compulsory licence—

(*a*) is limited, in scope and duration, to the purpose for which it was authorized, and in the case of semi-conductor technology, shall only be for public non-commercial use or to remedy a practice determined after a judicial or administrative process to be anti-competitive;

(*b*) is limited predominantly for the supply of the domestic market;

(*c*) does not entitle the licensee to grant further licences, without the consent of the owner of the patent;

(*d*) is non-exclusive; and

(*e*) provides for the payment to the owner of the patent of remuneration which is equitable with due regard to all the circumstances of the case, including the economic value of the licence.

(3) A representative of the Institute and of the Government shall have the right to appear and be heard at the hearing of an application for a compulsory licence, before the Tribunal.

The Industrial Property Tribunal is entitled to grant compulsory licenses based on the following terms. The compulsory license must:

- be limited in scope and duration;
- not entitle the licensee to grant further licenses;
- be non-exclusive; and
- provide for the payment of remuneration to the owner of the patent.

Furthermore, a compulsory license may be transferred only with that part of the industrial undertaking or its goodwill in which the relevant invention is used and upon the acceptance of the Tribunal (Section 76). If all these conditions and terms are not met, the compulsory license may be cancelled (Section 77).

Part XI of the Industrial Property Act deals with the exploitation of patented inventions by the Government or third persons authorized by the Government. Pursuant to Section 80, where the public interest, in particular national security, health, environmental conservation, or the development of other vital sectors of the national economy, so demands, or if the manner of exploitation of an invention is not competitive, the competent Minister may order the exploitation of a patent by a Government Ministry, a public entity or a third party designated for that purpose. Still, in any case of *ex officio* licensing, remuneration must be paid to the owner of the patent. The amount of remuneration is fixed by the Managing Director of the Kenya Institute of Industrial Property.

Mauritius

Two types of compulsory licenses are provided under the Patent, Industrial Designs and Trademarks Act 2002: exploitation of the patent by the Government or a third party on its behalf; and the non-voluntary license regime.

Two situations may entail exploitation of a patent by the Government or a third party on its behalf: cases of the public interest, including national security, nutrition, health, or the development of other vital sectors of the national economy; and anti-competitive practices of a patent owner (Section 23.1).

Section 23(1) provides as follows:

> (1) Where the competent authority—
> (*a*) is satisfied that the public interest including, national security, nutrition, health or the development of other vital sectors of the national economy so requires; or
> (*b*) has, on the application of any party, determined that the manner of exploitation, by the owner of the patent or his licensee, is anti-competitive and that it is necessary to remedy such anti-competitive practice, it may, upon a request being made, authorise, even without the agreement of the owner of the patent, a Government agency or a third person to exploit the patented invention.

In both cases, reasonable remuneration is to be paid to the patent owner. In the first situation, the competent authority shall take into account the economic value of the authorization and, in the second, the need to correct anti-competitive practices. It is required under the law that the competent authority hears the patent owner or any interested party before making its decision (Section 23.3). The person seeking the authorization must prove a failure to obtain a voluntary license from the patent owner on reasonable commercial terms and within a reasonable time (Section 23.4). However, the requirement of prior negotiation with the patent owner does not apply in cases of national emergency or other circumstances of extreme urgency, for public non-commercial use or where it is necessary to remedy anti-competitive practices.

With regard to the non-voluntary license regime, all the common situations and conditions prescribed under the TRIPs Agreement and most national patent laws are set forth in Section 24 of the Act, which provides as follows:

> (1) Upon request made to the Controller after the expiration of a period of 4 years from the date of filing of the patent application or 3 years from the date of the grant of the patent, whichever period expires last, the Controller may issue a non-voluntary licence if he is satisfied that the patented invention is not exploited or is insufficiently exploited, by working the invention locally or by importation, in Mauritius.

(2) Notwithstanding subsection (1), a non-voluntary licence shall not be issued if the owner of the patent satisfies the Controller that circumstances exist which justify the non-exploitation or insufficient exploitation of the patented invention in Mauritius.

(3) The decision issuing the non-voluntary licence shall fix—
(a) the scope and the function of the licence;
(b) the time limit within which the licensee must begin to exploit the patented invention; and
(c) the amount of the adequate remuneration to be paid to the owner of the patent and the conditions of payment.

(4) The holder of the non-voluntary licence shall—
(a) have the right to exploit the patented invention in Mauritius according to the terms set out in the decision issuing the licence;
(b) commence the exploitation of the patented invention within the time limit fixed in the said decision; and
(c) thereafter, exploit the patented invention sufficiently.

(5) Where—
(a) the invention claimed in a patent (later patent) cannot be exploited in the country without infringing a patent granted on the basis of an application benefiting from an earlier filing or, where appropriate, priority date (earlier patent); and
(b) the invention claimed in the later patent involves an important technical advance of considerable economic importance in relation to the invention claimed in the earlier patent; the Controller, upon the request of the owner of the later patent, may issue a non-voluntary licence to the extent necessary to avoid infringement of the earlier patent.

(6) Where a non-voluntary licence is issued under subsection (5), the Controller, upon the request of the owner of the earlier patent, shall issue a non-voluntary licence in respect of the later patent.

(7) In the case of a request for the issuance of a non-voluntary licence under subsections (5) and (6), subsection (3) shall apply *mutatis mutandis* with the proviso that no time limit needs to be fixed.

(8) In the case of a non-voluntary licence issued under subsection (5), the transfer may be made only with the later patent, or, in the case of a non-voluntary licence issued under subsection (6), only with the earlier patent.

(9) The request for the issuance of a non-voluntary licence shall be subject to payment of a prescribed fee.

(10) Sections 23(2) to 23(12) shall apply *mutatis mutandis* to a non-voluntary licence issued under this section.

This law creates a kind of confusion between the *ex officio* license or exploitation of the patent right by the Government or by a third party on its behalf and the normal compulsory licensing regime based on the request of a third party.

Morocco

The Industrial Property Law sets out two types of compulsory licenses, namely compulsory licenses and *ex officio* licenses.

Pursuant to Article 60, a compulsory license may be accorded to a third party after a period of three years from the granting of a patent or four years from the filing date in the following circumstances:

> • in case of non-working of the patented invention on the territory of Morocco;
> • if patented products are not commercialized in sufficient quantity to satisfy the need of the Moroccan market; or
> • if working or commercialization of the patented invention in Morocco has been abandoned for more than three years.

Articles 61 and 62 set forth conditions for the grant of a compulsory license. Article 61 provides as follows:

> The application for a compulsory license shall be made to the court. It must be accompanied by evidence establishing that the applicant has been unable to obtain a license from the owner of the patent amicably under reasonable conditions and commercial terms and that he is in a position to work the invention in order to satisfy the needs of the Moroccan market.

Article 62 provides as follows:

> A compulsory license may only be non-exclusive.
> Any compulsory license shall be granted mainly for the supply of the Moroccan market.
> It shall be granted on conditions laid down by the court, particularly in respect of its duration and its field of application, which shall be limited to the purposes for which the license has been granted, and to the amount of royalties to be paid in respect thereof. Those royalties shall be laid down on a case-by-case basis, taking into account the economic value of the license.
> Those conditions may be amended by the court on a request by the owner or by the licensee.

The interested party should first seek amicably to conclude a license with the patentee, and the interested party must prove that he/she has the means to exploit the patented invention to satisfy the needs of Morocco's market. The compulsory license shall be non-exclusive and should be accorded principally to supply the national market. The court is competent to grant a compulsory license and to fix the amount of royalties to be paid to the patent owner.

Article 63 provides as follows:

> Where the circumstances that led to the grant of a compulsory license cease to exist and are unlikely to reoccur, the license to work may be withdrawn, subject to adequate protection of the legitimate interests of the licensees. The court may review, at the reasoned request of any party having an interest therein, whether the circumstances continue to exist.
> If the holder of a compulsory license does not comply with the conditions under which such license was granted to him, the owner of the patent and, where appropriate, the other licensees may request the court to withdraw that license.
> Any assignment of rights deriving from a compulsory license shall be subject, on pain of nullity, to the authorization of the court.

If the court realizes that the compulsory license is no longer necessary for various reasons, it may suspend or terminate it. Another reason for suspension or termination of the compulsory license may be the non-satisfaction by the licensee of the requirements (and conditions) stipulated by the court prior to the grant.

Other situations in which a compulsory license may be granted are laid down in Article 66 as follows. Where an invention protected by a patent cannot be worked without infringing rights deriving from an earlier patent of which the owner refuses a license under reasonable conditions and commercial terms, the owner of the later patent may obtain from the court a compulsory license under the same conditions as set out in Articles 60–62 above, provided that:

> (a) the invention claimed in the later patent represents substantial technical progress and economic interest in relation to the invention claimed in the earlier patent;
> (b) the owner of the earlier patent shall be entitled to a reciprocal license under reasonable conditions in order to use the invention claimed in the later patent;
> (c) the license relating to the earlier patent shall be assignable only if the later patent is also assigned.

Under Morocco's Industrial Property Law, another type of compulsory license, called the *ex officio* license, is provided. This type of compulsory license may be applied for or granted for public health reasons, for national defense purposes, or when there is a need to satisfy the national economy. In all those situations, the owner of the patent must be notified and due remuneration must be paid.

Article 67 provides as follows:

> Where the interests of public health demand, patents granted for medicines, for processes for obtaining medicines, for products necessary in obtaining such medicines or for processes for manufacturing such products may be worked ex officio in the event of such medicines being made available to the public in insufficient quantity or quality or at an abnormally high price.

> Ex officio working shall be ordered by administrative act at the request of the office responsible for public health.

Article 75 provides as follows:

> The State may at any time obtain ex officio, in order to meet its defense requirements, a license to work an invention that is the subject matter of a patent application or a patent, whether the working is to be done by the State itself or on its behalf.
> The ex officio license shall be granted at the request of the administration responsible for national defense by means of an administrative act.
> That act shall lay down the conditions of the license, but excluding those relating to the amount of royalties to be paid in consideration thereof. The license shall take effect on the date of the request for an ex officio license.
> Failing amicable agreement between the patent owner and the administration concerned, the amount of the royalties shall be laid down by the Administrative Court of Rabat.

Article 71 provides as follows:

> The competent administration may issue formal notice to the owners of patents other than those referred to in Article 67 above to work them in such a manner as to satisfy the needs of the national economy.

South Africa

Under the South African Patent Act, a compulsory license may be granted in two situations: in respect of dependent patents (Section 55); and in case of abuse of patent rights (Section 56).

Section 55 provides as follows:

> Where the working of a patent (hereinafter referred to as a dependent patent) without infringement of a prior patent is dependent upon the obtaining of a licence under that prior patent, the proprietor of the dependent patent may, if agreement cannot be reached as to such licence with the proprietor of the prior patent, apply to the commissioner for a licence under the prior patent, and the commissioner may grant such a licence on such conditions as he may impose, but including a condition that such licence shall be used only for the purpose of permitting the dependent patent to be worked and for no other purpose: Provided that the commissioner shall not grant such a licence unless—
> (a) the invention claimed in the dependent patent involves an important technical advance of considerable economic significance in relation to the invention claimed in the prior patent;

(b) the proprietor of the dependent patent granted the proprietor of the prior patent on reasonable terms a cross-licence to use the invention claimed in the dependent patent; and

(c) the use authorised in respect of the prior patent is not assignable except with the assignment of the dependent patent.

Section 56 sets out situations that may be considered to constitute abuse of the exclusive rights of the patentee and which may therefore lead to the issuance of a compulsory license to any interested party. These include the following:

(1) Any interested person who can show that the rights in a patent are being abused may apply to the commissioner in the prescribed manner for a compulsory licence under the patent.

...

(2) The rights in a patent shall be deemed to be abused if—

(a) the patented invention is not being worked in the Republic on a commercial scale or to an adequate extent, after the expiry of a period of four years subsequent to the date of the application for the patent or three years subsequent to the date on which that patent was sealed, whichever period last expires, and there is in the opinion of the commissioner no satisfactory reason for such non-working;

...

(c) the demand for the patented article in the Republic is not being met to an adequate extent and on reasonable terms;

(d) by reason of the refusal of the patentee to grant a licence or licences upon reasonable terms, the trade or industry or agriculture of the Republic or the trade of any person or class of persons trading in the Republic, or the establishment of any new trade or industry in the Republic, is being prejudiced, and it is in the public interest that a licence or licences should be granted; or

(e) the demand in the Republic for the patented article is being met by importation and the price charged by the patentee, his licensee or agent for the patented article is excessive in relation to the price charged therefor in countries where the patented article is manufactured by or under licence from the patentee or his predecessor or successor in title.

...

(4)

(c) A licence granted under this section shall include a provision that, subject to adequate protection of the legitimate interests of the licensee, the licence shall, on application by the patentee, be terminated if the circumstances which led to its grant cease to exist and, in the opinion of the commissioner, are unlikely to recur.

(5) Any licence granted under this section shall be non-exclusive and shall not be transferable except to a person to whom the business or part of the business in connection with which the rights under the licence were exercised has been transferred.

Section 78 provides that an invention may be acquired by the State for defense reasons.

Tunisia

The Patent Law of Tunisia has limited the rights of patentees by allowing the Minister responsible for industry, on a proposal by the authorities concerned, to rule that notwithstanding the grant of a patent, capital goods, accessories, and spare parts relating to the patent in question may be imported for non-commercial purposes to safeguard the public interest. This limitation for non-commercial purposes coupled with the public interest is provided generally under the heading of compulsory licensing.

Article 50 provides the general rule regarding dependent patents by stipulating that without prejudice to the provisions of Article 67 of the Law (compulsory licenses) the owner of a patent relating to an improvement made to an invention already patented may not work his invention without the authorization of the owner of the earlier patent, who himself may not exploit the patented improvement without the authorization of the owner of the improvement patent.

Another obligation placed on the patentee is to work or exploit the invention. Pursuant to Article 51, the owner of the patent is obliged to work the patented invention within a period of four years from the filing of the application or three years from the grant of the patent, whichever period is longer, except where the product to which the invention relates is subject to prior administrative marketing approval, in which case the period shall be extended by two years following the expiry of the periods mentioned.

Pursuant to Article 69 of the Tunisian Law, any interested party may, after the expiry of the period provided for in Article 51, obtain a compulsory license at any time in any of the following cases:

- where the invention to which the patent relates has not started to be worked industrially in Tunisia, or where no real and effective preparations have been made for such working, within the period provided for in Article 51 of this Law;
- where the product which is the subject matter of the invention has not been marketed in sufficient quantities to meet the needs of the Tunisian market;
- where the industrial or commercial exploitation of the invention to which the patent relates has been abandoned for more than three years in Tunisia.

In no event shall a compulsory license for non-working or insufficient working be granted if the owner of the patent provides evidence of a legitimate excuse.

It is prescribed in Article 70 that any application for the grant of a compulsory license shall be filed with the competent court. The law requests that the applicant provide evidence of failure to contract a voluntary license with the holder of patent rights on reasonable terms and conditions or within a reasonable period.

The compulsory license shall be non-exclusive. The rights deriving from the license may only be transferred together with the business, the company or the part of the company to which they are attached.

It is required under the Law that before appearing in the court for the grant of a compulsory license the applicant must convey a copy of the writ of summons by registered letter with advice of receipt to the entity responsible for industrial property within a period of 15 days from the date of the summons to appear before the competent court. The legal representative of the entity responsible for industrial property may submit to the court a memorandum containing his observations on the application for a compulsory license.

The court shall lay down the conditions governing the compulsory license, including in particular its duration, its scope, and the amount payable to the owner of the patent, which shall be proportionate to the importance of the working of the invention. These conditions may be amended by order of the court at the request of the owner of the patent or the beneficiary of the compulsory license where new circumstances dictate.

Any legal decision taken in connection with compulsory licenses shall be immediately notified to the entity responsible for industrial property by the licensee. Final decisions shall be entered directly in the National Register of Patents.

Ex officio licensing is also provided under the Tunisian Law in the context of compulsory licensing. Where the Minister in charge of industry observes that a patentee has not worked his/her patented invention to meet the needs of the national economy or to safeguard the environment, he may request the patent holder to undertake working of the patent within one year. Where the non-working or the qualitative or quantitative inadequacy of the working undertaken seriously prejudices economic development and the public interest, the patent to which the notice relates may be made subject to the *ex officio* license regime by order of the Minister responsible for industry, unless the owner of the patent provides proof of legitimate reasons attributable to the demands of the national economy.

Where public health interests dictate, patents granted for drugs, for the products necessary for the production of such drugs or for processes for the manufacture of such products may, where the drugs are made available to the public at levels of quality or quantity that are inadequate or at abnormally high prices, be made subject, at the request of the Minister responsible for public health, to the *ex officio* license regime by order of the Minister responsible for industry.

The State may at any time, for the purposes of national defense or national security, obtain an *ex officio* license for the exploitation of an invention covered by a patent application or patent, whether that exploitation is engaged in by itself or through a third party.

The *ex officio* license shall be granted at the request of the Minister concerned by order of the Minister responsible for industry. That license shall be granted by order of the said Minister on specific conditions, notably regarding its duration and scope, but to the exclusion of the financial remuneration payable to the owner of the invention. In the absence of amicable agreement, remuneration shall be fixed by the court. The *ex officio* license shall be non-exclusive. The rights deriving from that license may only be transferred together with the business or the company or part of the company to which they are attached.

The owner of the patent may apply for the withdrawal of the *ex officio* license for failure to comply with the obligations imposed on the licensee.

Conclusion

The laws of Botswana, Burundi, Egypt, Ghana, Kenya, Mauritius, Morocco, South Africa, and Tunisia all provide compulsory licensing regimes. In most of these countries, two types of compulsory licenses are set out, namely compulsory or non-voluntary licenses and *ex officio* licenses, though under the laws of some countries different terminologies may be used.

The granting authorities vary from one country to another. Three governmental entities may be empowered to grant compulsory licenses, namely the Patent Office, the relevant Ministry, and the courts. Most of the countries dealt with empower the relevant Ministry to issue *ex officio* licenses and the courts to issue normal compulsory licenses.

The prerequisite of an effort to conclude a voluntary license and failure to do so on reasonable terms and conditions is provided under the laws of all the countries dealt with. What is interesting is that Burundi has set the maximum reasonable period of negotiation at six months from the date of request of the applicant to conclude a voluntary license with the holder of a patent.

This effort is not required in case of national emergency or circumstances of extreme urgency. It is also clear under these laws that a situation of national emergency is a ground for issuing a compulsory license. In addition, the patent holder is entitled to remuneration in whatever circumstances.

Failure to work a patent within a certain period of time is included in most of these laws as a situation that may lead to the grant of a compulsory license, unless the patent holder proves his/her inability to exploit the patented invention for legitimate reasons.

Abuses of patent rights by the holder of a patent may be considered a situation that can lead to the grant of a compulsory license to a third party. Not all countries have included such a provision in their laws, and the definition of what shall be considered abuse differs from one country to another.

It is provided under the laws of all of these countries that compulsory licenses must be issued predominantly to supply the domestic market.

Compulsory licenses are non-exclusive and not transferable. In case of dependent patents, cross licensing is recommended if the second patent is important for the national economy.

Most of the countries have included public health concerns as a ground for issuing a compulsory license or an *ex officio* license.

Non-Traditional Marks

Article 15 of the TRIPs Agreement defines what may constitute a trademark and establishes the scope of protection. TRIPs Article 15(1) prescribes as follows:

> Any sign, or any combination of signs, capable of distinguishing the goods or services of one undertaking from those of other undertakings, shall be capable of constituting a trademark. Such signs, in particular words including personal names, letters, numerals, figurative elements and combinations of colours as well as any combination of such signs, shall be eligible for registration as trademarks. Where signs are not inherently capable of distinguishing the relevant goods or services, Members may make registrability depend on distinctiveness acquired through use. Members may require, as a condition of registration, that signs be visually perceptible.

Any sign that is not appropriated may be used by anyone as a trademark, provided that it is distinctive. It is likewise stipulated in the same Article that a country may condition the registrability of a mark upon the visibility of the sign.

Nowadays, with the development of new technologies, a new category of trademarks, called 'non-traditional marks', has been generated. Falling under this category are both visible signs and non-visible signs. The following are deemed to be visible signs: three-dimensional marks; color marks; position marks; gesture marks; holograms; titles of films or books; motion or multimedia signs; and slogans. Non-visible signs include, *inter alia*: sound marks; olfactory marks (smell marks); taste marks; and feel or texture marks.

It is questionable whether the existing (conventional) trademark system is able to provide adequate protection to non-traditional marks. In addition, it is still unclear how to apply the well-established trademark principles to non-traditional marks. The protection or registration of non-traditional marks has given rise to several important issues. Conflicts between the traditional trademark system and the protection of these new types of marks are more evident in the realm of non-visible signs. A large number of trademark laws set out that the sign shall be visible or perceivable by the eyes in order to qualify for trademark protection. Furthermore, the general principle is that a trademark shall be graphically represented in order to be eligible for registration. How is it possible to represent graphically a non-visible sign? Is the mere description of a non-visible sign able to serve that purpose?

In order to avoid prospective conflicts, one may say that the easiest approach would be to deny protection to non-traditional marks because it is difficult to accommodate them within the purview of the conventional trademark system. However, this reasoning is likely to prove unrealistic because it is undeniably true that non-traditional marks are gaining more popularity amongst competitors, and consumers may well consider a non-traditional mark to be a valuable source identifier and information provider.

Meanwhile, it is true that if all five human senses become hostage to business and trade, concerns over the availability of marks as well as other issues pertaining to the public interest and the public domain are likely to come to light. Consequently, it may seem reasonable to establish some limitations within the existing trademark system in order to delineate the scope of protection of these non-traditional marks. Some adjustment of the existing trademark system to accommodate these new marks is clearly required. Overprotection of non-traditional marks, however, is not acceptable, as this would undermine the entire system.

A number of countries have already provided protection for non-traditional marks, particularly for three-dimensional marks. On the other hand, a large number of countries are reluctant to grant protection to non-visible signs, such as olfactory marks (smell marks), taste marks, feel marks and sound marks, on the ground that they cannot be represented graphically and also that they may not be inherently distinctive.

Most of the countries dealt with in this study have generally excluded non-visible signs and single-color marks from the purview of protection. However, Article 133 of the Industrial Property Law of Morocco defines trademarks and service marks and enumerates items that may constitute signs in the following terms:

> For the purposes of this Law, a trademark or a service mark means a sign capable of graphic representation which serves to distinguish the goods or services of a natural or legal person.
>
> The following, in particular, may constitute such a sign:
>
> (a) Denominations in all forms, such as: words, combinations of words, surnames and geographical names, pseudonyms, letters, numerals, abbreviations;
> (b) Figurative signs such as: devices, labels, seals, selvedges, reliefs, holograms, logos, synthesized images; shapes, particularly those of a product or its packaging or those that identify a service; arrangements, combinations or shades of color;
> (c) sound signs such as: sounds, musical pieces;
> (d) olfactory marks.

Pursuant to these provisions, any sign which is capable of being represented graphically and which serves to distinguish products or services of one undertaking from those of others may constitute a trademark or a service mark. Under the same provisions, and following the 2006 amendment of the Industrial Property Law, sound marks and olfactory marks (smell marks) have been included as signs that may qualify as trademarks. In addition, only a combination of colors is protectable; no protection is available for a single color. Given that graphical representation of a mark is a *sine qua non* for the registration of a mark, the main question here is how sound marks and olfactory marks could be graphically represented to meet this condition.

Under the Kenyan Trademarks Act, Section 19 stipulates that a trademark may be limited in whole or in part to one or more specified colors and in any such case the fact that it is so limited shall be taken into consideration by the court or the Registrar having to decide on the distinctive character of the trademark. In addition, if and so far as a trademark is registered without limitation of color, it shall be deemed to be registered for all colors. South Africa provides a similar provision in Section 32 of its Trademarks Act.

Under the laws of Egypt and Mauritius, marks that are not visible may not be registered as trademarks. Consequently, most non-traditional marks—those non-visible signs such as smell marks, sound marks, taste marks, and feel marks—may not be registered as trademarks. Single colors may be excluded on the ground that the law prescribes for 'combination of colors' to constitute a trademark, if such combination is distinctive enough. In Burundi, in the event that the mark consists of a sign that is not visually perceptible, the application must contain a graphical representation of the mark. This reproduction must be specific and may not consist of a mere general description of the sign. This provision of the Industrial Property Law of Burundi may lead to two confusions. Graphical representation is required for any mark to be registered, on the one hand, and requesting a graphical representation for non-visible marks ignores the difficulty in registering these kinds of marks as they are not able to be graphically represented. Consequently, in countries where these marks are registered, what is required is a description of the mark (not a graphical representation) to enable the trademark office to appraise the mark's qualification for registration. Burundi's Law needs to be more explicit on this.

According to Article 288 of Burundi's Industrial Property Law, a mark may not be validly registered if it is not capable of distinguishing the goods or services of one undertaking from the goods or services of other undertakings. The smell, taste, or any other material characteristic of a product shall not be deemed to distinguish the product if these are the normal result of the product's ordinary composition. By interpretation of this provision, it can be said that in Burundi smell and taste may be considered as distinguishing signs if they are not descriptive. Tunisia sets out that signs may consist of phonetic signs such as musical tunes and sentences. In other words, in Tunisia sound marks are protected as trademarks, provided that they are distinctive.

Well-Known Marks Protection

According to Article 6*bis* of the Paris Convention, registration of a mark may be refused or cancelled if it constitutes a reproduction, an imitation, or a translation, liable to create confusion, of a well-known mark in connection with identical or similar goods. A likelihood of confusion is presumed. TRIPs Article 16(2) and (3) requires WTO Members to accord special protection to well-known trademarks or service marks in accordance with the Paris Convention. These provisions have extended the protection of well-known marks to services and to dissimilar goods or services, provided that there is a likelihood of connection or association and that the prior owner of the registered mark (well-known mark owner) is likely to suffer damage by such use.[12] They further add that account shall be taken of the knowledge of the trademark in the relevant sector of the public, including knowledge in that Member obtained as a result of the promotion of the trademark.

Hence, the TRIPs Agreement has expanded the ambit of applicability of well-known marks not only to services but also to goods or services which are not similar but when use of a mark would mislead consumers by associating the infringing mark with the well-known mark. There is a presumption of likelihood of association or connection. Thus, under the TRIPs Agreement, WTO Members must consider different sectors as well when determining whether a mark conflicts with a well-known one.

The Joint Recommendation Concerning Provisions on the Protection of Well-Known Marks[13] provides guiding norms that Member States of the Paris Union and/or WIPO may consider and implement at the national level. In its Article 2(1)(b), the Joint Recommendation sets out factors to be considered in determining whether or not a mark is well known. These factors are, *inter alia*, the degree of knowledge or recognition of the mark in the relevant sector of the public; the duration, extent, and geographical area of any use of the mark; the duration, extent, and geographical area of any promotion of the mark, including advertising or publicity and the presentation, at fairs or exhibitions, of the goods and/or services to which the mark applies; the duration, extent, and geographical area of any registrations, and/or any applications for registration, of the mark, to the extent that they reflect use or recognition of the mark; the record of successful enforcement of rights in the mark, in particular, the extent to which the mark was recognized as well known by competent authorities; and the value associated with the mark.

---

12 See, Kongolo, T. (2002), 'Are Well-Known Marks well known in African Countries?', *Journal of World Intellectual Property* 5:2, 273–289.

13 Joint Recommendation Concerning Provisions on the Protection of Well-Known Marks, adopted by the Assembly of the Paris Union for the Protection of Industrial Property and the General Assembly of the World Intellectual Property Organization (WIPO) at the Thirty-Fourth Series of Meetings of the Assemblies of the Member States of WIPO, September 20–29, 1999, WIPO, Geneva, 2000; available at: http://www.wipo.int/about-ip/en/development_iplaw/pdf/pub833.pdf (last accessed on December 3, 2011).

A general limitation is that if a trademark has been registered in good faith, in accordance with the Paris Convention, the owner of the well-known mark has at least five years to claim the cancellation. However, if the mark is registered in bad faith in order to gain unfair advantages or to mislead consumers as to the origin of the products or services, no time limit applies to such claim.

As seen, there is no worldwide definition of what constitutes a well-known mark. Well-known marks being specific to each country, it is appropriate to deal with each country's practice separately.

Botswana

In Botswana, a mark shall not be registered if it is identical to, or confusingly similar to, or constitutes an imitation, translation, or transliteration of a mark or trade name which is well known in Botswana for identical or similar goods or services of another enterprise, or if it is well known in Botswana for goods or services which are not identical or similar to those in respect of which registration is applied for if the use of the mark in relation to those goods or services should indicate a connection between them and the owner of the well-known mark and the interests of the owner of the well-known mark would be prejudiced by such use. Due regard shall be given to the knowledge of the mark in the relevant sector of the public, including knowledge which has been attained as a result of the promotion of the mark.

Burundi

As in other countries covered in this study, in Burundi a mark shall not be registered if it is identical or similar to such an extent that it leads to confusion with a trademark or name that is widely known in Burundi for identical or similar goods of another undertaking. Nor may it be registered if it constitutes a translation of such a trademark or name or if it is widely known and registered in Burundi for goods or services which are not identical or similar to those for which the registration of the mark is sought, provided that the use of this mark for these goods or services indicates a connection between said goods or services and the holder of the registered mark and that this use is likely to harm the interests of the holder of the registered mark. The knowledge of the mark in the relevant sector of the public is not referred to by the law.

Egypt

In accordance with the Paris Convention and the TRIPs Agreement, Egypt's Law No. 82/2002 establishes protection for well-known marks in two different ways:

- in case of identical products; and
- in case of non-identical products.

The owner of a trademark which is well known in Egypt and worldwide shall enjoy the protection prescribed in the Law even if such mark has not been registered in Egypt. The Trade Registry Department shall, *ex officio*, reject any application to register any mark which is identical with a well-known mark and which is intended for products which are identical with those of the well-known mark, unless the application for registration is filed by the owner of the well-known mark.

This provision applies to applications intended for products which are not identical with those of the well-known mark where the well-known mark is registered in a country Member of the WTO and in Egypt, and where the use of the mark in relation to those non-identical products is meant to lead people to believe that a connection exists between the owner of the well-known mark and those products and such a use may be prejudicial to the interests of the owner of the well-known mark.

For trademarks pertaining to identical products, a prior national registration of the well-known mark in Egypt is not required for it to benefit from special consideration and protection. If a trademark is deemed a well-known mark in Egypt, the Trade Registry Department shall *ex officio* reject the registration of any identical trademark for identical products unless the application is filed by the owner of the well-known mark.

However, in respect of trademarks pertaining to non-identical products, a prior registration of the well-known mark in Egypt and in one of the Members of the WTO is required for it to be awarded special protection. A likelihood of association or connection between the confusing mark and the well-known mark must be apparent. The fulfillment of three conditions is required for a well-known mark to be acknowledged special protection for non-identical products:

- Registration of the well-known mark in Egypt and in one of the countries Members of the WTO;
- Existence of a likelihood of connection or association between the well-known mark and the confusing mark; and
- Use or connection prejudicial to the legitimate interests of the owner of the well-known mark.

The Law has not explicitly mentioned service or service marks in relation to well-known marks. Is it correct to interpret the law in a broad sense and include service marks as provided under the TRIPs Agreement?

Ghana

A mark will not be registered if it is identical to or confusingly similar to or constitutes a translation of a trademark or trade name which is well known in the country for identical or similar goods or services of another enterprise. Nor may such a mark be registered if another trademark is well known and registered in the country for goods or services which are not identical or similar to those under application but the use of the new trademark would indicate a connection between those goods or services and the owner of the well-known trademark and the interests of the owner of the well-known trademark are likely to be damaged by the use of the new trademark.

Kenya

Protection of well-known marks is provided under the Trademarks (Amendment) Act 2002 as follows:

> (1) Reference in this act to a trademark which is entitled to protection under the Paris Convention or the WTO Agreement as a well-known trademark, are to a mark which is well known in Kenya as being the mark of a person who-
> (a) is a national of a convention country; or
> (b) is domiciled in, or has a real and effective industrial or commercial establishment in, a convention country, whether or not that person carries on business or has any goodwill in Kenya.
>
> (2) Subject to the provisions of Section 38B, the proprietor of a trademark which is entitled to protection under the Paris Convention or the WTO Agreement as a well-known trademark, is entitled to restrain by injunction, the use in Kenya of a trademark which is identical or the essential part of which is identical or similar to his, in relation to identical or similar goods or services, where the use is likely to cause confusion among the users of the goods or services.
>
> (3) Nothing in subsection (2) shall affect the continuation of any *bona fide* use of a trademark begun before the commencement of this section.
>
> (4) A trademark shall not be registered if that trademark, or an essential part thereof, is likely to impair, interfere with or take unfair advantage of the distinctive character of the well-known trademark.

In Kenya, protection of well-known marks is set out for both goods and services. The law is silent as to the likelihood of association between a mark for dissimilar goods and/or services and a well-known mark.

Mauritius

In Article 36.2(e) and (f) of the Patent, Industrial Designs and Trademarks Act 2002, well-known marks have been granted special protection in accordance with the Paris Convention and the TRIPs Agreement. Registration may be barred or cancelled for identical or similar goods or services and for non-identical or dissimilar goods or services as provided below:

36.2 No mark shall be registered, where it –

...

(e) is identical with, or confusingly similar to, or constitutes a translation of, a mark or trade name which is well known in Mauritius for identical or similar goods or services of another enterprise;

(f) is registered in Mauritius for goods or services which are not identical or similar to those in respect of which registration is applied for, provided, in the latter case, that use of the mark in relation to those goods or services would indicate a connection between those goods or services and the owner of the well-known mark and that the interests of the owner of the well-known mark are likely to be damaged by such use.

In the case of goods or services identical or similar to those associated with well-known marks, the confusing marks will not be registered to prevent misleading consumers. In the case of goods or services which are non-identical or dissimilar to those associated with the well-known marks, a likelihood of association or connection with the well-known marks may damage the interests of the owner of the well-known marks, which must be avoided.

Morocco

According to Article 162 of Industrial Property Law No. 17-97, the owner of a well-known mark within the meaning of Article 6*bis* of the Paris Convention may claim cancellation of the registration of a mark liable to lead to confusion with his own mark. Such nullity proceedings must be commenced no later than five years after the registration date of the mark, unless registration was applied for in bad faith.

The law does not elaborate very much in regard to well-known marks. It has not defined a well-known mark and has not limited the extent of its application. Further, the law is silent as to the conditions set out under the TRIPs Agreement relating to the likelihood of association or connection with well-known marks.

South Africa

Section 35 of the Trademarks Act lays down the protection system for well-known marks in conformity with the Paris Convention as follows:

(1) References in this Act to a trademark which is entitled to protection under the Paris Convention as a well-known trademark, are to a mark which is well known in the Republic as being the mark of—

(a) a person who is a national of a convention country; or

(b) a person who is domiciled in, or has a real and effective industrial or commercial establishment in, a convention country, whether or not such person carries on business, or has any goodwill, in the Republic.

(1A) In determining for the purposes of subsection (1) whether a trademark is well known in the Republic, due regard shall be given to the knowledge of the trademark in the relevant sector of the public, including knowledge which has been obtained as a result of the promotion of the trademark.

(2) A reference in this Act to the proprietor of such a mark shall be construed accordingly.

(3) The proprietor of a trademark which is entitled to protection under the Paris Convention as a well-known trademark is entitled to restrain the use in the Republic of a trademark which constitutes, or the essential part of which constitutes, a reproduction, imitation or translation of the well-known trademark in relation to goods or services which are identical or similar to the goods or services in respect of which the trademark is well known and where the use is likely to cause deception or confusion.

(4) Where, by virtue of section 10(8), the authorization of the competent authority of a convention country or an international organization is required for the registration of a mark as a trademark, such authority or organization is entitled to restrain the use in the Republic of such a mark without such authorization.

According to this Section, due consideration must be given to the knowledge of the trademark in the relevant sector of the public, and the owner of a well-known mark is entitled to prevent the use of similar or identical signs for goods or services which are identical or similar to those associated with his well-known mark. The law is silent as to the likelihood of association or connection as prescribed under the TRIPs Agreement.

In addition, there are some limitations to the protection of well-known marks based on prior use, as follows:

> Nothing in this Act shall allow the proprietor of a trademark entitled to protection of such trademark under the Paris Convention as a well-known trademark, to interfere with or restrain the use by any person of a trademark which constitutes, or the essential parts of which constitute, a reproduction, imitation or translation of the well-known trademark in relation to goods or services in respect of which that person or a predecessor in title of his has made continuous and bona fide use of the trademark from a date anterior to 31 August 1991 or the date on which the trademark of the proprietor has become entitled, in the Republic, to protection under the Paris Convention, whichever is the later, or to object (on such use being proved) to the trademark of that person being registered in relation to those goods or services under section 14.

This provision may bar owners of well-known marks from preventing the use of similar or identical marks that have acquired a secondary meaning through use before August 31, 1991.

Tunisia

Unlike other countries, Tunisia has not elaborated in detail on the protection of well-known marks. Article 5 of the Trademark Law sets out that a sign shall not be registered as a mark if it represents an infringement of a prior right, especially a well-know mark. Further, in Article 11, the Law stipulates that the application for trademark registration may be opposed by the owner of a previous well-known mark. The Law prescribes in Article 25 that the user of a well-known mark with respect to goods or services which are not similar to those listed in the registration shall be held liable for civil responsibility if this results in damage to the owner of the well-known mark or if this use represents an unjustifiable exploitation of the mark. The Law further maintains that this provision shall be implemented in accordance with international agreements ratified by the Republic of Tunisia.

Trademarks and the Internet

The protection of a mark is territorial, and the decision whether or not to register a mark lies within the discretion of each country. Also, signs that are registered as trademarks for particular products or services in one country may be freely used in countries where there is no protection unless the mark in question qualifies as a well-known mark. Any signs or marks will be considered to be part of the public domain in the countries where they are not registered or protected.

The Internet has a global nature. Any information uploaded onto the Internet is in principle accessible to/by anyone and from anywhere. The Internet is a market where all business actors are present. Trademarks being a major business tool, it is obvious that all competitors will use their trade/service marks on the Internet to sell their products or to provide services. The global nature of the Internet brings about new issues pertaining to the use of trademarks and related infringements. The scope of the public domain may be limited or expanded depending on how territorial 'use' of a mark on the Internet is defined. The question arises how a trademark could be deemed to be used in a particular country if it is used via the Internet. Borrowing the terminology of WIPO's Joint Recommendation Concerning Provisions on the Protection of Marks, and Other Industrial Property Rights in Signs, on the Internet,[14] the 'commercial effect' may be determinant

14 Joint Recommendation Concerning Provisions on the Protection of Marks, and Other Industrial Property Rights in Signs, on the Internet, Adopted by the Assembly of the Paris Union for the Protection of Industrial Property and the General Assembly of the World Intellectual Property Organization (WIPO) at the Thirty-Sixth Series of Meetings of

in defining 'use' and the scope of the public domain in connection with the use of marks on the Internet. Article 3 of the Joint Recommendation sets forth non-exhaustive factors for determining 'commercial effect':

- business circumstances;
- level and character of commercial activity;
- connection of an offer of goods or services on the Internet with the Member State;
- connection of the manner of use of the sign on the Internet with the Member State; and
- relation of the use of the sign on the Internet with a right in that sign in the Member State.

The determination of 'territorial use' on the Internet may vary from one country to another and from one jurisdiction to another. Some countries have opted for different components to define this use, such as 'targeted customers', 'substantial effect on commerce', 'purpose and effect of the use', and 'commercial market'.

The use of marks on the Internet has been further complicated by the occurrence of new forms of trademark infringement which have raised questions about the liability of search engines for the sale of trademarks as keywords as well as the liability of Internet auction sites which offer trademarked goods for (re)sale.

It will be interesting to see how, in the short run, African countries will regulate the use of marks on the Internet and the new issues brought about by the Internet in the field of trademarks.

Among the pioneers, Botswana's Industrial Property Law, in defining what constitutes use of a mark in the course of trade, has clearly included:

- use of the mark on the Internet or other electronic communication media or networks open to the public, where the use is intended for Botswana or has a commercial market in Botswana; and
- adoption or use of the mark as part of a domain name or other similar identification or designation on the Internet or other electronic communication media or networks open to the public.

The most important element in determining the 'territorial use' of a mark via the Internet in Botswana is 'the commercial market' in Botswana.

---

the Assemblies of the Member States of WIPO, September 24 to October 3, 2001; available at: http://www.wipo.int/about-ip/en/development_iplaw/pub845.htm (last accessed on February 15, 2012).

Exceptions and Limitations to Breeders' Rights

The TRIPs Agreement, in determining the purview of patent protection, has recommended that WTO Members provide protection for inventions in all fields of technology and to set out protection for plant varieties by means of either patents, an effective *sui generis* system or any combination thereof. While it grants Members the discretional authority to exclude plants and animals, other than micro-organisms, and essentially biological processes for the production of plants or animals, other than non-biological and microbiological processes, from the ambit of patent protection, the TRIPs Agreement nonetheless acknowledges the necessity of protecting new varieties of plants.

This section will highlight exceptions and limitations to breeders' rights as provided under the laws of some of the countries dealt with that have provided a *sui generis* system of protection of new varieties of plants. Among those exceptions, a close look will be taken at the farmer's exception.

Egypt, Kenya, Morocco, South Africa, and Tunisia have provided *sui generis* systems for protection of plant varieties. The conditions for such protection are the same in each of these: novelty; stability; uniformity/homogeneity; and distinctiveness.

Exceptions and limitations are also provided within each of these systems. Non-commercial activities and activities related to experiments and scientific research purposes are set out by all of these countries to fall outside the ambit of the exclusive rights of the breeder. Activities related to teaching and training are also permitted in Egypt and Tunisia. By interpretation, it can be said that those activities are also permitted in other countries, given the broad scope that scientific activities may encompass.

With the exception of Kenya and Tunisia, the farmers' exception is set out under the laws of the countries providing the *sui generis* system of protection, albeit in somewhat different terms. In Egypt, the law stipulates that protection shall not prevent third parties from carrying out non-commercial activities and permits the use of the result of propagating material by farmers on their own holdings for private propagating purposes. Morocco's law exempts acts done by farmers for breeding or propagation purposes, on their own holdings, using the proceeds of the harvest which they have obtained by the cultivation of the protected variety, except for trees, ornamental plants, and flowers. South Africa maintains that a person who has procured any propagating material of a variety in a legitimate manner does not infringe the plant breeder's right in respect of the variety if he or she is a farmer who uses harvested material obtained on land occupied by him or her from that propagating material for purposes of propagation on the same land. At the same time, it prohibits use of harvested material obtained from the replanted propagating material for purposes of propagation by any person other than that farmer.

In Egypt, activities of breeding, cross-breeding, and selection for the purpose of breeding new varieties are permitted by the law and may be undertaken by a third party without the consent of the breeder. In Morocco, acts done in the process of creating a new variety are permitted, provided that the protected variety is not used repetitively or that the new variety does not derive from the essentially protected variety and is distinct from the protected variety. Kenya permits acts undertaken to develop new varieties in the breeder's own nursery, and such acts shall not be deemed to be at variance with the exclusive right of the holder of plant breeder's rights. Kenya sets out another limitation in Section 20(2) of its Seeds and Plant Varieties Act as follows:

> Paragraph (a) of subsection (1) of this section shall not apply to the sale of reproductive material which is not in Kenya when it is sold, but if any person purchases such material outside Kenya and uses it in Kenya as reproductive material, the purchase and subsequent use shall together constitute an infringement of the plant breeder's rights and the purchaser shall be liable to be proceeded against in respect of such infringement, and reference in this subsection to using reproductive material of a plant variety as reproductive material in Kenya includes reference to so disposing of that material (otherwise than by way of sale) while it is in Kenya as to make it available for use in Kenya as reproductive material.

In South Africa, a person who procured any propagating material of a variety in a legitimate manner is not considered to infringe the plant breeder's right in respect of the variety if he or she uses or multiplies that propagating material in the development of a different variety.

Other exceptions and limitations are specific to each country. In Egypt, according to Article 199 of the Law on the Protection of Intellectual Property Rights (Book Four on Plant Varieties), the Minister of Agriculture may, on the recommendation of the Ministerial Committee, limit the exercise by the breeder of all or some of his rights provided for in the Law in any manner with the aim of safeguarding the public interest and, in particular, if it appears that the protected plant variety:

> (a) has harmful effects on the natural environment, the safety of biological diversity, the agricultural sector, the life or health of humans, animals or plants, in Egypt; [or]
>
> (b) has harmful economic or social effects, hampers local agricultural activities, or it appears that its use is incompatible with the values and beliefs of the community.

In South Africa, a person who has procured any propagating material of a variety in a legitimate manner shall not infringe the plant breeder's right in respect of the variety if he or she resells that propagating material or, under certain conditions, sells any plant, reproductive material, or product derived from that propagating material for purposes other than the further propagation or multiplication thereof.

A compulsory licensing regime is provided in respect of plant varieties in all these countries, although this may be available under different circumstances, such as to safeguard the public interest, where the breeder fails to produce the variety on his own or in case of non-exploitation of the protected variety or to provide others propagating material of the protected variety, where he refuses to grant third parties a license for the exploitation of the variety despite the offer of appropriate terms and conditions, where he practices unfair competition, or if he has not commercialized the variety in sufficient quantity to satisfy the needs of the domestic market. In Tunisia, for instance, certain new plant varieties of extreme importance for the life of man or animals may be subject to a compulsory authorization to exploit.

The breeder is entitled to fair compensation for the use and exploitation by third parties during any compulsory licensing period.

Traditional Knowledge, Traditional Cultural Expressions, and Genetic Resources

This section will address TK, TCEs, and GRs in the context of those African countries which have adopted any legal mechanism for their protection or are in the process of adopting one. No reference will be made to folklore or expressions of folklore protected under the copyright system by some of the countries covered in this study. The countries covered in this section therefore include only Botswana, Burundi, Kenya, and South Africa.

Botswana

Botswana provides in Part XII of its Industrial Property Law protection for traditional knowledge and handicrafts. Only a few provisions of this Law will be covered here because this author questions its very *raison d'être* as it fails to respond to the expectations of TK holders. From the definition to the registration process, the established protection is far from what may be called a *sui generis* system of protection of TK and handicrafts. The established system is closer to a patent system.

Traditional knowledge is defined under the law as an idea, knowledge, practice, use, or invention, written or unwritten, which may be associated with biological diversity and is a cultural, traditional, or spiritual belief or value of a group of people.

According to Article 115 of the Industrial Property Act:

> (1) Traditional knowledge shall be registered together with a description of such knowledge where —
>
> *(a)* it has not been disclosed to the public through any means; or

> *(b)* if it has been disclosed, such disclosure has not led to any commercial or industrial exploitation in Botswana.
>
> (2) A description shall disclose traditional knowledge in a manner which is sufficiently clear and complete to permit any third party to reproduce or utilize the traditional knowledge to obtain results similar or identical to those obtained by the holder of such traditional knowledge.
>
> (3) Any element of traditional knowledge may be registered separately or individually in conformity with its technical characteristics without prejudice to its holistic nature, or as a whole in its integrity combining, if necessary, all elements of traditional knowledge into a single registration.

This provision says that TK shall be registered in order to be protected and, in addition, that the TK should not have been disclosed by any means prior to such registration. If it has been already disclosed, it can still be registered, provided that there is no commercial or industrial exploitation of the TK in Botswana.

Pursuant to this Law, a local traditional practitioner, a representative of any local community or any individual may apply to register traditional knowledge. Where two or more local communities that occupy the same territory have created and are in possession of identical or similar elements of traditional knowledge, they may register those elements individually, on behalf of each community.

The beneficiary of protection is the owner of the TK. Where traditional knowledge is collectively owned, rights over it shall be exercised and enjoyed collectively in accordance with cultural practices. However, local communities which have registered individually for similar or identical elements of TK shall have the option to exercise and enjoy their rights over the traditional knowledge individually.

An applicant community which comprises individuals from different countries, including Botswana, shall have the right to register and acquire rights over TK in Botswana and in the other countries.

The Law indicates that protection of registered TK shall expire when it has lost its value in the following circumstances:

> *(a)* as an element of cultural identification;
>
> *(b)* as a result of willful and expressed abandonment by its owner or owners; or
>
> *(c)* as a result of non-use or use in a distorted manner by third parties of which the owner or owners are aware.

The exclusive rights conferred on the owners of TK are similar to the exclusive rights provided to any IPR holder without any consideration of the special nature of TK. In a similar fashion, exhaustion of rights is dealt with as if TK were a patent or trademark. This is disappointing. Under the Law, no person shall distort registered TK in any way, especially by distortion of the spiritual or cultural identity of a community that owns the TK or by any act that implies direct or indirect use of the knowledge for any purpose, including scientific or academic research, without the owner's consent. On the other hand, the Minister may, on grounds of the public interest, after hearing any local community that owns TK, authorize the scientific, commercial, or industrial exploitation of that knowledge or any element of it by a third party where the exploitation does not distort or offend the cultural identity of the local community and when the local community is granted an equitable share of any benefit derived from such scientific, commercial, or industrial exploitation.

The local community owning a handicraft may cause individual pieces of the product of the handicraft that are created after such registration to also be registered, and those pieces may be added to the general registration.

Any title of industrial property, including but not limited to patents, trademarks, industrial designs, or plant variety certificates that are granted, irrespective of any rights of TK under this Act, shall not be enforceable against third parties until the written consent of the local community owning the TK is obtained.

Local communities may, where applicable and at their discretion, seek protection for the elements of their TK in an alternative or complementary manner by means of other regimes of industrial property without prejudice to the rights and interests protected by this Act.

In sum, as stated above, the prescribed protection system has failed to take into consideration the objective of protecting TK and its nature, which requires a system of protection different from the common IP protection system.

Burundi

Under Title V of the Industrial Property Act of Burundi, protection of TK has been provided as an industrial property right. The Law prescribes that the provisions of Title V shall be designed to provide for industrial property rights for all aspects of the TK of the local indigenous communities of Burundi by means of a system of registration. The protection system is similar to the one provided under Botswana's Law. A system of registration is established and registration of TK is required to benefit from protection. The criticisms stated above of the system provided by Botswana are *mutatis mutandis* valid here.

According to the Law, any element of TK protected thereunder may be registered separately and individually, in accordance with its technical characteristics, without prejudice to its holistic nature. That is, independent elements of TK may be registered, or the TK may be registered as a whole in a single registration combining all of the elements of the knowledge.

Title and other rights in the protected TK shall be collective in nature and shall be exercised by each local community in accordance with its customary practices. These customary practices shall also determine the exploitation of the TK by the various members of the local communities. The means for distributing the profits arising from the exploitation of the TK within each local community shall also be established in accordance with the community's customary practices.

In the event that several local communities which occupy the same territory have created and hold identical or similar elements of TK, they may register these elements individually on behalf of each community. Each community concerned may also individually enforce its rights in these elements of TK. Nevertheless, nothing shall prevent these communities from joining forces to exploit jointly the TK they have in common.

Crafts shall be registered in a register separate from the one for TK by the Industrial Property Director, at the request of the local community concerned.

All industrial property titles, in particular patents, marks, industrial designs, or plant variety certificates, which have been granted in violation of rights in registered TK shall not be binding on third parties if the local community to which this TK belongs has not given its consent.

Local communities may also protect elements of their TK in a complementary or different fashion by means of other industrial property regimes, without prejudice to the rights and interests protected by this Law.

Kenya

In July 2009, Kenya adopted the National Policy on Traditional Knowledge, Genetic Resources and Traditional Cultural Expressions.[15] The Policy provides a national framework for recognition, preservation, protection, and promotion of the sustainable use of TK, GRs, and TCEs. This will enhance mainstreaming of such knowledge systems into national development planning and decision-making processes at all levels.

The Preamble of the Policy recognizes that the three themes of TK, GRs, and EoF/TCEs are closely intertwined and hence need to be addressed together. Their common characteristics, the similar issues they raise, and the question of intellectual property rights for their protection render it difficult to deal with them separately and sequentially. According to the Preamble, the Policy aims to develop a system that does more than merely document and preserve traditional knowledge created in the past which may be on the brink of disappearance. It also envisages a system that contributes to the promotion and dissemination of innovations which are based on the continuing use of tradition while also preserving what exists as an indispensable and powerful tool for fostering continuous traditional innovation and creativity to contribute to national development.

The Preamble underlines that Kenya's people are diverse, with very rich cultural heritages. These include but are not limited to: traditional literature; traditional arts and crafts; music; visual arts; ceremonies; traditional beliefs; traditional architecture associated with particular sites; forms of TK related to traditional medicines and traditional medical practices; agriculture; forest management; and

15 Kenya, National Policy on Traditional Knowledge, Genetic Resources and Traditional Cultural Expressions, 2009; available at: http://www.wipo.int/wipolex/en/details.jsp?id=11300 (last accessed on November 27, 2012).

conservation and sustainable use of biological diversity. Therefore, TK and TCEs form a body of knowledge vital to the day-to-day life of local communities derived through generations of living in close contact with nature.

It is also stressed in the Preamble that TK and TCEs are holistic, inherently dynamic, and constantly evolving through experimentation and innovation, fresh insight, and external stimuli. A great deal of TK and TCEs have cultural or spiritual values that cannot be quantified in any monetary sense.

The Preamble further points out that TK and TCEs have contributed significantly to the present body of knowledge possessed by scientists, including ethnobotanists and ethnopharmacologists, and by agriculturists, foresters, and food technologists. The fact that TK and TCEs are being widely disseminated and commercially exploited, with only a small proportion of the benefits flowing back to the people and communities that have provided them, raises the question of ownership and equity. Finally, according to the Preamble, lack of enabling policy and a legal framework for the recognition and protection of TK, GRs, and TCEs has led to a situation where custodians of knowledge and innovations derived from their traditional innovations and practices are not rewarded for their contributions.

The Policy underscores several challenges that impede the integration of TK, TCEs, and GRs into the national development planning and decision-making processes at all levels. The main challenges include:

- lack of recognition and mainstreaming of TK, GRs and TCEs into national policies and decision-making processes;
- lack of a comprehensive database of TK, GRs and TCEs;
- high cost of collation and documentation of TK, GRs and TCEs;
- weak community institutional linkages;
- inadequate capacities; and
- intellectual property rights.

The objectives of the National Policy on TK, TCEs, and GRs are to:

- provide a legal and institutional framework to support the integration of various aspects of TK, GRs and TCE into national development planning and decision making processes;
- promote the preservation, protection and development of TK, GRs and TCEs for multiple applications and use;
- promote and foster the documentation, use and dissemination of TK, GRs and TCEs with mechanisms to acknowledge, protect and benefit the sources and/or custodians;
- promote the protection of TK associated with conservation and sustainable use of biological diversity and equitable sharing of accrued benefits; and
- enhance collaboration and partnership in the generation, access to and utilization of TK, GRs and TCEs.

The Policy's guiding principles are as follows: the principle of respect; the principle of full disclosure; the principle of prior informed consent; the principle of confidentiality; the principle of good faith; the principle of compensation; the principle of equitable benefit-sharing; the principle of access; the principle of sustainable development; and the principle of international cooperation.

The Policy contains specific statements on: the policy framework; research and development in agriculture and food security, medicine and public health, biodiversity conservation, TK and TCEs, and IPRs and access; the legal and institutional framework; and linkage with other sectors. It is not the aim here to examine all of these policy statements; only those deemed to be closely related to TK, and their underlying *raison d'être*, will be addressed.

Policy framework

The Policy framework underlines that over the years communities have raised concerns about unauthorized reproduction of their fixed and tangible and intangible TCEs such as artistic works, handicrafts, designs, dances, and musical and dramatic performances. As a result, not only do foreigners frequently neglect to seek authority to do so but they also fail to acknowledge the source of creativity and even pass off productions and works as their authentic expressions or products when they are not. In addition, GRs and the TK associated with them are being appropriated and patented by multinationals, a situation that conflicts with the tenets underpinning TK and TCEs.

The Policy therefore sets out that the Government in collaboration with stakeholders will endeavor to:

(1) Support, promote and protect traditional knowledge, genetic resources and traditional cultural expressions and their associated innovations and practices.

(2) Develop mechanisms to facilitate integration of traditional knowledge and traditional cultural expressions into the policy, development planning and decision making processes at the local, national, regional and global levels.

(3) Ensure that communities have effective control over traditional knowledge, genetic resources and traditional cultural expressions, documentation and databases based on their know-how, practices and skills.

(4) Establish a registry of inventions in which communities can register their traditional innovations and a clearing house for horizontal networking and innovation market.

(5) Establish traditional knowledge, genetic resources and traditional cultural expressions searchable databases and networks.

(6) Put in place guidelines and laws to govern and regulate material transfer and information transfer agreements for genetic resource materials as well as traditional knowledge-related information for research and application.

(7) Develop standards for best practices in traditional knowledge, genetic resources and traditional cultural expressions.

(8) Mobilize and harness grassroots technological innovations and traditional knowledge values and institutions.

(9) Compulsory Acquisition: where the Government or any other international or national body compulsorily acquires TK, TCEs or GRs for the benefit of mankind, the owners of such TK, TCEs or GRs will be duly compensated in accordance with other national and international laws.

(10) Cross-border laws shall apply with regard to TK, GRs and TCEs which are owned across national borders (ARIPO and other regional bodies).

(11) This policy shall propose mechanisms for recovery and/or compensation or acknowledgement of stolen artifacts.

(12) This policy takes cognizance of international laws and treaties Kenya is a signatory to in the field of TK, TCEs and GRs.

Intellectual property rights and access

The existing IPR regimes are inadequate and do not address all the issues involved in the protection of TK and folklore. Yet there is widespread unfair exploitation of the cultural heritage for commercial and business interests. Furthermore, important elements of TK and folklore are being lost and will continue to be lost in the absence of a proper legal protection mechanism. The Policy therefore establishes that the Government will endeavor to:

1. Through a *sui generis* system, protect, integrate, enhance and validate traditional knowledge know-how and practices while ensuring that the owners of the traditional knowledge directly benefit on a equitable basis and on mutually agreed terms from any commercial exploitation of it or from any technological development derived from it and its derivatives.
2. Protect traditional knowledge systems from unauthorized intellectual property claims based on traditional artistic, literary and cultural works.
3. Ensure mandatory disclosure of source of origin of genetic resources and traditional knowledge in intellectual property applications.
4. Develop mechanisms for certification, labeling, trademark, geographical indication, tracing or an appellation of origin authorized by the communities' concerned.
5. Protect the economic rights of performers in their unfixed performances.

Legal framework

There is no harmonized legal framework on the protection of TK, GRs, and TCEs. To facilitate their protection and utilization, it is imperative that an appropriate legal framework is put in place. Under the Policy, the Government will therefore endeavor to: 'Put in place a comprehensive enabling legislation on traditional knowledge, genetic resources and traditional cultural expressions with the legislation being implemented concurrently with relevant laws.'

The National Policy adopted by Kenya is a very important document that will lead to the design of a law on TK, TCEs, and GRs. Implementation mechanisms are also put in place. The lack of a clear policy on TK and TCEs has led some African countries covered in this study to adopt TK laws which do not reflect the African traditional community interests. These TK laws may rather be seen as mere adaptations of existing IP laws to accommodate some aspects of TK. This is unfortunate.

South Africa

Background

The Parliament of South Africa has passed a new Bill on the Protection of Traditional Knowledge. The Bill will become law once it is promulgated by the President to create a new sui generis system of IPRs to protect TK and to enable traditional communities to exploit it commercially for their benefit. The text comprises three categories of TK, namely traditional works, traditional designs, and traditional marks.

According to the Bill, 'traditional work' means a literary, musical, or artistic work as defined in Section 1 of the Copyright Act which evolved in, or originated from, a traditional community and in respect of which no individual maker is known. Further, 'traditional design' means any design applied to any article, whether for the pattern or the shape or the configuration thereof, or for any two or more of those purposes, and by whatever means it is applied, having features which appeal to and are judged solely by the eye, irrespective of the aesthetic quality, which evolved in, or originated from, a traditional community and in respect of which no individual maker is known. 'Traditional mark' is defined under the Bill as a certification trademark as described in Section 42(1) of the Trade Marks Act, a collective mark as described in Section 43(1) of the Trade Marks Act or a trademark as defined in Section 2 of the Trade Marks Act which evolved in, or originated from, a traditional community.

The common denominator among the three categories of TK is that they have been generated within a traditional community. It should be underlined that the Bill has established the Registration Office for Traditional Knowledge and the National Council for Traditional Knowledge. In addition to the two institutions, the Bill has set up the National Trust Fund for Traditional Knowledge.

Conditions for protection

In order to qualify for protection, a traditional work or design shall be reduced to a material form, by or on behalf of the originating traditional community, and recognized as being derived from, and characteristic of, that community by persons outside that community. To be eligible of protection, a traditional mark shall be represented graphically, thus represented by or on behalf of the originating traditional community, and recognized as being derived from, and characteristic of, that community by persons outside that community.

Once a traditional work has been reduced to a material form, protection will extend back to the work in its corresponding prior inchoate state.

Rights of the traditional community

In respect of *a* traditional work, Section 3 of the TK Bill sets out as follows:

> (1) The right in and to a protected traditional work comprises the exclusive do, or to authorise the doing of, any of the following acts in the Republic in relation to the work or a substantial part thereof:
> (a) reproducing it in any manner or form;
> (b) publishing it if it was hitherto unpublished;
> (c) performing it in public;
> (d) broadcasting it;
> (e) causing it to be transmitted in a diffusion service, unless such services transmits a lawful broadcast, including the work, and is operated by the original broadcaster;
> (f) making an adaptation of it;
> (g) doing in relation to an adaptation of the work any of the acts specified in relation to the work in paragraphs (b) to (e) inclusive;
> (h) in regard to a copy of the work made without the authority of the copyright owner,
> (i) selling or letting it for hire or by way of trade offering or exposing it for sale or hire;
> (ii) importing it into the Republic otherwise than for the private or domestic use of the importer;
> (iii) distributing it for purposes of trade;
> (iv) distributing it for any other purposes to such an extent that the owner of the right is prejudicially affected.
>
> (2) The traditional work right shall be infringed by any person, not being the owner of that right, who, without the license of such owner, does or causes any other person to do, in the Republic, any act detailed above if to his knowledge the work in relation to which the act is performed is a protected traditional work and his performance of the act in question was without the authority of the owner of the traditional work right.

In relation to traditional designs, according to Section 9 of the TK Bill, the traditional community is vested with the exclusive right to exclude other persons from making, importing, using, or disposing of any article embodying the protected design or a design not substantially different from the protected design, provided that the design of such article is a copy of the protected design. As a result, the traditional design right shall be infringed by any person, not being the owner of that right, who, without the license of such owner, does or causes any other person to do, in the Republic, any such act if to his knowledge the design in relation to which the act is performed is a protected traditional design and his performance of the act in question was without the authority of the owner of the traditional design right.

In relation to traditional marks, according to Section 14 and subject to Section 17, the right in and to a protected traditional mark comprises the exclusive right to register that mark as a certification mark, a collective mark, or a trademark under the Trade Marks Act and it shall be deemed to be eligible for registration as such under the Trade Marks Act by the owner thereof, subject to the provisions of that Act. Therefore, a protected traditional mark shall be deemed to be a mark falling within Section 10(12) of the Trade Marks Act and to be a mark open to objection when any other party besides the owner of that protected traditional mark or someone acting on his authority seeks to register it.

General exceptions from protection

Exceptions are provided for two categories of TK, namely for traditional work and traditional design. The right in a protected traditional work, in so far as it consists of a literary work or a musical work, shall not be infringed by performing any act described in Sections 12 and 14 of the Copyright Act, which sections shall apply *mutatis mutandis* to literary and musical works that are protected traditional works.

The right in a protected traditional work, in so far as it consists of an artistic work, shall not be infringed by performing the acts described in Section 15 of the Copyright Act, which section shall apply *mutatis mutandis* to artistic works which are protected traditional works. The traditional work right shall not be infringed by the performance of any act by a member of the originating community which is in accordance with the customs and traditional practice of that community. The disposal of an article embodying a protected traditional design by or with the authority of the owner of the traditional design right shall give the purchaser the right to use and dispose of that article.

The traditional design right shall not be infringed by a person who makes an article embodying the protected design, or a design not substantially different from it, for private purposes or for the sole purpose of evaluation, analysis, research or teaching. Further, the traditional design right shall not be infringed by the performance of any act by a member of the originating community which is in accordance with the customs and traditional practice of that community.

Duration of protection

The duration of the traditional work right shall, in the case of a published traditional work, be a period of 50 years from the date of its first publication or the date on which the act came into operation, whichever is the later. The duration of the traditional work right shall, in the case of an unpublished traditional work, be indefinite.

The duration of the traditional design right shall, in the case of a published traditional design, be a period of 15 years from the date of its first publication or the date on which the act came into operation, whichever is the later. The duration of the traditional design right shall, in the case of an unpublished traditional design, be indefinite.

Subject to Section 16, the traditional mark right shall endure indefinitely.

Lapsing of TK rights

The exclusive rights of protected TK shall lapse and cease to have any force or effect in the following circumstances:

- if a person who is a member of the originating community pursues a claim of copyright infringement in respect of that work under the Copyright Act with the consent of the community proxy;
- if the traditional design is registered as a design under the Designs Act by or with the authority of the owner; or
- if the traditional mark is registered as a certification mark, a collective mark, or a trademark under the Trade Marks Act by or with the authority of the owner.

Ownership and transmission of TK rights

Ownership of the TK right shall vest in a representative capacity in the person designated from time to time as the community proxy of the originating community, and, subject to sub-section (2), it shall not be transmissible by assignment or operation of law.

In the event that the identity of the community proxy should change from time to time in accordance with the rules and practices of the originating traditional community, the ownership of the TK right will pass automatically to the new incumbent of the position, who shall hold it in a representative capacity.

Moral rights

Where any work, design, or mark is, or is derived from, an item of protected TK, the owner of the TK right shall have the unlimited right to claim that it is such a work, design or mark, to require acknowledgement thereof and to object to any distortion, mutilation, or other modification thereof where such action is, or would be, prejudicial to the honor or public esteem of the originating traditional community. Any infringement of these provisions shall be treated as an infringement of copyright under Chapter 2 of the Copyright Act, and for the purposes of the provisions of the said Chapter, the owner of the TK right shall be deemed to be the owner of the copyright in question and the protected TK shall be deemed to be a work in which copyright subsists.

Effect on common law

Subject to sub-section (2), for the purposes of the common law relating to passing-off and unlawful competition, a protected traditional mark shall be deemed to be well-known and to enjoy a repute amongst a substantial number of persons. In proceedings for passing-off or unlawful competition in which reliance is placed on sub-section (1), the plaintiff must show that the defendant knew at the time of the commission of the act that is the subject matter of the claim that the mark was a protected traditional mark and that the act in question was committed without the authority of the owner.

Although the Bill intends to create a *sui generis* regime of protection of TK, in this author's view its content reflects more accurately an adaptation of IP laws—namely those governing copyright, designs, and trademarks—to accommodate TK.

Genetically Modified Organisms (GMOs)

Egypt

The Egyptian Biosafety Regulations and Guidelines were adopted in 1994.[16] The Egyptian National Biosafety Committee (NBC) was established under these Regulations and Guidelines, comprising policy makers and designers and scientific experts in agriculture, health, industry, and the environment from government and academic research institutes. The purpose of the National Committee is to establish policies and procedures to govern the use of modem biotechnology in the country. The Committee will also provide technical advice to the regulatory authorities and the institutions responsible for the development of biotechnology in the country.

Biosafety guidelines are designed to ensure that the products of biotechnology will not have adverse effects on the environment and agriculture, to prevent unintentional release of hazardous organisms, and to protect the surrounding communities as well as employees and researchers involved in the use of such products from the research stage up until commercialization.

In order to establish safety research policies,the NBC shall formulate guidelines for both contained and uncontained applications to cover laboratory practices, greenhouse facilities, small-scale field trials, and final commercial release. This will include guidelines for research with natural organisms that are exotic to the host country.

The NBC shall review new initiatives to evaluate the benefits and potential risk to the environment and to human communities of conducting research with GMOs. If a license is issued after performing a risk assessment analysis, the NBC should periodically review containment measures and facilities to ensure that adequate safety guidelines are being followed.

Based on the Regulations and Guidelines, Egypt has been importing GMO products since 1997. In Egypt, as in other African countries, some people are still reluctant to accept GMOs.

---

16 Egypt, Ministry of Agriculture and Land Reclamation, Agricultural Research Center, Agricultural Genetic Engineering Research Institute (Ageri), Biosafety Regulations and Guidelines, January 1994.

Kenya

On February 12, 2009, Kenya adopted the Biosafety Act, which regulates GMOs in Kenya. The Biosafety Act aims to ensure an adequate level of protection for the safe transfer, handling, and use of GMOs that may have an adverse effect on the health of the people and the environment and to establish a transparent, science-based, and predictable process for reviewing and making decisions on the transfer, handling, and use of GMOs and related activities.

The Act makes it clear that a person shall not conduct any activity involving GMOs without the written approval of the National Biosafety Authority. The Authority shall perform the following acts:

(a) consider and determine applications for approval for the transfer, handling and use of genetically modified organisms, and related activities in accordance with the provisions of this Act;
(b) co-ordinate, monitor and assess activities relating to the safe transfer, handling and use of genetically modified organisms in order to ensure that such activities do not have adverse effects on human health and the environment;
(c) co-ordinate research and surveys in matters relating to the safe development, transfer, handling and use of genetically modified organisms, and to collect, (d) collate and disseminate information about the findings of such research, investigations or surveys;
(d) identify national requirements for manpower development and capacity building in biosafety;
(e) advise the Government on legislative and other measures relating to the safe transfer, handling and use of genetically modified organisms;
(f) promote awareness and education among the general public in matters relating to biosafety; and
(g) establish and maintain a biosafety clearing house to serve as a means through which information is made available facilitate the exchange of scientific, technical, environmental and legal information on, and experience with, living modified organisms.

The Act also sets out that a person shall not introduce a GMO into the environment without the written approval of the Authority. Furthermore, a person shall not import a GMO into Kenya without the written approval of the Authority. As a logical consequence, a person shall not place a GMO on the market without the written approval of the Authority. Further, a person intending to export a GMO from Kenya shall provide the Authority with an advance written consent granted by a relevant authority of the country to which the GMO is destined to the effect that such relevant authority has no objection to the intended exportation. Finally, any person manufacturing or importing any GMOs shall ensure that their handling, packaging, identification, and transportation are carried out in the prescribed manner.

The New Kenyan Biosafety Act took effect on July 1, 2011, effectively allowing the production, importation, and exportation of genetically modified foods. This Law has divided Kenya into two groups, the one supporting it and the other opposing it. Supporters of the Law say genetically modified foods will help Kenya deal with chronic grain shortages. This issue will be covered in detail in Chapter 4.

Mauritius

The GMOs Act adopted in 2004[17] governs all undertakings related to GMOs in Mauritius. The Act aims to provide for measures to regulate the responsible planning, development, production, use, marketing, and application of GMOs. According to the Act, GMO refers to:

> (a) an organism, the genes or genetic material of which has been modified in a way that does not occur naturally through mating or natural recombination, or both; and
> (b) any of its derivatives.

According to Section 3 of the Act:

> (1) This Act shall apply to the genetic modification of organisms which occurs through –
> (a) recombinant nucleic acid techniques involving the formation of new combinations of genetic material;
> (b) techniques involving the direct introduction into an organism of foreign nucleic acid molecules; or
> (c) cell fusion, including protoplast fusion, beyond the same taxonomic family or hybridization techniques where live cells with new combination of genetic material are formed.
> (2) This Act shall not apply –
> (a) to techniques involving genetic manipulation of hSuman cells; or
> (b) in cases where recombinant nucleic acid molecules or genetically modified organisms are not employed.

In Mauritius, no person shall develop, use, market, produce, release into the environment, transport, import, or export GMOs unless he holds a GMO permit issued under the GMO Act.

17 *Government Gazette of Mauritius*, No. 40, April 30, 2004.

South Africa

GMOs are regulated in South Africa by the GMO Act, Act No. 15 of 1997,[18] as revised by the GMO Amendment of 2006 and promulgated by the President on April 11, 2007.[19] The *raison d'être* of the law is clearly provided in the Preamble as follows:

> To provide for measures to promote the responsible development, production, use and application of genetically modified organisms; to provide for adequate level of protection during all activities involving genetically modified organisms that may have an adverse impact on the conservation and sustainable use of biological diversity, human and animal health; to give attention to the prevention of accidents and the effective management of waste; to establish common measures for the evaluation and reduction of the potential risks arising out of activities involving the use of genetically modified organisms; to lay down the necessary requirements and criteria for scientifically based risk assessments, environment impact assessments, socio-economic considerations and risk management measures; to establish a Council for genetically modified organisms; to ensure that genetically modified organisms are appropriate and do not present a hazard to the environment; and to establish appropriate procedures for the notification of specific activities involving the use of genetically modified organisms; and to provide for matters connected therewith.

A GMO is defined under the Law as genes or genetic material which has been modified in a way that does not occur naturally through mating or natural recombination or both.

The scope of the GMO Act is prescribed as follows:

> (1) This Act shall apply to-
> (a) the genetic modification of organisms:
> (b) the development, production, release, use and application of genetically modified organisms (including viruses and bactcriophages); and
> (c) the use of gene therapy.
> (2) This Act shall not apply to techniques-
> (a) involving human gene therapy;
> (b in which recombinant DNA molecules or genetically modified organisms are not employed-
> (i) in *in vitro* fertilisation in humans and animals;
> (ii) in conjugation, transduction, transformation or any other natural process; and

18 As published in *UPOV Gazette*, No. 93, June 2002.

19 As amended by the GMOs Amendment Act of 2006; see *Government Gazette*, April 17, 2007.

(iii) in polyploidy induction,

(c) in which genetically modified organisms as recipient or parental organisms are not employed-

(i) in mutagenesis;

(ii) in the construction and use of somatic hybridoma cells; and

(iii) in cell fusion (including protoplast fusion) of plant cells.

Conclusion

For the selected subject matters examined in this chapter, the comparative analysis of the laws of the African countries included in this study reveals a wide array of convergences, few divergences, and some particularities.

In terms of scope of patents, more similarities than differences can be seen. However, while the 'new use' or 'second pharmaceutical/medical use' is clearly recognized under the laws of Egypt, Kenya, and Morocco, this concept is not acknowledged in Burundi, where the law is clear that this is not protectable. In Morocco, the term of protection of patents may be extended under certain circumstances, and this applies also in the pharmaceutical field.

So far as the disclosure requirement is concerned, all of the countries have provided for this, but only Burundi and South Africa have amended their laws to include also a requirement to disclose the country of origin/source of the GRs or associated TK in the patent application.

All countries in the study provide for similar exclusions, including the exclusion of plant varieties from protection under patents. However, Burundi is the only country which provides patent protection for computer programs.

Similarities are also enormous among these countries in terms of their provisions for exceptions to patent rights, notwithstanding that Morocco is the only country that provides for national exhaustion of patent rights.

The compulsory licensing regimes of all these countries are similar in terms of the conditions and situations that allow for the grant of such licenses, although some of the countries have dealt with the subject more extensively than others. It is somewhat remarkable that to date only Botswana and Burundi have made specific provision in their laws for making use of the waiver allowing a wider use of compulsory licenses for the production of pharmaceuticals established by the WTO General Council's Decision of August 30, 2003. This is a critical issue for meeting the public health needs of most African nations, so it should be anticipated that it will be addressed more widely by national IP laws in the future.

With regard to non-traditional marks, it must be noted that most of these countries require that marks be visible to be eligible for trademark protection. Morocco and Burundi are the exceptions in providing protection for some non-visible marks. In general, then, these countries have shown little inclination to offer protection to non-traditional marks.

In terms of the protection of well-known marks, the conditions for doing so are similar among those countries, even though some are silent in respect of the use of well-known marks for dissimilar goods or services.

Only one of these countries, Botswana, has dealt with the issue of use of marks on the Internet by at least defining what comprises such use. This is a lacuna in these countries' IP laws that may have a serious impact as they become more integrated into the global information economy.

Although TK and TCEs are regulated under the laws of Botswana, Burundi, Kenya, and South Africa, in this author's opinion the systems of protection provided therein are not fully satisfactory in addressing the concerns of the main stakeholders, who are the traditional communities. Most importantly, the legal regimes established appear to give little serious thought to the unique characteristics of TK and TCEs but, rather, to offer modest adaptations of systems of IP protection developed essentially for the protection of individually developed and owned inventions and creations.

GMOs are regulated under different legal frameworks in four of the African countries subjects of this study—Egypt, Kenya, Mauritius, and South Africa. In each of these countries, GMOs are acknowledged for use and are permitted to be imported or exported under certain conditions.

In sum, it can be said that African countries are becoming increasingly aware of the importance of intellectual property for their own development, although in some of these countries the political will to address this effectively is not yet apparent. To design a good IP policy or law, what is of utmost importance nowadays is that each African country must be aware of the interconnection between IP and other fields of technology.

Chapter 3
African Regional Intellectual Property Systems and Regional Initiatives

This chapter addresses the systems provided under the two regional African IP organizations, namely the African Regional Intellectual Property Organization (ARIPO) and the African Intellectual Property Organization (OAPI).[1] Furthermore, African regional initiatives on IP taken by the African Union (AU) or other regional organizations will be discussed.

The African Regional Intellectual Property Organization (ARIPO)

In this section, the historical background of the ARIPO will be looked at prior to an in-depth analysis of the Protocol on Patents and Industrial Designs within the Framework of the ARIPO, the Banjul Protocol on Marks, and the ARIPO–Patent Cooperation Treaty (PCT) relationship.

Background

The ARIPO was previously known as the Industrial Property Organization for English Speaking Africa (ESARIPO).[2] The idea of developing a regional patent system arose as early as 1972, when representatives of English-speaking African countries attending a seminar on copyright called on WIPO and the United Nations to assist in the establishment of a regional industrial property office for English-speaking Africa. ESARIPO changed its name to the African Regional Industrial Property Organization (ARIPO) when it became open to all Member countries of the Organization of African Unity (OAU, but now called the African Union, or AU). Its Headquarters is in Harare, Zimbabwe, and is composed of 18 member states. Recently, the name of the organization was changed again, and it is now known as the African Regional Intellectual Property Organization.

The Agreement on the Creation of the ARIPO, known as the Lusaka Agreement, was adopted at Lusaka, Zambia in 1976[3] and has been supplemented

---

1 OAPI is an acronym derived from the French name of the Organization: Organisation Africaine de la Propriété Intellectuelle.

2 English-Speaking Africa Regional Industrial Property Organization.

3 The Agreement on the Creation of the ARIPO, adopted on December 9, 1976, has been amended by the Administrative Council of ARIPO on December 10, 1982, December

by two Protocols, namely the 'Protocol on Patents and Industrial Designs within the Framework of the ARIPO', adopted at Harare on December 10, 1982 (the Harare Protocol),[4] and the 'Banjul Protocol on Marks', adopted at Banjul, Gambia, on November 19, 1993.[5]

The ARIPO system is a regional IP system which coexists with the national systems of Member States. The ARIPO is principally governed by the Agreement on the Creation of ARIPO and by the two Protocols mentioned above. This chapter will examine the Protocols before highlighting the relationship between ARIPO and the Patent Cooperation Treaty (PCT).

Article III of the Agreement on the Creation of the ARIPO lays down the objectives of the ARIPO as follows:

- To promote the harmonization and development of the industrial property laws, and matters related thereto, appropriate to the needs of its Members and of the region as a whole;
- To foster the establishment of a close relationship between its Members in matters relating to industrial property;
- To establish such common services or organs as may be necessary or desirable for the coordination, harmonization and development of the industrial property activities affecting its Members;
- To establish schemes for the training of staff in the administration of industrial property laws;
- To organize conferences, seminars, and other meetings on industrial property matters;
- To promote the exchange of ideas and experience, research and studies relating to industrial property matters;
- To promote and evolve a common view and approach of its Members on industrial property matters;
- To assist its Members, as appropriate, in the acquisition and development of technology relating to industrial property matters, and to do all such other things as may be necessary or desirable for the achievement of the objectives.

12, 1986, and November 27, 1996 and by the Council of Ministers on August 13, 2004. The latter amendment came into force on November 13, 2004.

4 The Protocol on Patents and Industrial Designs has been amended by the Administrative Council of ARIPO on December 11, 1987, April 27, 1994, November 28, 1997, May 26, 1998, November 26, 1999, November 30, 2001, November 21, 2003, and November 24, 2006.

5 The Banjul Protocol on Marks has been amended by the Administrative Council on November 28, 1997, May 26, 1998, and November 26, 1999 and by the Council of Ministers on August 13, 2004.

Protocol on Patents and Industrial Designs within the Framework of the ARIPO

This Protocol includes provisions in respect of patents, utility models, and industrial designs. On November 26, 1999, it was revised to include utility models as a subject matter of protection. The ARIPO is empowered to grant, register, and administer patents, utility models, and industrial designs on behalf of the Contracting States.[6] According to the ARIPO Regulations for Implementing the Protocol on Patents and Industrial Designs,[7] the ARIPO Office shall maintain a Patents Register and an Industrial Designs Register in which shall be recorded, respectively, all patents granted and all utility models and industrial designs registered under the Protocol. Applications for the grant of patents or for the registration of utility models and industrial designs by the ARIPO Office shall be filed by the authorized representative of the applicant or by the applicant with the industrial property office of a Contracting State (Section 2(1)).

The industrial property office with which the application is filed shall, within one month of receiving the application, transmit that application to the Office of the ARIPO (Section 2(5)). An application filed with the industrial property office of a Contracting State shall have the same effect as if it had been filed on the same date at the ARIPO Office. The application may contain a declaration claiming, in respect of one or several designated States, the priority, as provided for in the Paris Convention, of one or more earlier national, regional, or international applications filed by the applicant or his predecessor in title in or for any State Party to the Paris Convention.[8]

Patents

Under the ARIPO system, the applicant files a single application and designates any Member country of the Contracting States in which the patent will have validity, unless any Member country makes a prior renunciation on the patentability of the invention in its territory.[9] The ARIPO Office examines the application's

6 The Protocol on Patents and Industrial Designs within the Framework of the ARIPO, Section 1 provides: 'The African Regional Intellectual Property Organization (ARIPO) is empowered to grant patents and to register utility models and industrial designs and to administer such patents, utility models and industrial designs on behalf of Contracting States in accordance with the provisions of the Protocol, through its Secretariat (hereinafter referred to as 'the Office').'

7 Regulations for Implementing the Protocol on Patents and Industrial Designs within the Framework of the ARIPO, entered into force April 25, 1984, and amended by the Administrative Council of ARIPO on April 27, 1994, November 27, 1998, November 24, 2000, November 21, 2003, and November 24, 2006.

8 Ibid., Rule 8.

9 Before the expiration of six months from the date of the notification, a designated State may make a written communication to the Office that, if a patent is granted by the Office, that patent shall have no effect in its territory because either the invention is not patentable in accordance with the provisions of the Protocol or because of the nature of the

compliance with formal requirements and notifies each designated State when the prescribed requirements are met.[10] The ARIPO undertakes or arranges for substantive examination of the patent application. If it finds that the invention claimed in the application does not comply with the requirements of patentability referred to in sub-Section (10) of the Protocol, it will refuse the application.

Before the expiration of six months from the date of the notification, a designated State may declare that the patent shall have no effect in its territory because the invention is not patentable in accordance with the provisions of the Protocol or because the nature of the invention is outside the protected subject matter as stipulated under its own national law. After the expiration of the said six months, the ARIPO shall grant the patent, which shall have effect in those designated States which have not declared that it shall have no effect therein. The ARIPO shall publish the patent granted. At any time before the grant or refusal of a patent, an applicant may, upon payment of the prescribed fees, convert the application into an application for a utility model, which shall be accorded the filing date of the initial application.

The ARIPO system is designated to be an additional system of protection coexisting with the national patent systems of its Member States. Its main purpose is the grant of regional patents having effect in all designated Member countries through a common granting authority under its own rules and standards of patentability. Under the ARIPO Protocol, various provisions of substantive patent law are set out, namely conditions for patentability,[11] the patent granting procedure,[12] and the establishment of an independent patent system.[13] In addition, the ARIPO recommends that its Members adhere to the PCT.

A patent granted by the ARIPO Office shall have the same effect in each designated State as a patent registered, granted, or otherwise having effect under that State's applicable national law, and the duration of the patent shall be 20 years from the filing date (Section 3(10)). Under Section 3(11), a patent granted by the ARIPO Office shall be subject in each designated State to the provisions of the applicable national law on compulsory licenses, forfeiture, or the use of patented inventions in the public interest.

---

invention a patent cannot be registered or granted or has no effect under the national law of that State.

10 Nevertheless, the applicant may lodge an appeal against the decision of the ARIPO Office to the Board of Appeal.

11 The ARIPO's conditions for patentability are that the invention shall be new, involve an inventive step, and be industrially applicable.

12 The ARIPO is legally assigned the task of carrying out the procedure for the grant of regional patents.

13 Up until recently, the majority of the ARIPO's Member countries operated patent systems in which patents granted in the United Kingdom were registered. The ARIPO encourages them to build up their own patent systems.

The ARIPO, under its Protocol and Regulations, has provided special norms and rules in respect of patents relating to micro-organisms.

The Banjul Protocol on Marks

As its name indicates, this Protocol pertains to the protection of marks, i.e. trademarks and service marks. The ARIPO is empowered to register and administer marks on behalf of the Contracting States. All applications for the registration of a mark shall be filed either directly with the ARIPO Office or with the industrial property office of a Contracting State by the applicant or his duly authorized representative (Section 2(1)). The application shall indicate the goods and/or services in respect of which protection of a mark is claimed, including the corresponding class or classes provided under the Nice Agreement Concerning the International Classification of Goods and Services for the Purpose of the Registration of Marks. The application shall contain a declaration of the actual use of the mark or the intention to use the mark or shall be accompanied by an application for the registration of a person as a registered user of the mark.[14] Where an application is filed with the industrial property office of a Contracting State, within one month of receiving the application that office shall transmit the application to the ARIPO Office.[15]

In accordance with Sections 3(3) and 3(4), color marks and three-dimensional marks are subject to protection under certain conditions. These Sections provide as follows:

> 3.3 Where colour is claimed to be a distinctive feature of the mark, the applicant shall make a statement to that effect as well as the name or names of the colour or colours claimed and an indication, in respect of each colour, of the principal parts of the mark which are in that colour.
>
> 3.4 Where the mark is a three-dimensional mark, the applicant shall make a statement to that effect and attach to the application a reproduction of the mark consisting of a two-dimensional graphic or photographic reproduction either of a single view of the mark or several different views of the mark.

As was noted in Chapter 2, many African countries are reluctant to protect single-color marks, notwithstanding that most of them accept registration of combinations of colors as trademarks. It is not the intention of the author to review

14 The Banjul Protocol on Marks, Section 3(5). The phrase referring to a registered user was added by the 1999 amendment.

15 Regulations for Implementing the Banjul Protocol, adopted by the Administrative Council at Kariba, Zimbabwe on November 24, 1995 and amended by the Council on November 28, 1997, May 26, 1998, and November 26, 1999 and as amended by the Council of Ministers on August 13, 2004.

trademark laws of the Contracting States of ARIPO to find out whether all protect a single-color trademark if it is distinctive enough. Kenya, Ghana, and Botswana are Member States of ARIPO. Under the Kenyan Trademark Law, a single-color mark is eligible for protection as a trademark. Ghana and Botswana are silent as to the registration of a single-color mark or even a combination of colors. It will have to be seen in practice how this ARIPO provision will be interpreted. Each designated Member State may refuse to register a mark registered by the ARIPO on the ground of its national law, so a designated Member State may turn down the registration of a single-color mark if it is not eligible for protection in its country.

As for the protection of three-dimensional marks, the Trademark Law of Ghana is silent. Botswana sets out that a mark shall not be registered if it is a sign that consists exclusively of the shape which results from the nature of the goods themselves, the shape of goods which is necessary to obtain a technical result, or the shape which gives substantial inherent value to the goods. From this provision it can be said that not all three-dimensional forms are protectable under the Trademark Law of Botswana, particularly when they are functional. Kenya includes the protection of three-dimensional marks. As mentioned for a single-color mark, a designated country may refuse to register a three-dimensional mark if such protection does not exist in its national legislation.

Pursuant to Article 4 of the Paris Convention, the right of priority is acknowledged under Section 4 of the Banjul Protocol. In this regard, the applicant must apply within six months from the date of the earlier application to benefit from the right of priority.

Once an application is received by the ARIPO Office, a formal check is carried out. If the latter is satisfactory, the ARIPO Office will notify each country designated in the application without delay (Section 5(3)). Every application for the registration of a mark must be examined in accordance with the national laws of a designated State. Before the expiration of 12 months from the date of notification, each designated State may make a written communication to the Office that, if a mark is registered by the Office, that registration shall have no effect on its territory on the basis of any grounds, both absolute and relative, including the existence of third-party rights. The decision of an individual Member State to refuse registration of a mark is subject to appeal or review under the national laws of the designated State concerned (Section 6(4)).[16]

An application for registration of a mark which has been accepted by any designated State shall be published in the Marks Journal. At any time before the registration of the mark, any person may give notice of opposition to the application for registration in a designated State or States. Three months after publication of the mark in the Marks Journal, the ARIPO Office shall register the mark upon payment of the required registration fees. Such registration shall be recorded in the Marks Register and the ARIPO Office shall issue the applicant a

16 This paragraph was added by the 1999 amendment.

certificate of registration. The fact of the registration of a mark shall be published in the Marks Journal.

The period of protection of a mark is set at 10 years from the filing date, and it is renewable for further periods of 10 years conditional on the payment of the renewal fee. The registration of a mark shall have the same effect with respect to rights conferred by the mark in each designated State as if it were filed and registered under the national law of each such State. Accordingly, the national laws of each Contracting State shall apply to the cancellation of a registration, whether based on non-use or any other grounds.

According to Section 8(3) of the Banjul Protocol, the indication of classes of goods or services provided for by the ARIPO Office shall not bind the Contracting States with regard to their own determination of the scope of protection of the mark. In other words, a Contracting State may set up an extensive protection of the mark applicable to goods or services belonging to different classes.

Rule 2 of the Banjul Regulations has provided the principle of independence of protection for marks. Accordingly, an application for the registration of a mark may not be refused, nor may a registration be invalidated, on the ground that filing, registration, or renewal has not been effected in the country of origin as defined in Article 6*quinquies*A(2) of the Paris Convention.[17]

Where a mark has been registered by the ARIPO Office or is pending registration in the ARIPO Office, the owner or applicant or, where applicable, his successor in title shall have the right to designate any other State which becomes a party to the Protocol subsequent to the registration or filing of the application for registration of the mark. In other words, subsequent designation is provided under the Protocol.

The ARIPO Office is empowered to register assignments, licenses, and other similar rights pertaining to marks registered or applied for under the Protocol.

The ARIPO–PCT Relationship

The ARIPO recommends that its Members adhere to the Patent Cooperation Treaty. The ARIPO's patent system operates *mutatis mutandis* in the same way as does the PCT. It is stipulated in Article 3*bis*(3) of the Protocol on Patents and Industrial Designs pertaining to international applications that the ARIPO Office may act as a Receiving Office under Article 2(xv) of the PCT[18] in relation to an international application filed by an applicant who is a resident or national of a Contracting

17 According to Article 6*quinquies*A(2) of the Paris Convention, the country of origin is the country where the applicant has a real and effective industrial or commercial establishment, or, if he has no such establishment within the Union, the country of the Union where he has his domicile, or, if he has no domicile within the Union but is a national of a country of the Union, the country of which he is a national.

18 Under the PCT, 'receiving Office' means the national office or the intergovernmental organization with which the international application has been filed.

State which is also bound by the PCT. Also, any international application in which a Contracting State which is also bound by the PCT is designated for the purposes of obtaining a patent under the provisions of the Protocol shall be considered to be an application for the grant of a patent under the Protocol. The provisions of the PCT shall apply to such international applications in addition to the provisions of the Protocol and its Regulations. In case of conflict between the ARIPO's Protocol and the PCT, the provisions of the PCT shall prevail.

African Intellectual Property Organization (Organisation Africaine de la Propriété Intellectuelle) (OAPI)[19]

Background

After some former French colonies in Africa gained their independence in 1960, they joined hands and created in 1962 the African and Malagasy Office of Industrial Property. The Agreement establishing the Office was signed at Libreville, Gabon, on September 13, 1962, and was known as the Agreement Relating to the Creation of an African and Malagasy Office of Industrial Property.[20] This Agreement was revised at Bangui, Central African Republic, on March 2, 1977[21] by the Agreement Relating to the Creation of an African Intellectual Property Organization,[22] which replaced the African and Malagasy Office of Industrial Property Agreement. The Bangui Agreement (the OAPI Agreement) was revised on February 24, 1999 in order to be in conformity with the TRIPs Agreement. OAPI has its headquarters in Yaoundé, Cameroon, and is composed of 16 Member States.

The Annexes and related categories embodied in the Bangui Agreement are as follows: Patents (Annex I); Utility Models (annex II); Trademarks and Service Marks (Annex III; Industrial Designs (Annex IV); Trade Names (Annex V); Geographical Indications (Annex VI); Literary and Artistic Property (Annex VII); Protection Against Unfair Competition (Annex VIII); Layout-Designs (Topographies) of Integrated Circuits (Annex IX); and Plant Variety Protection (Annex X). As set out in Article 4(3) of the Bangui Agreement, Annexes I to X inclusive form an integral part of it. Accordingly, the Agreement and its Annexes are applicable in their entirety to every State that ratifies or accedes to the Agreement.

19 Kongolo, T. (2000), 'The New OAPI Agreement as Revised in February 1999', *The Journal of World Intellectual Property* 3:5, 717–735.

20 The official French title was '*Accord relatif à la création d'un Office Africain et Malgache de la Propriété Industrielle*'.

21 The revised Agreement is known as the 'Bangui Agreement'; text available at: http://www.wipo.int/wipolex/en/other_treaties/text.jsp (last accessed on November 26, 2012).

22 The official French title is '*Accord relatif à la création d'une Organisation Africaine de la Propriété Intellectuelle*'.

In this study, only selected issues in the arena of the following IP categories will be addressed: patents; trademarks and service marks; and protection of plant varieties.

The main aim of OAPI is to have a uniform system of protection of intellectual property rights within the national framework of its Members.[23] Therefore, the OAPI countries have adopted a uniform system of protection whereby intellectual property rights are granted on their behalf by the Organization.

For each of the Member States, the Organization serves as both the national industrial property service within the meaning of Article 12 of the Paris Convention and the central patent documentation and information body. Therefore, the OAPI Member States do not have independent national laws on industrial property; the Bangui Agreement constitutes the law applicable directly on the territory of each Member State and functions as their national law on industrial property. For each of the OAPI Member States that are also parties to the Patent Cooperation Treaty, the OAPI serves as the national Office, the designated Office, the elected Office or the receiving Office within the meaning of Article 2(xii), (xiii), (xiv), and (xv) of the PCT.

Applications for patents; for the registration of utility models, trademarks or service marks, industrial designs, trade names, geographical indications or layout-designs (topographies) of integrated circuits; and for plant variety certificates must be filed directly with the Organization. However, any Member State may demand that the application be filed with the national administration of the State when the applicant is domiciled on its territory. A record will be taken, and a copy thereof issued to the applicant, by the national administration, which shall attest to every filing and specify the date and time of the filing of the documents. The national administration shall convey the application to the Organization within a period of five working days from filing.

According to Article 33(2), the High Commission of Appeal shall be responsible for ruling on appeals following:

- rejection of applications for titles of industrial property protection;
- rejection of requests for the maintenance or extension of terms of protection;
- rejection of requests for reinstatement;
- decisions on oppositions.

23 See, the Preamble of the Bangui Agreement: 'Considering the advantages of establishing a uniform system for the protection of literary, artistic and industrial property, in particular, in the latter field, a system for the single deposit of applications for patents, registration of utility models, trademarks, service marks, industrial designs, trade names and appellations of origin, on the one hand, and a common system of protection against unfair competition, on the other hand, in order to facilitate recognition of the rights provided for in the laws of their countries.'

Patents

Annex I of the Bangui Agreement sets out the scope of protection, rights conferred to the patentee, the period of protection, the working of patents and compulsory licenses, and enforcement of rights.[24]

An invention is defined as an idea that permits a specific problem in the field of technology to be solved in practice. Under the Bangui Agreement, to be eligible for a patent, an invention shall be new, involve an inventive step, and be industrially applicable. Further, the Bangui Agreement reaffirms that an invention may relate to a product, a process, or to a use thereof.

Under the Bangui Agreement, prior art consists of everything made available to the public, in any place and by any means or method, before the filing date either of the patent application or of a patent application filed abroad, the priority of which has been validly claimed.

As is recognized under the Paris Convention, an invention's novelty will not be denied if, during the 12 months preceding the first filing, it was disclosed by a third party without the consent of the applicant or was disclosed by the applicant at an official or officially recognized international exhibition.

Annex I, Article 6 sets forth non-patentable subject matter, providing that patents shall not be granted for the following:

- *(a)* inventions the exploitation of which is contrary to public policy or morality, provided that the exploitation of the invention shall not be considered contrary to public policy or morality merely because it is prohibited by law or regulation;
- *(b)* discoveries, scientific theories and mathematical methods;
- *(c)* inventions having as their subject matter plant varieties, animal species and essentially biological processes for the breeding of plants or animals other than microbiological processes and the products of such processes;
- *(d)* schemes, rules or methods for doing business, performing purely mental acts or playing games;
- *(e)* methods for the treatment of the human or animal body by surgery or therapy, including diagnostic methods;
- *(f)* mere presentations of information;
- *(g)* computer programs;
- *(h)* works of an exclusively ornamental nature;
- *(i)* literary, architectural and artistic works or any other aesthetic creation.

Under the OAPI provisions, plant varieties are excluded from the sphere of patent protection but *sui generis* protection is provided under Annex X of the Bangui Agreement, adopted in 1999. Computer programs as well as business

24 See, Kongolo, T. (1999c), 'The African Patent Systems and TRIPs', *Patent World* 117, 17–20.

methods are excluded from the ambit of patents, so in the OAPI region there will be no issue as to the protection of these two items under patents.

A patentee is entitled to the exclusive right to work his invention and may prohibit any other person from exploiting or working his invention without his prior consent. Annex I, Article 8 defines the working of a patented invention as follows:

> (3) For the purposes of this Annex, the working of a patented invention means one or other of the following acts:
> *(a)* where the patent has been granted for a product:
> (i) manufacturing, importing, offering for sale, selling and using the product,
> (ii) holding the product for the purposes of offering it for sale, selling it or using it;
> *(b)* where the patent has been granted for a process:
> (i) using the process,
> (ii) engaging in the acts mentioned in subparagraph (a) above in relation to a product resulting directly from the use of the process.

Limitations to rights conferred are also provided under Annex I, Article 8 as follows:

> (1) The rights deriving from the patent shall not extend
> *(a)* to acts in relation to subject matter brought on to the market on the territory of a member State by the owner of the patent or with his consent;
> *(b)* to the use of objects on board foreign aircraft, land vehicles or ships that temporarily or accidentally enter the airspace, territory or waters of a member State;
> *(c)* to acts in relation to a patented invention that are carried out for experimental purposes in the course of scientific and technical research;
> *(d)* to acts performed by any person who in good faith on the filing date, or where priority is claimed, on the priority date of the application on the basis of which the patent is granted on the territory of a member State, was using the invention or making effective and genuine preparations for such use, in so far as those acts are not different in nature or purpose from the actual or planned earlier use.

The Bangui Agreement thus clearly acknowledges regional exhaustion of patent rights, in accordance with which the patent rights of products put onto the market in any one of the Member countries of OAPI will be exhausted for all of the Members.

Another important limitation on patent rights under the Bangui Agreement concerns the research exemption/exception, which provides that acts carried out for experimental purposes in the course of scientific and technical research shall not be considered to infringe the exclusive rights of patentees or of holders of certificates of registration of utility models, layout designs (topographies) of integrated circuits, or plant varieties.[25]

The Bangui Agreement is silent as to the new application of known methods or processes. This silence implies that the second pharmaceutical/medical use may not be recognized as a protectable subject matter under its patents regime.

Prior use is included among the limitations to patent rights.

The term of protection is 20 years from the filing date (Annex I, Article 9).

Title IV of Annex I provides for a non-voluntary licensing regime. Three situations that may lead to the grant of a non-voluntary license are prescribed, as follows:

- non-voluntary license for non-working;
- non-voluntary license for dependent patents; and
- *ex officio* licenses (Article 56, Annex I).

After the expiration of a period of four years from the date of the filing of an application for a patent or three years from the date of the grant of a patent, a non-voluntary license may be granted at the request of any interested person for any of the following reasons:

- if the patented invention is not worked on the territory of a Member State at the time the request is made;
- if the working of the patented invention does not meet the demand for the protected product; or
- if the patentee refuses to grant licenses on reasonable terms.

However, if the patentee can show that there is any legitimate reason for his not working the patent, a compulsory license will not be granted to a third party.

A non-voluntary license may also be granted in the case of dependent inventions that cannot be worked without infringing each other. Where a patented invention cannot be worked without infringing the rights under an earlier patent whose owner refuses to authorize its use on reasonable commercial terms and procedures, the owner of the latter patent may obtain a non-voluntary license for such use from the court on the same terms as those that apply to the grant of other non-voluntary licenses but with the following additional conditions:

25 See, the Bangui Agreement, Annex I, Article 8(c); Annex II, Article 9(c); Annex IV, Article 6(a); and Annex X, Article 30(b).

(a) the invention claimed in the latter patent must represent substantial technical progress, of considerable economic interest, in relation to the invention claimed in the earlier patent;

(b) the owner of the earlier patent has the right to a reciprocal license on reasonable terms for the use of the invention claimed in the latter patent;

(c) the use authorized in relation to the earlier patent shall not be transferable except where the latter patent is also transferred.

An *ex officio* license is issued not by the court but by a competent Ministerial authority in the case where patents are of vital interest to the economy of the country, public health, or national defense, or where non-working or insufficient working of such patents seriously compromises the satisfaction of the country's needs. Royalties are paid to the owner of patent.

A request for the grant of a non-voluntary license must be made to the civil court of the domicile of the patentee or, if the latter is domiciled abroad, to the civil court of either his elected domicile or the place in which he has named an agent for the purposes of filing. Further, only requests made by persons domiciled on the territory of a Member State will be considered.

If a non-voluntary license is granted, the decision of the civil court shall specify the scope of the license, the period for which it is granted, and the amount of the remuneration to be paid by the licensee to the owner of the patent. A means for making an appeal to the court's decision is likewise provided.

The grant of a non-voluntary license shall not affect either normal or non-voluntary licenses in force and shall not preclude the conclusion of other license contracts or the grant of other non-voluntary licenses. In these cases, the patentee may, however, not grant to other licensees more favorable terms than those applicable to any non-voluntary license granted by the courts; the law requires that the non-voluntary licensee receive treatment equal to that afforded any subsequent voluntary licensees. At the same time, a non-voluntary licensee may not without prior permission of the patent holder authorize any third party to use the non-voluntary license. However, upon the authorization of the court, a non-voluntary license may be transferred together with the establishment of the beneficiary of the non-voluntary license or with the portion of his establishment that exploits the patented invention.

At the request of the owner of the patent or the beneficiary of the non-voluntary license, the civil court may amend the decision on the grant of the non-voluntary license where new facts justify such amendment. In addition, the civil court shall withdraw the non-voluntary license, at the request of the owner of the patent, if the grounds for its grant have ceased to exist, if the beneficiary exceeds the prescribed scope of the license, or if the beneficiary is in arrears with the payment of the remuneration. An appeal to the competent higher jurisdiction against a decision taken by one of the parties is set out under the OAPI regime.

Under the OAPI system, any beneficiary of a contractual or non-voluntary license may, by registered letter, summon the owner of a patent in order to bring the necessary judicial actions for civil or criminal sanctions for any violation by the latter of the licensee's rights under the patent.

The OAPI Agreement was revised in February 1999; the Doha Declaration on the TRIPs Agreement and Public Health was adopted in September 2001. As the most recent revision of the Bangui Agreement preceded the Doha Declaration, it is not surprising that issues addressed therein are not included in the OAPI provisions. In the same context, the issue of the granting of non-voluntary or *ex officio* licenses in situations of national emergency or circumstances of extreme urgency was not yet on the international agenda of IP law in 1999.

Both civil and criminal remedies are laid down in the case of infringement of a patentee's exclusive rights. The prior working of the patented invention is no longer a requirement for the recognition of an action for infringement.[26]

According to Article 7(2) of the Bangui Agreement, any filing of an international patent application that includes the designation of at least one Member State shall be equivalent to a national filing in each Member State that is also Party to the PCT.

Within the OAPI patent system, only a formal examination is carried out; there is no substantive examination of a patent application. A patent is granted or issued by the Director General of the OAPI at the applicant's own risk.

Pursuant to Annex 1, Article 12, any patent application that fulfills the conditions specified in Annex II concerning utility models may be converted into an application for a utility model. In such cases, the patent application shall be deemed to have been withdrawn and the Organization shall enter a withdrawal notice in the Register of Patents.

If the subject matter of the patent is a process for making a product, the judicial authority shall be authorized to order the defendant to prove that the process used to make an identical product is different from the patented process in one of the following situations:

- the product made by the process is new;
- there is a strong probability of the identical product having been made by means of the process and of the owner of the patent having been unable, in spite of reasonable effort, to establish what process was actually used (Annex I, Article 66).

Trademarks and Service Marks

Under the Bangui Agreement, trademarks and service marks are optional. However, Member States may exceptionally declare them compulsory for any goods or services that they may specify.

26 Kongolo, T. (2000b), 'The African Intellectual Property Organizations—The Necessity of Adopting One Uniform System for All Africa', *The Journal of World Intellectual Property* 3:2, 265–288, at 276.

Annex III, Article 2(1) defines what may constitute a trademark or service mark as follows:

> Any visible sign used or intended to be used and capable of distinguishing the goods or services of any enterprise shall be considered a trademark or service mark, including in particular surnames by themselves or in a distinctive form, special, arbitrary or fanciful designations, the characteristic form of a product or its packaging, labels, wrappers, emblems, prints, stamps, seals, vignettes, borders, combinations or arrangements of colors, drawings, reliefs, letters, numbers, devices and pseudonyms.

The OAPI provisions condition the registration of a trademark or a service mark upon its ability to be perceived visually and to be able to distinguish the goods or services of an enterprise from those of other undertakings. Since what is required is that the mark be visible, most non-traditional marks pertaining to non-visible signs, such as smell, taste, feel, and sound marks, may be excluded from the sphere of protection of trademarks or service marks under the OAPI system. The same may be said for some visible signs, such as a single color mark, which may not be considered to constitute a distinctive sign. The significance of this is that any trademark holder of a single-color mark or non-visible signs registered in other parts of the world who intends to do business in the OAPI region must redesign his trademark or service mark to meet the requirements of the Bangui Agreement, which provides explicitly that only arrangements or combinations of colors may qualify as trademarks. On the other hand, the Agreement establishes protection within the trademark system for three-dimensional marks, including packaging.

Annex III also provides protection for collective marks. It has adopted the first-to-file principle to accord exclusive rights to the person who has first filed. Every right stems from registration of the mark. Annex III, Article 3 further specifies those marks that are not eligible for registration as follows:

> A mark may not be validly registered if
>
> *(a)* it is devoid of distinctiveness, notably owing to the fact that it consists of signs or matter constituting the necessary or genetic designation of the product or the composition thereof;
>
> *(b)* it is identical to a mark that belongs to another owner and is already registered, or the filing or priority date of which is earlier, and which relates to the same or similar goods or services, or where it so resembles such a mark that it is liable to mislead or confuse;
>
> *(c)* it is contrary to public policy, morality or the law;
>
> *(d)* it is liable to mislead the public or business circles, notably as to the geographical origin, nature or characteristics of the goods or services in question;

> *(e)* it reproduces, imitates or incorporates armorial bearings, flags or other emblems, the abbreviated name or acronym or an official sign or hallmark indicating control and warranty of a State or intergovernmental organization established by an international convention, except where the competent authority of that State or of that organization has given its permission.

This list of non-protectable marks is in conformity with the general trend on the matter.

In accordance with Article 6*bis* of the Paris Convention and TRIPs Article 16(2) and (3), Annex III, Article 6 of the Bangui Agreement sets out protection with regard to well-known marks. It provides:

> The owner of a well-known mark within the meaning of Article 6*bis* of the Paris Convention for the Protection of Industrial Property and Article 16, paragraphs (2) and (3), of the Agreement on Trade Related Aspects of Intellectual Property Rights may apply to the court for the invalidation, on the national territory of one of the member States, of the effects of the filing of a mark liable to be confused with his own. Such action may not be taken after a period of five years has expired following the date of the application in so far as the latter was filed in good faith.

Accordingly, the owner of a well-known mark may apply to the national court for invalidation of a registered mark that may create confusion with his mark. However, if the applicant has registered his mark in good faith, the owner of the well-known mark cannot carry out any action against him after the expiration of five years from the filing date of the trademark application. Like most legislation, the Bangui Agreement has not defined what a well-known mark is. It remains to be seen in practice how the courts will define a well-known mark, taking into consideration the national context. Notwithstanding that the Agreement refers explicitly to the Paris Convention and the TRIPs Agreement in relation to well-known marks, it has not elaborated much on the subject. The question here is whether the provisions of the Paris Convention and the TRIPs Agreement on this subject form parts of the OAP-prescribed provisions. Interpretations on this matter may vary. Some may argue that the OAPI Agreement does not include those provisions by mere reference. In this case, the only determining factor would be the likelihood of confusion with a well-known mark, and under these circumstances protection of a well-known mark would be limited to its usage in relation to similar goods and services. The Bangui Agreement has not expressly extended the scope of coverage to also include dissimilar goods and services. Thus, it gives no consideration to the likelihood of association with or connection to the well-known mark for dissimilar goods or services, on the one hand, and no consideration to the damages that may be caused by such association, on the other hand. In addition, the Agreement is silent as to the consideration of the degree of public knowledge of the well-known mark or to the size of the segment of consumers who do possess such knowledge. Some may assert that the provisions of the Paris Convention and the TRIPs Agreement on well-known marks are an integral part of the OAPI Agreement. In this case, what are mentioned under the two provisions apply *mutatis mutandis* in the context of OAPI. It will be interesting to see the factors and elements that courts from the OAPI region will take into consideration to determine what constitutes a well-known mark in the region.

A registered mark is protected for a period of 10 years and is renewable indefinitely every 10 years. Annex III, Article 7 (1) and (2) sets forth the exclusive rights conferred on the owner of a trademark or a service mark as follows:

> (1) Registration of a mark confers on its owner the exclusive right to use the mark, or a sign resembling it, in connection with the goods or services for which it has been registered and similar goods or services.
>
> (2) Registration of the mark likewise confers on the owner the exclusive right to prevent all third parties from making use in business without his consent, of identical or similar signs for goods or services that are themselves similar to those for which the trademark or service mark has been registered where such use is liable to cause confusion. Where an identical sign is used for identical goods and services, a risk of confusion shall be presumed to exist.

What is interesting here is that the owner of a trademark is entitled to both positive and negative rights—the positive right to use the mark, or a sign resembling it, in connection with the goods or services for which it has been registered and similar goods or services, as well as the negative right to exclude others from using his mark without his consent. The legal implication is that even for non-commercial purposes no one other than the trademark owner is entitled to use the mark in connection with the goods or services for which it has been registered. Competitors also will not be permitted to use the trademark even for good reason, such as for comparison of products. In sum, the scope of protection offered under the Bangui Agreement is stronger and wider than that found in most other trademark protection systems.

Some limitations on the rights conferred are provided by the Bangui Agreement by stating that another party is not prohibited from using the mark if the use is in good faith and if the use in question is limited to the purpose of mere identification or information and cannot mislead the public as to the source of the goods or services. A second limitation pertains to the exhaustion of rights, whereby the registration of a mark does not confer on its owner the right to prohibit a third party from making use of the mark in relation to goods that have been lawfully sold under the mark on the national territory of the Member State in which the right of prohibition is exercised, provided that the products are not altered.

Rights subsisting in a mark are transferable in whole or in part, separately or together with an enterprise. Any interested person may oppose the registration of a mark within six months of its publication. The publication of the mark occurs after its registration. A post-grant opposition regime is also provided. Any registered mark which has not been used for an uninterrupted period of five years on the national territory of one of the Member States may be cancelled if any interested party files a suit with the civil court. In this context, the use of a mark has a regional meaning. What is important is to use the mark within the prescribed period in one of the Member States of the OAPI.

According to Article 7(3) of the Bangui Agreement, any international trademark registration effected under the provisions of the Trademark Registration Treaty and including the designation of at least one OAPI Member State shall have the effect of a national filing in each Member State that is also Party to that Treaty.

Protection of Plant Varieties

Annex X of the Bangui Agreement sets out a protection regime for plant varieties. This Annex was included by the 1999 amendment.

To be protected, the plant variety must be registered. To be registered, as set out in Annex X, Article 4, five criteria and conditions must be met. The plant variety must be new, distinct, homogenous, stable, and bear a denomination. Each criterion of eligibility has been defined in Articles 5–8. A plant variety certificate is issued upon registration, and it is granted only for one variety.

The denomination shall constitute the genetic designation of the variety. The denomination of the variety is protected, and no one is entitled to use it in the territory of any Member country in a manner that may create confusion. A plant variety certificate grants to its owner the exclusive right to exploit the plant variety which is the subject of the certificate. It also confers upon its holder the right to prohibit any other person from exploiting the variety and to institute legal proceedings against any person who infringes his rights. The owner is also entitled to the exclusive right to license or assign his rights.

Under Annex X, Article 29(1), 'exploitation' means the following acts carried out with respect to propagating material of a protected variety:

(a) production or reproduction (multiplication);
(b) conditioning for the purpose of propagation;
(c) offering for sale;
(d) selling or other marketing;
(e) exporting;
(f) importing;
(g) stocking for any of the purposes mentioned in *(a)* to *(f)* above.

Paragraphs 2 and 3 of the same Article add to the above-mentioned list acts carried out in respect of propagating and harvested material, including entire plants and parts of plants, obtained through the unauthorized use of such material of the protected variety, unless the holder of the rights has had reasonable opportunity to exercise his rights in relation to that propagating material. Those acts shall extend:

> *(a)* to varieties which are essentially derived from the protected variety, where the protected variety is not itself an essentially derived variety;
> *(b)* to varieties which are not clearly distinguishable in accordance with Article 6 from the protected variety; and
> *(c)* to varieties whose production requires the repeated use of the protected variety.

Some exceptions to the exclusive rights of the owner are provided in Annex X, Article 30. Acts carried out for private use and non-commercial purposes, acts carried out for research or experimental purposes, acts accomplished for the creation of new varieties that are in conformity with the Bangui Agreement, utilization by a farmer for reproduction or multiplication purposes on his own farm of a protected variety (this exception does not apply to forest trees, fruit trees, and ornamental trees), and acts accomplished by a third party in good faith before the filing of application are all such exclusions.

The Annex recognizes the exhaustion of rights regime by allowing third parties to use (exploit) a plant variety that has been put into circulation by the owner or with his consent. The right to prevent propagation of the variety, however, is not exhausted. Annex, X Article 31 provides:

> The rights conferred by a plant variety certificate shall not extend to acts concerning material of the protected variety or a variety covered by Article 29(4) which has been sold or otherwise marketed on the territory of a member State by the holder or with his consent or any material derived from such material, unless such acts:
> *(a)* involve further propagation of the variety in question; or
> *(b)* involve an export of material of the variety, which enables the propagation of the variety, into a country which does not protect varieties of the plant genus or species to which the variety belongs, except where the exported material is for final consumption purposes.

The period of protection is set at 20 years from the issue date of the plant variety certificate.

Governments may use the plant variety without the prior consent of its owner under some circumstances and conditions (a kind of *ex-officio* license).

African Regional Initiatives

As will be seen in Chapter 4, pertaining to initiatives of African countries at the international level, these countries have been very active since early 2000 on the international IP scene. This is also reflected at the regional level, where a number of initiatives on specific IP subject matters have been undertaken by the two regional IP organizations. In addition, in recent years the AU has been very dynamic at the regional level by adopting model laws in the field of IP and biotechnology. The AU's adoption of the Model Law for the Protection of the Rights of Local Communities, Farmers and Breeders, and for the Regulation of Access to Biological Resources in 2000 is a breakthrough initiative at the regional level. The AU also adopted a Model Law on Biosafety in 2001 which is under revision. In addition, an initiative for the establishment of a Pan-African Intellectual Property Organization was tabled in early 2006 by the AU, and in November 2012 the Ministerial Conference of the AU adopted a 'Final Draft Statute of the Pan-African Intellectual Property Organization (PAIPO)'. Recently, in August 2010, the ARIPO adopted a Protocol on the Protection of Traditional Knowledge and Expressions of Folklore, and an ARIPO Draft Protocol on Plant Varieties Protection has been on the table since 2011.

Protocol on the Protection of Traditional Knowledge and Expressions of Folklore adopted by the ARIPO on August 9, 2010

Introduction

The Member States of the ARIPO adopted the Protocol on the Protection of Traditional Knowledge and Expressions of Folklore at a Diplomatic Conference held in Swakopmund, Namibia, on August 9, 2010. This Protocol is named after the city where it was adopted and is therefore called the 'Swakopmund Protocol on the Protection of Traditional Knowledge and Expressions of Folklore' (hereinafter the Swakopmund Protocol). This Protocol will come into effect three months after six States have deposited their instruments of ratification or accession. The Protocol is open to both Member States of the ARIPO and other Member States of the AU or the United Nations Economic Commission for Africa. Notwithstanding this openness, accession to the Protocol by such States shall entail acceptance of the Agreement on the creation of the ARIPO.

The Protocol comprises two main parts, namely the protection of TK and the protection of EoF. It is clearly stated in Section 1 that the purpose of the Protocol is:

> (a) to protect traditional knowledge holders against any infringement of their rights as recognized by this Protocol; and
> (b) to protect expressions of folklore against misappropriation, misuse and unlawful exploitation beyond their traditional context.

The Preamble of the Protocol underlines the *raison d'être* for adopting such a Protocol to protect both TK and EoF as follows:

> Convinced that traditional knowledge systems, traditional cultures and folklore are diverse frameworks of ongoing innovation, creativity and distinctive

> intellectual and creative life that benefit local and traditional communities and all humanity;
>
> …
>
> Mindful of the need to respect traditional knowledge systems, traditional cultures and folklore, as well as the dignity, cultural integrity and intellectual and spiritual values of traditional and local communities; to recognize and reward the contributions made by such communities to the conservation of the environment, to food security and sustainable agriculture, to the improvement in the health of populations, to the progress of science and technology, to the preservation and safeguarding of cultural heritage, to the development of artistic skills, and to enhancing a diversity of cultural contents and artistic expressions;
>
> …
>
> Desiring to preclude the grant and exercise of improper intellectual property rights in traditional knowledge, associated genetic resources and derivatives thereof, and in expressions of folklore and works and productions derived therefrom;
>
> …
>
> Emphasizing that legal protection must be tailored to the specific characteristics of traditional knowledge and expressions of folklore, including their collective or community context, the intergenerational nature of their development, preservation and transmission, their link to a community's cultural and social identity, integrity, beliefs, spirituality and values, and their constantly evolving character within the community concerned.

Protection of traditional knowledge

In this section, the criteria of protection, beneficiaries, rights conferred, equitable benefit-sharing, exceptions and limitations, compulsory licenses, and duration of protection as established by the Swakopmund Protocol will be addressed.

Criteria of protection Traditional knowledge is defined in Section 2 of the Protocol as any knowledge originating from a local or traditional community that is the result of intellectual activity and insight in a traditional context, including know-how, skills, innovations, practices, and learning, where the knowledge is embodied in the traditional lifestyle of a community or contained in the codified knowledge systems passed on from one generation to another.

The key components in the definition are local or traditional community, traditional context, traditional lifestyle, and generation to generation. In other words, for a practice to be called traditional knowledge under the Protocol these elements are determinant.

The Protocol sets out the scope of TK by maintaining that the term shall not be limited to a specific technical field and may include agricultural, environmental, or medical knowledge and knowledge associated with GRs. In other words, Member States of the ARIPO have opted for a wide coverage of TK to include all fields of technology. Section 4 of the Protocol lays down the criteria for protection of TK as follows:

> Protection shall be extended to traditional knowledge that is:
> (i) generated, preserved and transmitted in a traditional and intergenerational context;
> (ii) distinctively associated with a local or traditional community; and
> (iii) integral to the cultural identity of a local or traditional community that is recognized as holding the knowledge through a form of custodianship, guardianship or collective and cultural ownership or responsibility. Such a relationship may be established formally or informally by customary practices, laws or protocols.

Traditional knowledge that is generated, preserved, and transmitted in a traditional way from generation to generation, and which is distinctively associated with a local or traditional community, forming an integral part of its cultural identity, may be protected.

Protection of TK shall not be subject to any formalities. However, in the interests of transparency, evidence, and the preservation of TK, relevant competent national authorities of the Contracting States and the ARIPO Office may maintain registers or other records of the knowledge, where appropriate, and subject to relevant policies, laws and procedures and the needs and aspirations of the TK holders concerned. The registers shall not compromise the status of hitherto undisclosed TK or the interests of holders of TK in relation to undisclosed elements of their knowledge.[27]

The maintenance of relevant records by the Contracting States and the ARIPO and the registration of the owners of the TK are required where two or more communities in the same or different countries share the same TK.

Beneficiaries There is always some question in the context of TK as to who should be the beneficiaries of any protection. The Swakopmund Protocol lays down in Section 6 that the owners of the rights shall be the holders of the TK, namely the local and traditional communities, and recognized individuals within such communities, who create, preserve, and transmit knowledge in a traditional and inter-generational context.

Rights conferred Section 7 of the Protocol sets out the exclusive rights of the owners of TK as follows:

> 7.1. This Protocol shall confer on the owners of rights referred to in Section 6 the exclusive right to authorize the exploitation of their traditional knowledge.

27 See, Section 5 of the Protocol.

7.2. In addition, owners shall have the right to prevent anyone from exploiting their traditional knowledge without their prior informed consent.

7.3. For the purposes of this Protocol, the term 'exploitation' with reference to traditional knowledge shall refer to any of the following acts:

(a) Where the traditional knowledge is a product:

(i) manufacturing, importing, exporting, offering for sale, selling or using beyond the traditional context the product;

(ii) being in possession of the product for the purposes of offering it for sale, selling it or using it beyond the traditional context;

(b) Where the traditional knowledge is a process:

(i) making use of the process beyond the traditional context;

(ii) carrying out the acts referred to under paragraph (a) of this subsection with respect to a product that is a direct result of the use of the process.

The exclusive rights of the TK owners are designed *mutatis mutandis* in the same way as those of patent owners. The key element here is that prior informed consent from the beneficiary is required before any TK may be exploited outside its traditional context. The Protocol also sets out assignment and licensing of TK under Section 8, which provides as follows:

8.1. Owners of traditional knowledge shall have the right to assign and conclude licensing agreements; however, traditional knowledge belonging to a local or traditional community may not be assigned.

8.2. All access, authorizations, assignments or licences granted in respect of protected traditional knowledge shall be granted in writing; otherwise they shall be of no force or effect.

8.3. A document drawn up for the purpose of section 8.2 shall be approved by the national competent authority, failing which the document shall be void.

8.4. The ARIPO Office shall keep a register of all licences and assignments granted under this section.

Equitable benefit-sharing The Protocol regulates the equitable benefit-sharing regime. It maintains that the protection to be provided to TK holders shall include the fair and equitable sharing of benefits arising from the commercial or industrial use of their knowledge, which shall be determined by mutual agreement between the parties. In the absence of such mutual agreement, the national competent authority shall mediate between the concerned parties with a view to arriving at an agreement on the fair and equitable sharing of benefits. In addition, the right to equitable remuneration might extend to non-monetary benefits, such as contributions to community development, depending on the material needs and cultural preferences expressed by the traditional or local communities themselves.

It is provided that any person using TK beyond its traditional context shall acknowledge its holders, indicate its source and, where possible, its origin and use such knowledge in a manner that respects the cultural values of its holders.

In accordance with Section 15 of the Protocol, authorization to access protected TK associated with GRs shall not imply authorization to access the GRs derived from the TK.

Exceptions and limitations The only exception or limitation provided under Section 11 pertains to the continued availability of TK for use by the traditional community. It provides that:

> The protection of traditional knowledge under this Protocol shall not be prejudicial to the continued availability of traditional knowledge for the practice, exchange, use and transmission of the knowledge by its holders within the traditional context.

Compulsory licenses A compulsory license regime is established in case of insufficient use or exploitation of TK or in the case of a refusal to grant a license to a third party on reasonable commercial terms.

Section 12 provides:

> 12.1. Where protected traditional knowledge is not being sufficiently exploited by the rights holder, or where the holder of rights in traditional knowledge refuses to grant licences subject to reasonable commercial terms and conditions, a Contracting State may, in the interests of public security or public health, grant a compulsory licence in order to fulfil national needs.
>
> 12.2. In the absence of an agreement between the parties, an appropriate amount of compensation for the compulsory licence shall be fixed by a court of competent jurisdiction.

The inclusion of a 'patent regime'-like system for compulsory licensing of TK has particularly negative implications. First of all, the possibility of becoming subject to compulsory licensing seems to be ample justification for not registering some knowledge that might otherwise be secret. Also, how can one tell that a secret TK is not used or exploited? Second, granting compulsory licenses in the TK context seems to further defeat the rationale of protection because it leaves open to decision by persons outside the traditional community what or how much constitutes 'insufficient use or exploitation'. One may question whether the use of the knowledge within the traditional community may qualify as 'insufficient use'. Third, it likewise leaves up to the rationale of non-traditional authorities what shall constitute 'reasonable economic terms' for the grant of a license to third parties, so that TK can be 'forcibly' exploited by third parties under compulsory licenses at terms that may well be unacceptable to the traditional community.

Duration of protection Section 13 sets forth that TK shall be protected for so long as the knowledge fulfills the protection criteria referred to under Section 4, except that where the TK belongs exclusively to an individual protection shall last for 25 years following the exploitation of the knowledge beyond its traditional context by the individual. One may question the rationale behind granting protection to individual TK owners for only 25 years if the TK is exploited outside the community.

Protection of expressions of folklore

Unlike TK, which may be considered a new concept in the field of intellectual property, EoF have been included by several African copyright laws as protectable literary or artistic works. Within the WIPO Intergovernmental Committee on Intellectual Property and Genetic Resources, Traditional Knowledge and Folklore (IGC), whose work will be covered in Chapter 4, the term 'traditional cultural expressions' is preferred to the term 'expressions of folklore' because the latter may carry some pejorative meaning in certain contexts. Under the Swakopmund Protocol, the preference has been given to the term 'expressions of folklore'.

In this section, the criteria of protection, beneficiaries, protection of EoF against unlawful acts, exceptions and limitations, and duration of protection as established by the Swakopmund Protocol will be covered and discussed.

Criteria of protection Section 2 of the Protocol defines EoF as any forms, whether tangible or intangible, in which traditional culture and knowledge are expressed, appear or are manifested, and comprising the following forms of expressions or combinations thereof:

> i. verbal expressions, such as but not limited to stories, epics, legends, poetry, riddles and other narratives; words, signs, names, and symbols;
> ii. musical expressions, such as but not limited to songs and instrumental music;
> iii. expressions by movement, such as but not limited to dances, plays, rituals and other performances; whether or not reduced to a material form; and
> iv. tangible expressions, such as productions of art, in particular, drawings, designs, paintings (including body-painting), carvings, sculptures, pottery, terracotta, mosaic, woodwork, metal ware, jewelry, basketry, needlework, textiles, glassware, carpets, costumes; handicrafts; musical instruments; and architectural forms.

According to this Section, both tangible and intangible expressions may constitute EoF.

The Protocol sets out the criteria of protection for EoF as follows:

> Protection shall be extended to expressions of folklore, whatever the mode or form of their expression, which are:

(a) the products of creative and cumulative intellectual activity, such as collective creativity or individual creativity where the identity of the individual is unknown; and
(b) characteristic of a community's cultural identity and traditional heritage and maintained, used or developed by such community in accordance with the customary laws and practices of that community.

The main condition is that the EoF shall be a product of individual or collective creativity from unknown individuals and reflect the cultural identity of a community. The latter condition is not enough, in the sense that the EoF must also be maintained, used, or developed by the community, taking into consideration their customary laws and practices. The two sets of conditions are cumulative. What is quite disturbing here is that the identity of the individual who first created the EoF must be unknown for it to qualify for protection. EoF is not static; it is an evolving and dynamic subject matter. Denying protection to EoF merely because the identity of the individual first creator is known is unfortunate and may be contrary to one of the purposes for setting up a system to protect EoF, which is to contribute to innovation. Folklore is not necessarily identical with something that is old. The emphasis should be put on the mode of transmission and the form of EoF rather than on the identity of the person who created them. As a consequence, it might be asked how many generations must be considered for a work to be identified as folklore. In the context of the Protocol, as long as the grandfather is alive, or the great-grandfather is still known, the work will not be eligible for protection as an EoF. One could also question this by asserting that the Protocol refers to the identity of the person (alive or dead), which should be unknown. That may imply that as long as the identity of the person is known, alive or dead, no protection would be provided. In other words, by interpretation it may be said that many generations must pass for a work to be considered as an EoF and eligible for protection.

The Protocol has opted for no formality for the protection of EoF. On the other hand, for the purposes of evidence, measures for the protection of EoF may require that certain categories of the expressions for which protection is sought, particularly those with special cultural or spiritual value or significance or those that are sacred in character, be notified to the appropriate authority. The notification is not aimed at the granting of rights as it has only a declaratory function. Where two or more communities in the same or different countries share the same expressions of folklore, the relevant national competent authorities of Contracting States and the ARIPO Office shall register the owners of the rights in those expressions of folklore.

Beneficiaries According to Section 18, the owners of the rights in EoF shall be the local and traditional communities:

(a) to whom the custody and protection of the expressions of folklore are entrusted in accordance with the customary laws and practices of those communities; and

(b) who maintain and use the expressions of folklore as a characteristic of their traditional cultural heritage.

Essentially, the beneficiaries of protection of EoF are those local and traditional communities that meet the conditions set out in Section 16 of the Protocol. Based on the criteria of protection, which require that if a work was created by an individual that the identity of the individual must be unknown, and in view of the prescription of this provision, it can be said that the Protocol intends to provide rights only to the community and not to individuals.

Protection of expressions of folklore against unlawful acts Section 19 of the Protocol enumerates acts that may be considered as infringing the beneficiary's rights in the following terms:

> 19.1 Expressions of folklore shall be protected against all acts of misappropriation, misuse and unlawful exploitation.
>
> 19.2. In respect of expressions of folklore of particular cultural or spiritual value or significance to a community, the Contracting States shall provide adequate and effective legal and practical measures to ensure that the relevant community can prevent the following acts from taking place without its free and Prior Informed Consent:
>
> (a) in respect of such expressions of folklore other than words, signs, names and symbols:
>
> i). the reproduction, publication, adaptation, broadcasting, public performance, communication to the public, distribution, rental, making available to the public and fixation (including by still photography) of the expressions of folklore or derivatives thereof;
>
> ii). any use of the expressions of folklore or adaptation thereof which does not acknowledge in an appropriate way the community as the source of the expressions of folklore;
>
> iii). any distortion, mutilation or other modification of, or other derogatory action, in relation to the expressions of folklore; and
>
> iv). the acquisition or exercise of intellectual property rights over the expressions of folklore or adaptations thereof;
>
> (b) in respect of words, signs, names and symbols which are such expressions of folklore, any use of the expressions of folklore or derivatives thereof, or the acquisition or exercise of intellectual property rights over the expressions of folklore or derivatives thereof, which disparages, offends or falsely suggests a connection with the community concerned, or brings the community into contempt or disrepute.

19.3. In respect of the use and exploitation of other expressions of folklore, the Contracting States shall provide adequate and effective legal and practical measures to ensure that:

(a) the relevant community is identified as the source of any work or other production adapted from the expressions of folklore;

(b) any distortion, mutilation or other modification of, or other derogatory action in relation to expressions of folklore can be prevented and/or is subject to civil or criminal sanctions;

(c) any false, confusing or misleading indications or allegations which, in relation to goods or services that refer to, draw upon or evoke the expressions of folklore of a community or suggest any endorsement by or linkage with that community, can be prevented and/or is subject to civil or criminal sanctions; and

(d) where the use or exploitation is for gainful intent, there should be equitable remuneration or benefit-sharing on terms determined by the national competent authority in consultation with the relevant community.

19.4. Contracting States shall provide adequate and effective legal and practical measures to ensure that communities have the means to prevent the unauthorized disclosure, subsequent use of and acquisition and exercise of intellectual property rights over expressions of folklore that are held secret.

Authorizations to exploit EoF must be obtained from the national competent authority which acts on behalf of and in the interests of the communities concerned (Section 22.2). A prior appropriate consultation with the communities concerned and compliance with the scope of protection of the EoF, providing for the equitable sharing of the benefits arising from their use, are required. The national competent authority shall transfer directly to the communities concerned any monetary or non-monetary benefits arising from the use of the EoF.

The Protocol also prescribes that guidance on matters such as procedures for applications for authorization, fees that the national competent authority or the ARIPO Office may, where necessary, charge for its services, official publication procedures, dispute resolution, and the terms and conditions governing authorizations that may be granted by the national competent authority shall be provided by enabling legislation or administrative measures.

Exceptions and limitations Exceptions and limitations are established to ensure the continued use of EoF by the members of the traditional community in the traditional context and to permit certain uses of the EoF outside the traditional context under certain conditions for non-commercial use as set out under Section 20 as follows:

20.1. Measures for the protection of expressions of folklore shall:

(a) be such as not to restrict or hinder the normal use, development, exchange, dissemination and transmission of expressions of folklore within the traditional or customary context by members of the community concerned, as determined by customary laws and practices;

(b) extend only to uses of expressions of folklore taking place outside their traditional or customary context, whether or not for commercial gain;

(c) be subject to exceptions in order to address the needs of non-commercial use, such as teaching and research, personal or private use, criticism or review, reporting of current events, use in the course of legal proceedings, the making of recordings and reproductions of expressions of folklore for inclusion in an archive or inventory exclusively for the purposes of safeguarding cultural heritage, and incidental uses, provided that in each case, such uses are compatible with fair practice, the relevant community is acknowledged as the source of the expressions of folklore where practicable and possible, and such uses would not be offensive to the relevant community.

20.2 The measures put in place for the protection of expressions of folklore may make special provision for their use by the nationals of the country concerned.

The Protocol upholds the principle that where two or more communities in different countries share the same EoF, the ARIPO Office shall be responsible for raising awareness, education, guidance, monitoring, dispute resolution, and other activities relating to the protection of the EoF of those communities.

Duration of protection The Protocol lays down that EoF shall be protected against all acts of misappropriation, misuse, or unlawful exploitation for as long as they fulfill the protection criteria set out in Section 16. As will be discussed in Chapter 4, the question here is whether to provide protection to EoF in perpetuity or to limit it to a particular time period. The Protocol has opted for a middle-of-the-road solution which guarantees protection only if the EoF is the product of creative and cumulative intellectual activity, is characteristic of a community's cultural identity and traditional heritage and is maintained, used, or developed by such community in accordance with the customary laws and practices of that community.

Section 24.1 sets out that eligible foreign holders of TK and EoF shall enjoy benefits of protection at the same level as holders of TK and EoF who are nationals of the country of protection, taking into account as far as possible the customary laws and protocols applicable to the TK or EoF concerned.

Section 25 deals with transitional measures pertaining to TK and EoF that was used outside the traditional context before the entry into force of the Protocol and provides as follows;

25.1. Exploitation and dissemination of traditional knowledge prior to the entry into force of the protection under this Protocol shall comply with the provisions of section 9 relating to equitable benefit-sharing and section 10 relating to the recognition of the source, within twelve months following the entry into force of the protection, subject to equitable treatment of the rights acquired by third parties in good faith.

25.2. The continued use of expressions of folklore that had commenced prior to the introduction of this Protocol to protect the expressions of folklore shall comply with provisions of section 19 within twelve months of this Protocol entering into force, subject to equitable treatment of the rights and interests acquired by third parties through prior use in good faith.

The ARIPO Draft Protocol on Plant Varieties Protection

At the Twelfth Session of the Council of Ministers held in Gaborone, Botswana on November 26–27, 2009, the Council approved proposals for the ARIPO to develop a policy and legal framework which will form the basis for the development of an ARIPO Protocol on the Protection of New Varieties of Plants.[28]

Following the decision of the Council of Ministers, the ARIPO Secretariat requested technical assistance from the International Union for the Protection of New Varieties of Plants (UPOV) in the preparation of policy and legislative frameworks on the protection of new varieties of plants. As a result of the request, UPOV prepared a draft legislative framework for the Organization.[29] The Draft Regional Framework was developed on the basis of the 1991 Act of the UPOV Convention, which was adopted by the Council of UPOV at its Forty-Third Ordinary Session on October 22, 2009.[30]

The ARIPO Draft Protocol on Plant Varieties was discussed during the Thirteenth Session of the Council of Ministers that took place in Accra, Ghana, on December 1–2, 2011. The Draft Protocol encompasses, *inter alia*, the following subject matters: purpose; genera and species to be protected; conditions of protection; persons entitled to apply for protection; granting and rejection of a plant breeders' right; scope of the breeders' right; exceptions to the breeders' right; exhaustion of the breeders' right; duration of the breeders' right; variety denomination; appeals and enforcement procedures; and transitional provisions.

Preamble

The Preamble of the text explains the *raison d'être* for adopting such legislation for the Member States. Here are some of its statements:

---

28 See, *Draft Regional Policy and Legal Framework for Plant Variety Protection*, ARIPO Council of Ministers, Thirteenth Session, Accra, Ghana, December 1–2, 2011.

29 Ibid.

30 Ibid.

> *Convinced* that provision for plant breeders' rights in the region will allow farmers access to a wide range of improved varieties to contribute to the attainment of the regional goal of economic development and food security;
>
> ...
>
> *Convinced* of the importance of providing an effective system for the protection of new varieties of plants with the aim of encouraging the development of new varieties of plants for the benefit of the society.

At the outset, the issue of the definition of 'ARIPO territory' (vis-à-vis the UPOV Convention) was raised, and three plausible options have been put on the table as follows:

1. Option based on all ARIPO Member States:
   (a) 'territory of ARIPO' means the territories of the Members States of ARIPO to which the [constituting treaty of ARIPO/Lusaka Agreement] applies;
   (b) any application filed under this regional instrument with the ARIPO Office shall be valid in all the Members States of ARIPO; and
   (c) pursuant to [insert Article on filing of applications], any grant made by the ARIPO Office shall be valid in all the Members States of ARIPO.
2. Option based on all Contracting States to the regional instrument:
   (a) 'territory of ARIPO', for the purpose of this regional instrument, means the territories of the Contracting States to which this regional instrument applies;
   (b) any application filed under this regional instrument with the ARIPO Office shall be valid in all the Contracting States; and
   (c) pursuant to any grant made by the ARIPO Office shall be valid in all the Contracting States.
3. Option based on the Harare Protocol on Patents and Industrial Designs within the Framework of the African Regional Intellectual Property Organization (1982) (Harare Protocol):
   (a) an application for a breeder's right shall designate the Contracting States to the regional instrument for which the breeder's right is requested to be granted; and
   (b) under specific reasons, a designated State is entitled to make a written communication to the ARIPO Office that, if a breeder's right is granted by the ARIPO Office, that breeder's right shall have no effect in its territory.

The first option would require that any application for protection be valid in all Member States of the ARIPO, whist in the second option it would be valid only for Contracting States to which the Protocol on Plant Varieties Protection applies, and in the third option only in the Contracting States designated therein. The third option reflects the ARIPO's adopted format so far.

Purpose
According to the Draft Protocol, the purpose of the system is to grant and protect breeders' rights. The granted plant breeders' rights would, on the basis of one application, be valid in all the Contracting States. The ARIPO Office would be empowered to grant breeders' rights and to administer such breeders' rights on behalf of the Contracting States. This provision is not in line with the current format (option three) adopted by the ARIPO for other Protocols as it states that the granted breeder's rights will be valid in all the Contracting States (option two).

Genera and species to be protected
The Protocol shall be applied to the plant genera and species designated by decisions of the Administrative Council/the regulations and, after the expiration of a period of 10 years from the date of coming into force of this Legal Framework at the latest, to all plant genera and species. It can be said that the coverage of plant genera and species will be known once the Regulations are issued.

The ARIPO Office will have to maintain a register, to be known as the ARIPO Register of Plant Breeders' Rights.

Conditions of protection
The criteria of protection are similar to most of the legislation providing a *sui generis* system of protection of plant breeder's rights. The variety must be new, distinct, uniform, and stable. In addition, a variety must have a denomination. The Draft Protocol maintains that the grant of the breeder's right shall not be subject to any further or different conditions.

Persons entitled to apply for protection
The Draft Protocol enumerates persons entitled to apply for protection as follows:

(1) An application may be filed by the breeder of a new variety who is a national or resident of:
 (a) ARIPO member states; or
 (b) A Member of UPOV
 (c) Any other state which grants reciprocity of treatment to ARIPO.
(2) An application under Article 11(2)(b) and 11(2)(c) by a breeder who is not resident in ARIPO member states shall be submitted only through an agent or representative with residence in a member state of ARIPO.

The application would be required to be submitted through the National Authority, which would handle the application in the manner as prescribed in the Regulations.

Granting and rejection of the plant breeders' right
Where the plant variety fulfills the requirements of novelty, distinctness, uniformity, and stability and that the proposed denomination of the variety can be

registered, the ARIPO Office would grant a plant breeder's right, and where those requirements are not fulfilled the ARIPO Office would reject the application.

Scope of the plant breeders' right

The following acts in respect of the propagating material of the protected variety would require the authorization of the breeder:

- production or reproduction (multiplication);
- conditioning for the purpose of propagation;
- offering for sale;
- selling or other marketing;
- exporting;
- importing; or
- stocking for any of the purposes mentioned above.

The above-mentioned acts could not be undertaken in relation to the protected variety if they were not authorized by the breeder. In addition, the Draft Protocol gives leeway to the breeder to make such authorization subject to conditions and limitations.

The authorization of the breeder would be required as regards the harvested material obtained through the unauthorized use of propagating material of the protected variety, unless the breeder has had reasonable opportunity to exercise his right in relation to the said propagating material and has not done so.

In addition to the above-mentioned acts, the authorization of the breeder would be required in the following cases:

- varieties which are essentially derived from the protected variety, where the protected variety is not itself an essentially derived variety;
- varieties which are not clearly distinguishable from the protected variety; and
- varieties whose production requires the repeated use of the protected variety.

A variety shall be deemed to be essentially derived from another variety ('the initial variety') when:

- it is predominantly derived from the initial variety, or from a variety that is itself predominantly derived from the initial variety, while retaining the expression of the essential characteristics that result from the genotype or combination of genotypes of the initial variety;
- it is clearly distinguishable from the initial variety; and
- except for the differences which result from the act of derivation, it conforms to the initial variety in the expression of the essential characteristics that result from the genotype or combination of genotypes of the initial variety.

Exceptions to the plant breeders' right

The breeders' right would not extend to acts done privately and for non-commercial purposes, acts done for experimental purposes, acts done for the purpose of breeding other varieties, and acts carried out on varieties essentially derived from the protected variety except where the latter is itself an essentially derived variety.

The Draft Protocol would empower Contracting States, within reasonable limits, to set out any limitation to the breeder's right in relation to any variety in order to permit farmers to use for propagating purposes, on their own holdings, the product of the harvest which they have obtained by planting, on their own holdings, the protected variety or a variety covered, provided that the legitimate interests of the breeder are safeguarded. Ultimately, it may be up to each Contracting State to define the scope of application of farmer's rights or a farmer's exception.

Exhaustion of the plant breeders' right

The Draft Protocol provides for a regional exhaustion of the breeders' right within the ARIPO territory in the following terms:

> The breeder's right shall not extend to acts concerning any material of the protected variety, or of a variety covered by the provisions of Article 21(5), which has been sold or otherwise marketed by the breeder or with his consent in the territory of ARIPO, or any material derived from the said material, unless such acts
>
> (i) involve further propagation of the variety in question or
>
> (ii) involve an export of material of the variety, which enables the propagation of the variety, into a country which does not protect varieties of the plant genus or species to which the variety belongs, except where the exported material is for final consumption purposes.

Restrictions on the exercise of the plant breeders' right

Restrictions on the exercise of the breeders' right are equivalent to compulsory licensing. The Draft Protocol makes it clear that except where expressly provided, the free exercise of a breeder's right would not be restricted for reasons other than those of the public interest and that an equitable remuneration would be required to be provided when a third party might be authorized by the competent national authority to carry out any act, conditional upon the breeder's consent. It will be interesting to see how the ARIPO Contracting States will define public interest, which has various faces and which varies from one country to another.

Duration of the plant breeders' right

The breeders' right would be granted for a period of 20 years from the date of its grant. For trees and vines, the period would be 25 years from the date of the grant.

Appeals and enforcement procedures

Appeals and enforcement procedures are provided under the Draft Protocol.

Transitional provisions
A plant breeder's right could be granted for an existing variety that was no longer new on the date of entry into force of the Legal Framework in respect of the relevant species, provided that the application was filed within one year following the date that it came into force.

Finally, it should be pointed out that the Draft Protocol on Plant Varieties Protection is still under discussion and subject to any change that the ARIPO Member States may wish to make.

The African Model Law for the Protection of the Rights of Local Communities, Farmers and Breeders, and for the Regulation of Access to Biological Resources

The African Model Law for the Protection of the Rights of Local Communities, Farmers and Breeders, and for the Regulation of Access to Biological Resources (the Model Law)[31] was adopted in 2000 by the AU to empower African countries or their people to exercise their sovereign rights over their biological resources and also to recognize rights of local communities. The Model Law explicitly prescribes that it is the duty of the State and its people to regulate access to biological resources and to community knowledge and technologies. It also maintains that there is a need to promote and support traditional and indigenous technologies in the conservation and sustainable use of biological resources and to complement them by appropriately developed modern technologies.

According to the Model Law, there is a need to implement the relevant provisions of the CBD, in particular Article 15 on access to GRs and Article 8(j) on the preservation and maintenance of knowledge, innovations, and practices of indigenous and local communities. The Preamble also provides that the State and its people exercise sovereign and inalienable rights over their biological resources.

The Model Law clearly indicates that exclusive appropriation of any life form or part or derivative thereof violates fundamental human rights. Accordingly, the patenting of life forms shall not be permitted.

The merit of this Model Law is that it encompasses a hybrid system of protection covering biodiversity and plant varieties. It is a balanced *sui generis* system recognizing both breeders' rights and farmers' rights.

Objectives
The Model Law provides both general and specific objectives in Part I. The general or main objective is to ensure the conservation, evaluation, and sustainable use of biological resources, including agricultural GRs, and knowledge and technologies

31 Model Law for the Protection of the Rights of Local Communities, Farmers and Breeders, and for the Regulation of Access to Biological Resources (the Model Law); available at: http://www.flag-sa.org/downdocs/oaulocalfarmersrights-booklet.pdf. (last accessed on November 26, 2012).

in order to maintain and improve their diversity as a means of sustaining life support systems.

The specific objectives are as follows:

a. recognize, protect and support the inalienable rights of local communities including farming communities over their biological resources, knowledge and technologies;
b. recognize and protect the rights of breeders;
c. provide an appropriate system of access to biological resources, community knowledge and technologies subject to the prior informed consent of the State and the concerned local communities;
d. promote appropriate mechanisms for a fair and equitable sharing of benefits arising from the use of biological resources, knowledge and technologies;
e. ensure the effective participation of concerned communities, with a particular focus on women, in making decisions as regards the distribution of benefits which may derive from the use of their biological resources, knowledge and technologies;
f. promote and encourage the building of national and grassroots scientific and technological capacity relevant to the conservation and sustainable use of biological resources;
g. provide appropriate institutional mechanisms for the effective implementation and enforcement of the rights of local communities, including farming communities and breeders, and the conditions of access to biological resources, community knowledge and technologies;
h. promote the conservation, evaluation and sustainable utilization of biological resources with a particular focus on the major role women play;
i. promote improvements in the productivity, profitability, stability and sustainability of major production systems through yield enhancement and maintenance of biological diversity;
j. promote the supply of good quality seed/planting material to farmers; and
k. ensure that biological resources are utilized in an effective and equitable manner in order to strengthen the food security of the nation.

Through these self-explanatory objectives, the rights of local communities and breeders are acknowledged. Also, any access to biological resources is regulated and is conditional upon the prior informed consent (PIC) of the local traditional community and equitable sharing of the benefits derived from the utilization of those resources.

Scope

The Model Law clearly defines its scope of application. It covers biological resources in both *in situ* and *ex situ* conditions, derivatives of those biological resources, community knowledge and technologies, local and indigenous communities, and plant breeders. The extent of its coverage is the principal merit of this Model Law in comparison with other laws that attempt to cover the same subject matter.

The Model Law does, however, establish some limitations on its scope. It shall not affect traditional systems of access, use, or exchange of biological resources or access, use, and exchange of knowledge and technologies by and between local communities. The latter shall not apply to any person or persons not living in the traditional and customary way of life relevant to the conservation and sustainable use of biological resources.

Access to biological resources

Article 3 of the Model Law regulates access in the following manner:

- Any access to any biological resources and knowledge or technologies of local communities in any part of the country shall be subject to an application for the necessary prior informed consent and written permit.
- Any access to any biological resource in a protected area shall be subject to an application for the necessary prior informed consent and written permit.
- All applications for the necessary consent and written permit to access any biological resource, community knowledge or technology shall be directed to the National Competent Authority unless otherwise explicitly provided for by law.

This provision is complemented by Article 4, which enumerates in a non-exhaustive manner the information that any applicant seeking access to biological resources is required to provide. This includes, *inter alia*: the identity of the applicant; the resources to which access is sought, including the site; the purpose for which access to the resource is requested, including the type and extent of research, teaching, or commercial use expected to be derived from it; a description of the manner and extent of local and national collaboration in the research and development of the biological resource concerned; identification of the national institution or institutions which will participate in the research and be in charge of the monitoring process; the primary destination of the resource and its probable subsequent destination(s); the economic, social, technical, biotechnological, scientific, environmental, or any other benefits that are intended; and the proposed mechanisms and arrangements for benefit-sharing.

The Model Law in Article 5 confirms one of its aims by setting out that any access to biological resources, knowledge, and/or technologies of local communities shall be subject to the written PIC of the National Competent Authority and of the concerned local communities. Therefore, any access carried out without the PIC of the State and the concerned local community or communities shall be deemed to be invalid and shall be subject to penalties. In addition, the provision goes on by requesting the National Competent Authority to consult with the local community or communities in order to ascertain that its/their consent has been sought and granted. Consequently, any access granted without consultation will be deemed to be invalid.

Upon satisfaction of the conditions stated above, the National Competent Authority is entitled to grant access to the interested party within a time limit defined by the Authority. Following the grant of access, some other subsequent conditions that must be met by the interested party are provided. These include, *inter alia*, as follows:

- to inform immediately the National Competent Authority and the concerned local community or communities of all findings from research and development on the resource;
- not to transfer the biological resource or any of its derivatives or the community innovation, practice, knowledge, or technology to any third party without the authorization of the National Competent Authority and the concerned local community or communities;
- not to apply for any form of intellectual property protection over the biological resource or parts or derivatives thereof and not to apply for intellectual property rights protection over a community innovation, practice, knowledge, or technology without the prior informed consent of the original providers;
- to provide for the sharing of benefits;
- access shall be conditioned upon a commitment to contribute economically to the efforts of the State and concerned local community or communities in the regeneration and conservation of the biological resource, and the maintenance of the innovation, practice, knowledge, or technology to which access is sought.

In accordance with the Preamble, Article 9 of the Model Law regulates the protection of life forms in the following manner:

> Patents over life forms and biological processes are not recognized and cannot be applied for.
> The collector shall, therefore, not apply for patents over life forms and biological processes under this legislation or under any other legislation relevant to the regulation of access and use of a biological resource, community innovation, practice, knowledge and technology, and the protection of rights therein.

The Model Law also sets out particular conditions of access for academic and research institutions, public agencies, and intergovernmental institutions. The bottom line is that all access is conditioned on PIC. Specific conditions are to be established by the National Competent Authority in accordance with the Model Law. In addition, any academic institution seeking access for research purposes shall clearly state the objective of the research and the relationship (if any) of the applicant to industry.

Pursuant to the Model Law, benefit-sharing must be provided. Consequently, the access permit should be subject to the payment, made before commencement of collection, of a fee, the sum of which will depend on whether or not the collection is to be used for commercial purposes, the number of samples, the area of collecting, the duration of collection, and whether or not the collector is granted exclusive rights. The State and the local community or communities shall be entitled to a share of the earnings derived when any biological resource and/or knowledge collected generates, directly or indirectly, a product used in a production process.

The National Competent Authority may unilaterally withdraw consent and repossess the written permit under the following conditions:

- when there is evidence that the collector has violated any of the provisions of the legislation;
- when there is evidence that the collector has failed to comply with the agreed terms; and
- when there is failure to meet any of the conditions of access;
- for reasons of overriding public interest; or
- for the protection of the environment and biological diversity.

Any termination or withdrawal of consent shall be done in consultation with the concerned local community or communities.

Community rights

Part IV of the Model Law recognizes the rights of local and indigenous communities. States must recognize the rights of communities over the following:

- their biological resources;
- collective benefit from the use of their biological resources;
- their innovations, practices, knowledge, and technology acquired through generations;
- collective benefit from the utilization of their innovations, practices, knowledge, and technologies;
- use of their innovations, practices, knowledge, and technologies in the conservation and sustainable use of biological diversity; and
- the exercise of collective rights as legitimate custodians and users of their biological resources.

Pursuant to the Model Law, local communities have the right to refuse access, to withdraw their consent, or to place restrictions on the activities relating to access where such activities are likely to be detrimental to their socio-economic life or their natural or cultural heritage.

Some limitations are placed on access by permitting local communities to continue to exercise their inalienable right to access, use, exchange, or share their biological resources in sustaining their livelihood systems as regulated by their customary practices and laws. In addition, no legal barriers shall be placed on the traditional exchange system of the local communities in the exercise of their rights.

States are vested with the obligation to ensure that at least 50 percent of the benefits derived from their resources or knowledge are channeled to the concerned local community or communities.

Community Intellectual Rights are recognized under this Model Law. These are set forth in Article 23 as follows:

> (1) The Community Intellectual Rights of the local communities, including traditional professional groups, particularly traditional practitioners, shall at all times remain inalienable, and shall be further protected under the mechanism established by this legislation.
> (2) An item of community innovation, practice, knowledge or technology, or a particular use of a biological or any other natural resource shall be identified, interpreted and ascertained by the local communities concerned themselves under their customary practice and law, whether such law is written or not.
> (3) Non-registration of any community innovations, practices, knowledge or technologies, is not to mean that these are not protected by Community Intellectual Rights.
>
> The publication of a written or oral description of a biological resource and its associated knowledge and information, or the presence of these resources in a gene bank or any other collection, or its local use, shall not preclude the local community from exercising its community intellectual rights in relation to those resources.

Farmers' rights

Part V of the Model Law covers farmers' rights. Article 24 prescribes as follows:

> 1) Farmers' Rights are recognized as stemming from the enormous contributions that local farming communities, especially their women members, of all regions of the world, particularly those in the centres of origin or diversity of crops and other agro-biodiversity, have made in the conservation, development and sustainable use of plant and animal genetic resources that constitute the basis of breeding for food and agriculture production; and
> 2) For farmers to continue making these achievements, therefore, Farmers' Rights have to be recognized and protected.

What is interesting in this Model Law is that farmers are entitled to the protection of their varieties and breeds. In addition, varieties with specific attributes identified by a community shall be granted intellectual property protection without being required to meet the criteria of distinctiveness, uniformity, and stability. Consequently, the community shall have the exclusive rights to multiply, cultivate, use, or sell the variety or to license its use without prejudice to the Farmers' Rights recognized by the Model Law.

Article 26(1) provides for rights that constitute farmers' rights as follows:

1) Farmers' Rights shall, with due regard for gender equity, include the right to:
   a. the protection of their traditional knowledge relevant to plant and animal genetic resources;
   b. obtain an equitable share of benefits arising from the use of plant and animal genetic resources;
   c. participate in making decisions, including at the national level, on matters related to the conservation and sustainable use of plant and animal genetic resources;
   d. save, use, exchange and sell farm-saved seed/propagating material;
   e. use a new breeders' variety protected under this law to develop farmers' varieties, including material obtained from gene banks or plant genetic resource centres; and
   f. collectively save, use, multiply and process farm-saved seed of protected varieties.

Paragraph 2 of the same provision sets out that the farmer shall not sell farm-saved seed/propagating material of a breeders' protected variety in the seed industry on a commercial scale. This is a clear limitation to the farmers' rights. Paragraph 3 of the same Article places some limitations on the breeders' rights over a new variety when necessary to achieve the objectives of protecting food security, health, biological diversity, and any other requirements of the farming community for propagation material of a particular variety.

Plant breeders' rights

Plant breeders' rights are recognized in this Model Law. These stem, according to Article 28, from the efforts and investments made by persons/institutions for the development of new varieties of plants which constitute the basis for providing recognition and economic reward.

The following conditions of eligibility for protection of a new variety are provided under the Model Law: it must be new; distinguishable; stable; and sufficiently homogenous.

Exclusive rights of the breeder are provided in Article 30. These are as follows:

1. A Plant Breeders' Rights, in respect of a new variety, is:
   a. the exclusive right to sell, including the right to license other persons to sell plants or propagating material of that variety;
   b. the exclusive right to produce, including the right to license other persons to produce, propagating material of that variety for sale;

2. A Plant Breeders' Rights in respect of a plant variety is subject to the conditions provided in Part V, the Farmers' Rights Part of this Act.

Exceptions to the rights of the breeder are set forth under Article 31 of the Model Law as follows:

1. Notwithstanding the existences of Plant Breeders' Rights in respect of a plant variety, any person or farmers' community may:
   a. propagate, grow and use plants of that variety for purposes other than commerce
   b. sell plants or propagating material of that variety as food or for another use that does not involve the growing of the plants or the propagation of that variety
   c. sell within a farm or any other place at which plants of that variety are grown any plants or propagating material of that variety at that place
   d. use plants or propagating material of the variety as an initial source of variation for the purpose of developing another new plant variety except where the person makes repeated use of plants or propagating material of the first mentioned variety for the commercial production of another variety
   e. sprout the protected variety as food for home consumption or for the market
   f. use the protected variety in further breeding, research or teaching
   g. obtain, with the conditions of utilization, such a protected variety from genebanks or plant genetic resources centres.
2. Farmers will be free to save, exchange and use part of the seed from the first crop of plants which they have grown for sowing in their own farms to produce a second and subsequent crops subject to conditions specified in Part V, the Farmers' Rights Part of this Act.

These provisions are self-explanatory. Importantly, farmers' rights are amongst the exceptions provided here.

Besides exceptions, there are situations specified in the Model Law in which the breeder may be restricted from using his exclusive right when the Government considers it necessary to do so for the public interest. These situations are:

a. where problems with competitive practices of the Rights holder are identified;
b. where food security or nutritional or health needs are adversely affected;
c. where a high proportion of the plant variety offered for sale is being imported;
d. where the requirements of the farming community for propagating material of a particular variety are not met; and

e. where it is considered important to promote public interest for socio-economic reasons and for developing indigenous and other technologies.

Some conditions are attached to the grant of a compulsory license for such purposes. The following must be complied with:

a. Where restrictions are imposed on a Plant Breeders' Rights:
   i. the grantee shall be given a copy of the instrument setting out the conditions of the restriction;
   ii. a public notice shall be given;
   iii. the compensation to be awarded to the holder of the Rights shall be specified;
   iv. the Rights-holder may appeal against the compensation award.
b. In particular, and without prejudice to the generality of the foregoing provisions, the relevant Government authority shall have the right to convert the exclusive Plant Breeders' Rights granted under this Act to non-exclusive Plant Breeders' Rights (compulsory licence of right).

Regarding the duration of protection, plant breeders' rights in respect of a plant variety shall exist for a period of 20 years in the case of annual crops and 25 years in the case of trees, vines, and other perennials, commencing on the day on which the successful application for plant breeders' rights in respect of the plant variety was accepted.

A dispute settlement mechanism is provided under the Model Law. Where conflicts arise over whether a plant variety qualifies as a new plant variety under the legislation, they will be handled administratively through the National Competent Authority, an *ad hoc* tribunal and, finally, through a court of law. Decisions on approval, disapproval or cancellation of agreements regarding access to biological resources, community knowledge, or technologies may be appealed through appropriate administrative channels. Recourse to the courts shall be allowed after exhaustion of all administrative remedies.

In case of infringements of breeders' rights, the Model Law sets out actions that can be carried out in Article 36. These are as follows:

1) An action or proceedings for an infringement of a Plant Breeders' Rights may be instituted in writing in a court or, if agreeable to both parties, it may be submitted to a binding arbitration.
2) A defendant in an action or proceeding for an infringement of a Plant Breeders' Rights in respect of a variety may apply by way of counter-claim for the revocation of that Plant Breeders' Rights:
   a) on the grounds that the variety was not a new plant variety;
   b) on the grounds that facts exist which, if known to the National Competent Authority before the grant of that Plant Breeders' Rights, would have resulted in the refusal of the grant.

3) If, in an action or proceedings for an infringement of a Plant Breeders' Rights in respect of a plant variety in which a defendant has applied by way of counter-claim for the revocation on the grounds referred to in paragraph 2)a) or b), the court is satisfied that the grounds exist, the court may revoke that Plant Breeders' Rights.
4) Where, in an action or proceedings for an infringement of a Plant Breeders' Rights, the court, on an application by the defendant by way of counter-claim, revokes the Plant Breeders' Rights, the court shall order the defendant to serve on the National Competent Authority a copy of the order revoking that Plant Breeders' Rights.

The Model Law vests the National Competent Authority with the competency to receive applications, to examine such applications, and to grant plant breeders' rights.

The Model Law regulates, *inter alia*, the following matters: uniform testing and assessment procedures; the characteristics of plant varieties originating from outside the country; plant varieties' trials; opposition to grants of plant breeders' rights; publication of grants of plant breeders' rights; the effects of grants on certain persons; the assignment of plant breeders' rights; and the revocation of plant breeders' rights.

The Model Law sets out a *sui generis* system of plant varieties protection. Under this system, both plant breeders' rights and farmers' rights are provided.

The main merit of the Model Law is that it has provided an alternative for all countries, but especially those in Africa, to choose an effective *sui generis* model which is based on their own realities and interests. The African Group, while discussing the relationship between the TRIPs Agreement and the UPOV Convention in the context of the review of TRIPs Article 27.3(b), stressed the importance of this Model Law for African countries. Another advantage of the Model Law is that it has provided a hybrid system of protection for both plant varieties and biodiversity.

The main question is whether the Model Law has brought change in Africa. Have African countries taken into consideration the Model Law to design their legislation or policy on the matter? Have African countries domesticated the Model Law?

At the time of its development, the African Model Law also sought to fulfill two strategic objectives on the international front. First, it was representative of an African common position on these issues at the WTO, the CBD, and the International Undertaking on Plant Genetic Resources for Food and Agriculture. Second, the African Model Law was facilitative in Africa's strategy to meet international obligations, such as those required under the TRIPs Agreement and the CBD. In this context, it served also as a framework for African Union (then OAU) Member States to craft specific national legislation in compliance with international commitments and consistent with their political orientation, national objectives, and level of socio-economic development.[32]

However, beyond the mere willingness reflected through the core content of the African Model Law, the real challenge in Africa is the translation of some of its core principles into national measures. It is therefore necessary that concrete moves from African countries be initiated at the national level for the development and implementation of measures. [33]

Since the adoption of the Model Law, new issues pertaining to biodiversity and genetic resources in particular have been raised and discussed in various fora. It is obvious that some of the provisions of the Model Law may not be up-to-date vis-à-vis the current stage of discussion. Some have called for revision of the Model Law to fill the gaps, while others have proposed creating a set of complementary guidelines as an Annex to the Model Law to fill the gaps.

At this stage, it might be difficult to assess the impact of the Model Law in Africa even though it may have exerted influences on some countries' legislation on plant varieties or biodiversity. The main success of the Model Law which should be underscored is that it has guided African countries in the negotiation of the Nagoya Protocol so that most of the aspirations contained in the African Model Law are reflected in the Nagoya Protocol. This is a great achievement.

The AU Model Law on Biosafety

The aim of this section is not to examine the complete legal framework of the African Model Law on Safety in Biotechnology (AU Model Law on Biosafety). Rather, the purpose is to highlight briefly how the Model Law regulates GMOs for African countries.

In February 1999, when the negotiations of the Cartagena Protocol on Biosafety were stalled, the African Group in the CBD and the Organization for African Unity (OAU, now the AU) started to develop the African Model Law on Biosafety. Its first purpose was to provide for a harmonized approach toward biosafety in Africa to serve as a model legal instrument for the development of national biosafety legislations in case the international negotiations should fail. The first draft was developed by an OAU workshop of experts from Africa and other developing countries in Addis Ababa in June 1999. This draft was based on the proposal of the African Group for a biosafety protocol which was submitted to the CBD Secretariat during the Third Conference of the Parties in Buenos Aires in 1996 and which was introduced at the second meeting of the working group to

32 See, *A Gap Analysis Report on The African Model Law on the Protection of the Rights of Local Communities, Farmers and Breeders, and for the Regulation of Access to Biological Resources*, Commissioned by the Department of Human Resources, Science and Technology of the African Union Commission. February 2012.

33 Ibid.

negotiate the Biosafety Protocol in 1997. In May 2001, this draft was finalized by an OAU working group in Addis Ababa.[34]

The Forty-Seventh OAU Council of Ministers in Lusaka in July 2001 supported the work of the working group and called for finalization of the Model Law. The Thirty-Seventh Assembly of Heads of State and Government, which followed it, confirmed this resolution.[35] The Model Law was subjected to a complete review in 2006–2007 after new issues not covered under the first adopted Model Law on Biosafety arose. This section addresses the text of the Draft Revised Model Law published in January 2008, which is still under review.

Preamble

In the Preamble, the key motivation for having such a Model Law is stressed. Some of the statements are as follows:

> *Whereas,* it is the responsibility of the Government to ensure the safety of the people and the environment with respect to the risks arising from genetically modified organisms (GMOs) and products of genetically modified organisms resulting from modern biotechnology;
>
> …
>
> *Whereas,* with the potential risks posed by genetic modification it is consistent with the precautionary principle to regulate any undertaking for the making, import, contained use, release or placing on the market of genetically modified organisms and products of genetically modified organisms.

Objectives

The objectives of the Model Law are twofold:

> (a) To contribute to ensuring an adequate level of safety for the protection of biological diversity, human and animal health, socio-economic conditions and ethical values in the making, safe transfer, handling and use of genetically modified organisms and products of genetically modified organisms resulting from modern biotechnology.
>
> (b) To enable countries that are members of the Cartagena Protocol on Biosafety to implement the provisions of the Protocol at the national level.

Scope

The Model Law's scope of application is large and extends to the making, import, export, transport, contained use, release, or placing on the market of any GMO or any product of a GMO.

---

34 See, 'African Model Law on Biosafety' on the AU website at: http://www.africa-union.org/root/au/auc/departments/hrst/biosafety/AU_Biosafety_2b.htm (last accessed on July 19, 2012).

35 Ibid.

National Biosafety Committee
AU Member States are requested to establish a National Biosafety Committee comprising representatives of governmental and non-governmental organizations and the private sector that are relevant to the issues of biotechnology and biosafety.

Application
The Model Law recommends that AU Member States include in their national biosafety laws the following requirements at the outset of the process:

(1) No person shall make, import, make contained use of, release, place on the market or cause the movement in transit of a genetically modified organism or a product of a genetically modified organism without the approval of the Competent Authority.
(2) Any person who intends to make, import, release, make contained use of or place on the market a genetically modified organism or a product of a genetically modified organism.
(3) Any approval for the making, import, contained use, release or placing on the market of a genetically modified organism or a product of a genetically modified organism shall require the applicant to carry out monitoring and evaluation of risks on a continuing basis.
(4) No approval shall be given by the Competent Authority unless there is firm and sufficient evidence that the genetically modified organism or the product of a genetically modified organism poses no significant risks to the environment, biological diversity or human health.

Risk assessment
The responsibility of carrying out the risk assessment is vested with the applicant, who shall carry out or cause to be carried out an assessment of any risks associated with a GMO or a product of a GMO which is the subject of an application. In any case where the evaluation of the assessment shows that risks cannot be avoided, the Competent Authority shall refuse approval for the making, import, contained use, release, or placing on the market of the GMO or a product thereof.

Identification and labeling
The Competent Authority shall put in place measures to ensure that any GMO or any product of a GMO is handled, packaged, and transported under conditions of safety. In addition, any GMO or product of a GMO shall be clearly identified and labeled as such, and the identification shall specify the relevant traits and characteristics given in sufficient detail for purposes of traceability. This requirement is very important to enable consumers to make the right choice if they have any choice at all.

Export
Any person who intends to export a GMO or a product of a GMO shall provide to the Competent Authority a written advance informed agreement from the

Competent Authority of the importing country. This will also enable traceability of GMOs and products of GMOs and ensure that before their export they went through a due process of control.

Liability and redress

Irrespective of the authorization given by the Competent Authority, a person who makes, imports, makes contained use of, releases, or places on the market a GMO or a product of a GMO shall be liable for any harm caused by it. Liability shall attach to the applicant as well as to the provider, supplier, or developer of the GMO or of the product of a GMO for any damage, injury, or loss caused by it. Liability shall also extend to harm or damage caused directly or indirectly by the GMO or product of the GMO to the economy, social or cultural conditions, livelihood or indigenous knowledge systems or technologies of a community or communities.

Community rights for GMO-free zones

The Competent Authority shall develop policies that protect the rights of communities to declare GMO-free zones. As a result, the Competent Authority shall take measures for the creation of geographical areas that are declared as 'GMO-free zones' where the release of any GMO is prohibited.

Conclusion

In sum, the AU Model Law on Biosafety intends to provide African Countries with a tool to regulate GMOs. The Model Law recommends that AU Member States take appropriate measures to provide a legal framework for the use, making, importing, and exporting of GMOs in their territory. Kenya, South Africa, Mauritius, and Egypt have referred to the Model Law in the establishment of their own legislation or legal framework for control and authorization of GMOs.

The Establishment of the Pan-African Intellectual Property Organization

This author wrote an article entitled 'The African Intellectual Property Organizations: Necessity of Adopting One Uniform System for All Africa', which was published in the March 2000 issue of *The Journal of World Intellectual Property*. In this article, the author advocated the establishment of a single African organization that would deal with IP matters, including TK.[36] The African IP environment has greatly evolved since then.

This section will be divided into two parts. The first part will refer to the main ideas contained in the published paper with no amendments.[37] The second

36 Kongolo, T. (2000b), 'The African Intellectual Property Organizations—The Necessity of Adopting One Uniform System for All Africa', *The Journal of World Intellectual Property* 3:2, 265–288.

37 In fact, some of the criticisms originally raised by the author may no longer be applicable as the result of the revision of the OAPI Agreement and its Annexes in 1999 and

part will highlight current discussions on the establishment of the Pan-African Intellectual Property Organization by examining its Final Draft Statute, which was adopted in November 2012 at the Fifth Ordinary Session of the African Ministerial Conference on Science & Technology which took place in Brazzaville (Republic of Congo).[38]

The African Intellectual Property Organizations: necessity of adopting one uniform system for all Africa[39]

In this part, some portions of the article mentioned above that are deemed important will be referred to with no amendments to reflect the original ideas of the author in 1999–2000:

> Notwithstanding that the African IP Organizations have played a significant role in the harmonization of the intellectual property laws of their Members, it should be pointed out that these Organizations are not without shortcomings. Their systems would be more effective if they would take into consideration African needs, priorities and realities. They should guide African countries for the setting up of a unique African system of protection of intellectual property which would enable the international community to acknowledge the African vision.[40]
>
> …
>
> With this perspective, the need to restructure the existing African Organizations dealing with intellectual property matters is evident, to enable them to cope with new issues brought about by globalization and at the same time ensure the establishment of a system reflecting the African vision. Under this approach, via these organizations, African folklore and traditional knowledge which reflect the African identity should be promoted as advocated by the OAPI. It should be stated that the existing systems contain only a few specific rules or provisions that aim to safeguard African traditional assets.[41]
>
> …
>
> It should be noted that the ARIPO and the OAPI have both contributed to the harmonization of the intellectual property laws of their members. The second step and the most important one is to go forward in displaying African values which should form new components to be included in the list of protected intellectual property matters. In other words, the new African intellectual

---

the ARIPO Agreement and its Protocols later.

38 African Union, Fifth Ordinary Session of the African Ministerial Conference on Science & Technology (Amcost V), November 12 to 15, 2012, Brazzaville, Congo, Final Draft Statute of the Pan-African Intellectual Property Organization (PAIPO), AU/STRC/522, November 2012. See, also, www.au.int (last accessed on November 28, 2012).

39 Kongolo, T. (2000b).

40 Ibid., p. 265.

41 Ibid., p. 266.

property organization should lead and contribute to the recognition within the international framework of the African vision.[42]

…

It is said that economic co-operation between African countries still has a long way to go, in the sense that most African countries prefer co-operating with European or American countries than fostering the economical interchanges between themselves. It should likewise be pointed out that this administrative cooperation between African countries is lacking in many areas. That is also true in the area of intellectual property. One thing is sure, African nations should all have the same vision as to the protection of traditional assets and intellectual property rights.[43]

…

The new Organization must combine both the ARIPO and OAPI systems. That is to say that, notwithstanding that the principal objective is to create a unique African intellectual property organization which will incorporate (involve) one legal intellectual property system that will override any other existing (or pre-existing) systems of its members, should permit at the first phase, the coexistence of national intellectual property laws of its members and the provided norms under the Organization. That would enable and ensure the uniformity of rules. In the case of conflict between regional rules and any national law, regional rules should prevail. The second phase would be the establishment of one system that member countries should be bound to. The national offices would be considered as branches of the main office which would be the organization Office.[44]

…

From this perspective, in order to foster the promotion of African culture and heritage, and to ensure the harmonization between modern intellectual property rights and the traditional assets, the creation or establishment of a unique African intellectual property organization that would integrate all African countries without regard to their location and their spoken languages should be established. It could be called 'Folklore and Intellectual Property Organization of Africa (FIPOA)'.[45]

…

In a globalized world, with respect to intellectual property, the FIPOA should play a leading role in the recognition of African folklore and traditional assets at the international level. At the same time, the system provided must contribute and lead to the welfare of people living in those countries.[46]

42 Ibid., p. 280.
43 Ibid., p. 282.
44 Ibid.
45 Ibid., p. 284.
46 Ibid., p. 287.

Many of the ideas embodied in that paper are *mutatis mutandis* valid today. It is also worthwhile acknowledging the tremendous efforts carried out by the ARIPO and OAPI to cope with the new challenges engendered by the globalization of the world and to consider at the same time African TCEs (folklore) and TK through adoption of related Protocols or Annexes to their respective Agreements.

Discussions on the establishment of PAIPO

Before examining the newly adopted Final Draft Statute of the Pan-African Intellectual Property Organization, it is worth looking at the background and the past discussions on the subject that took place in various fora.

Background and premise to the adoption In May 2006 a WIPO-supported meeting of the African Group on Intellectual Property recommended the decision to establish a Pan-African Intellectual Property Organization (PAIPO).[47] A concept paper in this regard was presented by the African Union's Scientific, Technical and Research Commission (STRC) at the Extraordinary Conference of the African Ministers of Council on Science and Technology held in Cairo, Egypt, November 20–24, 2006.[48]

The concept paper attempted to explore the following questions:[49]

- Why would Africa need to establish a Pan-African Intellectual Property Organization?
- What benefits would such an institution generate for Member States?
- Would the new Pan-African entity add value to the intellectual property activities of Member States?
- Would the Continent be better off with this new entity?
- Would countries' capacity for inventiveness and innovation suffer in the absence of such an umbrella body?
- Conversely, would creativity and innovation be catalyzed by the operations of such a body?

According to the concept paper, the establishment of an Africa-wide IP structure would sharpen the visibility of IP issues as they relate to economic development. This in turn would add impetus to the leaders' political will and

---

47 See, Extraordinary Conference of the African Ministers of Council on Science and Technology (AMCOST), November 20–24, 2006, Cairo, Egypt, 'Establishing a Pan-African Intellectual Property Organization (PAIPO)—A Concept Paper', African Union Doc. No. EXT/AU/EXP/ST/8(II), para. 2.

48 See, Extraordinary Conference of the African Ministers of Council on Science and Technology (AMCOST), November 20–24, 2006, Cairo, Egypt, 'Report of the Meeting of Experts', African Union Doc. No. EXT/AU/EXP/ST/Rpt.(II).

49 African Union Doc. No. EXT/AU/EXP/ST/8(II), para. 3.

commitment to inventiveness and innovation, thus emphasizing the significance of political leadership in such a strategic field of development.[50]

The paper further maintained that the formation of an umbrella body would not imply the dismemberment of the two existing regional IP organizations. To the contrary, the new structure would envisage sustaining OAPI and the ARIPO as regional arrangements under its umbrella. The modalities of how the whole set-up would look (where OAPI and the ARIPO would fit in) would be determined on the basis of various proposals and options yet to be considered.[51]

The intended objectives of the proposed organization were as follows:

1. set IP standards that reflect the needs of Member States;
2. set benchmarks for best practices on intellectual property;
3. promote the growth of knowledge-based economies in Africa;
4. facilitate the rationalization and harmonization of IP standards;
5. collect, process, and disseminate relevant information on intellectual property to Member States;
6. facilitate the utilization of relevant IP information by Member States;
7. assist Member States in training and capacity building on a wide range of IP matters.

The AU Assembly supported the establishment of PAIPO in January 2007 while deciding on the Report of the Extraordinary Conference of the African Ministers of Council on Science and Technology.[52]

At the fourth session of the African Ministerial Conference on Science and Technology (AMCOST-IV) it was agreed to constitute a team of Intellectual Property Rights (IPR) Experts to evaluate and thoroughly consider the existing PAIPO documents and submit them to the next Bureau Meeting in a bid to expedite the implementation of the AU Assembly decision on PAIPO.[53] It appears that the initial draft of the Draft Statute and Governance Structure did not fully meet the expectations of the African Ministers of Science and Technology (AMCOST). AMCOST thus mandated the STRC to engage another set of consultants to critically review both documents.[54]

50 Ibid., para. 6.

51 Ibid., para. 8.

52 See, Assembly of the African Union, Eighth Ordinary Session, January 29–30, 2007, Addis Ababa, Ethiopia, 'Decisions and Declarations', African Union Doc. No. Assembly/AU/Dec. 134–164 (VII) and Assembly/AU/Decl.1–61 (VIII), Decision 138 (VII).

53 See, Ministerial Decisions of the Fourth Ordinary Session of the African Ministerial Conference on Science and Technology (AMCOST IV), March 10, 2010, Cairo, Egypt, African Union Doc. No. AU/MIN/ST/DEC (IV), Decision 2.2.5.

54 Ibid.; see also, *Recent Intellectual Property Developments in the Africa Region and Proposals for the Harmonization of ARIPO and OAPI Systems*, ARIPO Council of

Those consultants reviewed the Draft Statute of PAIPO and produced a new draft legal instrument called 'The Agreement on the Establishment of the Pan African Intellectual Property Organization'. The Governance Structure was also revised. The consultants proposed that PAIPO should be a specialized agency of the AU and that initially it should be funded by AU Member States until such time that it would generate its own income by granting and registering IP rights and titles. The consultants also proposed a Business Plan for PAIPO which is structured into various phases spanning a period of 25 years. The consultants proposed that the ARIPO and OAPI should coexist with PAIPO for the 25 years, after which the three may become one harmonized system within the African Union. It was recommended that the ARIPO and OAPI be granted Observer Status at PAIPO meetings.[55]

A Validation Workshop was organized by the STRC in Dakar, Senegal on September 7–8, 2011 for the validation of the Agreement as produced by the consultants. At this Validation Workshop, the ARIPO and OAPI reiterated the need for the STRC to build upon the work that has already been done by them in Africa in the field of IP. The ARIPO strongly argued that since the resources of the continent have been used to develop IP to its current state in Africa, it will not be useful and progressive to brush that work aside and start with a totally new organization. The ARIPO further urged that the STRC rather establish a unit within the AU to work to unify the ARIPO and OAPI and to bring other African states on board.[56]

Final Draft Statute of the Pan-African Intellectual Property Organization (PAIPO) As mentioned above, African Ministers of Science and Technology adopted this final draft during the AU Ministerial Conference, which took place in Brazzaville (Republic of Congo) from November 12–15, 2012. This final draft, if approved and endorsed by the Assembly of Head of States and Government of the Union, will become a treaty and will enter into force immediately.

In this part, the following matters will be addressed: the preamble; objectives of the organization; functions of the organization; and other matters.

Preamble It is not the aim of this study to indicate all the preamble texts prescribed under the draft statute but to highlight some, as follows:

> We the African Union Head of States and governments,
>
> **DETERMINED** to promote the development of the continent through an effective intellectual property system in order to achieve objectives of the African Union;

Ministers, Thirteenth Session, Accra, Ghana, December 1–2, 2011, ARIPO Doc. No. ARIPO/AC/XIII/13, October 31, 2011.

55 ARIPO/AC/XIII/13, *supra*, note 55, para. 4.

56 Ibid., para. 5.

RECOGNIZING that Intellectual Property rights are tools for economic growth and dissemination of knowledge;
BEING FULLY AWARE of the urgent and requisite need to provide a broad-based Intellectual Property platform that would provide a forum for policy based discussions and formulation of common African position on global and emerging Intellectual Property issues; and the valuable benefits that the Member States would derive from an effective, continuous and well-coordinated stock of specialized Intellectual Property information, knowledge and services that would be instrumental in promoting and protecting creativity, invention, innovation, facilitating technology transfer, techno-industrial competitiveness and economic growth in Africa;
……….
DESIRING to encourage creativity as well as to promote, protect and exploit Intellectual Property rights throughout Africa;
BEING DESIROUS to formulate and implement strategies for the effective combating piracy and counterfeit in Africa;
………….
APPRECIATING and **RESPECTING** the crucial role played by national Intellectual Property offices of Member States, as well as the autonomy of ARIPO and OAPI, in recognizing the need to modernize and harmonize Intellectual Property legislation throughout Africa and to render more efficient the administration of Intellectual Property rights;
………….
RECOGNIZING the cross-cutting nature of Intellectual Property and the need to have a streamlined co-ordination system for Intellectual Property within the framework of the African Union, and the importance of addressing Intellectual Property matters within the African Union;
……………..

The most important part of this text relates to the desire of the organization to create a forum for policy-based discussions to enable formulation of a common African position on IP matters. Is this spirit reflected throughout the entire text?

According to Article 2.2 of the draft text, PAIPO shall be a specialized agency of the AU responsible for IP and other emerging issues related to IP in Africa. One may question the relationship between PAIPO and the existing two IP organizations, namely the ARIPO and OAPI. The same question may be asked vis-a-vis Member States of these organizations.

Objectives of the organization According to Article 5, the objectives of the organization shall be to:

(i) Ensure the effective use of the intellectual property system as a tool for economic, cultural, social and technological development of the continent;
(ii) Contribute to the accelerated achievement of the objectives of the African Union as stated in the Constitutive Act of the African Union;

(iii) Promote the harmonization of intellectual property systems of its Member States, with particular regard to protection, exploitation, commercialization and enforcement of intellectual property rights;
(iv) Provide common services to Member States and/or regional economic communities in the administration and management of intellectual property rights that maximizes and builds upon the solid achievements of ARIPO, OAPI and/or WIPO;
(v) Provide a forum for policy discussions and formulation, addressing political issues and developing African common positions relating to Intellectual Property matters, particular regard being given to genetic resources, traditional knowledge, geographical indications, expressions of folklore, matters pertaining and arising from the Convention on Biological Diversity (CBD) and emerging topics in the field of intellectual property;
(vi) Initiate activities that strengthen the human, financial and technical capacity of Member States to maximize the benefits of the intellectual property system to improve public health and eradicate the scourge of piracy and counterfeits on the continent;
(vii) To foster and undertake positive efforts designed to raise awareness on intellectual property in Africa and to encourage the creation of a knowledge-based and innovative society as well as the importance of creative industries including, in particular, cultural and artistic industries; and
(viii) To lead the African negotiation in the international IP issues and to ensure the African common position.

These objectives are self-explanatory. Among them, two conflict with the mandates of the ARIPO and OAPI, namely the harmonization of IP systems of Member States with a particular emphasis on the protection, exploitation, commercialization, and enforcement of IPRs, and the provision of services to Member States in the administration and management of IPRs.

The objectives which may well fit with this kind of organization are those to ensure African common positions relating to IP issues in international negotiations, and to create a forum for policy discussions.

Functions of the organization Very ambitious functions of the organization are provided in Article 6 as follows:

> In order to attain the objectives described in this Statute, the Organization through its appropriate organs shall:
> (i) Set intellectual property standards that reflect the needs of both the African Union and its Member States and Regional Economic Communities of the Organization;
> (ii) To grant and register industrial property titles;

(iii) Facilitate the realization and harmonization of national legislation and regional treaties and intellectual property standards in all the AU levels;
(iv) Facilitate the use of intellectual property to promote creativity and innovativeness on the continent;
(v) Assist its Member States in formulating policies and addressing current and emerging Intellectual Property issues in conformity with the Objectives of the Organization;
(vi) Initiate strategies that will promote and develop the Intellectual Property system;
(vii) Strengthen the existing regional organizations or such other organizations as may be necessary;
(viii)Strengthen the existing collective management organizations and facilitate their establishment in the Member States which have no collective management organization in the field of copyright and related rights ;
(ix) Take deliberate measures to promote the protection and exploitation of Intellectual Property rights within the Member States, including conclusion of bilateral and multilateral agreements;
(x) Collect, process and disseminate relevant information on Intellectual Property to Member States and support the establishment of databases on genetic resources, traditional knowledge and traditional cultural expressions and folklore in order for Member States to derive regular and maximum benefit;
(xi) To develop updated policy guide lines and training modules to support Member States to achieve a world-class IP systems; and
(xii) Do such other things as may be necessary for the achievement of the Objectives of the Organization.

The most ambitious function is formulated in sub-paragraph, which aims to set IP standards reflecting the needs of Member States and other Regional Economic Communities of the organization.

The function that is most in conflict with those of the existing African IP organizations relates to PAIPO's granting and registration of industrial property titles. The author cannot support this function, which he deems premature for an organization which is at the stage of learning the ABCs of the IP system. The ideal would be for this organization to concentrate on the policy level and leave the administration and management of IPRs to the ARIPO and OAPI. The risk of this is that IP may be politicized and used just as a bargaining tool that will serve no one's interests in the end.

Other matters PAIPO will be composed of four organs, namely the Council of Ministers; the Experts Committee and its Bureau; the Board of Appeal; and the Office. The Board of Appeal is empowered to hear appeals from decisions made by the Office on any aspect of the grant or registration of any IPR. It should be pointed out that a special relationship with other institutions, co-operating States and organizations has been set out in Article 6, which prescribes that the organization shall establish and maintain close and continuous working relationships with the ARIPO, OAPI, WIPO, the International Confederation of Authors and Composers Societies (CISAC) and the WTO.

Article 20 lays down that this Statute shall come into force on the day of the endorsement by the Assembly of Head of States and Government of the AU. This provision embodies some legal inconsistencies and incoherencies. It is stipulated in Article 22 that no reservations to this Statute shall be permitted.

The movement to establish PAIPO has raised concerns on the part of some stakeholders. Some fear that Africa, by setting up a new organization, would embark in a direction that may lead to stronger protection of IPRs. Another concern relates to the relationship between the proposed PAIPO and the two existing regional organizations. The IP systems developed under the ARIPO and OAPI are different. The proposed PAIPO would be under the umbrella of the AU. The concern is that, while the AU may help to gather in Member States that are not Contracting Parties to either of the two regional organizations, it could nonetheless serve to politicize IP matters. The main issue here is that the ARIPO and OAPI have gained experience in the field and are well equipped to understand and cope with IP matters at both regional and international levels.

The way forward The format of the proposed PAIPO is not welcomed by many stakeholders.. The key point at this stage is to understand what added value this institution would bring to the continent in IP matters at both the regional and international levels. Most of the countries who are advocating the establishment of PAIPO are Members of neither the ARIPO nor OAPI. Consequently, one may question the motivations behind this move. In other words, is there any hidden agenda? Some have suggested that PAIPO should be established as a political body dealing with IP policy and its development dimension, whereas the ARIPO and OAPI would continue to offer technical services, including registration of intellectual property for their respective Member States.[57] Regrettably PAIPO purports to register and grant IP titles and such an attempt to replicate existing IP expertise is unfortunate.

The concerns of those opposed to the establishment of PAIPO should not be underestimated. Their fears are justified, particularly in the African context, given the fact that the level of understanding of IP matters in general and IP policy in particular is still low. As a result, at this stage strong cooperation among the ARIPO, OAPI, and the proposed PAIPO is required. As proposed originally by the author in 1999–2000, the establishment of a single body dealing with IP in Africa is a good initiative. However, there is a need to define and delimit the boundaries

57 See, 'Concern Rises Over Proposed Pan-African IP Organisation', IP Watch, 30 August 2007, available at: http://www.ip-watch.org/weblog/2007/08/30/concern-arises-over-proposed-pan-african-ip-organisation, accessed January 10, 2012.

of the proposed PAIPO in order not to conflict with the ARIPO and OAPI. The proposed PAIPO system must be clearly defined. In addition, a transitional period of at least 15 years would be required before the new institution becomes operational in order to equip it with relevant human resources and to facilitate a smooth harmonization with the existing regional IP organizations. Another option would be to provide just a political/policy mandate to PAIPO and to leave the substance of the subject matters, including registration of titles, to the ARIPO and the OAPI.

Conclusion

The existing regional organizations on IP, namely the ARIPO and OAPI, embody two systems that have important differences. The ARIPO's system is solely regional, and coexistence with the national system of each Member State is the norm. The OAPI system is unique; it includes both a regional system and national systems. There is no need for OAPI Member States to have separate laws in the field of industrial property because the Bangui Agreement has direct effect on the territory of each OAPI Member State and constitutes a national law for each Member.

The new initiatives taken by the ARIPO to deal with TK, EoF, and new plant varieties protection have raised expectations among Member States to benefit from IP systems that are based on their own assets.

The leadership of the AU on matters that are of concern for African countries has been demonstrated in the areas of biodiversity, breeders' rights, community rights, farmers' rights, and biosafety. Only the future will tell how the newly proposed PAIPO will be able to respond to the expectations of the stakeholders.

Overall, the African regional initiatives are promising. It will be seen in the short run how African contributions on the international scene will impact at the national and regional levels.

Chapter 4
African Initiatives at the International Level

Introduction

Previous chapters of this book have examined the existing national and regional African IP systems with a focus on selected IP issues. The two African IP organizations, the ARIPO and OAPI have taken significant initiatives at the regional level. The ARIPO has adopted a new Protocol on the Protection of TK and EoF and is also discussing the Draft Protocol on Plant Varieties Protection. African regional initiatives are reflected through the adopted African Model Law for the Protection of the Rights of Local Communities, Farmers and Breeders, and for the Regulation of Access to Biological Resources, the African Model Law on Biosafety, and the proposed establishment of a Pan-African Intellectual Property Organization.

The present chapter will take a close look at the contributions of African countries as a group in shaping the worldwide IP system. Most of these contributions made at the international level remain unnoticed. The initiatives and proposals made by the African Group that have led to the adoption of a number of international instruments may constitute the primary windows through which those contributions may be recognized and identified.

This chapter does not intend to analyze all unsettled issues that have been debated within international organizations but will focus on select IP issues where African countries have made tremendous contributions or where initiatives/positions taken by the African Group have changed the course of debates. These issues have been debated under the auspices of WIPO, the WTO, the World Health Organization (WHO), and the United Nations Environment Program (UNEP), among others.

Within WIPO, issues pertaining to the protection of TK and TCEs, as well as GRs, have been discussed in the Intergovernmental Committee on Intellectual Property and Genetic Resources, Traditional Knowledge and Folklore (IGC), where the African Group has made valuable contributions in the last 10 years. Some argue that the future of the international IP system may depend on the outcome of these important issues at the international level. While in the past Member States were hesitant to discuss the issue of IPRs and public health, recently this has also been addressed within WIPO. The African Group has made valuable proposals.

Within the WTO, several issues have been debated in the context of the review of Article 27.3(b) of the TRIPs Agreement, including the relationship between the TRIPs Agreement and the Convention on Biological Diversity (CBD), and IP and TK and folklore. The issue of IP and public health has been addressed in the framework of the Doha Declaration on the TRIPs Agreement and Public Health, the Decision of the General Council on the Implementation of Article 6 of the Doha Declaration on the TRIPs Agreement and Public Health, and the proposed amendment of the TRIPs Agreement. The African Group has made tremendous contributions mainly in the context of IP and public health and IP and TK and folklore.

In the context of WHO, the issue relating to the relationship between IP and public health has been dealt with by different means, including the work of the Commission on Intellectual Property Rights, Innovation and Public Health and, more recently, the Global Strategy and Plan of Action on Public Health, Innovation and Intellectual Property adopted in 2008.[1] The main concern here is how to strike a balance between access to medicines, as advocated by WHO, and the exclusive rights of owners of patented medicines that may impede access. On the other side of the coin, lack of incentives may prevent research and investment in the medical field in general and pharmaceuticals in particular in areas where African countries are the most in need of medicines (e.g. tropical diseases and orphan medicines). African countries are the most exposed among the developing countries when this balance is not achieved.

The CBD, administered by UNEP, is at the core of debates regarding access to GRs. The newly adopted Nagoya Protocol attempts to set up an international regime of access and benefit-sharing. African countries are very rich in biodiversity. They are keen to benefit from IP protection, particularly with the growing importance of biotechnology. During the negotiations that led to the adoption of the Nagoya Protocol, African countries participated actively in the debates and voiced their positions with regard to the international regime of access and benefit-sharing.

To pave the way for a better understanding of the issues and the African contributions, this chapter is divided into four sections: TK, TCEs, and GRs; IP and public health; exceptions and limitations to copyright; and selected IP issues. In each section, the background of the issue, the African position(s) and initiatives, and the current status will be examined.

Traditional Knowledge, Traditional Cultural Expressions or Expressions of Folklore, and Genetic Resources

This section will display the African positions and initiatives related to TK, TCEs, and GRs within the framework of WIPO and the WTO.

---

1 More information on the Global Strategy can be found on the WHO website at http://www.who.int/phi/implementation/phi_globstat_action/en/index.html (last accessed on January 11, 2012).

Work Done Within WIPO

Background and premises to the debates

The need for protection of TK came to light as a result of the fact-finding missions undertaken by WIPO in 1998–1999 to assess the needs and expectations of indigenous people relevant to their knowledge which had been subject to widespread misappropriation all over the world. Consequently, in 2000, the Intergovernmental Committee on Intellectual Property and Genetic Resources, Traditional Knowledge, and Folklore (IGC) was set up to debate these issues.

The IGC held its first session from March 30 to April 3, 2001 in accordance with the Decision of the WIPO General Assembly[2] with a clear mandate stated by the Chair of the first session as follows:

> The decision to establish this body signaled consensus that the issues referred to in the title of this Committee, 'Intergovernmental Committee on Intellectual Property and Genetic Resources, Traditional Knowledge and Folklore,' should be addressed in this Organization. He noted that the task was to advance consensus on how those important issues should be addressed. He pointed out that the emergence of the knowledge economy rendered all forms of creativity and innovation even more valuable, and that, with modern biotechnologies, genetic resources had assumed increasing economic, scientific and commercial value to a wide range of stakeholders. He added that traditional knowledge and other tradition-based creations, such as expressions of folklore, had at the same time taken on new economic and cultural significance within a globalized information society.[3]

In the first session of the IGC, most of the Groups and Member States made their first commitment toward protection of TK, TCEs, and access to GRs. All the Group representatives welcomed the establishment of the IGC to serve as a forum for discussion of the issues relating to the protection of TK and TCEs, as well as access to GRs.

Many Delegations raised the issue of misappropriation of TK or TCEs due to the lack of an international mechanism that could protect them. Therefore, these Delegations emphasized the need to explore international mechanisms for the protection of TK and TCEs to prevent them from being abused or misappropriated given that there were cases where TK had been inappropriately patented in foreign countries.

---

2 See, Report of the WIPO General Assembly, Twenty-Sixth (Twelfth Extraordinary) Session, Geneva, September 25 to October 3, 2000, WIPO Doc. WO/GA/26/10, para. 71.

3 Report of the Intergovernmental Committee on Intellectual Property and Genetic Resources, Traditional Knowledge and Folklore, First Session, Geneva, April 30 to May 3, 2001, WIPO Doc. WIPO/GRTKF/IC/1/13, para. 19.

Some Delegations asserted that while supporting the establishment of the IGC, they had some reservations, especially as regards folklore. They felt that further discussion was needed on the issues such as a proper definition of the subject matter to be protected; the acts against which possible protection should apply; the beneficiaries of the protection; and the nature of such protection, including to what extent the existing protection systems could apply and if and to what extent that protection should be improved.[4]

Some Delegations pointed out that the IPR system was not appropriate to protect TK and TCEs given that IPR regimes were generally intended to grant exclusive rights for a certain period of time to new knowledge created by an individual or corporation, while TK, on the other hand, tended to evolve incrementally over time, was passed on orally, was improved over generations, and was often held collectively by one or several communities.[5]

The African Group welcomed the establishment of the IGC and stated that it represented a real and decisive step forward in dealing with the important issues of GRs, TK, and folklore within WIPO. It considered that the setting up of the IGC represented a historic opportunity enabling the imbalance inherent in current IP systems in the international community to be corrected. The Delegation pointed out that this question was of particular importance for developing countries, which have a wealth of GRs, TK, and folklore as part of their natural and cultural heritage. The African Group stressed that TK, folklore, and the works of African countries were subjects of illicit use and were inadequately protected by the existing IP system.[6]

Representatives of regional Groups welcomed the establishment of the IGC to seek ways or means of protecting TK and TCEs and to regulate access to GRs. The first statements of the delegates demonstrated goodwill among Member States to fight against misappropriation.

African initiatives, positions, and proposals in the context of the IGC

The African initiatives, positions, and proposals in the context of the IGC may be displayed in two different phases of the negotiations: the pre-text-based negotiation period (or non-text-based negotiation); and the text-based negotiation period.

The pre-text-based negotiation period At the beginning of the exercise, Member States agreed that a survey of existing forms of IP protection for TK and TCEs was required. In general, Members were supportive of the concept that the survey should focus on two major sub-issues: whether existing mechanisms of IP can and/or have been applied to protect TK and TCEs; and what sort of *sui generis* IP measures have been established for the protection of TK or TCEs.[7] Upon completion

4 Ibid.

5 Ibid.

6 Ibid., para. 25.

7 See, ibid., paras. 130–155.

of the initial survey, it was noted that a few IP mechanisms are to a certain extent more suitable for the protection of TK or TCEs than others.[8] However, a holistic approach to the protection of TK or TCEs is required to take into consideration particular features of TK or TCEs that might not be accommodated within the current IP system.

As a starting point, the African Group presented a position paper to the third session of the IGC[9] which was the result of the 'Decision on Intellectual Property, Genetic and Biological Resources, Traditional Knowledge and Folklore in Africa' taken by the Council of Ministers and adopted by the Heads of African States at the Seventy-Fourth Ordinary Session/Ninth Ordinary Session of the African Economic Community of the OAU and was a synthesis of views and proposals developed by African States at several meetings held in Africa and within the context of the IGC. The paper covered access to GRs and benefit-sharing, TK, and EoF. It included a broad Preamble and the African Position on Specific Agenda Items of the IGC.

According to the paper, there is a need to put in place measures and mechanisms to prevent misappropriation of GRs. Paragraph 1, 'Access to Genetic Resources and Benefit Sharing', reads as follows:

> In view of the alarming rate of loss and misappropriation of genetic resources, States are urged to put in place legislative, administrative and strategic policy measures and mechanisms for the conservation and sustainable use of biological diversity, while protecting the rights of the owners and users of genetic resources. Such measures and mechanisms should include:
>
> (a) the preparation of national laws on the protection of the rights of local communities in respect of their genetic resources;
> (b) the development of national policies and laws on the protection, conservation, preservation and sustainable use of genetic resources;
> (c) the creation of a competent national authority responsible for the regulation, monitoring and coordination of developmental activities, including access to and the fair and equitable sharing of benefits in respect of genetic resources and all other matters relating to traditional knowledge;

8 See, *Survey on Existing Forms of Intellectual Property Protection for Traditional Knowledge—Preliminary Analysis and Conclusions*, document prepared by the WIPO Secretariat for the Intergovernmental Committee on Intellectual Property and Genetic Resources, Traditional Knowledge and Folklore, Second Session, Geneva, December 10–14, 2001, WIPO Doc. WIPO/GRTKF/IC/2/9, para. 28.

9 *The Position of the African Group*, paper presented by the African Group to the Intergovernmental Committee on Intellectual Property and Genetic Resources, Traditional Knowledge and Folklore, Third Session, Geneva, June 13–21, 2002, WIPO Doc. WIPO/GRTKF/IC/3/15

(d) regional cooperation among genetic resource supplier States, and the drafting of harmonized regional legislation on the management of genetic resources that are multi-cultural in nature and cut across national borders within regional economic integration areas, such as the draft African Model Law on the Protection of the Rights of Local Communities, Farmers and Breeders and for the Regulation of Access to Biological Resources;

(e) the promotion and recognition of research and development of genetic resources and associated traditional knowledge, and the responsible dissemination of the results of such research;

(f) the design, implementation, monitoring and evaluation of programs of information, education, communication and awareness, particularly at the local community level;

(g) consolidation of regional coordination efforts;

(h) African States, particularly those less developed, should benefit, in case of need, from the assistance of intergovernmental organizations for capacity building and in the areas cited above.

The Group proposed that the IGC develop 'guide contractual practices', guidelines and model intellectual property clauses for contractual agreements on access to and use of GRs, and the fair and equitable sharing of benefits. Paragraph 2, 'Access to Genetic Resources and Benefit Sharing', reads as follows:

> The African Group considers as an important stage the development by the IGC of 'guide contractual practices', guidelines and model intellectual property clauses for contractual agreements on access to and use of genetic resources, and the fair and equitable sharing of benefits. In this regard:
>
> (a) contractual arrangements on access to genetic resources should take into account the following points and principles:
>
> (i) any access to genetic resources for industrial, commercial or research purposes should be the subject of a prior request in writing addressed to the competent national authority or any other relevant body responsible for genetic resources, in accordance with national laws;
>
> (ii) adoption of the principle of prior informed consent in the process of access and the fair and equitable sharing of benefits;
>
> (iii) the subject matter of each contract, the rights and obligations of all parties, the nature of the benefits and the method of their distribution, and the identity of the beneficiaries must be clearly specified;
>
> (iv) the protection of the supplier's interests, subject to assurance of the preservation and permanency of the genetic resource for present and future generations.

(b) the African Group supports enhancing, nationally, regionally and internationally, the negotiating capacity of traditional communities and governmental and research institutions, by, for example, creating awareness, information-sharing, and providing targeted legal education.

(c) the African Group supports putting into place national and international regulatory mechanisms and frameworks for monitoring the compliance by the parties of the terms and conditions of contracts relating to access to genetic resources and the fair and equitable sharing of benefits.

In respect of the protection of biotechnology and biological resources, the Group maintained as follows:

(a) in accordance with the precautionary principle, endeavours for respect for the rights of biotechnology inventors and innovators, with due regard to the rights of the owners of genetic resources;

(b) the protection of all inventions and innovations with due regard to the rules of bioethics;

(c) the establishment of national biosafety regulatory frameworks;

(d) assistance to researchers and innovators in the protection of their inventions.

With regard to TK, the position paper made a number of recommendations. It stressed that *sui generis* forms of protection must be provided to include the subject matter of protection, the type of protection, rights to be conferred, term of protection, and identification of beneficiaries. Paragraph 1, 'Traditional Knowledge', reads as follows:

> The African Group believes that in considering *sui generis* forms of protection for traditional knowledge, attention should be paid to determining and identifying the subject matter of protection; the type of protection desired; the content of the rights to be granted; the duration of rights granted; and, the identity of the owners of the rights. In this respect:
>
> (a) in developing effective national, regional and international systems of protection, it is necessary to develop flexible *sui generis* systems that take customary laws, protocols and practices into account, to provide protection not adequately provided by existing rights and systems;
>
> (b) strategies for identifying the subject matter to be protected could inter alia include compiling inventories of traditional knowledge and the natural heritage, with the assistance of ethics committees; the better organization of the sector comprising traditional knowledge; cooperation between traditional medicine and modern medicine suppliers; and, the teaching of traditional knowledge at primary,

secondary and tertiary levels. National authorities should be continuously and fully involved in all phases of the development and implementation of these activities;

(c) the owners of traditional knowledge are at the outset the individuals, families and/or local communities from which the knowledge has come. If these cannot be identified, then the State should stand in for them.

It further supported development by the IGC of a legally binding instrument to be adopted at the international level. Paragraphs 2–4, 'Traditional Knowledge', read as follows:

(2) In respect of the IGC, the African Group:

(a) favors the development of a legally binding international instrument that recognizes, protects and rewards traditional knowledge and innovations;

(b) supports the development by the IGC of a working definition of 'traditional knowledge' that is illustrative and inclusive, and which establishes its characteristic features and the criteria according to which it should be protected;

(c) supports the compilation of an inventory of documents related to traditional knowledge for inclusion in the minimum documentation list of the Patent Cooperation Treaty (the PCT), and the classification of relevant traditional knowledge documentation for patent search purposes;

(d) notes with interest this step of the development and publication of appropriate databases of traditional knowledge that is already in the public domain, taking into account, however, the characteristics and needs of African Traditional Knowledge Systems, which are largely orally-held, as well as the use of databases to provide positive protection for traditional knowledge, particularly 'secret knowledge.' Further, the Group encourages African States to establish traditional knowledge databases and make them available, in cases where 'defensive protection' of disclosed traditional knowledge is desired. The Group also calls upon WIPO to provide intellectual property assistance to African documentation initiatives in this regard, particularly in respect of the intellectual property implications of such documentation.

(3) More generally, States should:

(a) speed up the formulation of national policies and legislation in regard to the recognition, preservation, development and popularization of the inherent elements of traditional knowledge which impact on the life of the people and the environment;

(b) create national competent authorities for the management and promotion of traditional knowledge;
(c) intensify efforts to create public awareness among all stakeholders on all issues relating to the development, promotion and protection of traditional knowledge;
(d) translate regulatory texts linked to traditional knowledge into the local languages with a view to the involvement of all the communities.

(4) The African Group also believes that traditional communities have a key responsibility for identifying, preserving, and promoting their knowledge systems, and national governments should support and assist them in these endeavours.

As for folklore, while the position paper recognized that copyright, trademarks, and industrial designs may provide adequate protection to EoF where creators are identifiable, these protection regimes lag behind where that is not the case. Paragraph 1, 'Expressions of Folklore', reads as follows:

> The African Group believes that existing intellectual property rights, such as copyright, trademarks (including certification and collective marks), and industrial designs, may provide adequate protection for expressions of folklore in respect of tradition-based creations where the creator (or creators) of the expression is (or are) identifiable. In such cases, the creator should be the owner and beneficiary of the rights. On the other hand, where there is no identifiable creator, recourse should be had to a *sui generis* intellectual property system, which should provide for the State to hold the rights. In such cases, the State should pay any financial proceeds either to the relevant community or to a fund for the promotion of cultural heritage.

Consequently, recourse to a *sui generis* regime of protection would be required. At the international level, the Group proposed that the IGC develop a binding legal instrument for protection of EoF. Paragraph 2, 'Expressions of Folklore', reads as follows:

In respect of the IGC:

(a) the IGC should examine the means by which intellectual property registration systems, particularly the trade mark and industrial designs systems, could be adapted to enhance the protection provided to expressions of folklore, without prejudice to the examination of these questions within other organs of WIPO.

(b) the African Group supports the study of the relationship between customary laws, protocols and practices governing custodianship, use and transmission of expressions of folklore, on the one hand, and the formal intellectual property system, on the other, in relation *inter alia* to the establishment of *sui generis* systems of protection and so as to ensure that intellectual property rights do not preclude continued customary creation and use of expressions of folklore;

(c) the WIPO/UNESCO Model Provisions, 1982 provide a useful reference point for the development of effective national, regional and international systems of protection, although they could be updated and improved upon;

(d) the African Group favors the establishment of a comprehensive international binding instrument on the protection of expressions of folklore, with some form of dispute settlement mechanism either similar to that which is obtainable under the TRIPS Agreement or a mediation process as is provided by the WIPO Arbitration and Mediation Centre.

The WIPO General Assembly decided on October 1, 2003 to extend the mandate of the IGC for two more years and urged it to continue its work on questions included in its previous mandate. Under its new mandate, the IGC was directed to focus on a consideration of the international dimension of those questions, without prejudice to the work pursued in other fora. No outcome of its work was excluded, including the possible development of an international instrument or instruments.[10]

Commenting on the mandate prior to its extension by the General Assembly, the African Group had considered that the time was ripe during the upcoming biennium for the IGC to go beyond its deliberative mandate and to enter into a norm-setting mode, with a view to reaching agreement on an international legally binding instrument. The Group believed that such an instrument was fundamental to combat biopiracy and to ensure effective protection and enforcement of rights related to the issues under discussion. The Group was aware that to arrive at such an international legally binding instrument it was first necessary to develop relevant elements and principles of such instruments, as in any norm-setting process.[11]

As a follow-up to this statement, at the sixth session of the IGC in March 2004, the African Group submitted a document[12] which may be considered a landmark proposal and which was supported by most Delegations, including that of the developed countries' Group B.[13] The document is reproduced below.

---

10 See, Report of the WIPO General Assembly, Thirtieth (Sixteenth Ordinary) Session, Geneva, September 22 to October 1, 2003, WIPO Doc. WO/GA/30/8, para. 93.

11 Ibid., para. 58.

12 *Submission by The African Group: Objectives, Principles and Elements of an International Instrument, or Instruments, on Intellectual Property in Relation to Genetic Resources and on the Protection of Traditional Knowledge and Folklore*, document submitted by the African Group to the Intergovernmental Committee on Intellectual Property and Genetic Resources, Traditional Knowledge and Folklore, Sixth Session, Geneva, March 15–19, 2004, WIPO Doc. WIPO/GRTKF/IC/6/12.

13 See, Report of the Intergovernmental Committee on Intellectual Property and Genetic Resources, Traditional Knowledge and Folklore, Sixth Session, Geneva, March 15–19, 2004, WIPO Doc. WIPO/GRTKF/IC/6/14, para. 191.

OBJECTIVES, PRINCIPLES AND ELEMENTS OF AN INTERNATIONAL INSTRUMENT, OR INSTRUMENTS, ON INTELLECTUAL PROPERTY IN RELATION TO GENETIC RESOURCES AND ON THE PROTECTION OF TRADITIONAL KNOWLEDGE AND FOLKLORE, SIXTH SESSION OF THE IGC, MARCH 2004

Objectives

1. Prevent the misappropriation of genetic resources, traditional knowledge and expressions of folklore
2. Ensure prior informed consent and equitable sharing of the benefits arising from the use of genetic resources, traditional knowledge and expressions folklore
3. Ensure that these benefits are harnessed for the benefit of traditional knowledge holders and custodians, in particular local and indigenous communities
4. Ensure the conservation and sustainable use of bio-diversity
5. Protect and reward innovations and creative works derived from traditional knowledge and expressions of folklore

Principles

1. Reaffirm the principle of national sovereignty over genetic resources
2. Recognize the role of the State in the preservation and protection of traditional knowledge and expressions of folklore
3. Recognize the economic rights of traditional knowledge holders and custodians as well as their moral rights against the culturally offensive use of their traditional knowledge and expressions of folklore
4. Recognize the role of customary law and protocols in the protection of traditional knowledge and expressions of folklore
5. Recognize the complementary nature of defensive and positive measures relating to the protection of genetic resources, traditional knowledge and expressions of folklore

General Elements

— National Treatment/ Mutual recognition of national legislation
— Definitions

Genetic Resources

— Recognition of the right of States to take measures to ban the patenting of life forms
— Compliance with access and benefit sharing laws of the country of origin of genetic resources to ensure implementation of prior informed consent and equitable benefit sharing
— Introducing a disclosure requirement in patent laws as well as evidence of compliance with national access and benefit sharing laws of the country of origin of genetic resources (disclosure of the source and country of origin of the genetic resource in claimed inventions and of the associated traditional knowledge used in the invention)
— Contractual arrangements

Traditional Knowledge
Developing a *sui generis* system of protection
— Establish scope of protected subject matter
— Establish nature of rights
— Address ownership of rights, moral and economic rights, acquisition, exercise, expiry and enforcement of rights
— Establish registration mechanisms
Expressions of Folklore
Developing a *sui generis* system of protection
— Establish scope of protected subject matter
— Establish nature of rights,
— Establish ownership of rights, moral and economic rights of performers, acquisition, exercise, expiry and enforcement of rights
— Establish registration and administration mechanisms
Institutional Mechanism
— Capacity building and technical assistance
— Sensitization and awareness building
— Networking and exchange of information
— Promotion of documentation and codification of traditional knowledge and expressions of folklore
— Institutional mechanism for fostering the transfer of technology
— Establishment of national focal points of implementation
— Establishment of a follow up body
Enforcement
Dispute Settlement

This document received widespread support from both developed and developing countries. One Delegation considered the African Group proposal for an international instrument to be excellent food for thought in furthering discussions on the international dimension of the Committee's work.[14] Another Delegation considered this document to be a very constructive contribution to the work of the Committee, and found it a useful identification of some of the issues requiring further consideration.[15] Another stated that it shared many of the objectives set out in the submission and supported discussion of the objectives and principles identified in it. It did not, however, agree with all the elements, such as the banning of patents on life forms.[16] Several other Delegations also supported the African proposal.[17]

14 Ibid., para. 194.
15 Ibid., para. 191.
16 Ibid., para. 218.
17 Ibid., paras. 195, 197, and 192, respectively.

The African Group's representative stressed in his statement that the main goal in presenting the document was to focus the work of the Committee in a structured manner.[18] Further, the African Group requested the WIPO Secretariat to prepare for the next session a basic proposal containing provisions which could be included in an instrument addressing one or more of the issues at hand.[19]

As requested by Committee members in the sixth session of the IGC,[20] the WIPO Secretariat produced two documents containing overviews of the core principles and policy objectives in relation to protection of TCEs and TK which were set out in a structure that closely followed the African Group's proposal at that session.[21] Similarly, in line with the request of Committee members,[22] the principles were articulated in the form of 'provisions which could be included in an instrument addressing one or more of the issues at hand'.

At this stage, there is no need to examine these two documents. However, what should be underlined is that the African Group submission shaped a new direction as to how these issues could be discussed in a more structured way to advance the work of the Committee leading to the adoption of international instrument(s) aimed at protecting both TK and TCEs. The African Group reaffirmed that discussions of the draft policy objectives and core principles were not an end in themselves but should be the basis for further discussions on the legal status of protection and, in particular, for the development of an international legally binding instrument(s) on IP in relation to GR and the protection of TK and folklore.

These documents have been revised by Member States at each session of the IGC. The revised policy objectives and principles well reflect the evolution/state of the discussion on TKs and TCEs since the sixth session of the IGC.

At the twelfth session of the IGC, several questions were raised by Member States with regard to both TK and TCEs. These questions related to the following issues:

- definition of TK and TCEs/EoF that should be protected;

---

18 Ibid., para. 188.

19 Ibid.

20 See, for example, ibid., paras. 188 (Egypt), 222 (the African Group), and 217 (Pakistan).

21 See, *The Protection of Traditional Cultural Expressions/Expressions of Folklore: Overview of Policy Objectives and Core Principles*, document prepared by the WIPO Secretariat for the Intergovernmental Committee on Intellectual Property and Genetic Resources, Traditional Knowledge and Folklore, Seventh Session, Geneva, November 1–5, 2004, WIPO Doc. WIPO/GRTKF/IC/7/3; and *Protection of Traditional Knowledge: Overview of Policy Objectives and Core Principles*, document prepared by the WIPO Secretariat for the Intergovernmental Committee on Intellectual Property and Genetic Resources, Traditional Knowledge and Folklore, Seventh Session, Geneva, November 1–5, 2004, WIPO Doc. WIPO/GRTKF/IC/7/5.

22 See, for example, WIPO Doc. WIPO/GRTKF/IC/6/14, paras. 188, 196 (The African Group), 195 (Brazil), and 217 (Pakistan).

- who should benefit from any such protection or who would hold the rights to protectable TK and TCEs/EoF;
- what objective is sought to be achieved through according intellectual property protection (economic rights, moral rights);
- what forms of behavior in relation to protectable TK and TCEs/EoF should be considered unacceptable and illegal;
- exceptions or limitations to rights attaching to protectable TK and TCEs/EoF;
- length of protection;
- to what extent do existing IPRs already afford protection and what gaps need to be filled;
- what sanctions or penalties should apply to behavior or acts considered to be unacceptable/illegal;
- which issues should be dealt with internationally and which nationally, or what division should be made between international regulation and national regulation; and
- how should foreign rights holders/beneficiaries be treated.

To respond to these questions and issues, in the thirteenth session of the IGC in October 2008, the African Group made a proposal reflecting the views of its members.[23] The proposal covered the following three items: TK, TCEs, and GRs. A brief summary of the African views with regard to each issue follows.

As regards the definition of TK, the African Group proposed a concise, flexible, and non-rigid definition complemented by a list of examples, also emphasizing that TK should not be limited to a single technical field and should be inclusive of all knowledge systems.

The same view was expressed for the definition of TCEs, which should be flexible, descriptive, and not rigid. According to the Group, the Berne Convention's definition is limited to copyright, which is suitable only for certain forms of TCEs and does not extend to protecting the universe of TCEs.

According to the proposal, the beneficiaries of protection should be the indigenous and traditional communities.[24]

---

23 *African Group Proposal on the Protection of Traditional Knowledge, Traditional Cultural Expressions and Genetic Resources*, document submitted by the African Group to the Intergovernmental Committee on Intellectual Property and Genetic Resources, Traditional Knowledge and Folklore, Thirteenth Session, Geneva, October 13–17, 2008, WIPO Doc. WIPO/GRTKF/IC/13/9. See, also, *African Group Submission on Document WIPO/GRTKF/IC/13/9*, document prepared by the WIPO Secretariat for the Intergovernmental Committee on Intellectual Property and Genetic Resources, Traditional Knowledge and Folklore, Fourteenth Session, Geneva, June 29 to July 3, 2009, WIPO Doc. WIPO/GRTKF/IC/14/9.

24 See, also, WIPO/GRTKF/IC/11/5C, Reproduction of Document WIPO/GRTKF/IC/9/5 'The Protection of Traditional Knowledge: Revised Objectives and Principles' and WIPO/GRTKF/IC/11/4C, Reproduction of Document WIPO/GRTKF/IC/9/4 'The

For TK, PIC, mutually agreed terms (MAT) and benefit-sharing are the means to achieve moral and economic rights through IP protection. With regard to TCEs, according to the Group, the objective of IP protection should be positive and defensive. It should cover both the economic and moral rights, as these are interlinked, and all TCEs should be protected at both national and international level.

According to the proposal, misappropriation of both TK and TCEs would be considered the main illegal act. For TK, Article 10*bis* of the Paris Convention relating to unfair competition may be the basis to identify unacceptable behavior. For TCEs, the list should include, *inter alia*, unauthorized disclosure of secret TCEs, distortion, disrespect and denigration, and unauthorized commercial exploitation.

Limitations and exceptions must take into consideration the public interest and continuing customary use and practices of the community (use in the traditional context). For TK, the African Group maintained that the duration of protection must be in perpetuity. For TCEs, it said that protection should not be limited in time as long as the TCEs satisfy the requirements of protection and as long as they remained integral to a traditional community's collective identity. It was also underlined that the terms of protection for both TK and TCEs could be influenced by the scope of exceptions and limitations.

According to the Group, TK and TCEs may not be adequately protected under the existing IP regime even though some attempts had been made in the past in the context of TCEs and, recently, for TK. A *sui generis* system of protection and a holistic approach were recommended by the proposal for both TK and TCEs. The proposal recommended that civil, criminal, and administrative sanctions be provided for infringement of the protected rights.

The question of which issues should be dealt with internationally and which nationally was considered by the Group to be the key one. According to the Group, the main purpose was to come up with an international instrument which would safeguard the rights of the beneficiaries of protection.

Finally, the proposal clearly indicated that the principle of national treatment must regulate the rights of foreigners.

Several options for the protection of GRs were proposed by the African Group. The latter proposed that WIPO:

(i) Consider developing a range of options for the IP related aspects of ABS arrangements that could ensure benefit-sharing. In doing so, also develop a structured menu of options to guide custodians of genetic resources to facilitate their decision making process.

(ii) Consider developing disclosure requirements and alternative proposals for dealing with the relationship between IP and GR as requested by the CBD.

Protection of Traditional Cultural Expressions/Expressions of Folklore: Revised Objectives and Principles'.

(iii) Consider developing guidelines and procedures with regards to dealing effectively with the IP aspects of access and benefit-sharing arrangements.
(iv) Consider supporting demand and needs driven capacity building initiatives in Africa relevant to the relationship within IP and GR as well as the interface amongst World Intellectual Property Organisation (WIPO), Convention on Biological Diversity (CBD), World Trade Organisation (WTO) and Food and Agriculture Organisation (FAO).
(v) Further emphasizes the linkages that exist amongst WIPO, CBD, FAO and WTO. In this regard, encourages these organizations to interact and participate actively amongst themselves, within their respective mandates, to foster synergistic implementation of related activities.[25]

As can be clearly seen, the African Group took a number of initiatives during the pre-text-based negotiation period not only to advance the work of the IGC but, more importantly, by presenting proposal papers that have changed the flow of debates within the Committee.

Several sessions of the IGC have taken place since its establishment. The discussions carried out under the IGC have contributed to a better understanding of TK and TCEs and helped to underline the issues involved.

Text-based negotiations In 2009, a new mandate for the IGC was discussed amongst the WIPO Member States. It was agreed that the new mandate should incorporate a text-based negotiation of the issues debated. At the fourteenth session of the IGC, the African Group submitted a proposal in this regard that was supported and endorsed by most of the countries from all the Groups.[26] The text of the African proposal is reproduced below.

> ELEMENTS FOR THE NEW MANDATE – AFRICAN GROUP PROPOSAL
> Bearing in mind the Development Agenda recommendations, agreed to recommend to the WIPO General Assembly that the mandate of the Committee be renewed as follows, namely that, the Committee will undertake during the next budgetary biennium (2010/2011) text-based negotiations on genetic resources, traditional knowledge and traditional cultural expressions.
>
> It will adopt, as set out in the Annex, a clearly defined work program and timeframe, including the holding of intersessional work sessions. The focus of its work, without prejudice to the work pursued in other fora, will build on the existing work carried out by the Committee and use WIPO documents WIPO/

25 WIPO Doc. WIPO/GRTKF/IC/13/9, Annex, p. 19.

26 See, *Proposal of The African Group on the Mandate of the Intergovernmental Committee*, document prepared by the WIPO Secretariat for the Intergovernmental Committee on Intellectual Property and Genetic Resources, Traditional Knowledge and Folklore, Fourteenth Session, Geneva, June 29 to July 3, 2009, WIPO Doc. WIPO/GRTKF/IC/14/8 Rev.

> GRTKF/IC/9/4, WIPO/GRTKF/IC/9/5 and WIPO/GRTKF/IC/11/8A (TCE, TK, and GR) which is to constitute the basis of the Committees' work on text based negotiations.
>
> The Committee is requested to submit to the 2011 GA a text for an internationally legally binding instrument/instruments on TCEs, TK and GR and recommend a date for the Diplomatic Conference as agreed in its work program.
>
> The General Assembly would further request the International Bureau to continue to assist the Committee by providing Member States with necessary expertise, funding of the participation of experts from developing countries and LDCs.

According to the mandate adopted by the WIPO General Assembly on October 1, 2009:

> the Committee [IGC] will, during the (next) budgetary biennium (2010/2011), and without prejudice to the work pursued in other fora, continue its work and undertake text-based negotiations with the objective of reaching agreement on a text of an international legal instrument (or instruments) which will ensure the effective protection of GRs, TK and TCEs.
>
> …
>
> The focus of the Committee's work in the 2010/2011 biennium will build on the existing work carried out by the Committee and use all WIPO working documents, including WIPO/GRTKF/IC/9/4 (Traditional Cultural Expressions), WIPO/GRTKF/IC/9/5 (Traditional Knowledge) and WIPO/GRTKF/IC/11/8A (Genetic Resources), which are to constitute the basis of the Committee's work on text-based negotiations.
>
> …
>
> The Committee (IGC) is requested to submit to the 2011 General Assembly the text (or texts) of an international legal instrument (or instruments) which will ensure the effective protection of GRs, TK and TCEs. The General Assembly in 2011 will decide on convening a Diplomatic Conference.[27]

In 2010 and 2011, the IGC followed a defined work program which included four sessions of the IGC and three inter-sessional working groups.[28] The Inter-sessional Working Group 1 (IWG1) covered TCEs; the IWG2 dealt with TK; and the IWG3 covered GRs.

---

27 *Matters Concerning the Intergovernmental Committee on Intellectual Property and Genetic Resources, Traditional Knowledge and Folklore, Agenda Item 28*, Decision of the WIPO General Assembly, Thirty-Eighth (Nineteenth Ordinary) Session, September 22 to October 1, 2009, WIPO Doc. WIPO/GRTKF/IC/15/REF-DECISION 28, paras. (a), (c), and (d).

28 Ibid., para. (b).

Each IWG undertook a text-based negotiation provision by provision. The respective draft texts, namely the main Articles 1 (definition of the subject matter), 2 (beneficiaries), 3 (scope of protection), and 5 (exceptions and limitations), were reviewed during the seventeenth, eighteenth, and nineteenth plenary sessions of the IGC. All the draft texts originally encompassed several options reflecting the differing positions of the Member States. 'Facilitators' further consolidated and streamlined the texts, which the nineteenth plenary session of the IGC then accepted as the basis for future work.

Current status of the negotiations

The text of the new mandate of the IGC as decided by the WIPO General Assembly in October 2011[29] is reproduced below.

> At its 19th session, the IGC agreed to recommend to the WIPO General Assembly the renewal of its mandate for the 2012–2013 biennium. In this regard, the IGC agreed to recommend the following decision to the General Assembly:
>
> Bearing in mind the Development Agenda recommendations, the WIPO General Assembly agrees that the mandate of the WIPO Intergovernmental Committee on Intellectual Property and Genetic Resources, Traditional Knowledge and Folklore be renewed as follows:
>
> (a) The Committee will, during the next budgetary biennium (2012/2013), and without prejudice to the work pursued in other fora, expedites its work on text-based negotiations with the objective of reaching agreement on a text(s) of an international legal instrument(s) which will ensure the effective protection of GRs, TK and TCEs.
>
> (b) The Committee will follow, as set out in the [table below], a clearly defined work program, based on sound working methods, for the 2012/2013 biennium. This work program will make provision initially for four sessions of the IGC, three of which will be thematic, as detailed in the future work program of the IGC, taking into account sub paragraph (d) with regard to the possible consideration by the General Assembly in 2012 of the need for additional meetings.
>
> (c) The focus of the Committee's work in the 2012/2013 biennium will build on the existing work carried out by the Committee and use all WIPO working documents, including WIPO/GRTKF/IC/19/4, WIPO/GRTKF/IC/19/5, WIPO/GRTKF/IC/19/6 and WIPO/GRTKF/IC/19/7, which are to constitute the basis of the Committee's work on text-based negotiations, as well as any other textual contributions by Members.
>
> (d) The Committee is requested to submit to the 2012 General Assembly the text(s) of an international legal instrument(s) which will ensure

29 Report of the WIPO General Assembly, Fortieth (Twentieth Ordinary) Session, Geneva, September 26 to October 5, 2011, WIPO Doc. WO/GA/40/19, para. 180.

the effective protection of GRs, TK and TCEs. The General Assembly in 2012 will take stock of and consider the text(s), progress made and decide on convening a Diplomatic Conference, and will consider the need for additional meetings, taking account of the budgetary process.

(e) The General Assembly requests the International Bureau to continue to assist the Committee by providing Member States with necessary expertise and funding, in the most efficient manner, of the participation of experts from developing countries and LDCs, taking into account the usual formula.

(f) With a view to enhancing the positive contribution of observers, the General Assembly invites the Committee to review its procedures in this regard. To facilitate this review, the General Assembly requests the secretariat to prepare a study outlining current practices and potential options.[30]

In line with this decision, the mandate of the IGC has been renewed for a further period of two years—2012–2013—with the aim of reaching agreement on a text(s) of an international legal instrument(s) which will ensure the effective protection of GRs, TK and TCEs. Pursuant to the mandate for the 2012–2013 biennium, and as indicated in the work program referred to in the mandate, the IGC met three times in 2012, as follows:

a. IGC 20, from February 14 to 22, 2012, on the subject of genetic resources (GRs);
b. IGC 21, from April 16 to 20, 2012, on the subject of traditional knowledge (TK); and,
c. IGC 22, from July 9 to 13, 2012, on the subject of traditional cultural expressions (TCEs).

This work program was respected in 2012. In each session, the relevant draft text was discussed by Member States and further reviewed by Facilitators to reduce or eliminate various options contained in each article. As agreed in the IGC, three main draft texts, namely one each on GRs, TK, and TCEs were submitted to the General Assembly 2012 for decision. Accordingly, the General Assembly decided in October 2012[31] as follows:

---

30 *Matters Concerning the Intergovernmental Committee on Intellectual Property and Genetic Resources, Traditional Knowledge and Folklore (IGC),* document prepared by the WIPO Secretariat for the WIPO General Assembly, Fortieth (Twentieth Ordinary) Session, Geneva, September 26 to October 5, 2011, WIPO Doc. WO/GA/40/7, para. 16.

31 *Matters Concerning the Intergovernmental Committee on Intellectual Property and Genetic Resources, Traditional Knowledge and Folklore (IGC)*, WIPO General Assembly, Decision, Forty-First (Twenty-First Extraordinary) Session, Geneva, October 1-9, 2012.

> In accordance with the mandate of the IGC for 2012/2013, the Assemblies of the Member States of WIPO agree to continue intensive negotiations and engagement in good faith, with appropriate representation, towards concluding the text(s) of an international legal instrument(s) which will ensure effective protection of GRs, TK and TCEs, and decide:
>
> a. The work of the Committee will be carried out through three thematic IGC sessions as set out in the table below.
> b. The work will build on the existing texts submitted by the IGC to the General Assembly (Annex A, Annex B, and Annex C of document WO/GA/41/15).
> c. The Committee is requested to submit to the 2013 General Assembly the text(s) of an international legal instrument(s) which will ensure the effective protection of GRs, TK and TCEs. The General Assembly in 2013 will take stock of and consider the text(s), progress made and decide on convening a Diplomatic Conference.
> d. The work of the IGC shall follow the program set out below:
> February 2013: IGG 23 – Genetic Resources (5 days)
> April/May 2013: IGC 24 – Traditional Knowledge. With a focus on, but not limited to, 4 key Articles *viz* Subject Matter of Protection, Beneficiaries, Scope of Protection and Limitations and Exceptions (5 days)
> July 2013: IGC 25 - Traditional cultural expressions. With a focus on, but not limited to, 4 key Articles *viz* Subject Matter of Protection, Beneficiaries, Scope of Protection and Limitations and Exceptions (5 days)
> Review and take stock of the text(s) of the International legal instrument(s) ensuring the effective protection of TCEs, TK, and GRs and make a recommendation to the General Assembly ([2][3] days)
> October 2013: WIPO General Assembly, decide on convening a diplomatic conference

The Decision of the General Assembly shed light on the continuous mandate of the IGC and its work program for 2013. It will be seen whether the IGC will be in a position to submit the text(s) of an international legal instrument(s) which will regulate TK, TCEs, and GRs to the 2013 General Assembly to decide on convening a diplomatic conference.

Before embarking on current negotiations taking place in the IGC, it is worth mentioning that the former Chair of the IGC for the 2010–2011 biennium submitted at the end of his mandate a very important report with regard to the three items, namely TK, GRs, and TCEs.[32] This report will be referred to in the

32 Report from His Excellency Ambassador Philip Richard Owade on Key Issues Pending from the 2010–2011 Biennium, WIPO/GRTKF/IC/20/INF/4, WIPO/GRTKF/IC/21/INF/4, WIPO/GRTKF/IC/22/INF/4.

following discussion where appropriate. However, the different draft texts/Articles as produced in February 2012 for GRs, in April 2012 for TK, and in July 2012 for TCEs and transmitted to the 2012 General Assembly will be the main documents.

Traditional cultural expressions

This part will review the key provisions of the Facilitators' text and others as discussed in the plenary session of the IGC Twenty-Second Session in July 2012. As mentioned above, the Facilitators' exercise aimed at narrowing gaps and eliminating various options or brackets in each provision that was originally produced in the IWG1, as revised. In other words, the present draft Text reflects the positions of Member States on the issues on the table. A particular focus on the African Group's inputs will be considered in the following items: subject matter of protection; beneficiaries; scope of protection; exceptions and limitations;[33] term of protection; and such other matters as administration of rights/interests; formalities; sanctions, remedies, and exercise of rights/interests; transitional measures; consistency with the general legal framework; national treatment; and trans-boundary cooperation. The comments of the Facilitators will be addressed where appropriate.

Subject matter of protection Article 1 of the Draft Text on TCEs deals with the subject matter of protection, which comprises both the definition of TCE and the conditions of eligibility, and stipulates as follows:

> 1. Traditional cultural expressions are any form of [artistic and literary] expression, tangible and/or intangible, or a combination thereof,
> *Alternative 1:* in which traditional culture [and knowledge] are embodied
> *Alternative 2*: which are indicative of traditional culture [and knowledge]
> [which pass from generation to generation and between generations], including, but not limited to:
>
> (a) phonetic or verbal expressions, [such as stories, epics, legends, popular stories, poetry, riddles and other narratives; words, signs, names, and symbols];
> (b) musical or sound expressions, [such as songs, rhythms, and instrumental music, the sounds which are the expression of rituals];
> (c) expressions by action, [such as dances, works of mas, plays, ceremonies, rituals, rituals in sacred places and peregrinations, games and traditional sports, puppet performances, and other performances, whether fixed or unfixed]; and
> (d) tangible expressions, [such as material expressions] of art, [handicrafts, handmade carpets, architecture, and tangible spiritual forms, and sacred places];
> (e) [adaptations of the expressions referred to in the above categories].

33 As proposed by the Chair of the Nineteenth Session of the IGC in July 2011, these first four items are the key issues.

> *Criteria for eligibility*
> 2. Protection extends to traditional cultural expressions that are:
> (a) [the result of the creative intellectual activity] of;
> (b) [distinctive of or the unique product of]/[associated with] the cultural and social identity of; [and/or]
> (c) [held], maintained, used or developed as part of the cultural or social identity [or heritage] by the beneficiaries as defined in Article 2.
> 3. The terminology used to describe the protected subject matter shall/should be determined in accordance with national law and where applicable, regional law.

Delegations agreed that the subject matter of protection, which incorporates both the definition and criteria for eligibility, is at the core of protection of TCEs. Notwithstanding this common understanding, Member States were unable to agree on some terminologies, concepts, or options to reach the main objective. In other words, despite convergence of views, divergence of opinions is present.

The Facilitators have identified a number of outstanding issues on the subject matter of protection of TCE.[34] Firstly, Member States have not agreed on whether or not to include the term 'artistic'. Some Delegations, such as the African Group and India, maintain that this term must be removed from the definition as it may narrow or limit the scope of expressions to protect because TCEs are not necessarily 'artistic'. On the other hand, some Member States are supportive of limiting the ambit of protection to 'artistic' TCEs.

The second divergence is on the approach mentioned in Alternative 1, whereby it would be required that traditional culture must be 'embodied' in the TCEs to be protected. This is deemed by some Members to be too restrictive and to affect the dynamic and evolving nature of TCEs. Consequently, Member States have not agreed whether to use the phrases 'in which traditional culture and knowledge are embodied' or 'which are indicative of traditional culture and knowledge'.

The third element of divergence is the reference to 'knowledge'. Some Delegations are not comfortable with the inclusion of 'knowledge', which relates to TK and which may therefore lead to the duplication of protection. However, several Delegations from developing countries, including the African Group, assert that for many indigenous peoples, TCEs and TK are closely connected, with TCEs being the outward manifestation of the TK.

The fourth divergence is whether the definition of TCEs should be based on general categories or should include lists of examples. This issue was also identified by the former Chair of the IGC. According to the former Chair, there was no agreement on whether to include a list or simply introductory categories. The general idea, expressed by many Delegations, is that an international instrument would provide a broad framework which would enable each country to specify

34 See, Draft Report of the Intergovernmental Committee on Intellectual Property and Genetic Resources, Traditional Knowledge and Folklore, Twenty-Second Session, Geneva, July 9–13, 2012, WIPO Doc. WIPO/GRTKF/IC/22/6/Prov. 2 of November 5, 2012.

which of its cultural elements may be protected. Other Delegations maintain that a list of examples provides certainty and clarity and ensures that particular items are protected. The African Group has mainly supported inclusion of a list of examples. According to the Group, any such list would only be illustrative and indicate the areas which need to be clearly included.[35]

Another issue in the definition relates to the phrase 'which pass from generation to generation and between generations'. One Delegation expressed reservation over the use of this phrase. On the other hand, another Delegation held that the phrase 'from generation to generation and between generations' was essential to the definition of TCEs. It was a central concept that needed to be retained. Some other Delegations stated that the phrase was an important ingredient of the definition of TCEs. The use of the term 'between generations' would take into consideration TCEs which had skipped generations.

The Facilitators have also identified several issues regarding the criteria for eligibility where divergence among Member States is still perceived. One question posed by some Delegations is whether or not the phrase 'creative intellectual activity' in paragraph 2(a) should be a criterion. The proponents of the concept argued that they could not conceive of situations where a TCE would not result from some intellectual activity. There were concerns from others that not all instances of TCEs would qualify as intellectual activity (e.g., rituals), and questions about how one would prove this criterion. Some maintained that TCEs are not necessarily intellectual activity and, consequently, there is no need to have such a criterion.

In paragraph 2(b), there is disagreement on whether to say 'distinctive of or the unique product' or 'associated with'. One delegation was concerned that 'associated with' is not adequate to exclude inauthentic TCEs and suggested that the issue be given further reflection and discussion. The Delegation of Norway was in favour of the inclusion of TCEs being 'distinctive of or the unique product of the cultural and social identity and cultural heritage of the beneficiaries'. The Delegation of Australia said that eligible TCEs needed to be 'distinctive' or 'the unique product of the culture', as opposed to the vague notion of being 'associated with', since this would better encapsulate the authentic and unique character of the TCEs worthy of protection.[36] Some Delegations maintained that the criteria should not be cumulative.

Beneficiaries Article 2 of the Draft text sets out as follows:

> Beneficiaries of protection are indigenous [peoples] or [local communities], [or as determined by national law or by treaty] [who hold, maintain, use or develop] the traditional cultural expressions as defined in/determined by Article 1.

---

35 Draft Report of the Intergovernmental Committee on Intellectual Property and Genetic Resources, Traditional Knowledge and Folklore, Nineteenth Session, Geneva, July 18–22, 2011, WIPO Doc. WIPO/GRTKF/IC/19/12/Prov. 2, para. 30.

36 WIPO Doc. WIPO/GRTKF/IC/22/6/Prov. 2, para 68.

According to the former Chair, the scope of beneficiaries is one of the key outstanding policy issues. There is no agreement on the extent to which the instrument should extend beyond indigenous peoples and local communities. The identification of the beneficiaries is closely related to the scope of the instrument as a whole. The African Group, supported the inclusion of 'peoples', 'local communities' and 'or as determined by national law or by treaty'.

Another issue where Members have divergent views concerns the extent of flexibility to empower a national law to determine who the beneficiaries should be. One Delegation recognized the need for flexibility at the national level and expressed support for the term 'indigenous peoples and local communities' as being the holders and beneficiaries of the rights to TCEs. In some jurisdictions, however, beneficiaries might not be 'local communities' but 'traditional communities', 'ethnic minorities', 'cultural communities', etc. Nonetheless, it believed that the phrase 'or as determined by national law' would be too vague, as this phrase would include the possibility that even a ministry or agency of the State or a museum could be so included.

Another Delegation said that it was clear that the beneficiaries should be indigenous peoples. However, it recognized that there needed to be flexibility for other Member States to be able to deal through national law with the beneficiaries of protection. It believed that the current text provided that flexibility and was a particularly useful articulation of a flexible approach. The Delegation supported the inclusion of 'peoples', 'local communities' and 'or as determined by national law or by treaty'.

Scope of protection Article 3 covers the scope of protection of TCEs. Two options comprising alternatives have been put on the table. Options for Article 3 are as follows:

Option 1

> The economic and moral interests of the beneficiaries concerning their traditional cultural expressions, as defined in Articles 1 and 2, shall/should be safeguarded as appropriate and according to national law, in a reasonable and balanced manner.

Option 2

> Adequate and effective legal, administrative or policy measures shall/should be provided to [safeguard the economic and moral interests of the beneficiaries, including but not limited to]:
>
> (a) prevent the unauthorized disclosure, fixation or other exploitation of [secret] traditional cultural expressions;
> (b) acknowledge the beneficiaries to be the source of the traditional cultural expression, unless this turns out to be impossible;
> (c) prevent use or modification which distorts or mutilates a traditional cultural expression or that is otherwise offensive, derogatory or diminishes its cultural significance to the beneficiary;

(d) protect against any false or misleading uses of traditional cultural expressions, in relation to goods and services, that suggest endorsement by or linkage with the beneficiaries; and [there are two options for paragraph (e), which deals with commercial exploitation]

(e) Alternative 1: where appropriate, enable beneficiaries to authorize the commercial exploitation of traditional cultural expressions by others.

(e) Alternative 2: ensure the beneficiaries have exclusive and [inalienable] collective rights to authorize and prohibit the following in relation to their traditional cultural expressions:

(i) fixation;
(ii) reproduction;
(iii) public performance;
(iv) translation or adaptation;
(v) making available or communicating to the public;
(vi) distribution;
(vii) any use for commercial purposes, other than their traditional use; and
(viii) the acquisition or exercise of intellectual property rights.

According to the former Chair, Option 1 would give States the maximum flexibility to determine the scope of protection. Option 2 is more detailed and prescriptive and contains two different approaches. One prescribes the acts that should be regulated but allows for flexibility on the types of measures to be implemented. The other prescribes a rights-based approach. In addition, Option 2 deals with adequate and effective measures and reflects four different elements of protection: first, protection for secret TCEs; second, acknowledgment of the source of TCEs; third, offensive use, distortion, or mutilation of TCEs; and fourth, preventing the misleading use of TCEs in relation to goods and services.

The African Group is in favor of the second option. According to the Group, the first option is too restrictive in the sense that it may be unable to establish a true international standard, which is what is required for better protection of TCEs. The Group has not supported Option 1 or the use of the word 'safeguard', given that safeguard comprises a more restrictive objective than what protection encompasses.

One Delegation expressed its preference for Option 1, which permits greater flexibility for Members. Another believed that Option 1 was a succinct and flexible formula. It felt that this option has the great virtue of providing an umbrella for divergent national and regional approaches to protecting the subject matter.

Exceptions and limitations Article 5 lays down exceptions and limitations as follows:

1. Measures for the protection of traditional cultural expressions shall/should not restrict the creation, customary use, transmission, exchange

and development of traditional cultural expressions by the beneficiaries, within and among communities, in the traditional and customary context [consistent with national laws of the contracting parties/member States/ members where applicable].

2. Limitations on protection shall/should extend only to the utilization of traditional cultural expressions taking place outside the membership of the beneficiary community or outside traditional or cultural context.
3. Contracting parties/Member States/Members may adopt appropriate limitations or exceptions under national law, provided that the use of traditional cultural expressions:

   Alternative 1:

   (a) acknowledges the beneficiaries, where possible;
   (b) is not offensive or derogatory to the beneficiaries; and
   (c) is compatible with fair practice.

   Alternative 2:

   (a) is limited to certain special cases;
   (b) does not conflict with the normal utilization of the traditional cultural expressions by the beneficiaries; and
   (c) does not unreasonably prejudice the legitimate interests of the beneficiaries.
4. Regardless of whether such acts are already permitted under Article 5(3) or not, the following shall/should be permitted [only with the free prior and informed consent of the beneficiaries]:
   (a) the use of traditional cultural expressions in archives, libraries, museums or cultural institutions for non-commercial cultural heritage purposes, including for preservation, display, research, presentation and education;
   (b) [the creation of an original work of authorship inspired by or borrowed from traditional cultural expressions].
5. [[Except for the protection of secret traditional cultural expressions against disclosure], to the extent that any act would be permitted under the national law for works protected by copyright or signs and symbols protected by trademark law, such act shall/should not bem prohibited by the protection of traditional cultural expressions].

In these options, the use of TCEs within a traditional context by the beneficiaries is considered to be the main exception, while use outside the community upon fulfillment of certain conditions is recognized as a limitation. In both options, the same three-step test requirements, as provided under the copyright system with regard to exceptions and limitations, are included.

According to the former Chair, there seems to be wide-ranging agreement in the IGC on respect for customary use, a test for developing domestic exceptions and an exception for cultural institutions. The areas of disagreement concern derivative works and the relevance of existing exceptions under conventional copyright and trademark law.

The African Group is in favor of limited exceptions and limitations, taking into account the legitimate interests of the beneficiaries. According to the Group, the degree of protection depends upon both Articles 3 and 5. One Delegation pointed out that Article 5 was of great importance because of its fundamental policies favoring freedom of speech and freedom of expression.

Term of protection The term of protection is dealt with in Article 6, where two options are provided, as follows:

> *Option 1*
>
> Protection of traditional cultural expressions should endure for as long as the traditional cultural expressions continue to meet the criteria for protection under Article 1 of these provisions; and,
>
> The protection granted to traditional cultural expressions against any distortion, mutilation or other modification or infringement thereof, done with the aim of causing harm thereto or to the reputation or image of the community, indigenous peoples and communities or region to which they belong, shall last indefinitely.
>
> *Option 2*
>
> At least as regards the economic aspects of traditional cultural expressions, their protection should be limited in time.

In the first option, protection will be enjoyed so long as the TCEs continue to meet the criteria of protection, and moral rights are protected indefinitely against any distortion or harmful acts to the image of the community. The second option gives leeway to national laws to limit the term of protection.[37] The African Group supports Option 1 with a few adjustments. According to the former Chair, the IGC could consider merging Options 1 and 2 as well as whether or not time limits should be imposed on the period of protection for moral and economic rights.

Other matters The Draft Text on TCEs covers also the following items:

Administration of rights (Article 4) This provision deals with how and to whom authorizations to use TCEs/EoF are applied for and related questions. The matters dealt with in this provision should apply regardless of whether communities or State-appointed bodies are the rights holders. The provisions as a whole envisage the exercise of rights by the relevant communities themselves.

37 *The Protection of Traditional Cultural Expressions/Expressions of Folklore: Revised Objectives and Principles*, document prepared by the WIPO Secretariat for the Intergovernmental Committee on Intellectual Property and Genetic Resources, Traditional Knowledge and Folklore, Seventeenth Session, Geneva, December 6–10, 2010, WIPO Doc. WIPO/GRTKF/IC/17/4 Prov, Annex, p. 41.

According to the former Chair, the IGC could discuss whether governments should be able to legislate or make decisions concerning the management of rights (for example through national authorities), whether to refer to 'prior informed consent' or 'approval and involvement' and whether there should be reporting requirements for competent authorities. The Facilitators worked on this Article in July 2012 and have proposed the following:

> Where so requested by the beneficiaries,
> *Alternative 1:* a competent authority (regional, national or local)
> *Alternative 2*: a national competent authority
> may, to the extent authorized by the beneficiaries, and in accordance with:
> *Alternative 1*: the traditional-decision-making and governance processes of the beneficiaries
> Alternative *2*: customary protocols, understandings, laws and practices
> *Alternative 3*: national law
> Alternative *4*: national procedure
> *Alternative 5*: international law

The point here is that the administration of rights is primarily a matter for indigenous peoples and local communities (etc.), so there is no need to be prescriptive. Where government assistance is sought, the specific functions would be a matter for the particular community and government to determine.

Formalities (Article 7) According to Article 7, the protection of TCEs shall/should not be subject to any formality. In this connection, the general comments made in the IWG1 may be summarized as follows. It has been suggested that the acquisition and maintenance of protection should be practically feasible, especially from the point of view of traditional communities, and not create excessive administrative burdens for either right holders or administrators. Equally important is the need, expressed by several stakeholders such as external researchers and other users of TCEs/EoF, for certainty and transparency in their relations with communities.

A key choice is whether or not to provide for automatic protection or for some kind of registration:

(a) a first option is to require some form of registration, possibly subject to formal or substantive examination. A registration system may merely have declaratory effect, in which case proof of registration would be used to substantiate a claim of ownership, or it may constitute rights. Some form of registration may provide useful precision, transparency and certainty on which TCEs are protected and for whose benefit;

(b) a second option would be to require automatic protection without formalities, so that protection would be available as of the moment a TCE is created, similar to copyright.

According to the former Chair, there seems to be a consensus that protection should not be subject to any formality.

Sanctions, remedies and exercises of rights (Article 8) The general comments made in the IWG1 which are still relevant may be summarized as follows:

> This provision concerns which civil and criminal sanctions and remedies may be made available for breaches of the rights provided.
>
> Communities and others have pointed out that the remedies available under current law may not be appropriate to deter infringing use of the works of an indigenous copyright holder, or may not provide for damages equivalent to the degree of cultural and non-economic damage caused by the infringing use. References have also been made to the desirability of alternative dispute resolution (ADR) in this area. Member States have pointed out the necessity of appropriate guidance and practical experiences with sanctions, remedies and enforcement.

According to the former Chair, one main point of disagreement is whether the text should prescribe sanctions or provide States with the flexibility to determine appropriate sanctions based on domestic law.

Transitional measures (Article 9) Two options are on the table here, but the common denominator is that these provisions shall apply to all TCEs which, at the moment of the provisions coming into effect/force, fulfill the criteria set out in Article 1.

The general comments made in the IWG1 which are still relevant may be summarized as follows:

> This provision concerns whether protection should operate retroactively or prospectively, and in particular how to deal with utilizations of TCEs/EoF that are continuing when the provisions enter into force and which had lawfully commenced before then.
>
> This question touches directly upon the notion of the 'public domain'. Committee participants have stated that the public domain was not a concept recognized by indigenous peoples and/or that as expressions of folklore *stricto sensu* had never been protected under IP they could not be said to have entered a 'public domain.'

According to the former Chair, Article 9 first states that the instrument would apply to the TCEs which, at the moment of entry into force, fulfill the criteria of protection. Thereafter, it contains two options. One protects the existing rights of third parties, while the other provides for continuing uses by third parties to be brought into conformity with the provisions.

Consistency with the general legal framework (Article 10) According to Article 10, protection under this instrument shall/should take account of, and operate consistently with, other international instruments, including those dealing with intellectual property and with cultural heritage.

National treatment (Article 11) According to this Article, the rights and benefits arising from the protection of TCEs under national measures or laws that give effect to these international provisions shall/should be available to all eligible beneficiaries who are nationals or residents of a prescribed country/contracting party/member State/member as defined by international obligations or undertakings. Eligible foreign beneficiaries shall/should enjoy the same rights and benefits as enjoyed by beneficiaries who are nationals of the country/contracting party/member State/member offering protection, as well as the rights and benefits specifically granted by these international provisions.

The general comments made in the IWG1 which are still valid may be summarized as follows:

> This provision deals with the technical question of how rights and interests of foreign holders of rights in TCEs/EoF would be recognized in national laws. In other words, on what conditions and in what circumstances foreign rights holders would have access to national protection systems, and what level of protection would be available to the benefit of foreign right holders.

Trans-national boundary cooperation (Article 12) In instances where traditional cultural expressions are located in territories of different contracting parties/member States/members, those contracting parties/member States/members shall/should co-operate in addressing instances of trans-boundary traditional cultural expressions.

Traditional knowledge

This part will review the key provisions of the Facilitators' text and others as discussed in the plenary session in April 2012. As mentioned above, the Facilitators' exercise aimed at narrowing gaps and eliminating various options or brackets in each provision originally produced in the IWG2, as revised. A particular focus on the African Group's inputs will be considered in the following items: subject matter of protection; beneficiaries; scope of protection; exceptions and limitations;[38] scope of protection and sanctions (newly included), term of protection; and such other matters as sanctions, remedies, and exercise of rights/application; disclosure requirements; administration of rights; application of collective rights; formalities; transitional measures; national treatment and other means of recognizing foreign rights and interests; and trans-boundary cooperation. Comments of the Facilitators will be considered where appropriate.

Subject matter of protection Article 1 of the Draft Text on TK sets out the subject matter of protection, which includes the definition of TK and criteria of eligibility. Article 1 prescribes as follows:

---

38 As proposed by the Chair of the Nineteenth Session of the IGC in July 2011, these first four items are the key issues.

Definition of TK

Facilitators' Option (Convergent Text)
1.1 For the purposes of this instrument, 'traditional knowledge' [refers to] <u>includes</u> know-how, skills, innovations, practices, teachings and learnings [developed within a traditional context]/[developed with an indigenous people or local community]/[and that is intergenerational]/[and that is passed on from generation to generation].
Optional Additions to the Facilitators' Text
(a) [is knowledge that is dynamic and evolving and]
(b) [resulting from intellectual activity]
(c) [and which may be associated with agricultural, environmental, healthcare and medical knowledge, biodiversity, traditional lifestyles and natural and genetic resources, and knowhow of traditional architecture and construction technologies]
(d) [and which may subsist in codified, oral or other forms]
(e) [traditional knowledge is part of the collective, ancestral, territorial, cultural, intellectual and material heritage of [indigenous peoples and local communities] beneficiaries as defined in Article 2.]
(f) [and are inalienable, indivisible and imprescriptible.]
Alternative
For the purposes of this instrument, traditional knowledge includes [collectively] generated and preserved from generation to generation or intergenerational know-how, skills, innovations, practices, teachings. [They exist or develop inter alia by indigenous or local communities.]
<u>Criteria of Eligibility</u>
Facilitators' Option (Convergent Text)
1.2 Protection extends to traditional knowledge that is associated with beneficiaries as defined in Article 2, [collectively] generated, shared/transmitted and preserved [and [integral]/[closely linked]] to the cultural identity of beneficiaries as defined in Article 2.
Optional Additions to the Facilitators' Text
(a) [the unique product of or is distinctively] associated to the beneficiaries or
(b) [integral]/[linked] identified/associated with [to] the cultural identity of beneficiaries
(c) [not widely known or used outside the community of the beneficiaries as defined in Article 2, [for a reasonable period of time]]
(d) [not in the public domain]
(e) [not protected by an intellectual property right]
(f) [not the application of principles, rules, skills, know-how, practices, and learning normally and generally well-known]
(g) whether the list should be cumulative or not (and therefore whether to include the term 'and' or 'or' after the next-to-last item in any list comprising any combination of (a) to (f) above)

(h) whether the provision should include a reference to 'generation-to-Generation'/'intergenerational'

Regarding the definition of TK, three schools of thought exist. The first school defines TK in its broadest sense.[39] The second school defines TK in a narrow sense.[40] The third school refuses to set out a strict definition of TK; rather, as an alternative, it provides salient components that could be significant to recognize and identify TK. This third approach is espoused by the author.[41]

According to the former Chair, the questions yet to be resolved are: (1) which kind of definition of TK is needed, a general and open definition or a more descriptive one; and (2) which concepts should be included as criteria for eligibility?

The current definition as presented by the Facilitators reflects the discussion that took place during the Twenty-First Session of the IGC in April 2012. Member States are divided into two groups: those who favor a more general definition and those opting for a more descriptive one with a list of matters/items which may be included or excluded from the definition of TK. With the exception of the first option, which is widely accepted even though some Members have reservations on the use of some terms and concepts, the optional additions well illustrate the wide variety of matters to be included in the definition.

For illustration purposes, the inclusion of the following provision was proposed by one Delegation in the plenary in April 2012: 'Traditional knowledge is knowledge that is dynamic, in constant evolution, resulting from intellectual activities passed from generation to generation. It is inalienable, indivisible, imprescriptible and include[s] among others know how, skills, innovation, processes, learning and teaching, and apprenticeship in codified, oral and other forms of traditional systems.' Most of these elements are included in the definition.

Some delegations maintained that many of the elements in the definition might be very important in the broad sense but there did not appear to be a strong policy rationale to include them to meet the purposes of the instrument. According to them, the increased number of listed elements appeared to decrease the value of the definition in terms of any legal certainty of the protection granted in the instrument.

The African Group asserted that the reference to 'knowledge that is dynamic and evolving' was essential, since the knowledge that had been passed on from generation to generation did not remain the same. The African Group pointed out that the knowledge changed as each generation adapted it to its own uses, it was passed on and another generation changed it. If that phrase was not included, TK

39 By including matters supposed to be covered under TCEs.

40 By excluding other domains supposed to be within the TK realm, such as agriculture.

41 Numerous IP concepts are not defined, such as inventions and well-known marks. See, Kongolo, T. (2002), 'Are Well-Known Marks Well Known in African Countries?', *Journal of World Intellectual Property* 5:6, 273–289.

would become static, frozen at a particular time, and the value that each generation added would not be captured.

One Delegation highlighted the importance of recognizing that TK was dynamic and susceptible to change but expressed its concerns about including such a descriptive phrase in the definition. It explained that if the definition incorporated such descriptive terms which could apply to TK, there was the eventual risk of limiting the definition only to TK which complied with those terms and excluding from protection TK which was not dynamic or evolving. It therefore suggested that in general the definition should exclude, as much as possible, descriptive terms which described potential characteristics but not essential features. On the other hand, one delegation argued that as a matter of fact TK which was not dynamic and evolving could be excluded.

The African Group maintained, however, that from the perspective of the knowledge holders and practitioners who held the knowledge from within knowledge systems, TK was a living knowledge. It called on delegations to look deeper into what made it distinctive as TK and to examine the 'evolving and dynamic' issue within the context of TK rather than a broader knowledge system which was outside the scope of TK.

Some delegations proposed that the concept of 'inalienable, indivisible and imprescriptible' be included in the scope of protection but not in the definition. Some others rejected the change. The Facilitators said in their comments that the phrase 'are inalienable, indivisible and imprescriptible' represents a substantive provision which should therefore not be part of a definition but rather, perhaps, part of the scope of protection.

One Delegation expressed its objection to the use of the word 'collectively' before 'generated, shared and preserved' because this imposed an obligation to demonstrate that the creation of the knowledge took place collectively. It explained that TK could sometimes start with an individual before spreading to the community and could also develop in a variety of other ways. The use of the word 'collectively' before 'generated, shared and preserved' only set further restrictions on the types of TK that could be protected under this instrument.

As for the criteria for eligibility, the common denominators of the options presented are that, to be eligible for protection, TK must be distinctively associated with a traditional community and generated, preserved, and transmitted from generation to generation and it should form part of the cultural identity of that community.

For some delegations, the most disturbing provision among the criteria for eligibility—which is not one supported by many experts—is the one stating that the TK should not be widely known to be eligible for protection. As maintained by some experts, misappropriation may be the cause of the wider knowledge of the TK. It clearly seems unfair to punish the owners of TK by excluding them from protection merely because their TK has become widely known.

The African Group is opposed to any restrictive or narrow definition of TK. In addition, regarding eligibility for protection, the Group does not share the opinion that widely known TK should be excluded from the ambit of protection.

According to the Facilitators, some of the phrases such as 'traditional knowledge is part of the collective, ancestral, territorial, cultural, intellectual and material heritage of indigenous peoples and local communities; and which may subsist in codified, oral or other forms; and which may be associated with agricultural, environmental, healthcare and medical knowledge, biodiversity, traditional lifestyles and natural and genetic resources, and know-how of traditional architecture and construction technologies' are descriptive or aspirational and could therefore be better suited for any preambular language than for a definition of TK.

Beneficiaries Article 2 sets forth who the beneficiaries of TK protection would be:

> Facilitators' Option (Convergent Text)
> Beneficiaries of protection of traditional knowledge, as defined in Article 1, are indigenous peoples and communities and local communities.
> Optional Additions to the Facilitators' Text
> (a) [traditional communities]
> (b) [families]
> (c) [nations]
> (d) [individuals within the categories listed above]
> (e) [and, where traditional knowledge is not specifically attributable or confined to an indigenous people or local community, or it is not possible to identify the community that generated it, any national entity that may be determined by national law]/[and/or any national entity that may be determined by national law]
> (f) [who develop, use, hold and maintain traditional knowledge]
> (g) even when traditional knowledge is held by [individuals] within the categories.
> Alternative
> Beneficiaries of protection of traditional knowledge, as defined in Article 1, are indigenous peoples and communities and local communities and similar categories as defined by national

The common denominator agreed by all Member States is that indigenous peoples and local and traditional communities are the first beneficiaries of TK protection.

Some argue that protection should be granted only to the traditional community/indigenous peoples, given the collective nature of TK. Some countries expressed the view that the collective nature of TK does not have any implications for ownership. TK may be owned collectively by a community in the same way as some rights may be owned collectively under the existing IP system (e.g. a collective trademark or, to some extent, geographical indications). Others assert that TK may belong to an individual within a community. The two options reflect the two positions of Member States.

According to the former Chair, the key issues are:

- Which term should be used, 'indigenous peoples' or 'indigenous communities'?
- Should families, nations and individuals be considered as beneficiaries?
- How should 'local communities' and 'traditional communities' be defined and should both be considered as beneficiaries? and
- Who would be the beneficiary where TK is not specifically attributable or confined to an indigenous people or local community or it is not possible to identify the community that generated it?

One Delegation explained the distinction between peoples and communities. It pointed out that under its national legislation, an indigenous people referred to a certain number of communities which shared culture, customs and language. Within such an indigenous people, however, clans, tribes, or communities could be identified. Consequently, it stressed the importance of explicitly indicating that identical TK was not necessarily shared by all communities of a single indigenous people. The Delegation further clarified that although 'indigenous communities' were included under the umbrella term 'indigenous peoples', not all indigenous communities which formed a part of an 'indigenous people' shared the same TK with other clans or families which were also part of that same 'indigenous people'.

One Delegation objected to the inclusion of the concept of nation, which it pointed out fell outside the ambit of this instrument. It noted that the terms indigenous peoples, local communities, and indigenous communities were broad enough to encompass all categories of beneficiaries. In reaction to this, some delegations of small island nations maintained that they could not accept any definition of beneficiaries that was restricted to indigenous peoples and communities, and they proposed the insertion of language which referred to small island States or took into account the realities of island States.

Scope of protection Article 3 covers the scope of TK protection, for which two options have been proposed.

> *Option 1*
>
> 3.1 [[Member States]/[Contracting Parties] should provide] adequate and effective legal, policy or administrative measures [should be provided], as appropriate and in accordance with national law, to:
>
> (a) prevent the unauthorized disclosure, use or other exploitation of [secret] [protected] traditional knowledge;
>
> (b) where [protected] traditional knowledge is knowingly used outside the traditional context:

(i) acknowledge the source of traditional knowledge and attribute its holders/owners where known unless they decide otherwise;
(ii) encourage use of traditional knowledge in a manner that does not disrespect the cultural norms and practices of its holders/owners;
(iii) [encourage]/[ensure, where the traditional knowledge] [is secret]/ [is not widely known] traditional knowledge holders and users to establish mutually agreed terms with prior informed consent addressing approval requirements and the sharing of benefits [arising from the commercial use of that traditional knowledge] in compliance with the right of local communities to decide to grant access to that knowledge or not.

Option 2

3.1 Beneficiaries, as defined in Article 2, [should]/[shall], [according to national law], have the following [exclusive] [collective] rights:

(a) [enjoy], control, utilize, maintain, develop, preserve and [protect] their traditional knowledge;
(b) authorize or deny the access to and use of their traditional knowledge;
(c) have a fair and equitable share of benefits arising from the [commercial] use of their traditional knowledge based on mutually agreed terms;
(d) prevent misappropriation and misuse, including any acquisition, appropriation, utilization or practice of their traditional knowledge without [their prior informed consent and] the establishment of mutually agreed terms;
(e) prevent the use of traditional knowledge without acknowledgment and attribution of the [source and] origin of their traditional knowledge and its holders/owners, where known;
(f) ensure that the use of the traditional knowledge respects the cultural norms and practices of the holders/owners; and
(g) [require [in the application for intellectual property rights involving the use of their traditional knowledge] the mandatory disclosure of the identity of the traditional knowledge holders and the country of origin, as well as evidence of compliance with prior informed consent and benefit sharing requirements, in accordance with the national law or requirements of the country of origin in the procedure for the granting of intellectual property rights involving the use of their traditional knowledge.]

3.2 For the purposes of this instrument, the term 'utilization' in relation to traditional knowledge [should]/[shall] refer to any of the following acts:

(a) Where the traditional knowledge is a product:
  (i) manufacturing, importing, offering for sale, selling, stocking or using the product beyond the traditional context; or
  (ii) being in possession of the product for the purposes of offering it for sale, selling it or using it beyond the traditional context.
(b) Where the traditional knowledge is a process:
  (i) making use of the process beyond the traditional context; or

(ii) carrying out the acts referred to under sub-clause (a) with respect to a product that is a direct result of the use of the process; or

(c) When traditional knowledge is used for research and development leading to profit making or commercial purposes.

Exclusive rights are to be granted to the beneficiaries, and prior informed consent, sharing of benefits, and disclosure of the country of origin have been provided for. Despite efforts made by the Facilitators in reviewing the text, Article 3 still remains a challenging one which will lead to further debates.

According to the former Chair, both options provide a list of exclusive rights that beneficiaries should have. One main point of disagreement is whether or not the rights of the beneficiaries should be collective. Another difference between the options is whether or not to include 'the mandatory disclosure of the identity of the TK holders and the country of origin, as well as evidence of compliance with prior informed consent and benefit-sharing requirements'. In addition, the degree to which Member States should have flexibility at a national level is one of the issues. A further issue is whether or not it is necessary to include a definition of 'utilization'.

One suggestion put forward is to restructure the text further by clustering the current provisions under four broad approaches: a rights-based approach; a broad and flexible framework; targeted provisions for the protection of secret TK; and a mixed approach. The African Group supports this suggestion.

Facilitators have identified both elements of convergence and elements of divergence. Elements of convergence include:

- the concept of mechanisms to agree on use and/or access to traditional knowledge;
- the concept of acknowledgment of the source;
- the concept of respect for the cultural norms of the holders/owners;
- provisions regarding mutually agreed terms; and
- provisions regarding the sharing of benefits

Elements of divergence include:

- a measures-based approach (Option 1) versus a rights-based approach (Option 2);
- the concept of 'use outside of the traditional context' as a trigger for provisions on acknowledgment of source, cultural norms, mutually agreed terms and the sharing of benefits (in Option 1 only);
- provisions regarding mandatory disclosure (in Option 2 only);
- provisions regarding prior informed concept (in Option 2 only); and
- whether or not benefit sharing should apply only to commercial use (in Option 2 only).

Scope of protection and sanctions Article 3 *bis* provides as follows:

> 3 BIS.1 Access to and use of traditional knowledge requires prior informed consent from the indigenous people or local community that is the beneficiary of protection according to Article 2.
>
> The use of such knowledge [should]/[shall] be in accordance with the terms the beneficiary may have set out as a condition for the consent. Such terms can, inter alia, determine that benefits arising from the use of the knowledge [should]/[shall] be shared with the beneficiary.
>
> 3 BIS.2 In addition to the protection provided for in paragraph 1, users of traditional knowledge which fulfills the criterion in Article 1, Subparagraph 2(a) [should]/[shall]:
>
> (a) acknowledge the source of traditional knowledge and attribute the beneficiary, unless the beneficiary decides otherwise; and
>
> (b) use the knowledge in a manner that respects the cultures and practices of the beneficiary.
>
> 3 BIS.3 When traditional knowledge is accessed or used in a manner that contravenes any of the provisions in paragraphs 1 and 2, the beneficiary [should]/[shall] have the right to:
>
> (a) request that the judicial authorities order the infringer to desist from further infringements; and
>
> (b) a fair compensation from an infringer who knowingly, or with reasonable grounds to know, engaged in infringing activity.
>
> 3 BIS.4 The Parties [should]/[shall] provide adequate and effective legal measures to ensure
>
> the application and enforcement of the provisions set out in paragraphs 1 to 3.
>
> 3 BIS.5 Protection of traditional knowledge under this instrument [should]/[shall] not affect:
>
> (a) access to or use of knowledge which is invented independently of traditional knowledge of indigenous peoples or local communities or is discovered from other sources than an indigenous people or local community; and
>
> (b) generation, sharing, preservation and transmission and customary use of traditional knowledge by the beneficiaries in the traditional and customary context.

With regard to this new provision, access and use of TK are conditioned upon prior informed consent of the beneficiaries.

Exceptions and limitations Article 6 provides exceptions and limitations to TK protection as follows:

> 6.1 Member States understand that measures for the protection of traditional knowledge should not restrict the generation, customary use, transmission,

exchange and development of traditional knowledge by the beneficiaries, within and among communities in the traditional and customary context, [in accordance with national law].

6.2 [Limitations on protection [should]/[shall] extend only to the utilization of traditional knowledge taking place outside the membership of the beneficiary community or outside traditional or cultural context.]

6.3 Member States may adopt appropriate limitations or exceptions under national law[, with the prior and informed consent of the beneficiaries], provided that the use of traditional knowledge:
  (a) acknowledges the beneficiaries, where possible;
  (b) is not offensive or derogatory to the beneficiaries; and
  (c) is compatible with fair practice.

Alternative

(a) does not conflict with the normal utilization of the traditional knowledge by the beneficiaries; and

(b) does not unreasonably prejudice the legitimate interests of the beneficiaries taking account of the legitimate interests of third parties.

Alternative

6.3 Contracting Parties may adopt appropriate limitations or exceptions under national law for the following purposes:
  (a) teaching, learning, but does not include research resulting in profit-marking or commercial purposes;
  (b) for preservation, display and presentation in archives, libraries, museums or cultural institutions for non-commercial cultural heritage purposes,

6.4 Contracting Parties may permit the use of traditional knowledge for epidemics and natural disaster response, provided that the beneficiaries are adequately compensated.

[End of alternative]

6.4 [Secret and sacred traditional knowledge shall not be subjected to exceptions and limitations.]

6.5 [Regardless of whether such acts are already permitted under Article 6.2 or not, the following shall be permitted:
  (a) the use of traditional knowledge in cultural institutions recognized under the appropriate national law, archives, libraries, museums for non-commercial cultural heritage or other purposes in the public interest, including for preservation, display, research and presentation should be permitted; and
  (b) the creation of an original work of authorship inspired by traditional knowledge.]

6.6 [There shall be no right to [exclude others] from using knowledge that:

Alternative

6.6 The provisions of Article 3 shall not apply to any use of knowledge that:

[End of alternative]

(a) has been independently created;
(b) derived from sources other than the beneficiary; or
(c) is known outside of the beneficiaries' community.]

6.7 [Protected traditional knowledge shall not be deemed to have been misappropriated or misused if the protected traditional knowledge was:
(a) obtained from a printed publication;
(b) obtained from one or more holders of the protected traditional knowledge with their prior informed consent; or
(c) mutually agreed terms for access and benefit sharing apply to the protected traditional knowledge that was obtained, and were agreed upon by the national contact point.]

6.8 [Except for the protection of secret traditional knowledge against disclosure, to the extent that any act would be permissible for this parties under the national law for knowledge protected by patent or trade secrecy laws, such act shall not be prohibited by the protection of traditional knowledge.]

6.9 [National authorities shall exclude from protection traditional knowledge that is already available without restriction to the general public.]

6.10 [National authorities may exclude from protection diagnostic, therapeutic and surgical methods for the treatment of humans or animals.]

6.11 [National authorities, in the case of a national emergency or other circumstances of extreme urgency or in cases of public non-commercial use, authorize the use of protected traditional knowledge, without the consent of the protected traditional knowledge holder.]

In these options, the use of TK within a traditional context by the beneficiaries is considered the main exception, while use outside the community upon fulfillment of certain conditions is recognized as a limitation. In both options, the three-step test requirements as provided under the copyright system with regard to exceptions and limitations are included. It is still under discussion whether or not secret and sacred TK shall be subjected to exceptions and limitations.

According to the former Chair, remaining issues to be addressed include:

- Should the prior and informed consent of the beneficiaries be required for the development of domestic/national limitations and exceptions?
- Should the text include more exceptions and limitations as provided in Option 2 or fewer exceptions and limitations as provided in Option 1?
- Should 'independent discovery or independent innovation' be included or not? and
- Should secret and/or sacred TK be included or not?

With regard to exceptions and limitations, Member States were very active in proposing new texts or complementary provisions to support their positions.

One Delegation stated that Article 6 dealt with a lot of possible exceptions and that it should be worded in a shorter and more general way. In accordance with

Article 30 of the TRIPS Agreement, it proposed a new text: 'Parties may adopt appropriate exceptions, provided such exceptions are limited and do not conflict with a normal utilization of the beneficiaries' rights according to Article 3 and do not unreasonably prejudice the legitimate interests of the beneficiaries, taking into account the legitimate interests of third parties.' It believed that the protection of TK should not hinder customary use or affect independent discoveries.

One Delegation proposed the following wording for Article 6: 'Measures for the protection of traditional knowledge should not restrict, [according to domestic/national law,] the generation, customary use, transmission, exchange and development of traditional knowledge by the beneficiaries, within and among communities in the traditional and customary context. The protection of traditional knowledge does not affect: (a) the use of traditional knowledge in archives, libraries, museums or cultural institutions for non-commercial cultural heritage purposes, including for preservation and display; (b) the reproduction of traditional knowledge on the part of an archive or library, for reasons of security and preservation and which would be at risk of disappearing; (c) the use of traditional knowledge in the academic and private scope and for non-commercial purposes; (d) the use of traditional knowledge in activities of scientific and technological research, purely experimental for teaching or for trials; (e) the reproduction in administrative or legal procedure.'

One Delegation maintained that a clear distinction should be established between the utilization of TK within and among indigenous peoples and local communities and its utilization outside.

Another Delegation proposed the insertion of the following alternative text for Article 6.3: 'Contracting Parties may adopt appropriate limitations or exceptions under national law for the following purposes: (a) teaching, learning, but does not include research resulting in profit-making or commercial purposes; (b) for preservation, display and presentation in archives, libraries, museums or cultural institutions for non-commercial cultural heritage purposes, taking account of the legitimate interests of third parties.' It also proposed the following for Article 6.4: 'Contracting Parties may permit the use of traditional knowledge for epidemics and natural disaster response, provided that the beneficiaries are adequately compensated.' Parts of this proposed text are already incorporated in the current text produced by the Facilitators.

One Delegation requested to add ', taking account of the legitimate interests of third parties' to the end of the new Article 6.3(b) as was also proposed by the first Delegation.

Term of protection Article 7 sets out the term of protection in two options as follows:

> *Option 1*
> [Member States]/[Contracting Parties] may determine the appropriate term of protection of traditional knowledge [which may] [should]/[shall] last as long as

the traditional knowledge fulfills/satisfies the criteria of eligibility for protection according to Article 1.

Optional additions to Option 1

(a) traditional knowledge is transmitted from generation to generation and thus is imprescriptible

(b) the protection [should]/[shall] applied and last for the life of indigenous peoples and local communities

(c) the protection [should]/[shall] remain while the immaterial cultural heritage is not accessible to the public domain

(d) the protection of secret, spiritual and sacred traditional knowledge [should]/[shall] last forever

(e) the protection against biopiracy or any other infringement carried out with the intention of destroying wholly or partially the memory, the history and the image of indigenous peoples and communities

Option 2

Duration of protection of traditional knowledge varies based upon the characteristics and value of traditional knowledge.

It is prescribed that the protection of TK against misappropriation should last as long as the TK fulfills the criteria of eligibility for protection according to Article 1.[42] Some Members are in favor of protecting TK in perpetuity.[43] In the first scenario, TK that ceases to be eligible for protection would fall into the public domain, whereas if TK were to be protected in perpetuity that would be possible only by the wish of the beneficiaries or TK owners.

According to the former Chair, the main issues seem to be: whether or not the term of protection should last as long as TK meets the eligibility criteria under Article 1 and whether or not the duration of protection should vary according to the characteristics and value of TK.

The different options on the table regarding the term of protection have been influenced by the existing terms of protection provided under other IPRs, such as copyright and trademark. Member States are agreeable to the first option, which was originally proposed by one Delegation and endorsed by Member States.

Another Delegation stated that two extremely divergent and mutually exclusive points of view—namely, that protection should be unlimited, and that protection should be subjected to limitations—had been taken into account in the text presented by the Facilitators. It reiterated, however, that it believed that an unlimited term

---

42 See, also, *The Protection of Traditional Knowledge: Revised Objectives and Principles*, document prepared by the WIPO Secretariat for WIPO/GRTKF/IC/16/5 Prov.

43 See, *Reproduction of Document WIPO/GRTKF/IC/9/5 'The Protection of Traditional Knowledge: Revised Objectives and Principles'*, document prepared by the WIPO Secretariat for the Intergovernmental Committee on Intellectual Property and Genetic Resources, Traditional Knowledge and Folklore, Eleventh Session, Geneva, July 3–12, 2007, WIPO Doc. WIPO/GRTKF/IC/11/5(c), Annex, p. 36, 'Commentary on Article 9'.

of protection was acceptable, provided that the criteria for eligibility continued to be met.

The African Group is supportive of the condition requiring that TK fulfill the criteria of eligibility to enjoy or continue to enjoy protection.

The Facilitators have identified areas of divergence and convergence among Member States in respect of the term of protection of TK. The principal element of divergence is whether the term of protection should/shall be automatically linked to the fulfillment of the criteria for eligibility found in Article 1 or whether the term of protection may be set by Member States but also based on the fulfillment of the criteria for eligibility.

Additional observations For Article 7, the Facilitators also noted that two main positions were presented in the Plenary: one that contemplates some form of perpetual protection; and another that would allow Member States/Contracting Parties to limit the protection based on the 'characteristics and value of traditional knowledge'.

Other matters The Draft Text on TK also covers the following matters:

Sanctions, remedies, and exercise of rights/application (Article 4) Should Article 4.2, which deals with the measures to be taken, be more general or more specific? Should the means of redress for safeguarding the protection granted be governed by the legislation of the country where the protection is claimed? And, should the sanctions and remedies reflect the sanctions and remedies that indigenous peoples and local communities would use?

According to one Delegation, one of the issues was whether to take a flexible or prescriptive approach. Further, the Delegation pointed out that Article 4 was not just an article which dealt with enforcement but also included provisions which dealt with application.

Another Delegation, in order to shorten Article 4, which comprises three paragraphs, proposed the following: 'Contracting Parties shall; (a) adopt, in accordance with their legal systems, the measures necessary to ensure the application of this instrument; (b) provide for adequate, effective and deterrent criminal and/or civil and/or administrative remedies, for the violation of the rights provided under this instrument; and (c) provide procedures for exercise of rights which are accessible, effective, fair, adequate and not burdensome for beneficiaries of traditional knowledge, and, where appropriate, may provide for [a] dispute resolution mechanism based on customary protocols, understandings, laws and practices of beneficiaries.'

The Facilitators identified elements of convergence and of divergence. The main element of convergence concerns the following alternate wording: '[Member States]/[Contracting Parties] [should]/[shall] [endeavor to/undertake to] adopt [as appropriate and] in accordance with national law], the appropriate legal policy and/or administrative measures necessary to ensure the application of this instrument.'

Elements of divergence include:

(i) the suitability of enforcement procedures; and
(ii) the concept of alternative dispute settlement mechanisms.

The disclosure requirement (Article 4bis) This provision on the disclosure requirement was proposed by one Delegation in the following terms: '1. Patent and plant variety applications that concern an invention that relates to or uses traditional knowledge shall include information on the country from which the inventor or the breeder collected or received the knowledge (the providing country), and the country of origin if the providing country is not the same as the country of origin of the traditional knowledge. The application shall also state whether prior informed consent to access and use has been obtained. 2. If the information set out in paragraph 1 is not known to the applicant, the applicant shall state the immediate source from which the inventor or the breeder collected or received the traditional knowledge. 3. If the applicant does not comply with the provisions in paragraphs 1 and 2, the application shall not be processed until the requirements are met. The Patent or Plant variety office may set a time limit for the applicant to comply with the provisions in paragraphs 1 and 2. If the applicant does not submit such information within the set time limit, the Patent Office or Plant variety office may reject the application. 4. Rights arising from a granted patent or a granted plant variety right shall not be affected by any later discovery of a failure by the applicant to comply with the provisions in paragraphs 1 and 2. Other sanctions, outside of the patent system and the plant variety system, provided for in national law, including criminal sanctions such as fines, may however be imposed.'

Another Delegation requested that Article 4*bis* be expanded to include all aspects of IP and not be limited to patents and plant varieties. The Delegation requested another change in replacing the words 'inventor or breeder' with 'applicant' and the word 'invention' with 'any process or product'. It proposed an alternative text for Article 4*bis*.4 as follows: 'Rights arising from a grant shall be revoked and rendered unenforceable when the applicant has failed to comply with the obligations of mandatory requirements as provided for in this article or provided false or fraudulent information.'

The current text of Article 4*bis* includes the two proposed texts.

Administration of rights (Article 5) The key issues here include (1) the extent of participation of the TK holders in the establishment/appointment of an authority and in the establishment of its functions and (2) the functions the authority would have.

Some delegations support the idea of establishing a national or regional authority for the administration of rights. One delegation maintains that the instrument should afford Member States considerable flexibility in addressing appropriate administration measures for protection of rights vested in indigenous communities.

The Facilitators have identified elements of both convergence and divergence. The principal element of convergence concerns the general suitability of Member

States/Contracting Parties establishing an authority (or authorities) in connection with this instrument.

Elements of divergence include:

(i) the specific functions of any authority; and
(ii) the concept of prejudice to national law and/or the right of owners/holders to administer their rights.

Application of collective rights (Article 5 bis) This new provision is similar to the one related to the administration of rights. It is a matter of establishing a national authority to guarantee the safeguarding of TK and assist TK beneficiaries in the exercise of their rights.

Formalities (Article 8) Should formalities be required or not? Should/may registers be established or not? Most of the Delegations are in favor of no formalities. The text proposed by one Delegation is worth mentioning in this regard: 'The protection of traditional knowledge shall not be subject to any formality. However, in the interest of transparency, certainty and the conservation of traditional knowledge, the relevant national authorities may maintain registers or other records of traditional knowledge.' On the other hand, another Delegation is in favor of formal requirements for the protection of TK.

Transitional measures (Article 9) There seems to be consensus that this instrument applies to all TK which, at the moment of its coming into force, fulfills the criteria. The main questions may be: (1) Would the protection for TK apply to ongoing uses of TK that began before such protection came into force? (2) Should rights already obtained by third parties be secured? (3) Should continuing acts in respect of TK that had commenced prior to the coming into force of these provisions and which would not be permitted or which would be otherwise regulated by these provisions be brought into conformity with them?

One Delegation supported the text of Article 9.1. It proposed a new paragraph as follows: 'Notwithstanding paragraph 1, anyone who, before the date of entry into force of this instrument, has commenced to utilize traditional knowledge which was legally accessed, may continue a corresponding utilization of the traditional knowledge. Such right of utilization shall also, on similar conditions, be enjoyed by anyone who has made substantial preparations to utilize the traditional knowledge. The provision in this paragraph gives no right to utilize traditional knowledge in a way that contravenes with the terms the beneficiary may have set out as a condition for access.'

Consistency with the general legal framework (Article 10) Should this instrument take account of and act consistently with other instruments or should it leave intact and not affect the protection provided for under other instruments? Should particular instruments be referred to in this instrument, such as the Nagoya Protocol, or not? Should Article 10.2 be kept or not?

According to one Delegation, 'Protection under this instrument should be consistent with other relevant international instruments including international intellectual property instruments.'

National treatment and other means of recognizing foreign rights and interests (Article 11): The main question is whether foreign rights and interests should be recognized through national treatment, reciprocity or the development of an alternative means.

Trans-boundary cooperation (Article 12) Where TK is located in the territories of different States, there seems to be consensus that Member States should cooperate by taking measures that are supportive of and do not run counter to the objectives of this instrument. The key issues would include: (1) Is the cooperation to be with the 'participation of' or with the 'consent'/'prior informed consent of' TK holders? (2) Would a global mutual benefit-sharing mechanism be necessary?

Genetic resources

The Draft Text on GRs, comprising objectives and principles, was discussed briefly during the nineteenth session of the IGC, based on the version produced by the IGW3. The African Group submitted a proposal on Genetic Resources and Future Work in December 2010.[44] The main proposals may be summarized as follows:

1. Mandatory disclosure requirement: this should be the basis for the negotiations on Genetic Resources in the IGC.
2. Guidelines and recommendations on defensive protection: it is proposed to have recommendations or guidelines for search and examination procedures for patent applications to ensure that they better take into account the disclosure of the origin of genetic resources.
3. Online database of IP clauses on MAT; expanded use, scope and accessibility of the online database on IP clauses in MAT for access and equitable benefit-sharing.
4. Draft Guidelines for contractual practices.

Unlike the other IWGs, the IWG3 has produced no draft text in the form of provisions. Discussions were limited to objectives and principles up until the Twentieth Session of the IGC, which was devoted to GRs, in February 2012.[45] At that Session, a 'Consolidated Document Relating to Intellectual Property and Genetic Resources' was produced by the IGC and was annexed to the Decisions

44 *Proposal of the African Group on Genetic Resources and Future Work*, document prepared by the WIPO Secretariat for the Intergovernmental Committee on Intellectual Property and Genetic Resources, Traditional Knowledge and Folklore, Seventeenth Session, Geneva, December 6–10, 2010, WIPO Doc. WIPO/GRTKF/IC/17/10.

45 See, Decisions of the Twentieth Session of the Committee, adopted by the Committee on February 22, 2012.

taken during the Session. The Text is also referred to by the title 'Intellectual Property and the Protection of Genetic Resources [Their Derivatives] and Associated Traditional Knowledge: Negotiating Text'.

The Negotiating Text starts by defining the key terms of the matters covered. The second part of the Text deals with objectives and guiding principles. The third part refers to the provisions, which address the following subject matter:

- Subject Matter of Protection (Article 1);
- Beneficiaries (Article 2);
- [Scope [of [Legal] Protection]] [[Mandatory] Disclosure Requirements] (Article 3);
- [Proposal on Complementary] [Protection] Measures (Article 4);
- Relationship with International Agreements (Article 5);
- International Cooperation (Article 6);
- Transboundary Cooperation (Article 7);
- Sanctions, Remedies, and Exercise of Rights (Article 8);
- Technical Assistance, Cooperation, and Capacity Building (Article 9).

Each provision contains several options and sub-options. The key provision—and the most controversial one—is Article 3, which deals with the scope of protection and mandatory disclosure requirements.

Traditional knowledge and the public domain[46]

The public domain is a multifaceted and multidimensional concept with no definite definition. It is commonly understood to be a state in which information/creation has no IP protection and may be used and accessed by anyone. The public domain varies from one IP area to another and from one jurisdiction to another because IPR protection is territorial. In other words, the sphere of the public domain in connection with patents is different from the public domain related to copyright, trademarks, designs, or traditional knowledge (TK), including traditional cultural expressions (TCEs), notwithstanding the existence of common denominators enabling the identification of a public domain. The duration of protection, exclusions, exceptions, and limitations with regard to any IP subject matter affect the realm of the public domain.

Defining the boundaries of the public domain is not an easy exercise. Some may argue that every creation or piece of information is first in the public domain before it is protected. Creations and information may then enjoy protection for a limited period of time before falling again into the public domain after the expiry

46 For a more comprehensive study of this issue, see, Kongolo, T. (2011b), 'IP and Misappropriation of the Public Domain', *European Intellectual Property Review* 33:12, 780–794.

of their term of protection.[47] Some others may assert that not all information and creations are in the public domain at the outset because of the nature of the information or the way the protection system is set up. This reasoning may apply to original copyright and related rights works enjoying automatic protection from the creation of the work without any formality as well as to TK, which is of a quite different nature.

The concept of the public domain is alien to traditional communities who are the owners of TK. Some TK is accessible to any person belonging to the community; some is restricted to a certain group of people; and some is secret, sacred, and inalienable. The accessibility of TK should not mean that such TK is in the public domain, a concept not shared by traditional communities.

It was claimed up until recently that TK was part of the public domain and formed part of a common heritage that anyone could access freely and utilize without any return to the community holder of the TK. This perception of TK continues to be supported by certain groups. Consequently, it is quite natural to see countries reacting against expansion of the realm of the public domain in relation to TK. The multifaceted nature of both TK and the public domain makes their relationship very complex.

Nowadays, it is widely understood that TK is owned by a particular traditional community and should be considered to be that community's creation, and that its public availability should not be interpreted to mean that the TK forms part of the public domain. TK is protectable subject matter. A mind shift is required in this regard. The issue here is how to delimit the boundaries of TK, since not all types of TK are protectable. So, what is in the public domain in the context of TK?

Within the concept of public availability, PIC from a TK holder that is identifiable could still be required, and provisions for benefit-sharing could also be made applicable, especially when a different use of the TK is proposed than that for which earlier PIC was provided. When a holder is not identifiable, beneficiaries could still be identified, for example by the State.[48]

Within WIPO's IGC, one Delegation stated that the content of 'the public domain' is limited to those things which had once been protected when this protection has lapsed. Traditional cultural expressions have never been protected

---

47 In this regard, the equation would be 'public domain → IP protection → public domain'. The equation would be comparable to water. It is observed that in a normal, natural condition, water is liquid; at a lower temperature, the same water takes on a solid shape; and it becomes liquid again when placed in its normal, natural condition. This reasoning may be extended to the public domain, with the 'solid shape' being the protection period of what was originally in the public domain.

48 Report of the Meeting of the Group of Technical and Legal Experts on Traditional Knowledge Associated with Genetic Resources in the Context of the International Regime on Access and Benefit-Sharing, Hyderabad, India, June 16–19, 2009, UNEP Doc. UNEP/CBD/WG-ABS/8/2, p. 21; available at: http://www.abs-alliance.org/version02/files/ABS%20WG-8/abswg-08-02-en.pdf.

under IP laws, yet this should not suggest that because a work is accessible it is already in the public domain and freely available.[49] The representative of Tupaj Amaru, an NGO that advocates for the rights of the indigenous peoples of the Americas, stated that putting TK and TCEs into the public domain would violate the confidential character of many intangible, sacred, and secret elements which belong to the living heritage and accentuate the deterioration of cultural values and the illicit appropriation of their cultural values by corporations.[50]

The representative of the Tulalip Tribes, a Native American people of Washington State, USA, underlined the importance of a clearer understanding of the role, contours, and boundaries of the public domain in the context of IP protection of TCEs. The concept of the public domain is not accepted by many indigenous peoples but is a peculiar development of the history of Western countries. For most indigenous peoples, knowledge is a gift from the Creator and there are complex systems regulating its use, in which some knowledge is held by individuals, clans, or other groups. Although individuals might hold knowledge, their right is collectively determined. It is rare that individuals have the right to use knowledge in a free and unconstrained manner; they are bound by the laws of their tribe and of the Creator. In the Western IP system, unprotected, disclosed knowledge is part of the so-called 'public domain', but this distinction is not typically made in indigenous communities. Open sharing in indigenous cultures does not automatically confer a right to use the knowledge. Even when knowledge is shared and used widely, it does not fall into the public domain but is shared among those who are trusted to know their roles and responsibilities in using the knowledge. In this context, misuse of this knowledge is not only 'derogatory, libelous, defamatory, offensive and fallacious' but could cause severe physical or spiritual harm to the individual caretakers of the knowledge or their entire tribe. For this reason, misappropriation and misuse is not simply a violation of 'moral rights' leading to a collective offense but a matter of cultural survival for many indigenous peoples. Traditional cultural expressions and TK are not in the 'public domain' because indigenous peoples have failed to take the steps necessary to protect the knowledge in the Western IP system but, rather, from a failure of governments, corporations, and individuals to recognize and respect the customary law regulating its use.[51]

African countries favor extensive use and broad definition of the public domain, except in the field of TK where they defend its narrow use where TK has been wrongly ascribed to the public domain and no protection has been offered. The African Group in several sessions of the IGC has taken the position that the 'availability' of TK does not have to be confused with the public domain.

49 Report of the Intergovernmental Committee on Intellectual Property and Genetic Resources, Traditional Knowledge and Folklore, Fifth Session, Geneva, July 7–15, 2003, WIPO Doc. WIPO/GRTKF/IC/5/15, para. 37.

50 Ibid., para. 80.

51 Ibid., para. 56.

Conclusion

The African Group has played a major role in the IGC since its inception, taking several initiatives that have changed the shape of debates pertaining to the protection of TK, TCEs, and GRs. Its breakthrough initiative relates to the first proposal on objectives and principles, which was adopted by the IGC as the first document giving a new direction to its work. Another important initiative concerned the IGC's mandate in 2009 in its proposal on the text-based negotiations on GRs, TK, and TCEs.

Other initiatives took place during the debates on each specific issue and item, where the African Group made significant inputs. Ultimately, the African Group will feel satisfied with the results of these negotiations if an international treaty is adopted in the fields of TK, TCEs, and GRs to prevent their widespread of misappropriation. In addition, in the sphere of GRs, African countries yearn for a patent system which incorporates the requirement to disclose the country of origin of GRs or associated TK or TCEs in a patent application at the filing stage. The latter will be discussed in the next section.

Finally, it has been demonstrated that TK is not in the public domain and it deserves protection if it meets conditions set out under the legislation.

Work Done Within the WTO

In the course of the negotiations that led to the adoption of the Agreement Establishing the WTO, most of the African trade delegates were not familiar with IP matters. Therefore, the real color of the accepted deal (package) was not apparent to them and came to light only afterwards. The African Group became very active during the review of Article 27.3(b) of the TRIPs Agreement, including the debate on the relationship between the TRIPs Agreement and the CBD, and the discussion on the protection of TK and folklore.

Background and premises to debates

Article 27.1 of the TRIPs Agreement sets out the scope of patent protection and the criteria of patentability.[52] Patents are obtainable for any invention meeting the three conditions, namely novelty, inventive step, and industrial application, without discrimination as to the field of technology.

52 TRIPs Article 27.1 reads as follows: 'Subject to the provisions of paragraphs 2 and 3, patents shall be available for any inventions, whether products or processes, in all fields of technology, provided that they are new, involve an inventive step and are capable of industrial application. Subject to paragraph 4 of Article 65, paragraph 8 of Article 70 and paragraph 3 of this Article, patents shall be available and patent rights enjoyable without discrimination as to the place of invention, the field of technology and whether products are imported or locally produced.'

Article 27.2[53] and 3 lays down exclusions and some exceptions to patentability. The first set of exceptions are aimed at protecting public order or morality, human, animal or plant life, or health, and the environment while the second set deals with exclusions in the medical field and biotechnology.

According to Paragraph 3:

> Members may also exclude from patentability:
> (a) diagnostic, therapeutic and surgical methods for the treatment of humans or animals;
> (b) plants and animals other than micro-organisms, and essentially biological processes for the production of plants or animals other than non-biological and microbiological processes.
>
> However, Members shall provide for the protection of plant varieties either by patents or by an effective *sui generis* system or by any combination thereof. The provisions of this subparagraph shall be reviewed four years after the date of entry into force of the WTO Agreement.

Paragraph 3 clearly prescribes that any Member has the freedom to exclude from patentability plants, animals, and essentially biological processes.[54] Nevertheless, Members are obliged to provide protection in respect of plant varieties in any of three different possible ways: patents; an effective *sui generis* system; or a combination of both.

The last part of this provision, stipulating that 'the provisions of this subparagraph shall be reviewed four years after the date of entry into force of the WTO Agreement', gave a mandate to the Council for TRIPs, as the competent Body within the WTO to handle matters pertaining to intellectual property, to review this subparagraph beginning in 1999, four years after the date of entry into force of the TRIPs Agreement for developed countries.

In the official first meeting of the Council for TRIPs in connection with the review of Article 27.3(b), the Chair noted that there was some debate over the mandate contained in Article 27.3(b). Some Members understood that the review called for in that provision should not be limited to gathering information on its implementation but also for a review of the provisions themselves. The difference seemed to relate to how the word 'review' should be interpreted.[55]

---

53 TRIPs Article 27.2 reads as follows: 'Members may exclude from patentability inventions, the prevention within their territory of the commercial exploitation of which is necessary to protect *ordre public* or morality, including to protect human, animal or plant life or health or to avoid serious prejudice to the environment, provided that such exclusion is not made merely because the exploitation is prohibited by their law.'

54 However, micro-organisms and non-biological and microbiological processes must be eligible for patents.

55 See, WTO, Council for TRIPs, Minutes of the Meeting of April 21–22, 1999, WTO Doc. IP/C/M/23, July 2, 1999, paras. 89–107.

Regarding the scope of the review, many developing countries called for the review of the substance of Article 27.3(b) and not to limit the review to information gathering on Members' implementation of the Article. In preparation for the 1999 WTO Ministerial Conference, in July 1999, the African Group submitted a paper[56] in which, among other things, its position on the review was presented. According to the African proposal, the mandated review was meant to be a review of the substance of the subparagraph itself and was not meant to be confined to its implementation.[57] As for the substance of the Article per se, the paper went on to present three proposals with regard to: the distinctions between biological and microbiological organisms and processes; the option of a *sui generis* system for plant varieties; and the relationships among TRIPs Article 27.3(b), the CBD, and the International Undertaking on Plant Genetic Resources.

As for the distinctions between biological and microbiological organisms and processes, the Group proposed as follows:

> (a) The review of the substantive provisions of Article 27.3(b) should clarify the following:
>
> – Why the option of exclusion of patentability of plants and animals does not extend to micro-organisms as there is no scientific basis for the distinction.
>
> – Why the option of exclusion of patentability of 'essentially biological processes' does not extend to 'microbiological processes' as the latter are also biological processes.
>
> (b) The review process should clarify that plants and animals as well as microorganisms and all other living organisms and their parts cannot be patented, and that natural processes that produce plants, animals and other living organisms should also not be patentable.[58]

Regarding the option of a *sui generis* system for plant varieties, the Group proposed the following:

> After the sentence on plant variety protection in Article 27.3(b), a footnote should be inserted stating that any *sui generis* law for plant variety protection can provide for:
>
> (i) the protection of the innovations of indigenous and local farming communities in developing countries, consistent with the Convention on

56 See, Communication from Kenya on Behalf of the African Group, WTO Doc. WT/GC/W/302, August 6, 1999; see, also, Review of the Provisions of Article 27.3(b)—Communication from Kenya on Behalf of the African Group, WTO Doc. IP/C/W/163, November 8, 1999.

57 Ibid.

58 WTO Doc. IP/C/W/163, ibid., para. 11.

Biological Diversity and the International Undertaking on Plant Genetic Resources;

(ii) the continuation of the traditional farming practices including the right to save, exchange and save seeds, and sell their harvest;

(iii) preventing anti-competitive rights or practices which will threaten food sovereignty of people in developing countries, as is permitted by Article 31 of the TRIPs Agreement.[59]

As for the relationships among Article 27.3(b), the CBD, and the International Undertaking on Plant Genetic Resources, the Group proposed as follows:

> The review process should seek to harmonize Article 27.3(b) with the provisions of the CBD and the International Undertaking, in which the conservation and sustainable use of biological diversity, the protection of the rights and knowledge of indigenous and local communities, and the promotion of farmers' rights, are fully taken into account.[60]

These proposals were supported by other developing countries.[61] Finally at the meeting of the Council for TRIPs held in March 2000, the Chair provided a list of issues raised under the review of Article 27.3(b) by Members. These are as follows:

- the link between the provisions of Article 27.3(b) and development;
- technical issues relating to patent under Article 27.3(b);
- technical issues relating to *sui generis* protection of plant varieties;
- ethical issues relating to the patentability of life forms;
- the relationship to the conservation and sustainable use of genetic material; and
- the relationship with the concepts of traditional knowledge and farmers' rights.

On September 18, 2000, the African Group submitted another paper relating to the review of the provisions of Article 27.3(b) which tried to develop those six issues.[62] Several views were expressed by the Members.

59 Ibid., para. 13.

60 Ibid., para. 15.

61 See, WTO, Council for TRIPs, Minutes of the Meeting of October 20–21, 1999, WTO Doc. IP/C/M/25, December 22, 1999.

62 WTO, Council for TRIPs, Review of the Provisions of Article 27.3(b)—Communication from Mauritius on Behalf of the African Group, WTO Doc. IP/C/W/206, September 20, 2000.

The review mandate was further strengthened in 2001 by the Doha Ministerial Declaration[63] adopted on November 14, 2001. Paragraph 19 of the Doha Ministerial Declaration sets forth as follows:

> We instruct the Council for TRIPs, in pursuing its work programme including under the review of Article 27.3(b), the review of the implementation of the TRIPs Agreement under Article 71.1[[64]] and the work foreseen pursuant to paragraph 12 of this Declaration,[[65]] to examine, *inter alia*, the relationship between the TRIPs Agreement and the Convention on Biological Diversity, the protection of traditional knowledge and folklore, and other relevant new developments raised by Members pursuant to Article 71.1. In undertaking this work, the TRIPs Council shall be guided by the objectives and principles set

---

63 WTO Doc. WT/MIN(01)/DEC/1.

64 TRIPs Article 71.1: Review and Amendment reads as follows:

> The Council for TRIPS shall review the implementation of this Agreement after the expiration of the transitional period referred to in paragraph 2 of Article 65. The Council shall, having regard to the experience gained in its implementation, review it two years after that date, and at identical intervals thereafter. The Council may also undertake reviews in the light of any relevant new developments which might warrant modification or amendment of this Agreement.

65 Paragraph 12, of the Doha Ministerial Declaration: Implementation-Related Issues and Concerns reads as follows:

> We attach the utmost importance to the implementation-related issues and concerns raised by Members and are determined to find appropriate solutions to them. In this connection, and having regard to the General Council Decisions of 3 May and 15 December 2000, we further adopt the Decision on Implementation-Related Issues and Concerns in document WT/MIN(01)/17 to address a number of implementation problems faced by Members. We agree that negotiations on outstanding implementation issues shall be an integral part of the Work Programme we are establishing, and that agreements reached at an early stage in these negotiations shall be treated in accordance with the provisions of paragraph 47 below. In this regard, we shall proceed as follows: (a) where we provide a specific negotiating mandate in this Declaration, the relevant implementation issues shall be addressed under that mandate; (b) the other outstanding implementation issues shall be addressed as a matter of priority by the relevant WTO bodies, which shall report to the Trade Negotiations Committee, established under paragraph 46 below, by the end of 2002 for appropriate action.

out in Articles 7[[66]] and 8[[67]] of the TRIPs Agreement and shall take fully into account the development dimension.

Under the new mandate, in addition to the review of TRIPs Article 27.3(b) as prescribed under Article 27.3(b) *in fine*, the Doha Ministerial Declaration demanded the Council for TRIPs to examine the relationship between the TRIPs Agreement, the Convention on Biological Diversity (CBD), and the protection of TK and folklore. The Declaration thereby considerably broadened the scope of the review. The three issues have subsequently been discussed in special sessions of the TRIPs Council in parallel.

African main positions relating to the review of Article 27.3(b),[68] *the relationship between the TRIPs Agreement and the CBD, and protection of traditional knowledge and folklore*

As mentioned above, before the Doha Ministerial Conference the African Group submitted two important papers on the review of Article 27.3(b), including their main position on the relationship between the CBD and the TRIPs Agreement, an effective *sui generis* system for protection of new plant varieties, and, to some extent, on protection of TK and folklore.

This part will cover the discussions that took place in the Council for TRIPs between 2002 and 2006. The African Group submitted a position paper entitled 'Taking Forward the Review of Article 27.3(b) of the TRIPs Agreement' in June 2003 which clearly displayed the African positions on the three issues.[69] The paper

66 TRIPs Article 7 reads as follows:

The protection and enforcement of intellectual property rights should contribute to the promotion of technological innovation and to the transfer and dissemination of technology, to the mutual advantage of producers and users of technological knowledge and in a manner conducive to social and economic welfare, and to a balance of rights and obligations.'

67 TRIPs Article 8 reads as follows:

1. Members may, in formulating or amending their laws and regulations, adopt measures necessary to protect public health and nutrition, and to promote the public interest in sectors of vital importance to their socio-economic and technological development, provided that such measures are consistent with the provisions of this Agreement.

2. Appropriate measures, provided that they are consistent with the provisions of this Agreement, may be needed to prevent the abuse of intellectual property rights by right holders or the resort to practices which unreasonably restrain trade or adversely affect the international transfer of technology.'

68 This includes the relationship between the TRIPs Agreement and the plant variety protection regime.

69 'Taking Forward the Review of Article 27.3(b) of the TRIPs Agreement', WTO Doc. IP/C/W/404, June 26, 2003.

had a great impact and many elements were endorsed not only by all developing countries but also by a number of developed countries.

The relationship between the TRIPs Agreement and the CBD The discussion on the relationship between the TRIPs Agreement and the CBD commenced somewhat before the Doha mandate. With the Doha mandate, this item was officially included on the agenda. The main issue put on the table was the determination of whether or not there was a conflict between TRIPs provisions and CBD principles and objectives. Positions of countries in this regard may be grouped into three categories:

- Group 1: No conflict between TRIPs and the CBD;
- Group 2: Inherent conflict between TRIPs and the CBD; and
- Group 3: Positive action required to avoid conflict.

According to the first group, there is no conflict between TRIPs and the CBD as the two treaties pursue different objectives and cover different subject-matter. Proponents of the first group maintain that the two treaties can be implemented in a mutually supportive way through national measures. They likewise hold that if the criteria for patentability are correctly applied this will ensure the grant of valid patents over inventions that use genetic material; such patents do not prevent compliance with the provisions of the CBD regarding the sovereign right of countries over their GRs, prior informed consent and benefit-sharing.[70]According to this group, no amendment of the TRIPs Agreement is required.

The second group states that there is an inherent conflict between the TRIPs Agreement and the CBD and the only way to redress it is to amend the TRIPs Agreement to incorporate the CBD principles, namely prior informed consent and benefit-sharing, into TRIPs. The amendment of the TRIPs Agreement may take the form of the inclusion of the disclosure requirement of the country of origin of GRs or associated TK.[71] Another argument supported by this group is that the Regulations of the PCT of WIPO should be amended so as to explicitly enable countries to require patent applicants to disclose the source of GRs and TK if the inventions are directly based on these resources or this knowledge.[72] The Swiss

70 See, for example, Article 27.3(b), Relationship between the TRIPS Agreement and the CBD, and the Protection of Traditional Knowledge and Folklore, Communication from the United States, WTO Docs. IP/C/W/257, April 2, 2001, and IP/C/W/434, November 26, 2004.

71 See, Article 27.3(b), Relationship between the TRIPS agreement and the CBD, and the Protection of Traditional Knowledge and Folklore, Joint Communication from the African Group, WTO Docs. IP/C/W/404, IP/C/W/206, IP/C/W/163, IP/C/M/40, paras. 76–79.

72 See, Article 27.3(b), Relationship between the TRIPS agreement and the CBD, and the Protection of Traditional Knowledge and Folklore, Communication from Switzerland, WTO Docs. IP/C/W/433, IP/C/W/423, IP/C/W/400/Rev.1, IP/C/M/49, para. 115. See, also,

proposal[73] on the declaration of the source of GRs and TK in patent applications further stated that, in general, the requirements with regard to patent applications can be categorized as follows:

> • *formal requirements* which are examined for the purposes of determining if a complete application has been filed;
> • *formal requirements strongly linked to substance* concerning the various parts of the patent application for the purposes of search, examination and grant, that is, requirements which could affect the scope of a search or result in the rejection of the claims during the substantive examination of the patent application; and
> • *substantive requirements*, under which the claims are evaluated for patentability, namely, definition of prior art, disclosure of the claimed invention, patentable subject matter, novelty, inventive step and industrial utility.[74]

Within this group, some believe that non-compliance with the disclosure requirement should not penalize the applicant in pursuing his patent application (no rejection). According to them, sanctions may be brought outside the patent system. Others maintain that failure to respect the disclosure requirement should result in a denial or rejection of the application.

According to the third group, the two treaties must be mutually supportive and if conflict occurs, positive actions must be taken to avoid it.

The African Group position The African Group's position on the relationship between the TRIPs Agreement and the CBD is reflected in the position paper.[75] According to the paper, both the TRIPs Agreement and the CBD, as well as the International Treaty on Plant Genetic Resources, should be implemented in a mutually supportive and consistent manner. In this regard, Members retain the right to require, within their domestic laws, the disclosure of the sources of any

---

Kongolo T. (2002b), 'Biodiversity and African Countries', *European Intellectual Property Review (EIPR)* 24:12, 579–584.

73 The disclosure requirement is, in the view of Switzerland, linked neither to the search, examination or grant of patents, nor to the evaluation of the claims for patentability. Accordingly, it has to be considered a formal requirement, not a formal requirement strongly linked to substance or even a substantive requirement. Switzerland proposed amending the PCT Regulations to explicitly enable national patent legislation to require declaration of the source of GRs and TK in patent applications. The proposals thus leave it up to national legislators to decide whether such a requirement is to be introduced in each country's national patent legislation.

74 See, WTO Doc. IP/C/W/433, November 25, 2004, and see, generally, WIPO, Report of the Standing Committee on the Law of Patents, Fifth Session, Geneva, May 14–19, 2001, WIPO Doc. SCP/5/6, para. 51.

75 WTO Doc. IP/C/W/404. See, also, Kongolo, T. (2004b), 'Panorama of the Most Controversial IP Issues in Developing Countries', *European Intellectual Property Review (EIPR)* 26:6, 258–262.

biological material that constitutes some input in the inventions claimed, and proof of benefit-sharing.

The Group pointed out that actions were needed to protect GRs as well as TK from being misappropriated and that this should be done through requirements for disclosure of the source of the GRs and TK involved in the claimed inventions and demonstration of compliance with the applicable domestic procedures in the Member where the GRs and TK originate.

According to the Group, compared to other alternatives, TRIPs Article 29 seemed to be the most suitable for an appropriate modification to contain these rights and obligations, by including the requirements for equity, disclosure of the community of origin of the GRs and TK, and a demonstration of compliance with applicable domestic procedures.

The Group suggested that Article 29 be modified by adding the following as paragraph 3:

> 3. Members shall require an applicant for a patent to disclose the country and area of origin of any biological resources and traditional knowledge used or involved in the invention, and to provide confirmation of compliance with all access regulations in the country of origin.

An effective sui generis system With regard to plant varieties, TRIPs Article 27.3(b) provides for possible protection of new varieties of plants through an effective *sui generis* system. The main question discussed in this regard was whether the UPOV Convention could be considered 'the effective *sui generis* system'. Countries were divided into three groups. The first group stated that UPOV could be considered as the 'TRIPs intended *effective sui generis* system'. The second group considered that UPOV was not an effective *sui generis* system. The third group said that UPOV could be considered as a reference (a model that may be followed) but not necessarily the said effective *sui generis* system. Each group put arguments forward to support its position. At the end of discussions, it was agreed that each country should have the leeway to select any 'effective' *sui generis* system for the protection of new plant varieties and that UPOV could serve as a reference.

The African Group position The position paper[76] summarized the main arguments developed by the African Group during discussions of 'an effective *sui generis* system' for protection of new plant varieties. According to the African Group, the requirement to protect plant varieties should not in any manner undermine, but should support, the right of Members to protect important public policy goals relating to food security, nutrition, the elimination of rural poverty, and the integrity of local communities. In this regard, there is no basis for requiring Members to adopt inappropriate regimes for protecting new plant varieties. Members have the right and the freedom to determine and adopt

76 WTO Doc. IP/C/W/404, supra, note 70.

appropriate regimes to satisfy the requirement to protect new plant varieties by effective *sui generis* systems. In this regard, and for purposes of illustration, such regimes may draw upon the International Treaty on Plant Genetic Resources, the CBD, the 1978 Act of the Convention of UPOV, and the African Model Law on the Protection of the Rights of Local Communities, Farmers and Breeders and the Regulation of Access to Biological Resources. The appropriate and beneficial approach is to have systems of protection which can address the local realities and needs. The African Model Legislation on the Protection of the Rights of Local Communities, Farmers and Breeders and the Regulation of Access to Biological Resources is one example of a *sui generis* system which has been developed to provide appropriate and effective protection for the rights and knowledge of farmers, as well as indigenous peoples and local communities, in a manner that suits the circumstances of Africa and possibly other developing Members.

According to the Group, any *sui generis* system should enable Members to retain their right to adopt and develop measures that encourage and promote the traditions of their farming communities and indigenous peoples in innovating and developing new plant varieties and enhancing biological diversity.

Protection of traditional knowledge and folklore Within the Doha mandate, protection of TK could be considered as a great achievement for developing countries that championed this issue first during the review process of Article 27.3(b).[77] Thankfully, the Doha Ministerial Declaration endorsed it as item to discuss in the new mandate.

In the view of developing countries, TK and folklore have been subjects of widespread misappropriation by the developed world. It was argued that the TRIPs Agreement must be amended to consider the protection of TK and folklore. On the other hand, most of the developed countries were reluctant to engage in a discussion of this matter.

The African Group position The African Group not only made their position known through the position paper but they also annexed a draft Decision of Traditional Knowledge.[78] The aim was to have a separate Decision that could be an integral part of the TRIPs Agreement.

First, TK and creations of local communities should be protected under appropriate regimes, on the understanding that the TRIPs Agreement provides only minimum standards and does not prevent Members from adopting additional areas of protection. In this regard, it is important to develop mechanisms to ensure equity in relation to the use of GRs and TK through appropriate international arrangements and mechanisms to supplement domestic laws and measures. Also, international mechanisms should be adopted within the framework of the TRIPs Agreement to protect GRs and TK.

77 See, ibid.

78 See, ibid.

Second, according to the Decision on Traditional Knowledge, TK is a category of intellectual property hereby recognised and protected in accordance with the Decision and Members shall protect and enforce rights accordingly. The existence of TK in any form or at any stage shall defeat the novelty and inventiveness requirements for purposes of patents and originality for purposes of copyrights under any laws of all Members.

> Where:
>
> (i) traditional knowledge has been a lead to the invention,
>
> (ii) any invention that qualifies for patentability has derived at any stage from traditional knowledge,
>
> (iii) any invention is based on in situ genetic resources of any Member,
>
> then, no intellectual property rights shall be granted or protected in any Member unless the requirements on access to genetic resources under the Convention on Biological Diversity have been fully complied with.[79]

Current status of the debate Discussions over TK and folklore protection are still taking place under the TRIPs Council, but with no tangible progress. The debate nowadays is more and more centered on the issue of disclosure of country of origin of GRs/biological resources and associated TK. In this connection, two important proposals made in the TRIPs Council may be highlighted:

- Proposal on the Disclosure of Origin of Biological/Genetic Resources and/or Associated TK of July 2006 (as amended on April 15, 2011, coupled with the proposed amendment of the TRIPs Agreement); and
- Draft Modality Text on TRIPs/CBD Disclosure of July 2008.

Proposal on the Disclosure of Origin of Biological/Genetic Resources and/or Associated Traditional Knowledge In June 2006, Norway submitted a proposal on amendment of the TRIPs Agreement to incorporate a mandatory obligation to disclose the origin of GRs and TK in patent applications. Such a disclosure obligation would be introduced in a new Article 29*bis* and would provide that patent applications should not be processed unless the required information has been submitted.[80] According to the Norwegian Proposal, a disclosure obligation should be based on the following key principles:

> (a) A binding international obligation should be introduced to include information on the supplier country (and the country of origin, if known and different) of genetic resources and traditional knowledge in patent applications. The supplier country (or country of origin, if relevant) of traditional knowledge must be disclosed even if the traditional knowledge

79 Ibid., Annex, 'Decision on Traditional Knowledge', para. 2(e).

80 WTO Docs. WT/GC/W/566, TN/C/W/42, IP/C/W/473, June 14, 2006.

has no connection with genetic resources. If the national law of the supplier country or country of origin requires consent for access to genetic resources or traditional knowledge, the disclosure obligation must also encompass a duty to state whether such consent has been given. If the country of origin is unknown, that fact must be disclosed.

(b) The disclosure obligation should apply to all patent applications (international, regional and national).

(c) If the applicant is unable or refuses to give information despite having had an opportunity to do so, the application should not be allowed to proceed.

(d) If it is subsequently discovered that incorrect or incomplete information has been given, this should not affect the validity of the granted patent, but should be penalised in an effective and proportionate way outside the patent system.

(e) A simple notification system should be introduced, under which patent offices send all declarations of origin they receive to the CBD Clearing-House Mechanism.

In July 2006, some WTO Members proposed a draft text for such an Article 29*bis*.[81] The draft text has been the subject of various amendments since its submission in 2006 which have led to changes in the terminologies used within the draft text, including its own title. The draft text was further amended on April 15, 2011.[82] The African Group is now one of the signatories of the draft text, which is supported by a large number of WTO Members.

The actual proposed Article 29*bis* comprises five paragraphs.

The April 15, 2011 draft text of proposed TRIPs Article 29*bis* reads as follows:

Disclosure of Origin of Genetic Resources and/or Associated Traditional Knowledge

1. For the purposes of establishing a mutually supportive relationship between this Agreement and the Convention on Biological Diversity, Members shall have regard to the objectives, definitions and principles of this Agreement, the Convention on Biological Diversity, and the Nagoya Protocol on Access to Genetic Resources and the Fair and Equitable Sharing of Benefits Arising from their Utilization, in particular its provisions on prior informed consent for access and fair and equitable benefit sharing.

2. Where the subject matter of a patent application involves utilization of genetic resources and/or associated traditional knowledge, Members shall require applicants to disclose: (i) the country providing such resources, that

81 See, WTO Docs. WT/GC/W/564/Rev.2; TN/C/W/41/Rev.2; IP/C/W/474, July 5, 2006.

82 Draft Decision to Enhance Mutual Supportiveness between the TRIPS Agreement and the Convention on Biological Diversity, WTO Doc. TN/C/W/59, April 19, 2011.

is, the country of origin of such resources or a country that has acquired the genetic resources and/or associated traditional knowledge in accordance with the CBD; and, (ii) the source in the country providing the genetic resources and/or associated traditional knowledge. Members shall also require that applicants provide a copy of an Internationally Recognized Certificate of Compliance (IRCC). If an IRCC is not applicable in the providing country, the applicant should provide relevant information regarding compliance with prior informed consent and access and fair and equitable benefit sharing as required by the national legislation of the country providing the genetic resources and/or associated traditional knowledge, that is, the country of origin of such resources or a country that has acquired the genetic resources and/or associated traditional knowledge in accordance with the CBD.

3. Members shall publish the information disclosed in accordance with paragraph 2 of this Article jointly with the publication of the application or the grant of patent, whichever is made first.
4. Members shall put in place appropriate, effective and proportionate measures so as to permit effective action against the non-compliance with the obligations set out in paragraph 2 of this Article. Patent applications shall not be processed without completion of the disclosure obligations set out in paragraph 2 of this Article.
5. If it is discovered after the grant of a patent that the applicant failed to disclose the information set out in paragraph 2 of this Article, or submitted false and fraudulent information, or it is demonstrated by the evidence that the access and utilization of genetic resources and/or associated traditional knowledge violated the relevant national legislation of the country providing genetic resources and/or associated traditional knowledge, that is, the country of origin of such resources or a country that has acquired the genetic resources and/or associated traditional knowledge in accordance with the CBD, Members shall impose sanctions, which may include administrative sanctions, criminal sanctions, fines and adequate compensation for damages. Members may take other measures and sanctions, including revocation, against the violation of the obligations set out in paragraph 2.

The first paragraph requests WTO Members to consider the guiding principles, definitions, and objectives embodied in the CBD and the Nagoya Protocol in order to establish a mutually supportive relationship between the TRIPs Agreement and the CBD, particularly the provisions on prior informed consent for access and equitable sharing of benefits.

The second paragraph is the key provision pertaining to the disclosure of countries of origin of GRs and/or associated TK. It obliges WTO Members to request applicants to provide such disclosure as well as evidence of compliance with the prior informed consent and fair and equitable sharing of benefits requirements of the country of origin. It also demands that Members require applicants to provide a copy of an Internationally Recognized Certificate of Compliance (IRCC),[83] where applicable.

Paragraph 3 obliges Members to publish the information disclosed and related additional information. Paragraph 4 deals with sanctions if disclosure of the country of origin is not made, and in Paragraph 5 further specific sanctions are set out if an applicant for a patent has not satisfied the disclosure requirement.

While over 100 WTO Members support amendment of the TRIPs Agreement to require applicants for patents to disclose the country of origin or source of GRs and/or associated TK used in their inventions and to provide evidence of prior informed consent and fair and equitable sharing of benefits, a number of Members reject amendment of the TRIPs Agreement for this purpose.

Opponents are of two types. The first group refuses to accept the disclosure requirement as a substantive condition for the grant of a patent. This group argues that the proposal goes against the spirit of TRIPs Article 27.1, in which three substantive conditions of patentability are set out, namely novelty, inventive step, and industrial application. These opponents maintain that requesting the disclosure of the country of origin of GRs may be burdensome for patent applicants. The second group accepts the disclosure requirement without, however, supporting amendment of the TRIPs Agreement for that purpose. It also opposes the sanctions contained in the proposed paragraphs 4 and 5 if an applicant fails to comply. According to this group, amendment of the TRIPs Agreement is not required. Thus, this group opposes the inclusion within the TRIPs Agreement of a provision requesting applicants to disclose the country of origin of GRs or, further, of associated TK. According to this group, Members may individually require the disclosure of the source or origin of genetic material, but any legal consequences of failure to meet such requirements should lie outside the scope of patent law.

Another argument developed by the opponents of amendment of the TRIPs Agreement has been that the CBD's objectives on access to GRs and benefit-sharing can best be achieved through national legislation and contractual arrangements based on such legislation, which could include commitments on disclosure of any commercial application of GRs or TK, rather than through patent requirements.

---

83 Article 17.3 of the Nagoya Protocol states:

> An internationally recognized certificate of compliance [IRCC] shall serve as evidence that the genetic resource which it covers has been accessed in accordance with prior informed consent and that mutually agreed terms have been established, as required by the domestic access and benefit-sharing legislation or regulatory requirements of the Party providing prior informed consent.

Article 17.4 states the minimum information that shall be contained in the IRCC when such information is not confidential.

According to this group, the disclosure issue may be taken care of by national laws and, to some extent, by private contracts between the parties involved.[84]

The African Group supports the disclosure of the country of origin and the amendment of the TRIPs Agreement for that purpose.

Draft Modalities Text for TRIPs related issues[85] Some WTO Members called for a procedural decision to negotiate the following issues in a parallel and horizontal process: the issue of the establishment of a multilateral system of notification and registration of geographical indications for wines and spirits; the disclosure issue requesting patent applicants to disclose the origin of GRs or associated TK used in their inventions; and the extension of the higher level of protection of geographical indications (as afforded to wines and spirits under TRIPs Article 23) to other products. The African Group is supportive of the Draft Modalities Text.

Pursuant to the Draft Modality Text on TRIPs/CBD Disclosure, which forms an integral part of the overall Draft Modalities Text, Members would agree to amend the TRIPs Agreement to include a mandatory requirement for the disclosure of the country providing/source of GRs, and/or associated TK for which a definition will be agreed, in patent applications. Patent applications would then not be processed without completion of the disclosure requirement.[86]

Furthermore, Members would agree to define the nature and extent of a reference to prior informed consent and access and benefit-sharing.[87]

The Draft Text also calls for text-based negotiations to be undertaken, in Special Sessions of the TRIPs Council and as an integral part of the Single Undertaking, to implement the above. Additional elements contained in Members' proposals, such as prior informed consent and access and benefit-sharing as an integral part of the disclosure requirement and post-grant sanctions, may also be raised and considered in these negotiations.[88]

Some Members have expressed concern over the modality that has been proposed to deal with the three issues in a horizontal manner and as part of the Single Undertaking. They maintain that each issue is different and should be dealt with on its own merit and addressed separately.[89] According to the opponents of the modality approach, this artificial marriage is not worth celebration. The proponents have asserted that this union is not a marriage of convenience.

---

84 See, Kongolo, T. (2008), *Unsettled International Intellectual Property Issues* (New York: Kluwer Law International), at 94. See, also, Kongolo, T. (2001b), 'Towards a More Balanced Coexistence of Traditional Knowledge and Pharmaceuticals Protection in Africa', *Journal of World Trade* 35:2, 349–361.

85 WTO Doc. TN/C/W/52, July 19, 2008.

86 Ibid., Annex, para. 4.

87 Ibid., Annex, para. 5.

88 Ibid., Annex, para. 6.

89 WTO, Council for TRIPs, Minutes of the Meeting of June 8–9, 2009, WTO Doc. IP/C/M/60, September 28, 2009, e.g. paras. 38, 43, 44, 46, 51, and 54.

One proponent of the modality approach has argued that the disclosure requirement was a major development component of the Doha Round and an agreement on disclosure would respond to a major demand of developing countries within the Doha Development Round.[90]

The Draft Modalities Text has been endorsed by more than 100 Members. The main idea of this proposal is for Members to agree to negotiate the three issues mentioned above in parallel in the Special Sessions of the TRIPs Council. Opponents have maintained that the proposal went beyond the mandate of the Special Session of the Council for TRIPs.

Conclusion

The issue of protection of TK and folklore first came to light in the course of the review of Article 27.3(b) as recommended by the TRIPs Agreement itself. It later became part of the new mandate of the Council for TRIPs provided under the Doha Ministerial Declaration, which instructed the Council to also discuss the relationship between the TRIPs Agreement and the CBD and the protection of TK and folklore.

The African Group's position paper of June 2003 may be considered a groundbreaking initiative which gained the support of many countries and also led to deeper examination of the issues. Another important proposal backed by the African Group and which is currently on the table is the proposal to amend the TRIPs Agreement to incorporate a new Article 29*bis* containing a requirement for disclosure of the country of origin of GRs and associated TK, along with appropriate sanctions for failure of compliance. In fact, the disclosure requirement is the key issue that has dominated the discussions. Despite support for the disclosure requirement by more than 100 countries, no consensus on the issue has been achieved so far. The Draft Modality Text also endorsed by the African Group is still on the table but appears to have little chance to succeed.

Ultimately, the disclosure requirement is the key to successful handling of issues of biopiracy and misappropriation of TK and TCEs/EoF. The amendment of the TRIPs Agreement by the inclusion of the proposed Article 29*bis* may be the way to go.

Patents and Public Health

Introduction

The conflict between the patent system and access to medicines drew the attention of the world community in the late 1990s with the HIV/AIDS pandemic and related issues. With the increased number of people infected and suffering from HIV/AIDS, the human rights dimension of the issue came to the forefront of

90 Ibid., para. 22.

international concerns. The main question put on the table was whether patent rights or public health should prevail in case of conflict of interests between owners of patent rights and the human right of access to medicines?

The need for more affordable HIV/AIDS drugs was expressed all over the world, particularly in developing countries. Governmental action was required to remedy the situation, or at least to provide alternative solutions to the conflict. In Africa, for instance, the South African case[91] raised several concerns over the conflict between patents and public health that could not find adequate responses. Meanwhile, developing countries were threatened with sanctions by some developed countries if they used compulsory licenses and parallel imports to acquire the needed medicines. In light of these considerations, African countries acknowledged, at the Summit on HIV/AIDS, Tuberculosis and Other Related Infectious Diseases held at Abuja, Nigeria, in April 2001, the necessity of adopting measures to tackle HIV/AIDS infection because of the exceptional threat it constitutes to Africa's development and the life expectancy of African peoples. These diseases entail a devastating economic burden through the loss of human capital, reduced productivity, and the diversion of human and financial resources to care and treatment.[92]

African countries declared in the Summit the following: 'We consider AIDS as a State of Emergency in the continent. To this end, all tariff and economic barriers to access to funding of AIDS-related activities should be lifted.'[93] They further declared that: 'We resolve to act and enact appropriate legislation and international trade regulations to ensure the availability of drugs at affordable prices and technologies for treatment, care and prevention of HIV/AIDS, tuberculosis and other infectious diseases.'[94]

The current section will cover the background and premises to the debate and the African contributions on the issue of patents and public health within the WTO, WHO, and WIPO.

91 See, Kongolo, T. (2001), 'Public Interest *versus* the Pharmaceutical Industry's Monopoly in South Africa', *The Journal of World Intellectual Property* 4:5, 609–627. See, also, Kongolo, T. (2003b), 'TRIPS, The Doha Declaration and Public Health', *The Journal of World Intellectual Property* 6:2, 373–378.

92 See, OAU, Heads of State and Government, African Summit on HIV/AIDS, Tuberculosis and Other Related Infectious Diseases, held at Abuja, Nigeria on April 26–27, 2001, 'The Abuja Declaration on HIV/AIDS, Tuberculosis and Other Related Infectious Diseases', para. 13, available at: http://www.uneca.org/adf2000/Abuja%20Declaration.htm (last accessed on November 26, 2012).

93 Ibid., para. 22.

94 Ibid., para. 31.

African Contributions within the WTO in the Context of Patents and Public Health

Background and premises to the debates

At the international level, during the Council for TRIPs meeting held on April 2–6, 2001, the African Group proposed that one day be set aside at the June session to clarify the interpretation and/or application of certain provisions of the TRIPs Agreement and to examine the relationship between intellectual property rights and access to medicines. This initiative was welcomed by all Members, who decided to hold a special session of the Council for TRIPs in June 2001 to kick off discussions on these issues.

In June 2001, the Council for TRIPs held its first session devoted to the TRIPs Agreement and access to medicines. It was the first time that the Council for TRIPs had discussed intellectual property issues in the framework of public health. At the meeting, two papers were put on the table: one submitted by the European Union (EU) on June 11;[95] and the other by the developing countries on June 19 on the initiative of the African Group.[96]

The EU paper provided clarification with regard to the extent of use of a compulsory license, including grounds for granting compulsory licenses, procedural requirements, national emergency, and public non-commercial use. The EU stressed that HIV/AIDS infection could be considered to be a 'national emergency' or a 'circumstance of extreme urgency'. The paper also touched upon the issue of the manufacture of patented products produced under compulsory license aimed to supply a WTO Member's domestic market. The paper maintained that TRIPs Article 30[97] allows limited exceptions to the exclusive rights conferred by a patent, provided that such exceptions are: (1) limited; (2) not unreasonable; and (3) do not prejudice the legitimate interests of the patent holder or of third parties. Protection of undisclosed information was also covered in the paper, mainly in relation to test data. It affirmed that the Agreement contains an obligation to protect test data against 'unfair commercial use'. The paper concluded that, although intellectual property rights play a role with regard to access to medicines, the TRIPs Agreement cannot be held responsible for the health crisis in developing

95 Communication from the European Communities and their Member States, WTO Doc. IP/C/W/280, June 12, 2001.

96 Submission by the African Group and other Developing Countries, WTO Doc. IP/C/W/296, June 29, 2001. See, also, Kongolo, T. (2002e), 'WTO DOHA Ministerial Declaration and Intellectual Property: African Perspectives', *African Yearbook of International Law* 9, 185–211.

97 Article 30 prescribes exceptions to rights conferred as follows:

> Members may provide limited exceptions to the exclusive rights conferred by a patent, provided that such exceptions do not unreasonably conflict with a normal exploitation of the patent and do not unreasonably prejudice the legitimate interests of the patent owner, taking account of the legitimate interests of third parties.

countries. At the same time, the Agreement must not stand in the way of action to combat the crisis.

The developing countries' submission on the TRIPs Agreement and Public Health contained a very useful and self-explanatory summary that is reproduced below.

> The special discussion on TRIPS and Public Health at the TRIPS Council is not a one-off event. It should be part of a process to ensure that the TRIPS Agreement does not in any way undermine the legitimate right of WTO Members to formulate their own public health policies and implement them by adopting measures to protect public health.
>
> The TRIPS Agreement allows for implementation of public health policy measures. Nevertheless, where the provisions of the Agreement may be considered insufficient to protect public health, Members may wish to bring further proposals for modifications in the Agreement, with a view to increase its flexibility.
>
> Nothing in the TRIPS Agreement should prevent Members from taking measures to protect public health.
>
> Each provision of the TRIPS Agreement should be read in light of the objectives and principles set forth in Articles 7 and 8. The protection of intellectual property rights, in particular patent protection, should encourage the development of new medicines and the international transfer of technology to promote the development of manufacturing capacities of pharmaceuticals, without restraining policies on access to medications.
>
> Compulsory licences are an essential tool for governments to carry out public health policies, as they may facilitate access to medicines through prevention of abuses of rights, encouragement of domestic capacities for manufacturing pharmaceuticals and in cases of national emergency or other circumstances of extreme urgency, or of public non-commercial use. Nothing in the TRIPS Agreement limits the grounds for governments to issue compulsory licences.
>
> Parallel imports can also be an important tool to ensure adequate access to medications. In light of Article 6 of the TRIPS Agreement, the TRIPS Council should confirm the unconditional right of Members to determine the way in which exhaustion of rights regimes are applied in their jurisdiction.
>
> While we favour discussions on differential pricing arrangements, they are only part of a broader set of initiatives to improve access to medications. Differential pricing should in no way be used to limit the flexibility of the TRIPS Agreement in any of its provisions. Given that the issue is not within the sphere of discussions on intellectual property rights, it should not be covered by the TRIPS Council, but rather by other intergovernmental international organizations, such as the World Health Organization.
>
> Other issues related to the provisions of the TRIPS Agreement also deserve further discussion by Members, such as the extension of transitional arrangements.

> Finally, the Ministerial Conference in Qatar in November 2001 will be the best opportunity to take such action as will ensure that the TRIPS Agreement does not in any way undermine the legitimate right of WTO Members to formulate their own public health policies and implement them by adopting measures to protect public health.

The Council for TRIPs held its second special discussion on IPRs and access to medicines on September 19, 2001. Two proposals, emanating respectively from the African Group, joined by 19 developing countries,[98] and the United States of America, joined by Australia, Canada, Japan, and Switzerland,[99] were put on the table. Members expressed their views during the discussion. After an informal discussion that took place on September 21, 2001, the responsibility was delegated to the Chairman of the General Council to prepare a draft text for consideration at the Fourth WTO Ministerial Conference due to take place in Doha, Qatar, in November 2001.

As the two papers put emphasis on the compulsory license provisions as set out under the TRIPs Agreement, for a better understanding of the discussion which will follow, it is worth noting here the main conditions and situations provided under TRIPs Article 31.

> The compulsory licensee must make efforts to enter into a license agreement with the right holder of the patent under reasonable commercial terms but without being successful in doing so within a reasonable time. This requirement may be waived by a WTO Member in the case of national emergency or other circumstances of extreme urgency or in cases of public non-commercial use (b).
> The compulsory license shall be non-exclusive and shall be granted on the basis of the individual merit of a specific request (d & a).
> The compulsory license shall be authorized predominantly for the supply of the domestic market of the Member authorizing such use (f).
> The right holder shall be paid adequate remuneration (h).
> The need to correct anti-competitive practices may be taken into account to determine the amount of the remuneration (k).
> Where the compulsory license is for a second patent that cannot be worked without infringing another patent, the license may be only if the second patent involves an important technical advance of considerable economic significance. In that case, the owner of the first patent shall be entitled to a cross-license on reasonable terms to use the invention covered by the second patent (l).

98 *'Draft Ministerial Declaration on the TRIPs Agreement and Public Health', Proposal by the African Group [and Others],* WTO Doc. IP/C/W/312, WT/GC/W/450, October 4, 2001.

99 'Access to Medicines for HIV/AIDS and other Pandemics', Proposal from a group of developed countries, WTO Doc. IP/C/W/313, October 4, 2001.

The African Group proposed text aimed at providing clarifications on the use of the so-called flexibilities contained in the TRIPs Agreement and at the same time at giving wider scope of discretion to WTO Members when making decisions on public health issues.

The Preamble of the African Group's text stressed, *inter alia*, the following:

> *affirming* that the protection and promotion of public health and nutrition is a fundamental obligation and prerogative of the State and that Members retain their sovereign power in this regard;
> *recalling* the Preamble of the TRIPS Agreement, which, among others, prescribes that measures and procedures to enforce intellectual property rights should not themselves become barriers to legitimate trade and recognizes the special needs of the least-developed country Members in respect of maximum flexibility in the domestic implementation of laws and regulations in order to enable them to create a sound and viable technological base;
> *realizing* that the inability of large segments of the population to obtain medicines and treatment at prices they can afford threatens the vital interest of States in protecting and promoting public welfare, preserving law and order, and maintaining social cohesion;
> *recognizing* that public health crises of unprecedented consequences, of which HIV/AIDS is a most dramatic example, afflict developing countries;
> *anticipating* that drawing attention to and reaffirming the context of the TRIPS Agreement and certain provisions thereof as an initial concrete step will further encourage Members, particularly developing and least-developed country Members, towards considering every possible policy option for the protection and promotion of public health.

The African Group proposed text contains 14 paragraphs.

The text, after the Preamble, reads as follows:

1. Nothing in the TRIPS Agreement shall prevent Members from taking measures to protect public health.
2. Each Member retains the right to establish its own policy and rules regarding the exhaustion of intellectual property rights.
3. Each Member has the right to allow other use(1) of the subject-matter of a patent without the authorization of the right holder, including use by the government or third parties authorized by the government, and to determine the grounds upon which such use is allowed.
4. In the case of a national emergency or other circumstances of extreme urgency or in cases of public non-commercial use, Members may grant compulsory licences without prior efforts on the part of the user to obtain authorization from the right holder.
5. A compulsory licence issued by a Member may be given effect by another Member. Such other Member may authorize a supplier within its territory

to make and export the product covered by the licence predominantly for the supply of the domestic market of the Member granting the licence. Production and export under these conditions do not infringe the rights of the patent holder.

6. Members are not obliged to apply the conditions set forth in subparagraphs (b) and (f) of Article 31 of the TRIPS Agreement where use of the subject-matter of a patent is permitted to remedy a practice determined after judicial or administrative process to be anti-competitive.
7. Nothing in the TRIPS Agreement shall prevent Members from establishing or maintaining marketing approval procedures for generic medicines and other healthcare products, or applying summary or abbreviated marketing approval procedures based on marketing approvals granted earlier for equivalent products.
8. Nothing in the TRIPS Agreement shall prevent Members from disclosing or using information held by its authorities or the patent holder where it is so required for reasons of public interest, including where such disclosure or use is necessary to implement effectively any compulsory licences or other measures adopted by public authorities in the public interest.
9. Under Article 30 of the TRIPS Agreement, Members may, among others, authorize the production and export of medicines by persons other than holders of patents on those medicines to address public health needs in importing Members.
10. Each Member shall, within or beyond the framework of the WTO, refrain from imposing or threatening to impose sanctions and refrain from employing the grant of incentives or other benefits in a manner which could curtail the ability of developing and least-developed country Members to avail themselves of every possible policy option to protect and promote public health.
11. Members shall exercise utmost restraint in initiating and pursuing dispute settlement proceedings relating to measures adopted or implemented, particularly by developing and least-developed country Members, to protect and promote public health.
12. In its examination of the scope and modalities for the possible application of subparagraphs 1(b) and 1(c) of Article XXIII of GATT 1994 to the settlement of disputes under the TRIPS Agreement, and without prejudice to recommendations that the Council for TRIPS may adopt and submit to the Ministerial Conference on other relevant aspects, in no event shall such subparagraphs be rendered applicable to measures adopted and implemented by Members, particularly developing and least-developed country Members, to protect and promote public health.
13. In view of the special needs and requirements of developing and least-developed country Members, their economic, financial and administrative constraints, and their need for flexibility to create a viable technological base, the transition period provided for their benefit under Articles 65.4

and 66.1 of the TRIPS Agreement shall be extended for another period of five (5) years from the expiration of the transition periods provided thereunder, particularly in respect of the obligation to render available patent protection on products or processes relating to public health, without prejudice to further extensions.

14. The TRIPS Council shall monitor and evaluate on an ongoing basis, in collaboration with relevant international organizations, the effects of the TRIPS Agreement on health, with particular emphasis on access to medicines and research and development on medicines for the prevention and treatment of diseases predominantly affecting people in developing and least-developed countries.

According to paragraph 1, Members have leeway to take appropriate measures to protect public health. This provision was considered to be the most controversial and challenging one as some developed countries saw this wording as creating a new rule that would override the present rules of the TRIPs Agreement, which do not allow for health exceptions that are inconsistent with the Agreement. The text prescribes that each Member must decide by itself about the exhaustion of rights regime and must also be permitted to use compulsory licenses and make its own determination of the grounds for doing so. It stressed that no prior efforts to obtain a voluntary license should be required in case of national emergency or circumstances of extreme urgency or in case of non-commercial use. Paragraph 5 was considered a most controversial one.

Paragraph 6 prescribed that Members would not be obliged to apply the conditions set forth in TRIPs Article 31(b) and (f) where use of the subject-matter of a patent is permitted to remedy a practice determined after judicial or administrative process to be anti-competitive.

Paragraph 7 prescribes that nothing in the TRIPs Agreement shall prevent Members from establishing or maintaining marketing approval procedures for generic medicines and other healthcare products, or applying summary or abbreviated marketing approval procedures based on marketing approvals granted earlier for equivalent products.

Paragraph 8 sets out that nothing in the TRIPs Agreement shall prevent Members from disclosing or using information held by their authorities or the patent holder where this is required for reasons of public interest, including where such disclosure or use is necessary to implement effectively any compulsory licences or other measures adopted by public authorities in the public interest.

Paragraph 9 sets out that under TRIPs Article 30 Members may, *inter alia*, authorize the production and export of medicines by persons other than holders of patents on those medicines to address public health needs in importing Members.

Paragraph 10 stipulates that each Member shall, within or beyond the framework of the WTO, refrain from imposing or threatening to impose sanctions and refrain from employing the grant of incentives or other benefits in a manner which could curtail the ability of developing and least-developed country Members to avail themselves of every possible policy option to protect and promote public health.

The US-sponsored draft text, comprised only wording for a preamble, which reads as follows:

> We Members of the WTO, recognize that access to medicines for treatment of HIV/AIDS and other pandemics, such as malaria and tuberculosis, especially by the poorest populations of the globe, is one of the major challenges for the global community and for its sustainable development;
> recognize that an effective response to this challenge requires a mix of complementary social, economic, health policies and practices, including education and prevention programmes;
> recognize that it is, therefore, the common responsibility of international organizations, governments, non-governmental organizations and private actors, through their areas of responsibility, to contribute to the promotion of the most favourable conditions for improving access to medicines for treatment of HIV/AIDS and other pandemics;
> recognize that among the determinant factors for improving access to medicines are efficient infrastructure to distribute, deliver and monitor drug usage and provide necessary information and education; increased research and development particularly targeted at the major communicable diseases of relevance for developing countries; mechanisms to finance drug purchases, and affordable pharmaceuticals; and the implementation of effective and sustainable healthcare systems;
> recognize that strong, effective and balanced protection for intellectual property is a necessary incentive for research and development of life-saving drugs and, therefore, recognize that intellectual property contributes to public health objectives globally.
> Therefore, we Members of the WTO reaffirm that the TRIPS Agreement contributes to the availability of medicines and reaffirm our commitment to the TRIPS Agreement and its implementation;
> reaffirm the appropriateness of Members using the flexibility afforded by the Agreement to ensure that medicines for treatment of HIV/AIDS and other pandemics are available to their citizens who need them, particularly those who are unable to afford basic medical care;
> take note of discussions held by the Council for TRIPS that have clarified Member's views of the flexibility provided under the Agreement;
> encourage Members, whatever the exhaustion regime that they may have chosen, to take measures to prevent pharmaceuticals provided to the poorest populations of the globe under discounted pricing schemes or supplied under aid-schemes from being diverted from those for whom they were destined to markets for which they were not intended;

pledge, in the context of the new global fund, to work with the private sector and with affected countries to facilitate the broadest possible provision of drugs in an affordable, medically effective, and WTO-consistent manner; and
reaffirm the importance for developing and least-developed country Members of technical assistance for implementing their obligations under the TRIPS Agreement, while taking into account health concerns.

The Draft text, while recognizing the challenges faced by the poorest countries to access medicines for treatment of HIV/AIDS and other pandemics, underlined the supportive role of the TRIPs Agreement for access and availability of medicines. It recognized the need for a balanced protection of IPRs to create incentives for research and appropriate infrastructure, *inter alia*, to distribute, deliver, and monitor drug use. Further, the text stressed that Members may use flexibilities to ensure that drugs for treatment of HIV/AIDS and other pandemics are available. In addition, it encouraged Members, whatever the exhaustion regime that they may have chosen, to take measures to prevent pharmaceuticals provided to the poorest populations of the globe under discounted pricing schemes or supplied under aid schemes from being diverted from those for whom they were destined to markets for which they were not intended.

The Doha Declaration on the TRIPs Agreement and Public Health

The Doha Declaration on the TRIPs Agreement and Public Health of November 14, 2001 attempted to clarify and interpret a number of related concepts that had been subjects of discussion, such as parallel imports and exhaustion of rights, the scope of a national emergency (including HIV/AIDS epidemics), compulsory licenses, flexibilities, etc.[100]

The text of the Declaration reads as follows:

1. We recognize the gravity of the public health problems afflicting many developing and least-developed countries, especially those resulting from HIV/AIDS, tuberculosis, malaria and other epidemics.
2. We stress the need for the WTO Agreement on Trade-Related Aspects of Intellectual Property Rights (TRIPS Agreement) to be part of the wider national and international action to address these problems.
3. We recognize that intellectual property protection is important for the development of new medicines. We also recognize the concerns about its effects on prices.
4. We agree that the TRIPS Agreement does not and should not prevent members from taking measures to protect public health. Accordingly, while reiterating our commitment to the TRIPS Agreement, we affirm

100 WTO Doc. WT/MIN(01)/DEC/2. See, also, Kongolo, T. (2006), 'Intellectual Property and Public Health—Unpleasant Marriage?', *The Geneva Post Quarterly: The Journal of World Affairs* 1:1, 185–208.

that the Agreement can and should be interpreted and implemented in a manner supportive of WTO members' right to protect public health and, in particular, to promote access to medicines for all.

In this connection, we reaffirm the right of WTO members to use, to the full, the provisions in the TRIPS Agreement, which provide flexibility for this purpose.

5. Accordingly and in the light of paragraph 4 above, while maintaining our commitments in the TRIPS Agreement, we recognize that these flexibilities include:
   a. In applying the customary rules of interpretation of public international law, each provision of the TRIPS Agreement shall be read in the light of the object and purpose of the Agreement as expressed, in particular, in its objectives and principles.
   b. Each member has the right to grant compulsory licences and the freedom to determine the grounds upon which such licences are granted.
   c. Each member has the right to determine what constitutes a national emergency or other circumstances of extreme urgency, it being understood that public health crises, including those relating to HIV/AIDS, tuberculosis, malaria and other epidemics, can represent a national emergency or other circumstances of extreme urgency.
   d. The effect of the provisions in the TRIPS Agreement that are relevant to the exhaustion of intellectual property rights is to leave each member free to establish its own regime for such exhaustion without challenge, subject to the MFN and national treatment provisions of Articles 3 and 4.
6. We recognize that WTO members with insufficient or no manufacturing capacities in the pharmaceutical sector could face difficulties in making effective use of compulsory licensing under the TRIPS Agreement. We instruct the Council for TRIPS to find an expeditious solution to this problem and to report to the General Council before the end of 2002.
7. We reaffirm the commitment of developed-country members to provide incentives to their enterprises and institutions to promote and encourage technology transfer to least-developed country members pursuant to Article 66.2. We also agree that the least-developed country members will not be obliged, with respect to pharmaceutical products, to implement or apply Sections 5 and 7 of Part II of the TRIPS Agreement or to enforce rights provided for under these Sections until 1 January 2016, without prejudice to the right of least-developed country members to seek other extensions of the transition periods as provided for in Article 66.1 of the TRIPS Agreement. We instruct the Council for TRIPS to take the necessary action to give effect to this pursuant to Article 66.1 of the TRIPS Agreement.

As noted above, the African Group and other developing countries made the case in their proposed draft for generous interpretation of the TRIPs Agreement by asserting the primacy of human health and other public policy concerns over the interests of private companies. The spirit of that draft is to a large extent reflected in the adopted Declaration.

In Paragraph 1, the Declaration notes that Members recognize the gravity of the public health problems afflicting many developing and least-developed countries, especially those resulting from HIV/AIDS, tuberculosis, malaria, and other epidemics. The Declaration goes on to stress that intellectual property protection is important for the development of new medicines and that Members recognize the concerns about such protection's effects on prices.

Paragraph 4 was the provision that provoked the greatest discussion, first during the negotiations when it was proposed by the developing countries, later when it was redrafted by the Chair of the General Council and then during further discussions by the Members. The compromise text still retained the flavour of the developing countries' proposal.

The Declaration confirmed that WTO Members have the freedom to adopt any regime of exhaustion of IPRs that they find appropriate. A country may wish to opt for national, regional, or international exhaustion. The Declaration further confirms that the scope of a national emergency shall be defined by each country faced with a crisis, as well as noting that an HIV/AIDS crisis, as well as one involving other diseases, could qualify as a situation of national emergency. The sphere of applicability of compulsory licenses regime was also left in the hands of each WTO Member. In addition, the Declaration affirmed the right of Members to make use of any flexibility encompassed within the TRIPs Agreement to deal with public health issues.

Of extreme importance, however, was the Declaration's failure to deal definitively with the situation of countries who lack manufacturing capacity to produce the needed drugs. There was therefore a need to further discuss this issue, and Paragraph 6 of the Declaration instructed the Council for TRIPs 'to find an expeditious solution to this problem and to report to the General Council before the end of 2002'.

Decision of the General Council of WTO of August 30, 2003 implementing Paragraph 6 of the Doha Declaration on the TRIPs Agreement and Public Health

To implement Paragraph 6 of the Doha Declaration on the TRIPs Agreement and Public Health, further discussions took place in the Council for TRIPs between 2002 and 2003 to find an adequate way to assist countries lacking manufacturing capacity to produce the needed drugs to fight against HIV/AIDS and other diseases.

It was questioned whether third countries who did possess the manufacturing capacity could be authorized to produce medicines or pharmaceutical products on behalf of the country lacking such capacity. There was no legal ground under the TRIPs Agreement to permit such action given that TRIPs Article 31(f) provides that a compulsory license must be used predominantly for the supply of the domestic market.

In the Council for TRIPs, Members centered their discussions on the following elements:

- scope and coverage of the disease:
- products coverage;
- beneficiary importing countries
- eligible supplying Members
- conditions
- legal mechanisms.

Five position papers were submitted to the Council for TRIPs in the course of the discussion on the implementation of Paragraph 6 of the Declaration on the TRIPs Agreement and Public Health.[101]

The original paper presented by the European Union and their Member States proposed possible solutions as follows:

> (1) amend Article 31 of the TRIPS Agreement in order to carve out an exception, under certain conditions, to Article 31(f) for exports of products needed to combat serious public health problems and produced under compulsory licences; or
>
> (2) interpret the limited exceptions clause of Article 30 of the TRIPS Agreement in a way which would allow production for export, to certain countries and under certain conditions, of products needed to combat serious public health problems.[102]

In a later submission, the EU focused its recommendation on the first of these options (i.e. creating an exception to TRIPs Article 31(f), expressing the concern that 'an authoritative interpretation on Article 30 of the TRIPs Agreement may fail to offer the same level of legal security for all parties involved as a textual addition to Article 31(f) would do').[103]

According to the paper presented by the United Arab Emirates,[104] the interpretation of Article 30, which allows Members to authorize limited exceptions, would be an alternative option.

In its paper,[105] the Group of developing countries called on the Council for TRIPs to recommend an authoritative interpretation of Article 30 of the TRIPs

---

101 See, WTO Doc. IP/C/W/363, July 11, 2002, para. 1.

102 WTO Doc. IP/C/W/339, March 4, 2002, para. 16 (1) and (2). In para. 18, the proposal recommends that 'the exception clause would state that Article 31(f) does not apply to compulsory licences granted for the purpose of supplying a poor country with a product needed to address serious public health problems'.

103 WTO Doc. IP/C/W/352, June 20, 2002, para. 6.

104 WTO Doc. IP/C/W/354, June 24, 2002.

105 WTO Doc. IP/C/W/355, June 24, 2002.

Agreement so as to recognize the right of WTO Members to authorize third parties to make, sell, and export patented public health-related products without the consent of the patent holder to address public health needs in another country.[106]

The US proposal[107] considered a waiver to Article 31(f) to be a better option than an authoritative interpretation of Article 30. Further, the paper maintained that an expeditious, workable, transparent, sustainable, and legally certain solution may more likely be achieved through a moratorium for dispute settlement.[108]

The African Group proposed a Draft Decision which contained the position of African countries with regard to the amendment of TRIPs Article 31.[109] It contained three options for doing so:

> Option 1: Article 31(f) would be completely revised.
> Option 2: Article 31(f) would be deleted.
> Option 3: Article 31(f) would not apply to any laws, measures and administrative regulations including compulsory licences, adopted to protect public health and in particular to ensure affordable access to pharmaceutical products.[110]

The conditions under Article 30, as interpreted by the proposed Decision, would continue to apply.

Further, the African Group maintained that there should be a comprehensive moratorium on disputes against any Member that takes measures to address international and national health concerns in countries with insufficient or no manufacturing capacity. Such a moratorium would operate for as long as it would take the international community to effectively combat the diseases, and such a determination could be made by WHO in accordance with its statutes.[111]

The African Delegation, when presenting the paper in the plenary session of the Council for TRIPs, stressed that its package proposal would facilitate the adoption of a Decision on this issue.[112] In another meeting of the Council for TRIPs held September 17–19, 2002, the African Group representative maintained as follows:

---

106 Ibid., para. 8. According to the Group, the proposed solution based on an authoritative interpretation of Article 30 would be preferable to those based on Article 31, as the former would be administratively less burdensome, involving fewer steps for implementation; ibid., para. 10.

107 WTO Doc. IP/C/W/358, July 9, 2002, paras. 29–31.

108 Ibid., para. 29.

109 WTO Doc. IP/C/W/351, June 24, 2002.

110 Ibid., Annex, para. 1.

111 Ibid., Annex, para. 10.

112 See, WTO Doc. IP/C/M/36, July 18, 2002, para. 7. The delegation concluded that: 'the African group believed that all the options, taken as a package, would provide essential elements for the solution required under paragraph 6 of the Declaration and that the various elements would address the various stages or aspects of the process of ensuring access to life-saving pharmaceutical products. Members with sufficient manufacturing capacity would be able to export to Members needing support in addressing public health concerns.

> The essence of the matter[is] the affordability and availability of pharmaceutical products. The solution should be simple, easy to use and economically viable as opposed to a legal solution with additional obligations. Some of the proposals, like moratoria and waivers, were not durable proposals that addressed the lack of manufacturing capacity of countries, especially those in Africa.[113]

In sum, positions of Members during the discussions may be grouped into four categories:

- extensive interpretation of Article 30 of the TRIPs Agreement which allows certain exceptions to exclusive rights of the patent owner by taking into account his/her legitimate interest or that of third parties;
- amendment of Article 31 which deals with compulsory licensing;
- a waiver of the export restriction provided under Article 31(f); and
- a dispute settlement moratorium in relation to the non-respect of the export restriction stipulated under Article 31(f) of the TRIPs Agreement.

In the course of the discussion, the representative of Norway made a valuable statement which helped to move the discussion ahead. As noted in the Minutes of the meeting:

> The representative of Norway said that the most significant criterion in choosing a solution was legal certainty. On this basis, his delegation favoured an amendment to the TRIPS Agreement. Such an arrangement would ensure that a paragraph 6 solution was not overridden by other substantive provisions of the TRIPS Agreement or the WTO Agreement or the GATT. If the Council should decide to go ahead with an amendment, he said that it would still be inapplicable before 1 January 2003 as the necessary ratifications had to take place. Hence, he said that there was need for an interim solution which, in his opinion, was a waiver. Such a waiver should be available until an amendment of the TRIPS Agreement entered into force.[114]

At its meeting of August 28, 2003, the Council for TRIPs approved the draft decision and agreed to forward it to the General Council for adoption.[115] The General Council adopted the Decision on the Implementation of Paragraph 6 of the Doha Declaration on the TRIPs Agreement and Public Heath on August 30,

---

Producers would be able to look at production facilities in Members with insufficient manufacturing capacity, assured that they will be able to serve the entire regional market and to some extent other Members outside the regional markets.'

113 WTO Doc. IP/C/M/37, October 11, 2002, para. 25.

114 Ibid., para. 65.

115 See, WTO Doc. IP/C/W/405, August 28, 2003.

2003 based on the recommendations of the Council for TRIPs.[116] The General Council decided to provide an exceptional arrangement whereby countries lacking manufacturing capacity to produce their own drugs for an emergency situation could import these drugs after issuing a compulsory license.

The Decision sets out conditions under which the obligation of an exporting Member under Article 31(f) of the TRIPs Agreement shall be waived with respect to the grant by it of a compulsory license to the extent necessary for the purposes of production of a pharmaceutical product(s) and its export to an eligible importing Member(s). Among these conditions are:

- Notification to the TRIPs Council by the eligible importing country of the names and expected quantities of the product(s).
- The importing country must prove its incapacity to locally manufacture the product(s) in question and confirm that a compulsory license has been granted in conformity with Article 31 of the TRIPs Agreement.
- The compulsory license issued by the exporting country shall cover only the amount necessary to meet the needs of the eligible importing country.
- The exporting country must pay remuneration to the owner of the patent rights in that country, taking into account the economic value to the importing Member of the use that has been authorized in the exporting Member.
- The importing country is waived from paying remuneration.
- Products produced under license shall be clearly identified (through specific labeling or marking), including special packaging and/or coloring/shaping of the products.
- The re-exportation of these products is strictly prohibited.
- Eligible importing Members shall take reasonable measures within their means, proportionate to their administrative capacities and to the risk of trade diversion to prevent re-exportation of the products that have actually been imported into their territories under the system.
- In case of regional trade agreement, it is permitted to re-export the products to a party member to the agreement facing the same incapacity.

To use the system, the eligible importing Member must first notify the Council for TRIPs of its intention to do so. What is required is that both the importing and the exporting countries must issue compulsory licenses. The exporting country is waived from the obligation provided under Article 31(f) relating to the issuance of compulsory licenses for the purpose of supplying the domestic market. The exporting Member must also pay remuneration to the patent owner in accordance with TRIPs Article 31(h) whilst the importing Member will be waived from such obligation.

116 Decision of the General Council of August 30, 2003, WTO Doc. WT/L/540. See, also, Kongolo, T. (2006) .

According to the Decision, least-developed countries are automatically deemed to lack manufacturing capacity. Therefore, there is no need for them to prove their manufacturing incapacity to produce needed medicines.

In addition to the Decision, the Chairman of the General Council issued a valuable statement that was read before the adoption of the Decision.[117] The Chair prompted Members to act in good faith when implementing this Decision. The key message is for countries benefiting or using the system to take appropriate measures to prevent diversion of these products from the intended market and also to prevent their re-exportation. It is important that Members seek to resolve any issues arising from the use and implementation of the Decision expeditiously and amicably.

According to Paragraph 11 of the Decision:

> This Decision, including the waivers granted in it, shall terminate for each Member on the date on which an amendment to the TRIPS Agreement replacing its provisions takes effect for that Member. The Council for TRIPS shall initiate by the end of 2003 work on the preparation of such an amendment with a view to its adoption within six months, on the understanding that the amendment will be based, where appropriate, on this Decision and on the further understanding that it will not be part of the negotiations referred to in paragraph 45 of the Doha Ministerial Declaration.

All Delegations welcomed the adoption of this Decision implementing Paragraph 6 of the Doha Declaration on the TRIPs Agreement and Public Health.[118]

It is in this context that the General Council, acting on behalf of the Ministerial Conference, adopted the Protocol amending the TRIPs Agreement on December 6, 2005.

The Protocol Amending the TRIPs Agreement

WTO Members embarked on further discussions within the Council for TRIPs sessions in 2004 and 2005 to amend the TRIPs Agreement to render the system provided under the Decision of August 30, 2003 permanent. In this exercise, some Members submitted proposals and some others presented their views in the plenary sessions of the Council for TRIPs.

On November 29, 2004, the African Group submitted a draft text that would modify Article 31 of the TRIPs Agreement.[119] This draft text was slightly revised in March 2005 to clarify one word.[120] The Proposal states the following:

---

117 The statement was prepared by the Chairman of the Council for TRIPs. See, WTO Doc. WT/GC/M/82, para. 29.

118 See, ibid., Agenda Item 3, pp. 3ff.

119 WTO Doc. IP/C/W/437, December 10, 2004.

120 WTO Doc. IP/C/W/437/Rev.1, March 23, 2005.

> This proposal by the African Group is aimed at providing the basis for the amendment. It is proposed to amend Article 31 of the TRIPS Agreement by adding a second paragraph to the Article so that the current text of Article 31 would become Article 31 paragraph 1 and the amendment text would become Article 31 paragraph 2. The proposed amendment would be based on the waivers with modifications, as appropriate. In essence, it is proposed to eliminate a number of provisions in the August 30 Decision as they would be redundant in the context of an amendment or where their purpose would otherwise be served by other provisions of the TRIPS Agreement, such as the Agreement's already existing provisions on compulsory licences read together with the provisions on enforcement.[121]

The proposed introductory text of the new TRIPs Article 31(2) must be read as follows:

> [2] The obligations under subparagraph 1(f) of this Article shall not apply to such use that is necessary for the purposes of production of a pharmaceutical product(s) and its export to an eligible importing Member(s) who notifies[[122]] the Council for TRIPS of its intention to use the system established under this paragraph in accordance with the terms set out below.[123]

The proposed terms are enumerated in Paragraph 2(a)–(g) as follows:

> (a) For the purposes of this paragraph:
>
> (i) 'pharmaceutical product' means any patented product, or product manufactured through a patented process, of the pharmaceutical sector needed to address the public health problems as recognized in paragraph 1 of the Doha Declaration. It is understood that, among others, active ingredients necessary for its manufacture and diagnostic kits needed for its use would be included;
>
> (ii) 'eligible importing Member' means any least developed country Member, and any other Member with no or insufficient manufacturing capacity in the pharmaceutical sector that has made a notification to the Council for TRIPS of its intention to use the system as an importer, it being understood that a Member may notify at any time that it will use the system in whole or in a limited way, for example, only in

121 Ibid., para. 3.

122 The text of the proposed amendment, ibid., para. 4, contains a footnote no. 4 at this point. It reads: 'It is understood that this notification does not need to be approved by a WTO body in order to use the system set out under this paragraph. The notification will be made available publicly by the WTO Secretariat through a page on the WTO website dedicated for this purpose.'

123 Ibid., para. 4.

the case of a national emergency or other circumstances of extreme urgency or in cases of public non-commercial use;

(iii) 'exporting Member' means a Member using the system set out in this paragraph to produce pharmaceutical products for, and export them to, an eligible importing Member.

(b) Where use is made by an eligible importing Member of the subject matter of a patent under this paragraph, adequate remuneration for purposes of subparagraph 1(h) of this Article shall be paid by the exporting Member taking into account the economic value to the importing Member of the use that has been authorized in the exporting Member. Where a compulsory licence is granted for the same products in the importing Member, the obligation of that Member under subparagraph 1(h) of this Article shall be waived in respect of those products for which remuneration in accordance with the first sentence of this subparagraph has been paid in the exporting Member.

(c) Products produced under the licence shall be clearly identified as being produced under the system set out in this paragraph through specific labelling or marking. Suppliers should distinguish such products through special packaging and/or special colouring/shaping of the products themselves, provided that such distinction is feasible and does not have a significant impact on price.

(d) Members shall ensure the availability of effective legal means to prevent the re-exportation or unlawful importation into, and sale in, their territories of products produced under the system set out under this paragraph, using the means available under Part III of this Agreement. If any Member considers that such measures are proving insufficient for this purpose, the matter may be reviewed in the Council for TRIPS at the request of that Member.

(e) With a view to harnessing economies of scale for the purposes of enhancing purchasing power for, and facilitating the local production of, pharmaceutical products; where a developing or least developed country Member is party to a regional trade agreement within the meaning of Article XXIV of the GATT 1994 or the Decision of 28 November 1979 on Differential and More Favourable Treatment Reciprocity and Fuller Participation of Developing Countries (L/4903), at least half of the membership of which is made up of countries on the United Nations list of least developed countries, the obligation of that Member under subparagraph 1(f) of this Article shall be waived to the extent necessary to enable a pharmaceutical product produced or imported under a compulsory licence in that Member to be exported to the markets of those other developing or least developed country parties to the regional trade agreement.

(f) Members recognize the desirability of promoting the transfer of technology and capacity building in the pharmaceutical sector in order to help importing Members establish their own manufacturing capacities in this sector. To this end, eligible importing Members and exporting Members are encouraged to use the system set out in this paragraph in a way which would promote this objective. Members undertake to cooperate in paying special attention to the transfer of technology and capacity building in the pharmaceutical sector in the work to be undertaken pursuant to Article 66.2 of this Agreement, paragraph 7 of the Declaration and any other relevant work of the Council for TRIPS.

(g) Members shall not challenge any measures taken in conformity with the provisions of this paragraph under subparagraphs 1(b) and 1(c) of Article XXIII of GATT 1994.

Paragraph 2(a) defined pharmaceutical products, eligible importing Member, and exporting Member. Paragraph 2(b) stipulated that where use is made by an eligible importing Member of the subject matter of a patent under the new paragraph, adequate remuneration for purposes of Article 1(h) must be paid by the exporting Member taking into account the economic value to the importing Member of the use that has been authorized in the exporting Member. Where a compulsory licence is granted for the same products in the importing Member, the obligation of that Member under Article 1(h) would be waived in respect of those products for which remuneration has been paid in the exporting Member.

Paragraph 2(c) dealt with the labeling and packaging of the medicines produced under the system, which should be clearly identifiable. Paragraph 2(d) prompts beneficiary Members of the system to take adequate measures to prevent the re-export of these products. Paragraph 2(e) enables a country beneficiary of the system to export the importing medicines to another country that is a member of the same regional trade agreement and also lacks manufacturing capacity to produce these drugs. Transfer of technology between the exporting and importing countries to develop their manufacturing capacity is recommended in Paragraph 2(f). The final Paragraph 2(g) maintains that Members shall not challenge any measures taken in conformity with the provisions of the new Article 31(2) under GATT Article XXIII:1(b) and (c).

The African Group stated that some of the provisions of the Decision of August 30, 2003 had become redundant and their incorporation in the proposed amendment would destroy the goal of the amendments. These included: the Preamble; the last part of paragraph 1(b) dealing with Members that may voluntarily not use the system or that may use the system only in limited circumstances; Paragraph 6(ii) on regional patent systems; Paragraph 8 on review of the Decision; Paragraph 9 on prejudice to other rights; and Paragraph 11 on an amendment replacing the Decision.[124]

After several discussions and informal consultation meetings with Delegates, the final text amending the TRIPs Agreement was agreed on December 5,

124 WTO Doc. IP/C/W/440, March 1, 2005, para. 10.

2005, enabling the General Council to adopt the text on December 6, 2005.[125] The amendment will enter into force for the countries that ratify the Protocol once two-thirds of the WTO Members notify their acceptance. The General Council has extended the deadline for acceptance several times. The current deadline is December 31, 2013 or such later date as may be decided by the Ministerial Conference.[126]

The Protocol amending the TRIPs Agreement consists of three parts: Article 31*bis* (Annex to the Protocol) to be incorporated after Article 31; an Annex to the TRIPs Agreement; and an Appendix to the Annex. According to the amending Protocol, the TRIPs Agreement shall be amended to insert Article 31*bis* and the Annex to the TRIPs Agreement (which incorporates the Appendix by reference). According to Paragraph 1 of Article 31*bis*, the obligations of an exporting Member under TRIPs Article 31(f) shall not apply with respect to the grant by it of a compulsory licence to the extent necessary for the purposes of production of a pharmaceutical product(s) and its export to an eligible importing Member(s).

Where a compulsory license is granted by an exporting Member under the system set out in the Article and the Annex to the TRIPs Agreement, adequate remuneration pursuant to TRIPs Article 31(h) shall be paid in that Member, taking into account the economic value to the importing Member of the use that has been authorized in the exporting Member. Where a compulsory license is granted for the same products in the eligible importing Member, the obligation of that Member under Article 31(h) shall not apply in respect of those products for which remuneration is paid in the exporting Member.

Furthermore, Paragraph 3 of Article 31*bis* stipulates that where a developing or least-developed country Member is a party to a regional trade agreement, the obligation of that Member under TRIPs Article 31(f) shall not apply to the extent necessary to enable a pharmaceutical product produced or imported under a compulsory license in that Member to be exported to the markets of those other developing or least-developed countries parties to the regional trade agreement that share the health problem in question. It is understood that this will not prejudice the territorial nature of the patent rights in question.

Article 31*bis* reiterates the possibility for WTO Members to use existing flexibilities contained in the TRIPs Agreement to deal with the relationship between IPRs and public health issues.

The Annex to the TRIPs Agreement encompasses most of the provisions of the Decision of the General Council of August 30, 2003 with few amendments. The Appendix to the Annex covers the assessment of Members' manufacturing capacities in the pharmaceutical sector. The text of the Appendix reads as follows:

---

125 WTO Doc. WT/l/641, December 8, 2005.

126 See, Decision of the General Council of November 30, 2011, WTO Doc. WT/L/829, December 5, 2011.

> Least-developed country Members are deemed to have insufficient or no manufacturing capacities in the pharmaceutical sector.
> For other eligible importing Members insufficient or no manufacturing capacities for the product(s) in question may be established in either of the following ways:
>
> (i) the Member in question has established that it has no manufacturing capacity in the pharmaceutical sector;
>
> or
>
> (ii) where the Member has some manufacturing capacity in this sector, it has examined this capacity and found that, excluding any capacity owned or controlled by the patent owner, it is currently insufficient for the purposes of meeting its needs. When it is established that such capacity has become sufficient to meet the Member's needs, the system shall no longer apply.

Least-developed countries are automatically deemed to have insufficient or no manufacturing capacities in the pharmaceutical area.

The new Article 31*bis* annexed to the Protocol reflects *mutatis mutandis* the proposal from the African Group as it was revised in March 2005, although the Group expressed reservations about some elements of the Annex to the TRIPs Agreement, which has incorporated the Decision of the General Council of August 30, 2003. These elements are:

> Paragraph 2(a) (i) relating to specifying the names and quantities needed;
> Paragraph 2(a) (ii) relating to the confirmation of lack of capacity and the Annex to the Decision;
> Paragraph 2(a) (iii) relating to confirmation of intention to grant a compulsory licence;
> Paragraph 2(b) (i) relating to importation of only the amount necessary to meet the needs of the importing Member;
> Paragraph 2(b) (iii) relating to posting information on the website;
> Paragraph 2(c) relating to notifying the TRIPS Council of the grant of the licence, etc; and
> Paragraph 4 of the Decision relating to re-exportation.[127]

Only a few African countries have accepted the Protocol amending the TRIPs Agreement. Most of them consider that the conditions included in the Annex to the TRIPs Agreement for making use of the system are too burdensome and cannot be met by a developing country or a least-developed country lacking pharmaceutical manufacturing capacity. On the other hand, developed countries assert that these conditions are safeguard measures to guarantee that products produced under the system are not diverted or re-exported somewhere else. It is, of course, up to each individual Member to weigh the merits and shortcomings of the system.

127 See, WTO Doc. IP/C/W/440, March 1, 2005, para. 10.

Conclusion

The relationship between patents and public health has raised numerous issues that cannot be easily or quickly resolved. The African Group brought the case before the WTO in 2001 to search for alternative solutions to the conflict. The first attempt was made through the Doha Declaration on the TRIPs Agreement and Public Health, which can be considered as a great achievement for developing countries in general and African countries in particular. The Draft Declaration by the African Group, which was also endorsed by many developing countries, can be considered to be a great initiative. The Declaration provided answers to the interpretation of some provisions of the TRIPs Agreement, such as exhaustion of rights and parallel imports, compulsory licenses, definition of emergency situations, and the leeway of Members to use the so-called flexibilities embodied in the TRIPs Agreement.

The second challenge, which would be considered a most difficult one, was to reply to the concerns of countries which lack manufacturing capacity to produce the needed drugs through the use of compulsory licenses. Finally, the General Council on August 30, 2003 decided to waive importing countries from paying remuneration to the rights holder and exporting countries from the obligation of producing products to supply their own domestic markets.

Amendment of the TRIPs Agreement was considered necessary to put in place a permanent system. The Protocol Amending the TRIPs Agreement was adopted and is open for acceptance by WTO Members. Few African countries have so far accepted the Protocol, primarily because of the contents of its Annexes. Most of them argue that the system is burdensome and complicated. The pace of acceptance has increased recently. It remains to be seen how African countries might benefit from the system.

African Contributions within WHO in the Context of Public Health, Innovation and Patents

Background and premises to the debates

Access to medicines has been considered to be one of the priorities of WHO, which is the directing and coordinating authority for health within the United Nations system. It is responsible for providing leadership on global health matters, shaping the health research agenda, setting norms and standards, articulating evidence-based policy options, providing technical support to countries and monitoring and assessing health trends.[128]

In the past, the high (and often unaffordable) price of medicines was considered to be the main obstacle to access to medicines by poor countries or countries in need of drugs to save the lives of their people. The prices of patented medicines have always been higher than those of generic ones. This becomes an issue when generic drugs are not available on the market in a country because patents are still

128 See, 'About WHO' on the WHO website http://www.who.int/about/en, accessed January 31, 2012.

valid there or when the patented drugs are deemed to be the only way to counter, cure, or relieve new diseases.

This latter dimension of the problem of access to medicines came to light two decades ago with the increase in people infected with HIV or suffering from AIDS.[129] Antiretroviral drugs were the only drugs that could save the lives of many people. Pharmaceutical companies, the owners of the patents on these drugs, however, were not ready to abandon some of their exclusive patent rights for the sake of humanity. They maintain that in the pharmaceutical sector business risks are higher than elsewhere because the likelihood of a successful outcome for extensive investment in research and development is very small and only a few of the many drugs that are developed ever actually reach the market.

Despite arguments from both sides, positive action on the part of WHO was expected to remedy the situation. The first major action that WHO undertook was the establishment in 2004 of the Commission on Intellectual Property Rights, Innovation and Public Health, which in 2006 submitted recommendations included in its final report. The second action was the adoption of the Global Strategy and Plan of Action on Public Health, Innovation and Intellectual Property in 2008. The third action was the strengthening of collaboration among WHO, the WTO, and WIPO to tackle public health crises through their combined efforts. Another initiative to highlight is the draft resolution on counterfeit medical products proposed by Gambia, Ghana, Nigeria, Tunisia, and the United Arab Emirates to the Sixty-First World Health Assembly in 2008.

At the regional level, through various forums, African countries took actions to remedy the situation facing them. Under the African Union, as stated above, 'The Abuja Declaration on HIV/AIDS, Tuberculosis and Other Related Infectious Diseases'[130] adopted in April 2001 was aimed at the issue of HIV/AIDS in particular. Other important actions have been taken by the WHO Regional Bureau for Africa.

Final report and recommendations of the Commission on Intellectual Property Rights, Innovation and Public Health of 2006

The Commission on Intellectual Property Rights, Innovation and Public Health was established in May 2003 at the Fifty-Sixth World Health Assembly which adopted resolution WHA56.27 and commenced its work in 2004. According to the resolution, the Director General was requested to:

> establish the terms of reference for an appropriate time-limited body to collect data and proposals from the different actors involved and produce an analysis

129 To understand the magnitude of the HIV/AIDS epidemic, please see the UNAIDS, *World AIDS Day Report*, 2011, http://www.unaids.org/en/media/unaids/contentassets/documents/unaidspublication/2011/JC2216_WorldAIDSday_report_2011_en.pdf, accessed January 31, 2012.

130 See, 'The Abuja Declaration on HIV/AIDS, Tuberculosis and Other Related Infectious Diseases' see; available at: www.who.int (last accessed on January 28, 2012).

> of intellectual property rights, innovation, and public health, including the question of appropriate funding and incentive mechanisms for the creation of new medicines and other products against diseases that disproportionately affect developing countries, and to submit a progress report to the Fifty-seventh World Health Assembly.[131]

The mission of the Commission was to review the interfaces and linkages between intellectual property rights, innovation and public health in the light of current evidence and examine in depth how to stimulate the creation of new medicines and other products for diseases that mainly affect developing countries.[132] The Commission presented its final report, including valuable recommendations, in 2006.[133] These included a number of recommendations which relate directly to the interface between intellectual property and public health. These are, *inter alia*:

Countries should seek through patenting and licensing policies to maximize the availability of innovations, including research tools and platform technologies, for the development of products of relevance to public health, particularly to conditions prevalent in developing countries. Public funding bodies should introduce policies for sensible patenting and licensing practices for technologies arising from their funding to promote downstream innovation in health care products.

Patent pools of upstream technologies may be useful in some circumstances to promote innovation relevant to developing countries. WHO and WIPO should consider playing a bigger role in promoting such arrangements, particularly to address diseases that disproportionately affect developing countries.

Developing countries need to consider in their own legislation what form of research exemption might be appropriate in their own circumstances to foster health-related research and innovation.

Countries should provide in their legislation powers to use compulsory licensing, in accordance with the TRIPS agreement, where this power might be useful as one of the means available to promote, *inter alia*, research that is directly relevant to the specific health problems of developing countries.

Governments should remove any tariffs and taxes on healthcare products, where appropriate, in the context of policies to enhance access to medicines. They should also monitor carefully the supply and distribution chain to minimize costs that could adversely influence the prices of medicines.

Developing country governments should make available full and reliable information on patents granted. WHO, in cooperation with WIPO and others, should continue to pursue the establishment of a database of information about

131 The Fifty-Sixth World Health Assembly, Agenda Item 14.9, Intellectual Property, Innovation and Public Health, May 28, 2003.

132 See, 'Public Health, Innovation and Intellectual Property' on the WHO website at: http://www.who.int/phi/about/en (last accessed on January 31, 2012).

133 *Public Health, Innovation and Intellectual Property: Report of the Commission on Intellectual Property Rights, Innovation and Public Health*, WHO, Geneva, 2006.

patents, in order to remove potential barriers to availability and access resulting from uncertainty about the patent status in a country of a given product.

Developing countries need to decide in the light of their own circumstances, what provisions, consistent with the TRIPS agreement, would benefit public health, weighing the positive effects against the negative effects. A public health justification should be required for data protection rules going beyond what is required by the TRIPS agreement. There is unlikely to be such a justification in markets with a limited ability to pay and little innovative capacity. Thus, developing countries should not impose restrictions for the use of or reliance on such data in ways that would exclude fair competition or impede the use of flexibilities built into TRIPS.

Developing countries should adopt or effectively implement competition policies and apply the pro-competitive measures allowed under the TRIPS agreement in order to prevent or remedy anti-competitive practices related to the use of medicinal patents.

Countries should provide in national legislation for measures to encourage generic entry on patent expiry, such as the 'early working' exception, and more generally policies that support greater competition between generics, whether branded or not, as an effective way to enhance access by improving affordability. Restrictions should not be placed on the use of generic names.

Bilateral trade agreements should not seek to incorporate TRIPS-plus protection in ways that may reduce access to medicines in developing countries.

Developed countries, and pharmaceutical companies (including generic producers), should take measures to promote the transfer of technology and local production of pharmaceuticals in developing countries, wherever this makes economic sense and promotes the availability, accessibility, affordability and security of supply of needed products.

WHO should develop a Global Plan of action to secure enhanced and sustainable funding for developing and making accessible products to address diseases that disproportionately affect developing countries.

WHO should continue to monitor, from a public health perspective, the impact of intellectual property rights, and other factors, on the development of new products as well as access to medicines and other health-care products in developing countries.

The work undertaken and accomplished by the Commission has been enormous. The final report touches upon most of the issues generated from the interface between intellectual property and public health. These issues range from components impeding access to medicines to research and innovation in the field of medicine.

The Global Strategy and Plan of Action on Public Health, Innovation and Intellectual Property

The Intergovernmental Working Group on Public Health, Innovation and Intellectual Property (IGWG) was set up in 2006 to draw up a global strategy and plan of action in order to provide a medium-term framework based on the recommendations of the Commission on Intellectual Property, Innovation and Public Health, and to secure, *inter alia*, an enhanced and sustainable basis for needs-driven, essential health research and development relevant to diseases that disproportionately affect developing countries, proposing clear objectives and priorities for research and development, and estimating funding needs in this area.[134] The IGWG on Public Health, Innovation and Intellectual Property held its first session on December 4–8, 2006 in Geneva, Switzerland, with the participation of more than 100 Member States, of which 24 were from the African Region.

The Global Strategy and Plan of Action on Public Health, Innovation and Intellectual Property was adopted at the Sixty-First World Health Assembly, which took place on May 19–24, 2008. The African Group Delegation supported the Global Strategy and Plan of Action in a statement which may be summarized as follows:

> The draft global strategy acknowledged that better understanding of developing countries' health needs and determinants is essential to sustainable research and development on new and existing products.
> Policies that enhance health innovation in developing countries, North–South and South–South cooperation, and support for partnerships in order to build and improve technology transfer related to health innovation are essential.
> Supporting and strengthening health systems, stimulating competition and adopting appropriate pricing and taxation policies for health products are vital.
> The application of international agreements that affect access to health products in developing countries should be regularly monitored.
> Africa welcomed the recommendation concerning the expert working group that would examine financing and coordination of research and development.
> The Member States of the African Region supported the draft resolution and would support implementation of the global strategy and plan of action.
> The Delegation called upon WHO and relevant international organizations and bodies to prioritize the global strategy and to launch activities as soon as possible.

The Global Strategy and Plan of Action established 10 principles to be taken into consideration in the implementation stage. These are:

> WHO shall play a strategic and central role in the relationship between public health and innovation and intellectual property within its mandates

134 See, The Fifty-Ninth World Health Assembly, WHA59.24, 'Public Health, Innovation, Essential Health Research and Intellectual Property Rights: Towards a Global Strategy and Plan of Action', May 27, 2006. See, also, Preamble of Resolution WHA61.21 on Global Strategy and Plan of Action on Public Health, Innovation and Intellectual Property, The Sixty-First World Health Assembly, Geneva, May 19–24, 2008.

(including those contained in relevant Health Assembly resolutions), capacities and constitutional objectives, bearing in mind those of other relevant intergovernmental organizations. In this context, WHO, including its regional and, when appropriate, country offices, needs to strengthen its institutional competencies and relevant programmes in order to play its role in implementing this global strategy with its plan of action.

The enjoyment of the highest attainable standard of health is one of the fundamental rights of every human being without distinction of race, religion, political belief, economic or social condition.

The promotion of technological innovation and the transfer of technology should be pursued by all States and supported by intellectual property rights.

Intellectual property rights do not and should not prevent Member States from taking measures to protect public health.

International negotiations on issues related to intellectual property rights and health should be coherent in their approaches to the promotion of public health.

The strengthening of the innovative capacity of developing countries is essential to respond to the needs of public health.

Research and development of developed countries should better reflect the health needs of developing countries.

The global strategy and the plan of action should promote the development of health products and medical devices needed by Member States, especially developing countries, that are:

developed in an ethical manner
available in sufficient quantities
effective, safe and of good quality
affordable and accessible
used in a rational way.

Intellectual property rights are an important incentive in the development of new health care products. However, this incentive alone does not meet the need for the development of new products to fight diseases where the potential paying market is small or uncertain.

Several factors contribute to the price of health products and medical devices, and public policies should address these factors to increase their affordability and accessibility. Among others, competition and reduction or elimination of import tariffs on these products and devices can contribute to the reduction of prices. Countries should monitor carefully supply and distribution chains and procurement practices to minimize costs that could adversely influence the price of these products and devices.

The Global Strategy and Plan of Action comprises eight elements 'designed to promote innovation, build capacity, improve access and mobilize resources' in the field of public health.[135] These are as follows:

- prioritizing research and development needs;
- promoting research and development;
- building and improving innovative capacity;
- transfer of technology;
- application and management of intellectual property;
- improving delivery and access;
- ensuring sustainable financing mechanisms;
- establishing monitoring and reporting systems.

African positions are reflected in the report of the Regional Consultation on Public Health, Innovation and Intellectual Property that was held in Brazzaville, Congo, in September 2007 in the framework of the draft Global Strategy and Plan of Action discussions.[136] These positions are presented following the summary of each element of the Plan of Action in the following sections.

Prioritizing research and development needs Actions to be taken are as follows:

(1.1) mapping global research and development with a view to identifying gaps in research and development on diseases that disproportionately affect developing countries

(1.2) formulating explicit prioritized strategies for research and development at country and regional and interregional levels

(1.3) encouraging research and development in traditional medicine in accordance with national priorities and legislation, and taking into account the relevant international instruments, including, as appropriate, those concerning traditional knowledge and the rights of indigenous peoples.

The African Regional Group takes the following positions:

> Regarding the definition of Type I, II and III diseases, currently 14 diseases are targeted. Member States should be able either to expand or narrow the list of diseases as appropriate;

135 See, 'The Global Strategy and Plan of Action on Public Health, Innovation and Intellectual Property' on the WHO website: http://www.who.int/phi/implementation/phi_globstat_action/en/index.html, accessed January 31, 2012.

136 See, Report of the Regional Consultation on Public Health, Innovation and Intellectual Property, WHO Regional Office for Africa, September 3–5, 2007, Brazzaville, Congo.

Research and development carried out by means of public funding should not be patented;
Disease determinants have not been followed through;
Biotechnology should be brought into the agenda;
There is progress with compound libraries, but more still needs to be done. Traditional medicines and biotechnologies may need another library;
Some of the progress indicators are not clear; terms such as 'accessible' and 'affordable' should be clearly defined.

Promoting research and development Actions to be taken are as follows:

(2.1) supporting governments to develop or improve national health research programmes and establish, where appropriate, strategic research networks to facilitate better coordination of stakeholders in this area
(2.2) promoting upstream research and product development in developing countries
(2.3) improving cooperation, participation and coordination of health and biomedical research and development
(2.4) promoting greater access to knowledge and technology relevant to meet public health needs of developing countries
(2.5) establishing and strengthening national and regional coordinating bodies on research and development.

The African Regional Group takes the following positions:

Infrastructure must be built;
Developing countries as well as developed countries should commit to fund R&D;
Setting up new research centers and strengthening existing ones are essential;
There is a need to engage with the pharmaceutical industry;
It is essential to decide whether or not R&D treaties are required;
Existing regional and sub-regional institutions and global forums to coordinate health research must be strengthened;
There is a need to find creative incentive mechanisms for research;
TRIPs flexibilities only apply to WTO Members;
Ethical review bodies should be established during development.

Building and improving innovative capacity Actions to be taken are as follows:

(3.1) building capacity of developing countries to meet research and development needs for health products

(3.2) framing, developing and supporting effective policies that promote the development of capacities for health innovation
(3.3) providing support for improving innovative capacity in accordance with the needs of developing countries
(3.4) supporting policies that will promote innovation based on traditional medicine within an evidence-based framework in accordance with national priorities and taking into account the relevant provisions of relevant international instruments
(3.5) developing and implementing, where appropriate, possible incentive schemes for health related innovation.

The African Regional Group takes the following positions:

There is a need for both qualitative and quantitative assessment of trained researchers;
Indigenous knowledge must be protected to promote ownership of innovation;
The pharmaceutical industry is already contributing to chemical libraries;
Use must be made of Regional Economic Communities for training to ensure efficiency;
Centers of excellence need to be explored.

Transfer of technology Actions to be taken are as follows:

(4.1) promoting transfer of technology and the production of health products in developing countries
(4.2) supporting improved collaboration and coordination of technology transfer for health products, bearing in mind different levels of development
(4.3) developing possible new mechanisms to promote transfer of and access to key health-related technologies.

The African Regional Group takes the following positions:

Technology transfer audits are required;
In collaboration with the pharmaceutical industry, tertiary institutions must also consider establishing technology transfer offices;
Principles governing the transfer of technology and preferential arrangements for developing countries are required;
Specific action should be taken to develop a list of essential technologies in relation to research and production of medicines relevant to developing countries. Particular attention should be paid to technologies of general application and which are production related. It is proposed that WHO should solicit, receive and document difficulties faced by developing countries and their entities in access;

Preferential treatment for developing countries and least developed countries is required;
The appropriateness of patent pools for medicines and other health technologies needs to be investigated;
The issue of technology transfer needs to be investigated for effectiveness;
Appropriateness and remedial measures should be taken, if required. (as revised)
Appropriate remedial measures should be taken.

Application and management of intellectual property Actions to be taken are as follows:

(5.1) supporting information sharing and capacity building in the application and management of intellectual property with respect to health-related innovation and the promotion of public health in developing countries
(5.2) providing as appropriate, upon request, in collaboration with other competent international organizations technical support
(5.3) exploring and, where appropriate, promoting possible incentive schemes for research and development on Type II and Type III diseases and on developing countries' specific research and development needs in relation to Type I diseases.

The African Regional Group takes the following positions:

The issue is not just about management of IP but about the 'right' type of IP policy to promote public health;
A better title for this element would be 'Management of IP from a Public Health Perspective';
Training in patent examination, negotiation skills, etc. is required;
An international legal instrument is needed to facilitate protection of traditional medicine and ensure appropriate benefit sharing;
Actions to enable access should be included;
Reducing IP protection is not a magic bullet. A balance of several other issues should be considered.

Improving delivery and access Actions to be taken are as follows:

(6.1) encouraging increased investment in the health-delivery infrastructure and financing of health products in order to strengthen the health system
(6.2) establishing and strengthening mechanisms to improve ethical review and regulate the quality, safety and efficacy of health products and medical devices
(6.3) promoting competition to improve availability and affordability of health products consistent with public health policies and needs.

The African Regional Group takes the following positions:

> TRIPs-plus and bilateral agreements should not be used to hinder broader access;
> Good Manufacturing Practices should apply to both developing and developed countries;
> Funding agencies must invest in health delivery infrastructure;
> Attention must be paid to the entire supply chain (cost, efficiency, effectiveness).

Ensuring sustainable financing mechanisms Actions to be taken are as follows:

> (7.1) endeavouring to secure adequate and sustainable financing for research and development, and improve coordination of its use, where feasible and appropriate, in order to address the health needs of developing countries
> (7.2) facilitating the maximum use of, and complementing as appropriate, existing financing, including that through public-private and product development partnerships, in order to develop and deliver safe, effective and affordable health products and medical devices.

The African Regional Group takes the following positions:

> A structure for the development of a resource mobilization plan is essential to enable easy access;
> Affordability is the major bottleneck;
> Financing must be linked to R&D incentives;
> Other funding mechanisms (e.g. prize funds, global fund, government contributions etc.) need to be explored. Identification of targeted projects will facilitate implementation.

Establishing monitoring and reporting systems Action to be taken is:

> (8.1) measuring performance and progress towards objectives contained in the strategy and plan of action.

The African Regional Group points out the need to ensure that the indicators are in some way measurable.

The Sixty-First World Health Assembly urged the Director General of WHO to undertake, *inter alia*, the following actions in implementing the Global Strategy and Plan of Action:

> to provide support for Member States, upon request, in implementing the global strategy and plan of action on public health, innovation and intellectual property and in monitoring and evaluating its implementation;

to coordinate with other relevant international intergovernmental organizations, including WIPO, WTO and UNCTAD, to effectively implement the global strategy and plan of action;

to reflect, as appropriate, the global strategy and plan of action on public health, innovation and intellectual property in the further development of WHO's research strategy;

to monitor performance and progress in implementing the global strategy and plan of action on public health, innovation and intellectual property, and to report progress to the Sixty-third World Health Assembly through the Executive Board, and subsequently every two years, until the fulfillment of the time frame, to the Health Assembly, through the Executive Board;

to establish urgently a results-oriented and time-limited expert working group to examine current financing and coordination of research and development, as well as proposals for new and innovative sources of funding to stimulate research and development related to Type II and Type III diseases and the specific research and development needs of developing countries in relation to Type I diseases, and open to consideration of proposals from Member States, and to submit a progress report to the Sixty-second World Health Assembly and the final report to the Sixty-third World Health Assembly through the Executive Board;

to reflect, as appropriate, the global strategy and plan of action on public health, innovation and intellectual property in the further development of WHO's research strategy.

In the course of implementation of the Global Strategy and Plan of Action, the African Network for Drugs and Diagnostics Innovation was launched in October 2008 with support from the UNICEF/UNDP/World Bank/WHO Special Programme for Research and Training in Tropical Diseases and from several African institutions. The Network aims to promote and sustain African-led R&D innovation and to support capacity and infrastructure development in Africa. Network activities to strengthen health innovation in Africa could be a critical regional contribution toward the implementation of the Global Strategy and Plan of Action.[137]

Pursuant to the Global Strategy and Plan of Action, the Sixty-Third World Health Assembly urged the Director General to establish a Consultative Expert Working Group on Research and Development: Financing and Coordination,[138] which will, *inter alia*, take forward the work of the Expert Working Group established at the Sixty-First World Health Assembly; deepen the analysis of the proposals in the Expert Working Group's report; and examine the appropriateness of different research and development financing approaches and the feasibility

137 WHO, Executive Board, EB124/16, Public Health, Innovation and Intellectual Property: Global Strategy and Plan of Action, Report by the Secretariat, 124th Session, November 20, 2008.

138 WHO, Sixty-Third World Health Assembly, Geneva, May 17–21, 2010.

of implementation of these approaches in each of the six WHO regions, with sub-regional analysis, as appropriate. The Director General was also requested to provide, upon request, within available resources dedicated to the financing of the Consultative Expert Working Group, technical and financial support for regional consultations, including meetings, in order to seek regional views to help inform the work of the Consultative Expert Working Group.

Collaboration among WHO, WTO, and WIPO on public health and patents

The Director General was urged under the Global Strategy and Plan of Action on Public Health, Innovation and Intellectual Property to coordinate with other relevant international intergovernmental organizations, including WIPO, the WTO, and UNCTAD, to effectively implement the Global Strategy and Plan of Action. Since the adoption of the Global Strategy and Plan of Action, the first three of these institutions have been involved in projects alone or in collaboration with pharmaceutical companies or various donors. In addition, joint technical symposia have also been held to discuss public health and IP matters.

The WHO, WIPO, and the WTO jointly organized a Symposium at the technical level on 'Access to Medicines: Pricing and Procurement Practices' on July 16, 2010 at the WTO Headquarters in Geneva. The purpose of the Symposium was to learn what international and regional agencies have experienced in the pricing and procurement of medicines as important determinants of access. It also provided an opportunity to discuss where to obtain information on access to medicines, their prices, and their availability. The core questions were about drug procurement, pricing, and relevant intellectual property issues.[139]

WHO, WIPO, and WTO held a second technical Symposium on 'Access to Medicines, Patent Information and Freedom to Operate' on February 18, 2011 at the WHO Headquarters in Geneva. The Symposium addressed the growing importance of patent information for public health in the fields of freedom to operate strategies, procurement of medicines, technology transfer, and setting of research priorities and strategies. The event raised awareness and provided insights on the availability and use of reliable patent information in the endeavor of ensuring access to medicines.[140]

Draft Resolution on Counterfeit Medical Products

Counterfeit medical products pose a significant danger to public health in both developing and developed countries. The distribution of counterfeit medical products has become increasingly extensive over the last three decades. They are

139 See, 'WHO-WIPO-WTO Holding Technical Symposium on Access to Medicines in July 2010', http://www.wto.org/english/news_e/news10_e/trip_21jun10_e.htm, accessed January 31, 2012.

140 See, 'WHO, WIPO, WTO to Hold 2nd Technical Symposium on Patents, Access to Medicines', http://www.wto.org/english/news_e/news11_e/trip_21jan11_e.htm, accessed January 31, 2012.

also a significant cause of death in many developing countries, including those in Africa.

A counterfeit medicine is one which is deliberately and fraudulently mislabeled as to its identity and/or source. Counterfeiting can apply to both branded and generic products, and counterfeit products may include products that contain either the correct ingredients or the wrong ingredients, those that have no active ingredients or insufficient active ingredient, or those sold with fake packaging.[141]

In light of this situation, 40 African countries proposed a draft resolution on counterfeit medical products at the Sixty-Third World Health Assembly that took place in May 2010.[142] The origin of this draft may be traced back to the Sixty-First World Health Assembly in 2008,[143] where it was initially introduced by four African countries—Gambia, Ghana, Nigeria, and Tunisia—and the United Arab Emirates. The Preamble of the draft resolution states that the Sixty-Third World Health Assembly was:

> Concerned about the situation in which counterfeit medical products continue to move in international commerce, representing a major threat to public health, especially in the poorer areas of developing countries where regulatory capacities and law enforcement authorities are weak, and in which counterfeit medical products pose a challenge to the credibility and effectiveness of health systems;
> Recognizing that the primary focus of combating the manufacture, distribution and use of counterfeit medical products is the protection of public health and that the main victims of counterfeiters are patients and the general public;
> Recognizing the importance of ensuring that combating counterfeit medical products does not result in hindering the availability of legitimate generic medicines;
> Requesting governments, pharmaceutical manufacturers and other concerned parties to cooperate in the detection, investigation and prevention of the increasing incidence of counterfeited or other substandard medical products moving in international commerce.

Member States of WHO were urged to do the following:

> (1) to reaffirm their commitment to develop, implement and monitor national policies and to take all necessary measures in order to ensure access to medical products that meet regulatory standards;

141 See, Report of the Situation of Counterfeit Medicines based on Data Collection Tool, WHO Regions for Africa and Eastern Mediterranean, 2010, WHO Doc. WHO/ACM/3.

142 WHO, Sixty-Third World Health Assembly, Geneva, May 17–21, 2010.

143 WHO, Sixty-First World Health Assembly, Geneva, May 19–24, 2008.

(2) to establish and enforce legislation and regulations that prevent counterfeit medical products from being manufactured, exported, imported or traded in international transactions as well as to regulate and monitor the supply and distribution systems;

(3) to establish effective mechanisms of coordination and collaboration, including exchange of information among health, law enforcement and other relevant authorities in order to improve prevention, detection, investigation and prosecution of cases of counterfeit medical products;

(4) to promote awareness among health professionals and consumers of the risks posed by the use of counterfeit medical products including those acquired through unauthorized outlets including Internet sites.

The Director General of WHO was requested to do the following:

(1) to continue to address counterfeit medical products as an integral part, within the existing framework, of standard setting for quality, safety and efficacy;

(2) to provide support to Member States in developing and implementing policies and programmes aimed at combating counterfeit medical products, including facilitating the exchange of information at the international level and the development of tools, guidelines, training and awareness initiatives, and methodology for evaluation and monitoring;

(3) to continue the development and dissemination of independent and timely information on instances of counterfeit medical products;

(4) to cooperate with Member States, at their request, and with international organizations and other relevant parties in detecting, monitoring and analysing cases of counterfeit medical products and their impact on public health;

(5) to report to the Sixty-fifth World Health Assembly, through the Executive Board, both on progress achieved and problems encountered in the implementation of this resolution.

This Resolution on Counterfeit Medical Products is a great achievement of African countries in the process of combating the widespread expansion of the counterfeiting business which poses a real threat to public health. It was one of the initiatives that formed the basis of the Decision taken by the Sixty-Third World Health Assembly to establish a time-limited and results-oriented working group on substandard/spurious/falsely-labeled/falsified/counterfeit medical products.

Conclusion

WHO has taken a number of initiatives that have facilitated access to medicines by developing countries. The final report, including its recommendations, of the Commission on Intellectual Property, Innovation and Public Health introduced new ways of resolving the issues relating to the relationship between patents and public health. The adoption of the Global Strategy and Plan of Action on Public Health, Innovation and Intellectual Property is another tool to implement objectives already adopted in 2006 to assist developing countries and enhance their research capacities in pharmaceutical field.

The Abuja Declaration on HIV/AIDS, Tuberculosis and Other Related Infectious Diseases sent a very strong message to the world community in general and WHO in particular to take action and be part of the solution and not act only as an observer to the situation facing African countries. Furthermore, the African Group played a very active role in the initiatives and actions undertaken by WHO. In the negotiation process of the Global Strategy and Plan of Action, proposals from the African Regional Office shed significant light on some of the issues discussed.

In addition, on the initiative of the African Group a draft resolution on Counterfeit Medical Products has been discussed in WHO since 2008. The fight against counterfeit medical products is among the priorities of the region, and the African countries support the mechanisms put into place to carry on this task.

The number of people infected with HIV/AIDS has declined dramatically since the height of the epidemic in 1997. Although the number of infected people is still high in sub-Saharan Africa, the drop in that number has been significant in the last five years.[144] Measures taken by WHO Member States to fight against HIV/AIDS have contributed to this success, and the collaboration among international organizations has facilitated the implementation of these measures in the field.

The African region is still behind other regions in the field of research and development in the medical and pharmaceutical areas and there is a need to prioritize positive action in this regard.

Patents and Public Health within WIPO

Currently, WIPO deals with patents and health through the tripartite scheme with WHO and the WTO and by means of significant projects in the health sector and within the Standing Committee on the Law of Patents (SCP), where two papers initiated by the African Group and the United States of America have been put on the table.

Tripartite cooperation between WHO–WIPO–WTO

WIPO has been always invited, as an observer, to a number of WHO meetings and negotiation processes where it has made substantive contributions. The main ones are the following:

- WHO Commission on Intellectual Property Rights, Innovation and Public

144 See, UNAIDS, *World AIDS Day Report*, 2011, p. 6. The total number of new HIV infections in sub-Saharan Africa has dropped by more than 26 percent, down to 1.9 million from the estimated 2.6 million at the height of the epidemic in 1997. In 22 sub-Saharan countries, HIV incidence declined by more than 25 percent between 2001 and 2009.

Health (CIPIH);

- Intergovernmental Working Group on Public Health, Innovation and Intellectual Property;
- Global Strategy and Plan of Action on Public Health, Innovation and Intellectual Property;
- Pandemic Influenza Preparedness: Sharing of Influenza Viruses and Access to Vaccines and other Benefits (PIP).

The WHO–WIPO–WTO tripartite cooperation is the result of the Global Strategy and Plan of Action adopted by the Sixty-First World Health Assembly in May 2008. Pursuant to this, WHO, WIPO, and the WTO have strengthened their collaboration to jointly discuss issues pertaining to the relationship between patents and public health. The three institutions have jointly organized symposia at the technical level covering IP and public health themes. The interface between intellectual property, trade rules, and public health has occupied center stage in the debates.

Patents and health in the WIPO Standing Committee on the Law of Patents (SCP) Two proposals from the African Group, made jointly with the Development Agenda Group, and from the United States have been put on the table in the SCP.

Joint proposal by the African Group and the Development Agenda Group, SCP Work Program on Patents and Health, SCP 16, May 16–20, 2011[145] In the context of the work of the SCP, the African Group and the Development Agenda Group submitted a proposal on the work program on patents and health in May 2011. This was an outgrowth of the African Group's proposal at the Fifteenth Session of the SCP that the Committee should undertake a work program on patents and health. Before introducing the work program, the paper outlined the context by recalling key messages included in the 2001 Doha Declaration on the TRIPs Agreement and Public Health, the 2008 WHO Global Strategy and Plan of Action, and the so-called flexibilities contained in the TRIPs Agreement. The proposed work program seeks to enhance the capacities of Member States, and particularly developing countries and least developed countries (LDCs), to adapt their patent regimes to make full use of the flexibilities available in the international patent system to promote public policy priorities related to public health.

The work program is composed of three components as follows:

1. the elaboration of studies to be commissioned by the WIPO Secretariat, following consultations with the Member States at the SCP, from renowned independent experts;

145 Standing Committee on the Law of Patents, Proposal Submitted by the Delegation of South Africa on behalf of the African Group and the Development Agenda Group, Sixteenth Session, Geneva, May 16–20, 2011.

2. information exchange among Member States and from leading experts in the field; and
3. the provision of technical assistance to Member States, and particularly developing countries and least developed countries (LDCs), in relevant areas, and building upon work undertaken in the first two elements of the work program.

At the Seventeenth Session of the SCP that took place December 5–9, 2011, written comments from Member States and observers on this proposal (Patents and Heath) were received by the Secretariat.[146]

The African work program was welcomed by many Member States, including observers, although some industrial countries maintained that WIPO should deal with issues relating to patents and public health only if there is an added value to the discussion. Some developing countries, as well as some observers, asserted that it is not a matter of WIPO adding value to the discussion on patents and health. The issue of patents is interlinked with the ability to take measures to protect health as noted in TRIPs Articles 7 and 8 as well as in the Doha Declaration on the TRIPs Agreement and Public Health. They therefore felt that it was time to reflect on current trends in patent law and whether these are advantageous or disadvantageous for health.[147]

In addition to the three components of the work program, the Third World Network (TWN) suggested additional activities to be considered:

(i) Establish a panel of experts on patents and development to review patent provisions in bilateral and plurilateral trade and investment agreements and its impact on public health. To facilitate the review, public hearings and/or other forms of consultations with Member states and civil society should be conducted.

(ii) Conduct a study on patenting strategies and practices employed by pharmaceutical companies to prevent or delay generic competition. To facilitate information gathering and the preparation of study, Member states and civil society should be given the opportunity to make written submissions.

(iii) Conduct a web-based hearing on patent examination practices to facilitate the grant good quality patents and prevent the grant of frivolous pharmaceutical patents. The hearing could be followed up with a discussion in the SCP.

146 Standing Committee on the Law of Patents, Seventeenth Session, Geneva, December 5–9, 2011.

147 Standing Committee on the Law of Patents, Patents and Health: Comments Received from Members and Observers of the Standing Committee on the Law of Patents (SCP), Seventeenth Session, Geneva, December 5–9, 2011.

(iv) Set up a database to facilitate prompt dissemination of information pertaining to pre-and post grant oppositions to patent applications and grants related to pharmaceutical products filed in WIPO member states. The database should be publicly accessible and contain information on the patent oppositions filed including the rationale for opposition, responses to the oppositions, appeals filed (if any) and the final decision made on the opposition.

(v) Compile information on the legislative implementation of the 30th August 2003 Decision by WIPO Member states and to convene a discussion panel at the next SCP on the operation and use of the 30th August 2003 decision of the World Trade Organization.[148]

Patents and Health: the US proposal[149] The US paper proposed non-exhaustive alternative approaches to foster the development of new medicines and delivery for countries in need. These approaches are, *inter alia*:

- voluntary licensing and funding schemes
  - patent pools;
  - Re:Search consortium at WIPO for neglected diseases;
  - global funding;
  - advanced market commitments;
  - GlaxoSmithKline malaria vaccine partnership;
  - access program;
- tiered pricing;
- efficient regulatory review;
- enforcement.
- The paper recommended that the SCP carry out two studies:
- a study on the impact of patent protection in promoting the development of life saving medicines; and
- a study on factors affecting availability of medicines that are not related to the patent system.

The United States made three proposals contributing to the work program, as follows:

- Inviting the WHO to make a presentation to the SCP on the availability of generic medicines in DC/LDCs, on the non-patent barriers to availability of safe and effective medicines that are encountered in many countries,

148 Ibid.

149 Standing Committee on the Law of Patents, Patents and Health: Proposal by the Delegation of the United States of America, Seventeenth Session, Geneva, December 5–9, 2011.

and on the effect of falsified medicines, both generic and patented, on the availability of proper medicines.

- Conducting a comprehensive study on the positive impact of patent systems in providing lifesaving medicines to developing countries.
- Conducting a comprehensive study to examine the availability of lifesaving medicines that are not protected by patents, and the reasons for their lack of availability.

Other Contributions of WIPO in the Field of Patents and Health

In order to facilitate the sharing of knowledge and the adaptation, transfer, and diffusion of technologies, WIPO has been developing platforms that build on partnerships and collaborations between technology holders and technology users.[150]

In the area of health, WIPO Re:Search–Sharing Innovation in the Fight Against Neglected Tropical Diseases was formed in 2011 and creates a partnership among WIPO, pharmaceutical companies, research and academic institutions, and a non-governmental organization, BIO Ventures for Global Health. It provides access to intellectual property for pharmaceutical compounds, technologies, and know-how and data available for research and development for neglected tropical diseases, tuberculosis, and malaria.

In addition, WIPO is developing a web-based patent data retrieval system, with the working title 'WIPO Essential', that will provide access to patent information related to essential health-related technologies on a jurisdiction-by-jurisdiction basis.

Conclusion

The Global Strategy and Plan of Action adopted by the WHO World Health Assembly in May 2008 helped to strengthen the tripartite collaboration between WHO, WIPO, and WTO.

The year 2011 may be considered the turning point. The African Group again proposed that the Standing Committee on the Law of Patents deal with the relationship between patents and health and this initiative was welcomed by many Member States. The US proposal submitted in the Seventeenth Session of the SCP has contributed to the debate on health issues.

The work program proposed by the African Group (with the joint sponsorship of the Development Agenda Group) was supported by several countries. The United States has requested that a number of studies be undertaken. If adopted, this work program will open another window for WIPO to closely examine the relevant issues.

150 Standing Committee on the Law of Patents, WIPO Activities on Patents and Health, Seventeenth Session, Geneva, December 5–9, 2011.

Exceptions and Limitations to Copyright

Exceptions and limitations to copyright to serve various purposes have been acknowledged by all copyright laws in accordance with the Berne Convention. Given the discretion provided to Member States, the exceptions and limitations are not always the same and the definitions of terms may vary from one country to another.

Background and Premises to the Debates

The delegation of Chile in a communication dated October 28, 2004, requested that the subject of exceptions and limitations to copyright and related rights for the purposes of education, libraries, and disabled persons be included on the agenda of the Twelfth Session of the WIPO Standing Committee on Copyright and Related Rights (SCCR).[151]

Further, as a follow-up to its first suggestion, at the Thirteenth Session of the SCCR in November 2005, the Delegation of Chile submitted a proposal on the analysis of exceptions and limitations.[152]

The Chilean paper proposed three areas of work to be undertaken in the SCCR:

1. Identification, from the national intellectual property systems of Member States, of national models and practices concerning exceptions and limitations.
2. Analysis of the exceptions and limitations needed to promote creation and innovation and the dissemination of developments stemming therefrom.
3. Establishment of agreement on exceptions and limitations for purposes of public interest that must be envisaged as a minimum in all national legislations for the benefit of the community; especially to give access to the most vulnerable or socially prioritized sectors.

The paper further maintained that comparison of the various national legislations revealed a disparity in the scope of exceptions and limitations to copyright, particularly in the area of digital uses. Consequently, within a given category of exceptions, substantial differences may exist in the way those exceptions are handled, both in terms of depth and scope.[153]

---

151 *Proposal by Chile on the Subject 'Exceptions and Limitations to Copyright and Related Rights'*, Twelfth Session of the WIPO Standing Committee on Copyright and Related Rights (SCCR), Geneva, November 17–19, 2004, Document prepared by the Secretariat, SCCR/12/3, November 4, 2004.

152 *Proposal by Chile on the Analysis of Exceptions and Limitations*, Thirteenth Session of the WIPO Standing Committee on Copyright and Related Rights (SCCR), Geneva, November 21–23, 2005, SCCR/13/5, November 22, 2005.

153 Ibid.

In a globalized world, this difference in handling exceptions and limitations at national level may constitute an obstacle for both the disclosure and transfer of ideas and also for the acceptable use of works by disabled persons, libraries, and public archives.[154]

The lack of a minimum common international standard for exceptions and limitations can inhibit the public availability of works which incorporate other works or are derived directly therefrom. This risk affects the dissemination of works produced today under both traditional and open licenses, thus affecting both models for exploiting works currently in use.[155]

Based on the Chilean initiative and proposal, several studies on exceptions and limitations were commissioned by WIPO. At the Sixteenth Session of the SCCR in March 2008, a proposal was received from Brazil, Chile, Nicaragua, and Uruguay concerning the SCCR's work related to exceptions and limitations.[156] This proposal first stressed Chile's earlier proposal to achieve a consensus on minimum mandatory exceptions and limitations particularly with regard to educational activities, people with disabilities, libraries and archives, as well as exceptions that foster technological innovation.[157] It went on to emphasize that while the set of mandatory minimum exceptions and limitations would be common to all Member States, any established baseline would not preclude Member States from adopting broader exceptions in the same or similar subject areas in accordance with their respective legal systems and international laws.[158] The proposal requested further studies on specific issues on exceptions and limitations as follows:

- How do educators use copyrighted works for the purpose of education?
- How do educators perceive current copyright norms affect their ability to provide educational services?
- What are the requirements under which educational institutions and individuals providing education, or receiving education in both developing and developed countries, can qualify for uncompensated utilization of works?
- What are the conditions or requirements under which compulsory licensing systems for educational purposes could be implemented in developing countries?

---

154 Ibid.

155 Ibid.

156 *Proposal by Brazil, Chile, Nicaragua and Uruguay for Work Related to Exceptions and Limitations*, Sixteenth Session of the WIPO Standing Committee on Copyright and Related Rights (SCCR), Geneva, March 10–12, 2008, WIPO Doc. SCCR/16/2, July 17, 2008.

157 Ibid. Examples of what are considered mandatory exceptions or user rights would be the right for the disabled community to export and import works produced under a copyright exception, or an exception to the public lending right in favor of libraries, when such right has been recognized.

158 Ibid.

- How can remuneration for compulsory licenses that are justified for educational purposes be reasonably calculated and fairly distributed?[159]

Proposals on Exceptions and Limitations and Debated Issues from 2009 to 2012

Many proposals and draft treaties or international instruments have been submitted to the SCCR by the Member States since 2009. Most of them have not been submitted in isolation, but the newer ones have been influenced by the former ones. At the commencement of the debates, countries were divided on the scope of exceptions and limitations. Some Groups proposed that the scope of coverage be limited to exceptions and limitations for visually impaired persons (VIP), whist some other Groups, mainly the African Group, favored a more comprehensive approach to include exceptions and limitations not only for VIP but also for educational and research institutions, libraries, and archives. Several proposals were put on the table, and Member States were divided on how to proceed. A common approach was required.

The following discussion will address these issues by subject matter in accordance with the work plan adopted by the SCCR at its Twenty-First Session in November 2010, even though some of the proposals which are on the table date back to 2009 and early 2010. The adopted conclusions of the Twenty-First Session read as follows:[160]

> Bearing in mind
> - the Development Agenda recommendations;
> - the agreement reached during the 19th session of the SCCR on December 2009, namely that 'all the aspects concerning limitations and exceptions will be maintained on the Agenda of the twentieth session of the SCCR with the aim of establishing a work program concerning those limitations and exceptions, following a global and inclusive approach, and taking into account their equal importance and different level of maturity, while recognizing the need for concurrently addressing all the issues with a view to achieving progress on all of them';
> - the international conventions in the field of copyright and related rights, including the SCCR's authority to make a recommendation to convene a Diplomatic Conference.

159 Ibid.

160 Conclusions of the Twenty-First Session of the SCCR, Geneva, November 8–12, 2010. See also, Report on the Work of the Standing Committee on Copyright and Related Rights, July 26, 2011, Fortieth (Twentieth Ordinary) Session, Geneva, September 26 to October 5, 2011, WIPO Doc. WO/GA/40/6.

> Following a global and inclusive approach, the SCCR agrees to work towards an appropriate international legal instrument or instruments[161] (whether model law, joint recommendation, treaty and/or other forms), taking into account the proposals already tabled or any additional submissions.
> The SCCR agrees to the following work program on exceptions and limitations for the two-year period 2011–2012:
> 1. Recognizing the need to advance the more mature areas, the Committee will undertake text-based work with the objective of reaching agreement on appropriate exceptions and limitations for persons with print disabilities and other reading disabilities. In a similar manner, the Committee will undertake text-based work on appropriate exceptions and limitations for libraries, archives, educational, teaching and research institutions, and persons with other disabilities.
> 2. The Committee will follow, as set out in this Annex, a clearly defined work program for the two-year period 2011–2012.[162]

According to the timetable on the SCCR Agenda Item on Limitations and Exceptions annexed to the Conclusions of the Twenty-First Session, the following timeframe was approved by the SCCR:

- SCCR/22 session, May/June 2011: limitations and exceptions for persons with print and other reading disabilities;
- SCCR/23 session, November 2011: limitations and exceptions for libraries and archives;
- SCCR/24 session, May/June 2012 (actually July): limitations and exceptions for educational, teaching and research institutions and persons with other disabilities.

This timetable was respected in 2011 and 2012. A new timeframe was agreed by the SCCR in July 2012 and approved by the WIPO General Assembly in October 2012 as follows:[163]

1. With regard to exceptions and limitations to copyright for visually impaired persons/persons with print disabilities, it was recommended to

161 This is without prejudice to any other process under negotiation in other WIPO bodies.

162 Conclusions of the Twenty-First Session of the SCCR, Geneva, November 8–12, 2010. See also, Report on the Work of the Standing Committee on Copyright and Related Rights, July 26, 2011, Fortieth (Twentieth Extraordinary) Session, Geneva, September 26 to October 5, 2011, WIPO Doc. WO/GA/40/6.

163 Report on the Work of the Standing Committee on Copyright and Related Rights, August 13, 2012, Forty-First (Twenty-First Extraordinary) Session, Geneva, October 1 to 9, 2012, WIPO Doc. WO/GA/41/17.

hold an inter-sessional meeting of the SCCR between the 2012 General Assembly and the Twenty-Fifth Session of the SCCR (actually October 17-19, 2012), followed by the Twenty-Fifth Session of SCCR from November 19 to 23, 2012; and that the General Assembly would convene an extraordinary session to make a decision on whether to convene a diplomatic conference in 2013.

2. In respect to exceptions and limitations to copyright for library and archives, the target is to submit recommendations to the General Assembly by the Twenty-Eighth Session of the SCCR in 2014.
3. For exceptions and limitations to copyright for educational and research institutions and persons with other disabilities, the deadline for submission of recommendations to the General Assembly is fixed for the Thirtieth Session of the SCCR in 2015.

In the following discussion, the first part will deal with exceptions and limitations for visually impaired persons/persons with print disabilities and other reading disabilities; the second part will address exceptions and limitations for libraries and archives; the third part will cover exceptions and limitations for educational, teaching, and research institutions and persons with other disabilities; and the fourth part will discuss the African proposal which is also considered as an integral part of each of the exceptions and limitations to copyright covered under different headings.

Exceptions and limitations for visually impaired persons/persons with print disabilities and other reading disabilities

This segment of exceptions and limitations is the most mature in terms of negotiations in comparison with those regarding exceptions and limitations for libraries and archives and for education, teaching and research. In the beginning of the discussion on exceptions and limitations to copyright for visually impaired persons, no one could predict the current status of development. In the near future, an international instrument will be adopted to provide more access to visually impaired persons to works which are not for the moment accessible to them for a variety of reasons. As historical background, it is worth recalling that Member States of WIPO made several proposals, and actually the proposal of the Chair has become the draft international instrument negotiated by Member States to produce a final result. Before analyzing the draft text, it is worth looking at the main proposals relating to copyright limitations and exceptions for the visually impaired persons/persons with print disabilities and other persons with print disabilities that were submitted to the SCCR. These are:

- Proposal by Brazil, Ecuador and Paraguay, Relating to Limitations and Exceptions: Treaty Proposed by the World Blind Union (WBU) (WIPO Doc. SCCR/18/5; hereafter 'Proposal of Brazil, Ecuador and Paraguay, also endorsed by Mexico');

- Draft Proposal of the United States of America for a Consensus Instrument (WIPO Doc. SCCR/20/10; hereafter 'Proposal of the United States of America'); and
- Draft Joint Recommendation concerning the improved access to works protected by copyright for persons with a print disability (European Union) (WIPO Doc. SCCR/20/12; hereafter 'Proposal of the European Union').

The draft WIPO Treaty on Exceptions and Limitations for the Disabled, Educational and Research Institutions, Libraries and Archive Centers proposed by the African Group incorporates the three segments of exceptions and limitations. Given its nature, it will be treated separately at the end of this section even though the part related to the exceptions and limitations for VIP has been discussed and covered by the working document produced by the Chair of the SCCR.

As a result of the negotiations, the Working Document on an International Instrument on Limitations and Exceptions for Visually Impaired Persons/Persons with Print Disabilities[164] was produced by the Chair (hereafter 'Proposal of the Chair.').

Proposal of Brazil, Ecuador and Paraguay[165] At the Eighteenth Session of the SCCR in May 2009, a proposal by Brazil, Ecuador, and Paraguay relating to limitations and exceptions to copyright and endorsing the treaty proposed by the World Blind Union (WBU) was received. This proposal was also later endorsed by Mexico.

The proposed Treaty, entitled WIPO Treaty for Improved Access for Blind, Visually Impaired and other Reading Disabled Persons, covers, *inter alia*, the following matters: purpose, nature and scope of obligations; relations to other agreements; limitations and exceptions to exclusive rights under copyright; acknowledgment and moral rights; circumvention of technological measures; relationship with contracts; imports and exports of works; notice to right owners for commercial reproduction and distribution of works; database on availability of works; remuneration for commercial exploitation of works; orphaned works; respect for privacy; limitations and exceptions applied to non-copyrighted elements of databases; and disabilities covered.

The proposed treaty defines a visually impaired person in Article 15 as:

> • a person who is blind; or
> • a person who has a visual impairment which cannot be improved by the use of corrective lenses to give visual function substantially equivalent to that of a

---

164 WIPO Doc. SCCR/22/16, as revised.

165 *Proposal by Brazil, Ecuador and Paraguay, relating to Limitations and Exceptions, Treaty proposed by the World Blind Union (WBU)*, Eighteenth Session of the WIPO Standing Committee on Copyright and Related Rights (SCCR), Geneva, May 25–29, 2009, WIPO Doc. SCCR/18/5, May 25, 2009.

> person who has no visual impairment and so is unable to access any copyright work to substantially the same degree as a person without a disability.

Under the same provision, Contracting Parties are given full discretion to extend the application of the treaty to persons with any other disability who, due to that disability, need an accessible format to access a copyrighted work to substantially the same degree as a person without a disability.

The proposed treaty sets out its purpose in Article 1 in the following terms:

> The purpose of this Treaty is to provide the necessary minimum flexibilities in copyright laws that are needed to ensure full and equal access to information and communication for persons who are visually impaired or otherwise disabled in terms of reading copyrighted works, focusing in particular on measures that are needed to publish and distribute works in formats that are accessible for persons who are blind, have low vision, or have other disabilities in reading text, in order to support their full and effective participation in society on an equal basis with others, and to ensure the opportunity to develop and utilize their creative, artistic and intellectual potential, not only for their own benefit, but also for the enrichment of society.

Further, according to Article 2(a), Contracting Parties are vested with the obligation to undertake certain measures to enable full and equal access to information and communication for persons who are visually impaired or have other disabilities in accessing copyrighted works.

The proposed treaty prescribes limitations and exceptions to copyright enabling disabled persons to use copyrighted material under certain circumstances without the prior consent of the owner of copyright. It would enable suppliers to make an accessible format of a work and supply that accessible format, or copies of that format, to a visually impaired person by any means, including by non-commercial lending or by electronic communication by wire or wireless means, and to undertake any intermediate steps to achieve these objectives, provided that the person or organization wishing to undertake such activity has lawful access to that work or a copy of that work. For such purpose, the work must be converted to an accessible format, which may include any means needed to navigate information in the accessible format but which does not introduce changes other than those needed to make the work accessible to a visually impaired person. Copies of the work may be supplied exclusively to be used by visually impaired persons, and the activity must be undertaken on a non-profit basis. Also, with regard to these works, a visually impaired person is permitted without the authorization of the owner of copyright to copy the work exclusively for his or her own personal use.

All these exceptions are also to be extended to for-profit entities to permit commercial rental of copies in an accessible format, so long as certain conditions are met. These are, *inter alia*: the activity is undertaken on a for-profit basis, but only to the extent that those uses fall within the normal exceptions and limitations to exclusive rights that are permitted without remuneration to the owners of copyright; the activity is undertaken by a for-profit entity on a non-profit basis only to extend access to works to the visually impaired on an equal basis with others; or the work or copy of the work that is to be made into an accessible format is not reasonably available in an identical or largely equivalent format enabling access for the visually impaired and the entity providing this accessible format gives notice to the owner of copyright of such use and adequate remuneration to copyright owners is available.

The proposed treaty defines the extent of availability of a work for both developed and developing countries. Consequently, for developed economies, the work must be accessible and available at a similar or lower price than the price of the work available to persons who are not visually impaired; and for developing countries, the work must be accessible and available at prices that are affordable, taking into account disparities of incomes for persons who are visually impaired.

Under the proposed treaty, imports and exports of works are permitted without prior authorization of the copyright owner by persons who meet the conditions set out under Article 4. In case of commercial reproduction and distribution of works for the visually impaired, reasonable efforts should be made to provide notice to the owner of a work protected by copyright. Contracting Parties must ensure that there is a mechanism for determining the level of adequate remuneration to be paid to the owner of copyright in the absence of voluntary agreement.

Proposal of the United States of America[166] The US proposal, known as the 'Consensus Instrument Proposal', was tabled during the Twentieth Session of the SCCR in June 2010. The draft instrument targeted persons with print disabilities or visual impairment.

The preamble of the US text maintains that a balance between the interests of authors and users, particularly the needs of those persons with print disabilities or visual impairment, must be maintained. Further, it recognizes the role of the copyright system in facilitating access to information and full engagement by persons who are blind or print disabled in civil, educational, political, economic, social, and cultural spheres.

According to Article 1 of the Consensus Instrument, a 'person with print disabilities' is:

1. a person who is blind; or
2. a person who has a visual impairment or a perceptual or reading disability which cannot be improved by the use of corrective lenses to give visual function substantially equivalent to that of a person who has no such impairment or disability and so is unable to read printed works

166 *Draft Consensus Instrument Proposal by the Delegation of the United States of America*, Twentieth Session of the WIPO Standing Committee on Copyright and Related Rights (SCCR), Geneva, June 21–24, 2010, WIPO Doc. SCCR/20/10, June 10, 2010.

to substantially the same degree as a person without an impairment or disability; or

3. a person who has an orthopedic- or neuromuscular-based physical disability that prohibits manipulation and use of standard print materials.

Article 2 sets out acts of exportation that can be undertaken without the authorization of the copyright holder. These are:

- The exportation to another Member of any physical Braille format copy of a published work made pursuant to an exception, limitation, or other special provision of the Member's copyright law for the benefit of persons with print disabilities;
- The exportation to trusted intermediaries in another Member of any other special format copy of a published work made pursuant to an exception, limitation, or other special provision of the Member's copyright law for the benefit of persons with print disabilities.

Article 3 prescribes acts of importation that can be undertaken without the permission of the copyright holder. These acts are:

- The importation from another Member of any physical Braille format copy of a published work made pursuant to an exception, limitation, or other special provision of that other Member's copyright law for the benefit of persons with print disabilities;
- The importation from trusted intermediaries in another Member of any other special format copy of a published work made pursuant to an exception, limitation, or other special provision of that other Member's copyright law for the benefit of persons with print disabilities.

In both situations (exportation and importation), Members may chose to limit the operation of this principle to published works which, in the applicable special format, cannot be otherwise obtained in the country of importation within a reasonable time and at a reasonable price.

Proposal of the European Union[167] The EU proposal is also known as a Draft Joint Recommendation concerning the improved access to works protected by copyright for persons with a print disability.

---

167 *Draft Joint Recommendation concerning the Improved Access to Works Protected by Copyright for Persons with a Print Disability, Proposal by the Delegation of the European Union*, Geneva, Twenty-First Session of the WIPO Standing Committee on Copyright and Related Rights (SCCR), Geneva, June 21–24, 2010, WIPO Doc. SCCR/20/12, June 17, 2010.

The preamble of the EU proposal stresses that Member States must adopt all necessary measures to facilitate access to works by persons suffering from a print disability which constitutes an obstacle to the use of the works themselves and to pay particular attention to accessible formats. In addition, it says that alternative measures are needed to improve access if the market is unable to provide an appropriate access to works for persons with a print disability.

The aim of the EU proposal is to increase the number and range of accessible format works available worldwide to citizens with a print disability wherever there is no appropriate commercial product on offer. Therefore, Member States should introduce in their national copyright law an exception to the right of reproduction, the right of distribution and the right of making the work available to the public, as defined in Article 8 of the WIPO Copyright Treaty. Exceptions should cover uses that are directly related to the print disability to the extent required by the specific print disability and that are of a non-commercial nature.

Article 1 of the EU proposal prescribes the definition of person with a print disability as follows:

a. who is blind; or
b. who has an impairment of visual function which cannot be improved, by the use of corrective lenses, to a level that would normally be acceptable for reading without a special level or kind of light; or
c. who is dyslexic; or
d. who is unable, through physical disability, to hold or manipulate a book; or
e. who is unable, through physical disability, to focus or move his eyes to the extent that would normally be acceptable for reading; and whose disability results in an inability to read commercially available standard editions of works; and who can be helped to read by reformatting the content (but, does not require the text itself to be re-written in simpler terms to facilitate comprehension).

Exceptions and limitations for persons with print disabilities are set out in Article 2, as follows:

- Member States should provide in their national copyright law for an exception to the right of reproduction, the right of distribution and the right of making the work available to the public, as defined in article 8 of the WCT, for the benefit of persons with a print disability. The exception should cover uses that are directly related to the print disability to the extent required by the specific print disability and that are of a non-commercial nature.
- Such exception may only be applied in certain special cases which do not conflict with a normal exploitation of the work and do not unreasonably prejudice the legitimate interests of the right holder.

- Member States may ensure that the rights holders receive an adequate remuneration for the use of their works covered by the exception. This claim may be exercised through a collective management society.
- The recommendation is not of application to the extent that there are sufficient and adequate market solutions for persons with a print disability.

Under Article 2, exceptions to the right of reproduction, the right of distribution, and the right of making the work available to the public are prescribed. These must be undertaken for non-commercial purposes, should meet the three-step test,[168] and adequate remuneration to the right holder may be required.

According to Article 3, Member States should encourage the setting up for their territory of at least one Trusted Intermediary. Such bodies should fulfill the conditions and qualify for the status of Trusted Intermediary.

The EU proposal acknowledges in Article 4 the cross-border transfer of physical works in accessible formats that are produced under a copyright exception in the following terms:

> Member States should recognize that if a work is made accessible under an exception provided for in their national legislation for the benefit of persons with a print disability, a copy of that work in an accessible format can be distributed to a Member State that has an exception for the benefit of persons with a print disability or, subject to a specific export license granted by the rights holder, through a Trusted Intermediary into another Member State.

The proposal also maintains that a copy of the work in an accessible format may not be directly distributed to a person with a print disability resident in a Member State but must be distributed through a Trusted Intermediary established for that Member State. It also provides for a system of making available across borders to the public of works in accessible formats that are produced under a copyright exception in the following terms:

> Member States should recognize that if a work is made available online under an exception provided for in their national legislation for the benefit of persons with a print disability, the work in an accessible format can be made available online, as defined in article 8 of the WCT, to a Member State that has an exception for the benefit of persons with a print disability or, subject to a specific export license granted by the rights holder, through a Trusted Intermediary into another Member State.

168 The 'three-step test' was provided under the Berne Convention, which set out that exceptions and limitations: (1) must be limited to certain special cases; (2) should not conflict with a normal exploitation of the work; and (3) should not unreasonably prejudice the legitimate interests of the right holder.

The proposal stipulates that works in an accessible format can only be made available online through a Trusted Intermediary established for that purpose for the Member State where the person with a print disability resides.

Trusted Intermediaries should provide notice within a reasonable time to the rights holders or to the collective management societies prior to any use of the work in cases involving the reproduction, distribution, and the making available to the public of works in an accessible format for the benefit of persons with a print disability.

Under the proposal, Member States should encourage the design and development of an enabling technologies framework so that these technologies become accessible to persons with a print disability at a reasonable cost.

International Instrument on Limitations and Exceptions for Visually Impaired Persons/Persons with Print Disabilities: Proposal of the Chair[169] This proposal was originally called 'Consensus document on an international instrument on limitations and exceptions for persons with print disabilities'.[170] A number of countries, including the African Group, were not comfortable with the original title because they did not consider that the text represented a consensus of all Members.

During the discussion of the so-called consensus document, the Delegation of Pakistan proposed two steps to move ahead the discussions. Step one would be to call the document a proposal on an international instrument on limitations and exceptions for persons with print disabilities. The second step would be not to lose the work already done and to collate all the comments made by the African Group and other countries.[171] This proposal was agreed to by all Members.

---

169 *Proposal on an International Instrument on Limitations and Exceptions for Persons with Print Disabilities*, Document prepared by the Chair, Twenty-Second Session of the WIPO Standing Committee on Copyright and Related Rights (SCCR), June 15–24, 2011, WIPO Doc. SCCR/22/16, November 4, 2011. See, also, Working Document on an International Instrument on Limitations and Exceptions for Visually Impaired Persons/ Persons with Print Disabilities, Twenty-Third Session of the WIPO Standing Committee on Copyright and Related Rights (SCCR), adopted by the Committee, WIPO Doc. SCCR/23/7, December 16, 2011. See, also, *Revised Working Document on an International Instrument on Limitations and Exceptions for Visually Impaired Persons/Persons with Print Disabilities*, Twenty-Fourth Session of the WIPO Standing Committee on Copyright and Related Rights (SCCR), WIPO Doc. SCCR/24/9, October 19, 2012, and the Draft Text SCCR/25/2 of November 23, 2012.

170 *Consensus Document on an International Instrument on Limitations and Exceptions for Persons with Print Disabilities, Presented by Argentina, Australia, Brazil, Chile, Ecuador, Mexico, Paraguay, and the United States of America*, Twenty-Second Session of the WIPO Standing Committee on Copyright and Related Rights (SCCR), June 15–24, 2011, WIPO Doc. SCCR/22/15.

171 Report adopted by the WIPO Standing Committee on Copyright and Related Rights (SCCR), WIPO Doc. SCCR 22/18, December 9, 2011.

The document was prepared on the authority of the Office of the Chair to act as a simple channel and under the terms of the conclusions of the Twenty-Second Session of the SCCR, which provided for the obligation of the Chair to submit such a document. It is the result of the contributions by the Delegations, whose comments have been taken into account without any position being compromised or future positions being prejudiced or affected in any way in the discussions on the subject, since they will remain open and subject to the changes based on the future contributions by all Delegations. This text was commented upon and debated during the Twenty-Third Session of the SCCR in November–December 2011.[172] The text was further discussed during the following Sessions: the Twenty-Fourth Session of the SCCR that took place on July 16–25, 2012,[173] the Inter-Sessional Meeting on Limitations and Exceptions for Visually Impaired Persons/ Persons with Print Disabilities, that took place from October 17 to 19, 2012[174]; and the Twenty-Fifth Session of the SCCR that was held from November 19 to 23, 2012.[175] This text, supported by all Member States, constitutes the basis for an international instrument on exceptions and limitations to copyright for visually impaired persons/persons with print disabilities. Although the final legal nature of the text is still unknown, it has been revised several times through negotiation and its provisions have been amended accordingly. The lastest version of the text was issued on November 23, 2012, and it is the basis of the discussion which follows.

The Preamble contains 12 paragraphs commented upon by Member States. It prescribes the following:

> *(First)*
> Recalling the principles of non-discrimination, equal opportunity, accessibility, and full and effective participation and inclusion in society, proclaimed in the Universal Declaration of Human Rights and the United Nations Convention on the Rights of Persons with Disabilities,
> *(Second)*
> Mindful of the challenges that are prejudicial to the complete development of persons with visual impairments/print disabilities, which limits their freedom of expression including the freedom to seek, receive and impart information and

172 WIPO Doc. SCCR 23/7.

173 *Revised Working Document on an International Instrument on Limitations and Exceptions for Visually Impaired Persons/Persons with Print Disabilities*, Twenty-Fourth Session of the WIPO Standing Committee on Copyright and Related Rights (SCCR), adopted by the Committee, WIPO Doc. SCCR/24/9, July 25, 2012.

174 Kongolo, T. (2012), 'Towards an International Legal Instrument on Exceptions and Limitations for Visually Impaired Persons/Persons with Print Disabilities', *European Intellectual Property* Review 34:12, 823–833.

175 The Draft Text adopted by the SCCR on November 23, 2012 is the most recent revised text.

ideas of all kinds on an equal basis with others, including through all forms of communication of their choice, their enjoyment of the right to education, and the opportunity to conduct research,

(Third)

Emphasizing the importance of copyright protection as an incentive and reward for literary and artistic creations and enhancing opportunities for everyone including persons with visual impairments/print disabilities to participate in the cultural life of the community, to enjoy the arts and to share scientific progress and its benefits,

(Fourth)

Aware of the barriers of persons with visual impairments/print disabilities to access published works in achieving equal opportunities in society, and the need to both expand the number of works in accessible formats and to improve the circulation of such works,

(Fifth)

Taking into account that the majority of persons with visual impairments/print disabilities live in developing and least-developed countries,

(Sixth)

Recognizing that despite the differences in national copyright laws, the positive impact of new information and communication technologies on the lives of persons with visual impairments/print disabilities may be reinforced by an enhanced legal framework at the international level.

(Seventh)

Recognizing that many Member States have established exceptions and limitations in their national copyright laws for persons with visual impairments/print disabilities, yet there is a continuing shortage of available works in accessible format copies for such persons, and that considerable resources are required for their effort of making works accessible to these persons, and that the lack of possibilities of cross-border exchange of accessible format copies has necessitated duplication of these efforts,

(Eighth)

Recognizing both the [preference for the rightholders to make] [importance of rightholders' role in making] their works accessible to persons with visual impairments/print disabilities and [the importance of] [the need for] appropriate exceptions and limitations to make works accessible to persons with visual impairments/print disabilities, [including] [particularly] when the market is unable to provide such access.

(Ninth)

Recognizing also the need to maintain a balance between the effective protection of the rights of authors and the larger public interest, particularly education, research and access to information, and that such a balance must facilitate effective and timely access to works for the benefit of persons with visual impairments/print disabilities,

> *(Tenth)*
> [Reaffirming the obligations of Members States under the existing international treaties on the protection of copyright and the importance and flexibility of the three-step test for limitations and exceptions established in Article 9(2) of the Berne Convention and other international instruments],
> *(Eleventh)*
> Recalling the importance of the Development Agenda recommendations, adopted in 2007 by the General Assembly of the Convention Establishing the World Intellectual Property Organization (WIPO), which aim to ensure that development considerations form an integral part of the Organization's work,
> *(Twelfth)*
> Recognizing the importance of the international copyright system and desiring to harmonize exceptions and limitations with a view to facilitating access to and use of works by persons with visual impairments/print disabilities.

This self-explanatory Preamble underlines the *raison d'être* of the system to be put in place to enable visually impaired persons to access works which are still inaccessible by most of them for several reasons.

Article A deals with definitions of the main concepts, including work, accessible format copy, authorized entity, and reasonable price for both developed and developing countries.

Article B sets out who the beneficiaries of this system are as follows:

> A beneficiary person is a person who:
> (i) is blind;
> (b) has a visual impairment or a perceptual or reading disability which cannot be improved to give visual function substantially equivalent to that of a person who has no such impairment or disability and so is unable to read printed works to substantially the same degree as a person without an impairment or disability; or
> (c) is otherwise unable, through physical disability, to hold or manipulate a book or to focus or move the eyes to the extent that would be normally acceptable for reading, regardless of any other disabilities.

Member States have agreed on who should be the beneficiaries of exceptions and limitations referred to above. The discussion during the Inter-Sessional Meeting focused on the phrase 'cannot be improved' in Article B(b). Some delegations proposed using the phrase 'is not improved'. At the end of the day, it was interpreted that nothing in this language implies that the phrase 'cannot be improved' (which appears in the agreed text) requires the use of all possible medical diagnostic procedures and treatments.[176]

176 See, Kongolo, T. (2012).

Article B*bis*, proposed by the African Group, dealing with the nature and scope of obligations, was added in the Twenty-Fourth Session of the SCCR. According to this provision, Member States/Contracting Parties should/shall adopt appropriate measures to implement the provisions of the international legal instrument/joint recommendation/treaty. Under the provision, it is also stressed that Member States/Contracting Parties should/shall apply the international/joint recommendation/treaty transparently, taking into account the priorities and special needs of developing countries as well as the different levels of development of the Member States/Contracting Parties. The provision also maintains that Member States/Contracting Parties should/shall ensure that the implementation of this international legal instrument/joint recommendation/treaty allows for timely and effective exercise of the actions covered, including expeditious procedures that are fair and equitable.

A number of Delegations were not comfortable with the wording of this provision. Some Delegations expressed reservations about its inclusion while others supported its incorporation in the text. Finally, it was agreed that some Delegations will work on the wording of the provision to respond to the concerns of all.

The following provisions of the text cover national law limitations and exceptions on accessible format copies, cross-border exchange of accessible format copies, importation of accessible format copies, obligations concerning technological measures, the relationship with contracts, respect for privacy, interpretation of the three-step test and registry of authorized entities.

Article C sets out exceptions or limitations to the right of reproduction, the right of distribution, and the right of making available to the public that are to be provided by each Member State in its copyright law to facilitate the availability of works in accessible formats for beneficiary persons. It also has stressed that the limitations and exceptions provided in national laws should permit any changes needed to make the work accessible in the alternative format. Delegations were divided on whether or not to include 'the right of public performance' and 'the right of translation'. Some delegations maintained that 'the right of translation' may be beyond the aim of this instrument, which is to provide equal access to copyright works to VIP. Other delegations asserted that this 'right of translation' is required for full access, particularly in the developing world.[177]

The provision prescribes that these exceptions may be fulfilled by a Member State by providing that authorized entities shall be permitted without the authorization of the copyright rights holder to make an accessible format copy of a work, obtain from another authorized entity a work in accessible format, and supply those copies to a beneficiary person by any means, including by non-commercial lending or by electronic communication by wire or wireless means, and that they may undertake any intermediate steps to achieve those objectives, under the following conditions:

177 See, ibid.

- the authorized entity wishing to undertake said activity has lawful access to that work or a copy of that work;
- the work is converted to an accessible format copy, which may include any means needed to navigate information in the accessible format, but does not introduce changes other than those needed to make the work accessible to the beneficiary person;
- copies of the work in the accessible format are supplied exclusively to be used by beneficiary persons; and
- the activity is undertaken on a non-profit basis.

A beneficiary person, or someone acting on his or her behalf, including a primary caretaker or caregiver, may make an accessible format copy of a work for the personal use of the beneficiary person or may otherwise assist the beneficiary person to make and use accessible format copies where the beneficiary person has lawful access to that work or a copy of that work

A Member State may fulfill Article C (1) by providing any other exception or limitation in its national copyright law. Also, the Member State may limit said exceptions or limitations to published works which, in the applicable special format, cannot be obtained within a reasonable time and at a reasonable price. Some delegations sought clarification and had reservations on these exceptions and limitations. They stressed that a Member State/Contracting Party may confine limitations or exceptions under this Article to published works which, in the particular accessible format, cannot be obtained commercially under reasonable terms, including at prices that take account of the needs and incomes of beneficiary persons in that market. Another matter of discretion is remuneration in the context of the provided exceptions and limitations; i.e each national law has to determine whether exceptions and limitations are subject to remuneration. Article D, dealing with cross-border exchange of accessible format copies sets forth as follows:

1. A Member State/Contracting Party should/shall provide that if an accessible format copy of a work is made under an exception or limitation or export license in accordance with the national law, that accessible format copy may be distributed or made available to a beneficiary person or an authorized entity in another Member State/Contracting Party by an authorized entity.
2. A Member State may fulfill Article D(1) by providing an exception or limitation in its national copyright law such that:
   (A) Authorized entities shall be permitted without the authorization of the rights holder to distribute or make available accessible format copies to an entity or organization in another Member State/Contracting Party that is an authorized entity.
   (B) Authorized entities shall be permitted, pursuant to Article A to distribute or make available accessible format copies to a beneficiary

person in another Member State/Contracting Party without the authorization of the right holder.]

Provided that prior to the making available or distribution of the originating authorized entity did not know or have reasonable grounds to know that the accessible format copy would be used for other than the beneficiary persons.

3. Alternative A [The Member State/Contracting Party may limit said distribution or making available of published works which, in the applicable accessible format, cannot be otherwise obtained within a reasonable time and at a reasonable price, in the country of importation.]
   Alternative B A Member/Contracting Party should/shall [/may] confine said distribution or making available to published works where the exporting authorized entity, prior to making available for distribution, knew or should have known that a copy in the particular accessible format could have been obtained through the distribution channels customary to the beneficiary persons,under reasonable terms, including at prices that take account of the needs and incomes of beneficiary persons in the country of importation][, as well as the cost of producing and distributing the work].
4. Alternative A: A Member State/Contracting Party may fulfill Article D(1) by providing any other exception or limitation in its national copyright law that is limited to certain special cases which do not conflict with a normal exploitation of the work and do not unreasonably prejudice the legitimate interests of the right holder.
   Alternative B: A Member State/Contracting Party may fulfill Article D(1) by providing any other limitation or exception in its national copyright law pursuant to Article Ebis.

According to Article E, to the extent that the national law of a Member State/ Contracting Party would permit a beneficiary person, someone acting on his or her behalf, or an authorized entity to make an accessible format copy of a work, the national law of that Member State/Contracting Party should/shall also permit [them/authorized entities] to import an accessible format copy for the benefit of beneficiary persons without the authorization of the rightholder.

One Delegation maintained in the Twenty-Third Session of the SCCR that the words 'importation' and 'exportation' usually mean the exchange of tangible goods or products and usually do not mean exchanging intangible goods such as those in digital format. If the words importation and exportation in this instrument include exchanging works in digital format, the Delegation felt that it would be better to explicitly write this point somewhere in this instrument in order to prevent ambiguity.[178]

---

178 Ibid., p. 40, para. E.01.

In the Twenty-Third Session of the SCCR, one Delegation proposed adding a new Article E*bis*, which encompasses two alternatives to be added to the current text, which read:

> Alternative A. [All[national implementation of] exceptions and limitations provided for in this instrument shall be limited to certain special cases which do not conflict with a normal exploitation of the work and do not unreasonably prejudice the legitimate interests of the right holder.]
> Alternative B. [Contracting Parties/Member States, in their national [law/legislation], shall/should provide [additional/any] limitations or exceptions [in conformity with/as per Article Bbis of] this treaty/instrument [only] in certain special cases which do not conflict with a normal exploitation of the work and do not unreasonably prejudice the legitimate interests of the right holder.]

This provision has, in fact, been included in the latest version of the text as a new Article E*bis*.

The obligations to provide technological protection measures are prescribed in Article F of the text, in two alternative versions in the following terms:

> Member State/Contracting Party should/shall ensure that beneficiaries of the exception provided by Article C are not prevented from enjoying the exception where technological protection measures have been applied to a work.

Article F contains three alternatives in Paragraph 2 which reflect the three positions taken by Member States on technological protection measures as follows:

> Alternative A
> 1. Member States/Contracting Party should/shall ensure that beneficiaries of the exception provided by Article C are not prevented from enjoying the exception in the exception where technological protection measures have been applied to a work.
> 2. A Member State/Contracting Party may fulfill Article F(1) by permitting, under its national copyright law, circumvention of technological protection measures for the purposes of, and to the extent necessary for benefiting from an Article C exception. Member States/Contracting Parties may encourage rightholders to take adequate, effective and readily accessible voluntary measures to ensure the exercise of limitations and exceptions by beneficiaries.
> Alternative B
> Where the national law of a Member State/Contracting Party provides adequate legal protection and effective legal remedies against the circumvention of technological measures, a Member State/Contracting Party should/shall/may adopt effective and necessary measures to ensure that a beneficiary person may enjoy limitations and exceptions provided in that Member State's/Contracting Party's national law, in accordance with this instrument/Treaty, where

> technological measures have been applied to a work and the beneficiary person has legal access to that work, in circumstances such as where appropriate and effective measures have not been taken by rights holders in relation to that work to enable the beneficiary person to enjoy the limitations and exceptions under that Member State/Contracting Party's national law.

Article H of the current text dealing with respect for privacy prescribes that in the implementation of these exceptions and limitations, Member States/ Contracting Parties should/shall endeavor to protect the privacy of beneficiary persons on an equal basis with others.

Member States also discussed the interpretation of the three-step test. Article I states that the three-step test should be interpreted in a manner that respects the legitimate interests of third parties, including: interests deriving from human rights and fundamental freedoms; interests in competition, notably on secondary markets; and other public interests, notably in scientific progress and cultural, educational, social, or economic development.

Member States or Contracting Parties, depending on the final legal nature of this instrument, have been given the opportunity to set up at the national level a voluntary registry of authorized entities which may be used by authorized entities to identify one another for the purpose of cross-border exchange of accessible format copies.

The cross-border exchange of accessible format copies is one of the most critical issues in this draft instrument, so close cooperation is required among Member States. The draft text prescribes as follows:

> [To foster the cross-border exchange of accessible format copies, Member States/Contracting Parties shall endeavor to facilitate the voluntary sharing of information to assist authorized entities in identifying one another. The International Bureau shall establish an information access point for this purpose.]
> [The International Bureau shall collect, where available, anonymous and aggregated data relating to the cross-border exchange of accessible format copies for the evaluation of the functioning of this instrument/Treaty.]

The "Principles of application" or Cluster Package, which incorporates the provisions for national implementation, development, respect of copyright, and respect for visually-impaired persons, has been annexed to the draft articles. It provides as follows:

> National implementation provision
> [first sentence]
> Member States/Contracting Parties should/shall adopt the measures necessary to ensure the application of this instrument/treaty.

[second sentence]
Nothing shall prevent parties from determining the appropriate method of implementing the provisions of this instrument/treaty within their own legal system and practice.
[third sentence]
[Member States/Contracting Parties may fulfill their obligations under this instrument/treaty through specific exceptions or limitations for beneficiary persons; general exceptions or limitations [such as fair dealing or fair use; or a combination thereof,] whether existing or established to fulfill this instrument/ treaty, [provided they are consistent with the Member States'/Contracting Parties' international obligations].]
This instrument/Treaty is without prejudice to other exceptions and limitations for persons with disabilities provided by national law.
"Development" provision
[A Member State/Contracting Party may implement in its national law other exceptions and limitations for the benefit of beneficiary persons than are provided by this instrument/Treaty having regard to that Member State/Contracting Party's economic situation, and its social and cultural needs, and in the case of a least-developed country taking into account its special needs, in accordance with that Member State's/Contracting Party's international rights and obligations.]
"Respect for copyright" provision
[In adopting measures necessary to ensure the application of this instrument/ Treaty, a Member State/Contracting Party may exercise its rights and shall comply with its obligations under the Berne Convention for the Protection of Literary and Artistic Works, and any other Treaties to which it is a party, including the obligations it has to confine exceptions and limitations to certain special cases, which do not conflict with a normal exploitation of the work and do not unreasonably prejudice the legitimate interests of the rightholders.]
[A Member State/Contracting Party may fulfill its obligations under this instrument/Treaty through specific exceptions or limitations for beneficiary persons; general exceptions or limitations [such as fair dealing or fair use; or a combination thereof], whether existing or established to fulfill this instrument/ treaty, [provided that such exceptions and limitations are consistent with the Member State's/Contracting Party's international rights and obligations].
"Respect for visually-impaired" provision
A Member State/Contracting Party should/shall implement in its law the provisions herein in a manner that fulfills its obligations under other international agreements [with respect to the treatment and protection] [to promote, protect and ensure the rights, freedoms and dignity] of visually-impaired persons/ persons with print disabilities.]

The draft text was adopted by the SCCR on November 23, 2012 during its Twenty-Fifth Session, which took place from November 19 to 23, 2012. The Committee concluded as follows:

> The Committee agreed to recommend that the WIPO General Assembly, convened in extraordinary session on December 17 and 18, 2012, evaluate the text of document SCCR/25/2 and decide whether to convene a diplomatic conference in 2013 to adopt a legal instrument/treaty on appropriate exceptions and limitations for persons with visual impairment and/or print disabilities. Should the General Assembly decide not to convene a diplomatic conference in 2013, the SCCR recommends that it be directed by the General Assembly to continue negotiations on the text and to reallocate its time in the next SCCR to give priority to that work.

Exceptions and limitations for libraries and archives
This is the second segment of exceptions and limitations to copyright agreed by Member States.

Three Proposals pertaining to copyright limitations and exceptions for libraries and archives and a compiled document prepared by the WIPO Secretariat and discussed by Member States are on the table:

- Proposal on Limitations and Exceptions for Libraries and Archives submitted by Brazil, Ecuador and Uruguay (WIPO Doc. SCCR/23/5);
- Proposal on Objectives and Principles for Exceptions and Limitations for Libraries and Archives submitted by the United States of America (WIPO Doc. SCCR/23/4);
- The Case for a Treaty on Exceptions and Limitations for Libraries and Archives: Background Paper by IFLA, ICA, EIFL, and INNOVARTE (WIPO Doc. SCCR 23/3, presented by Brazil); and
- Provisional Working Document Containing Comments on and Textual Suggestions Towards an Appropriate International Legal Instrument (in whatever form) on Exceptions and Limitations for Libraries and Archives (WIPO Doc. SCCR/23/8).

Proposal on Limitations and Exceptions for Libraries and Archives submitted by Brazil, Ecuador and Uruguay[179] This proposal was submitted by the three countries at the Twenty-Third Session of SCCR in November 2011. It aims at providing compulsory exceptions and limitations for libraries and archives, covering library lending, reproduction and distribution of copies by libraries and archives, obligations concerning technological protection measures, and limitation on liability for libraries and archives.

The text prescribes that a library shall be permitted to lend copyright works, or materials protected by related rights, to a user or to another library. The text also

179 *Proposal on Limitations and Exceptions for Libraries and Archives, Document Presented by Brazil, Ecuador and Uruguay*, Twenty-Third Session of the WIPO Standing Committee on Copyright and Related Rights (SCCR), Geneva, November 21–25, 28, and 29 and December 2, 2011, WIPO Doc. SCCR/23/5, November 22, 2011.

clearly provides that Member States who provide for a public lending right in their copyright laws may not discontinue such right.

As regards reproduction and distribution of copies by libraries and archives, the text clearly sets out the following:

> 1. It shall be permitted for a library or archive to reproduce and to distribute a copy of a copyright work, or of material protected by related rights, to a library user, or to another library or archive, for purposes of:
>   a. education;
>   b. requests by users for research or private study;
>   c. interlibrary document supply;
>
>   provided that such reproduction and distribution is in accordance with existing international obligations, among them the Berne Convention.
> 2. Libraries and archives shall be permitted to reproduce and distribute a copy of a copyright work or material protected related rights, to a user, in any other case where a limitation or exception in national legislation would allow the user to make such copy.

Member States or Contracting Parties shall ensure that libraries and archives have the means to enjoy the exceptions and limitations provided when technological protection measures have been applied to a work or other protected matter.

The text sets forth limitations on the liability for librarians and archivists acting in good faith within the scope of their duties for claims for damages, criminal liability, and copyright infringement.

Proposal on Objectives and Principles for Exceptions and Limitations for Libraries and Archives submitted by the United States of America[180] This proposal was submitted by the United States during the Twenty-Third Session of the SCCR. The objectives and principles are intended to underline the main purposes of each exception and limitation for libraries and archives, covering preservation, support for research and human development, legal deposit, and general exceptions. The self-explanatory proposal is reproduced below:

> **Adoption of National Exceptions**
>
> *Objective*:
>
> Encourage Member States to adopt exceptions and limitations in their national laws that facilitate the public service role of libraries and archives, maintaining the balance between the rights of authors and the larger public interest, particularly education, research, and access to information.

---

180 *Objectives and Principles for Exceptions and Limitations for Libraries and Archives document presented by the United States of America*, Twenty-Third Session of the WIPO Standing Committee on Copyright and Related Rights (SCCR), Geneva, November 21–25, 28, and 29 and December 2, 2011, WIPO Doc. SCCR/23/4, November 22, 2011.

Principles:
Exceptions and limitations, which are an integral part of national copyright systems, play a critical role in enabling libraries and archives to meet the needs of the public, helping individuals to achieve their full potential and engage with others.
Exceptions and limitations for libraries and archives help these institutions to assist individuals in seeking, receiving and imparting information so that they may participate meaningfully in public life.
Exceptions and limitations also advance knowledge by preserving and providing access to the world's cultural, artistic, and scientific heritage.
Both affirmative protections for authors and exceptions and limitations, including those for library and archival services, are vital to achieving the copyright system's goals of encouraging creativity, innovation, and learning.

Preservation

Objective:
Enable libraries and archives to carry out their public service role of preserving works.
Principles:
Exceptions and limitations can and should enable libraries and archives to carry out their public service role of preserving works that comprise the cumulative knowledge and heritage of the world's nations and peoples.
To that end, exceptions and limitations can and should enable libraries and archives to make copies of published and unpublished works for purposes of preservation and replacement, under appropriate circumstances.
The need for such preservation exists in a variety of media and formats and may include the migration of content from obsolete storage formats.

Support for Research and Human Development

Objective:
Enable libraries and archives to carry out their public service role of advancing research and knowledge.
Principles:
Libraries and archives advance knowledge by providing access to their collections, which together comprise the cumulative knowledge of the world's nations and peoples.
Libraries and archives are essential to the knowledge economy of the 21st century – supporting research, learning, innovation and creative activity; providing access to diverse collections; and providing information and services to the general public, including disadvantaged communities and vulnerable members of society.
Reasonable exceptions and limitations can and should establish the framework enabling libraries and archives to supply copies of certain materials to researchers and other users directly or through intermediary libraries.

Legal Deposit

Objective:

Encourage the adoption of national legal deposit laws and systems.

Principles:

Legal deposit systems help develop national collections and may help in preservation efforts, particularly if they include many categories of works published in multiple formats.

Libraries and archives also serve the public by maintaining essential government information. Copyright restrictions on government materials should not limit the ability of libraries and archives to receive, preserve, and disseminate government works.

Other General Principles

Other exceptions and limitations, including general use exceptions, may also play an important role in enabling libraries and archives to carry out their public service mission.

National copyright laws may recognize limitations on the liability of certain types of damages applicable to libraries and archives and their employees and agents that act in good faith, believing or having reasonable grounds to believe that they have acted in accordance with copyright law.

Existing national systems of exceptions and limitations for libraries and archives should be examined to determine whether they require updating for the digital era, to enable libraries and archives to continue to carry out their public service mission.

Right holders have a critical role in ensuring sustainable access to copyrighted works in developed and developing countries. Where rapidly changing technology requires flexible solutions, Member States should encourage collaborative and innovative solutions among all stakeholders.

Museums share many of the same public service roles as libraries and archives, and Member States may want to consider extending the same or similar exceptions and limitations for museums.

Adequate safeguards should be in place to ensure the responsible and lawful exercise of exceptions and limitations by libraries and archives.

The Case for a Treaty on Exceptions and Limitations for Libraries and Archives: Background Paper by IFLA, ICA, EIFL, and INNOVARTE[181] This paper was submitted at the Twenty-Third Session of the SCCR and was presented by Brazil on behalf of the International Federation of Library Associations and Institutions (IFLA), the International Council on Archives (ICA), Electronic Information for

181 *The Case for a Treaty on Exceptions and Limitations for Libraries and Archives: Background Paper by IFLA, ICA, EIFL and INNOVARTE, document presented by Brazil*, Twenty-Third Session of the WIPO Standing Committee on Copyright and Related Rights (SCCR), Geneva, November 21–25, 28, and 29 and December 2, 2011, WIPO Doc. SCCR 23/3, November 18, 2011.

Libraries (EIFL, an international non-profit organization), and INNOVARTE, a library NGO. The draft treaty contains two parts. The first part (background) explains different issues encountered by libraries and archives. The second part deals with the proposed treaty on exceptions and limitations for libraries and archives.

The issues encountered by libraries and archives are described as follows:

- The absence in many countries of exceptions to copyright for preservation, replacement, even for print materials, means that documentary heritage will disappear and may not be available to future generations. For example, libraries and archives contain a wide variety of print material often not available anywhere else in the world but which are of important historical, political and cultural value e.g. newspaper collections. Without an appropriate exception, a library or archive cannot copy or digitize the newspaper in order to preserve it.
- Exceptions to copyright which enabled libraries and archives to preserve and make available works in the print era have not been updated to the digital age. For example, libraries and archives now provide access to large quantities of 'born digital' works that are not available in print format. Without the legal certainty to preserve this material for future access, the world faces a digital 'black hole' of 21st century material.
- Imposed licences for the provision of digital information such as electronic journals are often used to undermine limitations and exceptions to copyright designed to support education, learning and creativity. In a study of 100 contracts offered to the British Library by commercial vendors, well over ninety percent undermined the public interest as expressed by limitations and exceptions in UK copyright law, particularly as regards fair dealing, archiving and access by the visually impaired.[182]
- Technological Protection Measures (TPM) are used by rights holders to control access and use of content, such as to restrict copying. This can conflict with the right of libraries and archives to undertake activities permitted by national copyright law. If libraries and archives cannot circumvent TPM they will be unable to preserve, archive and make permitted use of lawfully acquired digital content. Libraries and archives must not be prevented from exercising their lawful rights under national copyright law.
- The internet has opened up new opportunities for information and communication. The discoverability of published material has become easier and collaboration between researchers, students and citizens is

182 See, *British Library submission to the UKIPO on: 'Taking Forward The Gowers Review of Intellectual Property: Proposed Changes to Copyright Exceptions'*, http://pressandpolicy.bl.uk/imagelibrary/downloadMedia.ashx?MediaDetailsID=130, accessed February 21, 2012.

> increasingly global. Established practices of resource-sharing among libraries to advance knowledge are increasingly cross-border and multi-jurisdictional. Yet these practices are not always reflected in current copyright law. If libraries are unable to provide access to materials that are only available internationally through another library, education and scholarship will be impaired. This would be especially harmful for developing countries and for those living in rural or remote areas.

To resolve those major problems, IFLA, ICA, EIFL, and INNOVARTE have proposed the adoption of a legally binding international instrument that aims to create a basic foundation of exceptions and limitations for all countries and sets out a framework for national copyright laws that is consistent with international law. The beneficiaries of the proposed treaty would be libraries and archives, their users and society at large.

The proposed treaty relates to the use of all copyrighted works and all materials protected by related rights however those may be defined by national laws. It applies to materials in any format, digital and non-digital.

All the limitations and exceptions in the proposed treaty apply to non-commercial uses only. They would be limited exceptions to the exclusive rights of copyright holders in order to enable:

- Preservation of materials for posterity, with the flexibility to access cultural works in copy-protected formats;
- Support of education, research, and private study;
- Making or receiving of copies of works lawfully acquired by a library or archive for personal and private purposes;
- Supply of copies of works in response to requests from individual users;
- Provision or lending of lawfully acquired content on a not-for-profit basis;
- Support of people with disabilities in the exercise of their right to access content;
- Circumvention of TPM for the purpose of permitting a non- infringing use of a work;
- Limiting of the risk of liability to libraries and archives with respect to orphan works.

According to the proponents of this proposal, a treaty is the only instrument that would bind Member States to provide limitations and exceptions in their national laws to protect specific library and archive activities.

Provisional Working Document Containing Comments on and Textual Suggestions Towards an Appropriate International Legal Instrument (in whatever form) on Exceptions and Limitations for Libraries and Archives[183] This Working Document has been prepared by the WIPO Secretariat comprising comments and proposals of Member States on specific issues pertaining to exceptions and limitations for libraries and archives.

Member countries agreed to discuss the following items: (1) preservation; (2) right of reproduction and safeguarding copies; (3) legal deposit; (4) library lending; (5) parallel importations; (6) cross-border uses; (7) orphan works, retracted and withdrawn works and works out of commerce; (8) limitations on liability of libraries and archives; (9) technological measures of protection; (10) contracts; and (11) right to translate works. The 11 subject matters were discussed during the Twenty-Third and Twenty-Fourth Sessions of the SCCR. Each of them will be addressed here, taking into consideration key elements of the discussion as well as pending issues.

Preservation Throughout the discussions, there was an understanding among Member States that exceptions and limitations can and should enable libraries and archives to make copies of published and unpublished works for purposes of preservation and replacement, under appropriate circumstances. The key question was the scope of such preservation.

Some countries proposed that preservation focus on the ability of libraries and archives to preserve the work. Preservation copies should not be used as an item additional to the original work in the collection but must be used instead of the original work. First, the work has to have been legally and lawfully acquired; second, a copy can only be made in order to preserve works that are in the collection with no other purpose than to allow the work to remain in the collection; and, third, this has to be done not for profit purposes. The reproduction of works by libraries is permitted if the works have been actually damaged in a severe manner and the reproduction is necessary for their preservation.

Copying should be limited to the maintenance or management of a library, archive, or museum's own permanent collection, or that of another library, archive, or museum, so preservation or maintenance has six specific functions or purposes. First, a copy can be made if the original is rare or unpublished and is lost or at risk of deterioration or becoming damaged or lost. Second, it is for the purpose of onsite consultation if the original cannot be viewed, handled, or listened to because of its condition or because of the atmospheric conditions in which it must be kept. Third, a copy can be made in an alternative format if the original is currently in an obsolete format or if the technology required to

183 *Provisional Working Document Containing Comments on and Textual Suggestions Towards an Appropriate International Legal Instrument (in whatever form) on Exceptions and Limitations for Libraries and Archives*, document prepared by the Secretariat, Twenty-Third Session of the WIPO Standing Committee on Copyright and Related Rights (SCCR), Geneva, November 21–25, 28, and 29 and December 2, 2011, WIPO Doc. SCCR 23/8, May 25, 2012, available at http://www.wipo.int/edocs/mdocs/mdocs/en/sccr_23/sccr_23_8_prov.pdf, accessed July 31, 2012.

use the original is unavailable. There is also the possibility of making a copy if the technology or format is becoming unavailable in order to read the material. Fourth, a copy can be made by the library, museum, or archive for catalogue making. Fifth, copies can be made for insurance purposes or police investigations. And sixth, if necessary, a copy may be made for restoration. Among these six purposes, there is a limitation on the first three purposes in accordance with which the exception would not apply where an appropriate copy is commercially available in the medium and of a quality that is appropriate for those preservation purposes. If a person needs to make an intermediate copy to accomplish one of the purposes in the first section, that intermediate copy must be destroyed as soon as it is no longer needed.

Libraries and archives shall have the right to reproduce any works in any format for the purposes of digital preservation or replacement. Acts of reproduction for the purpose of preservation mainly concern works or other protected subject matters that are in danger of disappearing and that are old, rare, unique, or fragile, as well as works and other protected subject matters that are in an obsolete format.

Right of reproduction and safeguarding copies Article 11 of the proposal of the African Group basically deals with the supply of works. One of the main reasons to elaborate that particular part was to emphasize fair use practices as determined by national law. The possibility of producing safeguard copies is going to be limited to the strict minimum. It is not a question of giving that permission to allow libraries and archives not only to make a safeguard copy for themselves but also of making safeguard copies for other libraries or archives. The most important condition for being able to use this possibility is that the work is lawfully available. It is agreed that libraries and archives should be permitted to carry out appropriate reproduction and distribution of library materials for the purposes of education, research, or interlibrary loans. Nonetheless, it is acknowledged that due consideration must be given to rights-holders. In particular, the quantity that is to be supplied and the quality of copies supplied are issues that may require further discussion.

Legal deposit As regards legal deposit, although at the end of the discussion most of the Member States supported the deposit of a publication at the national library, it was also observed that legislation varies from one country to another; some have opted for mandatory deposit while for others such deposit is optional.

Legal deposit systems help develop national collections and may help in preservation efforts, particularly if they include many categories of works published in multiple formats. Member States shall have the freedom to decide the manner in which legal deposit is implemented, taking note of the different approaches followed.

Library lending Reasonable exceptions and limitations can and should establish a framework enabling libraries and archives to supply copies of certain materials to researchers and other users directly or through intermediary libraries. The main focus of having this particular provision is to ensure that libraries can interchange works, lending the works or supplying the works to other libraries for users within the acceptable limits of the law.

The aim of this proposal is to ensure that libraries can comply with an essential function, which is to lend works to users through any means, for which we believe that it is essential that countries recognize and acknowledge the right of lending to users, and there must be an exception that protects libraries when they carry out that particular function.

Parallel importations It shall be permissible for libraries and archives to purchase and import legally published works to be incorporated into their collections in cases where a Contracting Party does not provide for international exhaustion of the importation right after the first sale or other transfer of ownership of a work. The main purpose of this particular article was, taking into account the various laws that ordinarily do not allow for parallel importation of copyrighted works, to ensure that libraries and archives are able to buy or such works, within the provisions of the law, without breaking the law. It applies to works that are not available within the country and when there is a need for libraries to incorporate them into their collections. Member States were divided on the issue of parallel imports.

Cross-border uses It shall be permissible for libraries and archives located in the territory of a Contracting Party to send, receive or to exchange a copy of work, or material protected by related rights, legally made in the territory of another Contracting Party, including copies of works and materials protected by related rights made in accordance with this Treaty.

In the view of one Delegation, this issue is already covered by the subject area of work on reproduction and distribution of copies to the clients of libraries and archives. Also, the restrictions in national copyright law on the reproduction and distribution activities of these institutions apply to the addressed cross-border uses as well.

Orphan works, retracted and withdrawn works and works out of commerce It shall be permitted for the beneficiaries provided for to reproduce and use a work, and materials protected by related rights, for which the author or rights holder cannot be identified or located after reasonable inquiry.

The problem arises when these works are no longer orphaned, so certain steps should be provided for before a work may be declared to be orphaned. The African proposal refers to the carrying out of what is called a 'reasonable inquiry', but the question remains as to what should be considered the criteria for such an inquiry. Therefore, this should be left to the criteria established by national laws.

When addressing the issue of orphan works, there is a need to take into account the various interests involved in order to ensure optimal legal security.

Member States were divided on the definition of orphan works, and the definitions actually in use vary from one country to another. In addition the pending issue is on the steps to follow for declaring a work to be an orphan work and how one can ensure that there is no right holder that can be identified or located after the work is declared as such.

Limitations on liability of libraries and archives All Member States concurred that this provision is important in the sense that librarians and archivists must be immune from liability in the exercise of their work.

Any person working in any library or archive shall be protected for any action performed in good faith from claims for damages and criminal liabilities. While the importance of exempting librarians and archivists from liabilities when they act in good faith is recognized, such exceptions should be introduced appropriately for specific circumstances.

Technological measures of protection Contracting Parties shall ensure that beneficiaries of the exceptions and limitations for libraries and archives have the means to enjoy the exception where technical protection measures have been applied to a work, including when necessary the right to circumvent the technical protection measure so as to make the work accessible. On the technical circumvention of technological protection measures, there are a number of provisions in copyright laws that make such circumvention illegal, so the present provision is crafted to take into account the fact that there are certain users that ordinarily would fall under exceptions and limitations and this particular provision would allow those who would otherwise be entitled to the exceptions and limitations to be able to access the works in the digital environment.

There is a need to allow libraries and archives to circumvent technological protection measures, but care should be taken that this should not lead to piracy. Libraries and archives should have the right to circumvent technological protection measures applied to any work for the purposes of enjoying any act permitted under this treaty and in their national legislation.

The danger of technological protection measures arises in certain cases when they apply to works that have fallen into the public domain or others which are subject to exceptions in the field of education and scientific research. Here they should be restricted or, rather, banned if it is a matter of a work that is not protected. If the work is subject to such measures but it has fallen into the public domain, then in fact it does not need them.

In Japan, even the use of works that is made possible by circumvention of technological protection measures is not recognized as detrimental to the benefits of the owner of copyright.

Contracts Any contractual provisions that prohibit or restrict the exercise or enjoyment of the limitations and exceptions in copyright adopted by Contracting Parties according to the provisions of this Treaty, shall be null and void. While in Australia concerns have been raised by the libraries about their ability to negotiate arrangements with publishers, it is still recommended that this issue be best addressed by the publishing industry and the libraries coming together to negotiate a practical solution to this particular problem.

Right to translate works The question has been whether the library or archive must be entitled as an exception for the translation of existing works. Member States are divided on this issue.

The Committee in its Twenty-Fifth Session, which took place from November 19 to 23, 2012, concluded as follows:

> The Committee agreed to continue its text-based work at the SCCR/26 session, towards an appropriate international legal instrument or instruments (whether model law, joint recommendation, treaty and/or other forms), and to consider the structure of the document, as well as whether to hold a three-day inter-sessional meeting on limitations and exceptions for libraries and archives in the second half of 2013, between the SCCR/26 and SCCR/27 sessions, with the target to submit recommendations on limitations and exceptions for libraries and archives to the General Assembly by the SCCR/28 session.

Exceptions and limitations to copyright for educational, teaching, and research institutions

As stated above, the work on exceptions and limitations to copyright for educational, teaching, and research institutions, as well for persons of other disabilities, forms the basis of the third international instrument text on exceptions and limitations to copyright that WIPO Member States have been undertaking. Among these three documents, this is the one where the most further work and understanding among Member States are still required. There are two proposals on the table in addition to the African proposal, which includes a segment on this, and the 'Provisional working document containing comments on and textual suggestions towards an appropriate international legal instrument (in Whatever form) on limitations and exceptions for educational, teaching and research institutions and persons with other disabilities'. This compiled 'provisional working document' was produced by the WIPO Secretariat on July 25, 2012. The proposals are as follows:

- Proposal by the Delegation of Brazil on Draft Articles and Thematic Clusters on Limitations and Exceptions to Copyright for the Benefit of Educational, Teaching and Research Institutions (WIPO doc. SCCR/24/7/, July 16, 2012; hereinafter 'The Proposal of Brazil');[184]
- Proposal by the Delegations of Ecuador, Peru and Uruguay on Limitations and Exceptions regarding Education (WIPO doc. SCCR/24/6, July 16,

184 *Draft Articles and Thematic Clusters on Limitations and Exceptions to Copyright for the Benefit of Educational, Teaching and Research Institutions*, document proposed by Brazil, at the Twenty-Fourth Session of the WIPO Standing Committee on Copyright and Related Rights, July 16–25, 2012, WIPO Doc. SCCR/24/7, July 16, 2012, available at: http://www.wipo.int/edocs/mdocs/copyright/en/sccr_24/sccr_24_7.pdf, accessed July 31, 2012.

2012; hereinafter 'The Proposal of Ecuador, Peru and Uruguay');[185] and

- Provisional working document containing comments on and textual suggestions towards an appropriate international legal instrument (in Whatever form) on limitations and exceptions for educational, teaching and research institutions and persons with other disabilities, prepared by WIPO Secretariat (Working document (Rev. 5), July 25, 2012; hereinafter, 'Provisional Working Document').[186]

The proposal of Brazil According to this proposal, the following shall not constitute violation of copyright:

- The performance, recitation and exhibition of a work, as applicable, for teaching purposes in educational institutions in the context of educational or research activities, to the extent justified by the non-commercial purpose to be achieved, provided that the source, including the author's name is indicated, unless this turns out to be impossible.
- The reproduction, translation and distribution of excerpts of existing works of any kind, or of entire works in the case of works of visual arts or short compositions, as a pedagogical resource for the use by teachers with the purpose of illustration in the context of educational or research activities, to the extent necessary justified by the non-commercial purpose to be achieved, provided that the source, including the author's name is indicated, unless this turns out to be impossible.
- The note taking of lectures, conferences and classes by those to whom they are addressed. The publication of the notes of said lectures, conferences and classes in whole or in part is prohibited without prior written permission of the person who addressed them.
- The quotation in books, newspapers, magazines or in any other medium of excerpts of a work for the purposes of study, criticism or debate, to the extent justified by the purpose and in accordance with fair practice, provided that the source, including the author's name, is indicated, unless this turns out to be impossible.

185 *Limitations and Exceptions regarding Education*, document proposed by the Delegations of Ecuador, Peru and Uruguay at the Twenty-Fourth Session of the WIPO Standing Committee on Copyright and Related Rights, July 16–25, 2012, WIPO Doc. SCCR/24/6, July 16, 2012.

186 *Provisional Working Document Containing Comments on and Textual Suggestions Towards an Appropriate International Legal Instrument (in whatever form) on Limitations and Exceptions for Educational, Teaching and Research Institutions and Persons with other Disabilities*, produced by the WIPO Secretariat (Working document (Rev. 5)), July 25, 2012.

Brazil also submitted the following non-exhaustive list of thematic clusters for work on this instrument:

(1) access to withdrawn works and works out of print;
(2) technological protection measures;
(3) use for pedagogic and teaching purposes;
(4) reproduction of lectures and conferences; and
(5) quotations.

The proposal of Ecuador, Peru, and Uruguay This proposal puts forward the obligation to update and expand exceptions for educational purposes, in particular in the digital environment, in the following terms:

> Contracting Parties shall update, carry forward and appropriately extend into the digital environment limitations and exceptions in their national laws which have been considered acceptable under the Berne Convention, specially under article 10.1 and 10.2, and devise new exceptions and limitations that are appropriate in the digital network environment to protect educational and research activities.

On the interpretation of the three-step test requirements with regard to exceptions and limitations, the proposal maintains that when applying either Articles 9.2 of the Berne Convention, 13 of the TRIPS Agreement, or 10 of the WIPO Copyright Treaty, or a similar provision in any other multilateral treaty, nothing shall prevent the Contracting Parties from interpreting the test in a manner that respects the legitimate interests, including those of third parties, deriving from educational and research needs, other human rights and fundamental freedoms and other public interests, such as the need to achieve scientific progress and cultural, educational, social, or economic development, protection of competition and secondary markets.

Provisional Working Document According to the conclusions of the SCCR, as agreed by Member States, this present provisional working draft will be restructured with textual proposals and comments separated under each topic. The following discussion will be limited to highlighting the general positions of Member States on some specific issues with no further details.

Some countries maintain that there is a need to strike a balance between copyright protection, which is required to ensure top quality teaching material, and exceptions and limitations for educational purposes, which aim at achieving public interest objectives.

Talking about flexibilities, one Delegation maintained that the Berne Convention provides specific exceptions to allow uses of copyrighted works for the purpose of quotation and teaching. The same types of exceptions are permitted under the WIPO Copyright Treaty and, as far as related rights are concerned, under the Rome Convention and the WIPO Performances and Phonograms Treaty.

These exceptions leave a significant margin of maneuver for members of these conventions and treaties in their implementation (for instance, in the case of education, they make no distinction among levels of education or its nature). It is for individual countries to apply the framework provided at the international level, to put it into practice via their national legislation and adapt it to their local conditions while respecting the three-step test as that is provided for in each of the conventions and treaties. On the same subject, one Delegation stressed that strengthening of existing flexibilities and introduction of new flexibilities in the copyright system to ensure access to textbooks and educational material at affordable prices was called for.

On more specific items, such as the beneficiaries of these exceptions and limitations, one Delegation proposed that the Contracting Parties should provide them for the benefit of persons with disabilities and for public and private educational and non-profit research and teaching institutions. According to the Delegation, the Contracting Parties should extend the provisions of the Treaty to persons with any other disability who, due to that disability, need an accessible format of a type that could be made in order to access a copyright work to substantially the same degree as a person without any disability. Also in relation to exceptions and limitations for persons with other disabilities, the African Group has submitted a proposal on what shall be their scope as well as for remuneration to the right holder of copyright for the commercial exploitation of works.

In terms of use, distinctions have been made between access to educational materials in the classroom and outside the classroom. The African Group has provided a long list of exceptions and limitations related to each.

As to the broader topics with implications for education, the discussion focussed on technology, orphan works and withdrawn or out of print works, the public domain, contracts, ISP (Internet Service Provider) liability, importation and exportation and public health or security. The African Group has proposed specific exceptions for science; limits to database protection laws; special rules on computer programs and technical protection measures; and digital rights management. Regarding orphan works, the African Group proposed that it should be permitted for educational institutions, research organizations, libraries, and archives to reproduce and use a work, and materials protected by related rights, for which the author or rights holder cannot be identified or located after reasonable inquiry. Some delegations showed some reservations in this regard.

The Committee, in its Twenty-Fifth Session that took place from November 19 to 23, 2012, concluded as follows:

> The Committee agreed to continue text-based work on SCCR/24/8/Prov. at the SCCR/26 session, towards an appropriate international legal instrument or instruments (whether model law, joint recommendation, treaty and/or other forms), and to consider during that meeting the possible reorganization of the document and the possible identification of issues on which the Committee could focus its text-based work, with the target to submit recommendations on

limitations and exceptions for educational, teaching and research institutions and persons with other disabilities to the General Assembly by the SCCR/30 session.

Proposal of the African Group: Draft WIPO Treaty on Exceptions and Limitations for the Disabled, Educational and Research Institutions, Libraries and Archive Centers[187]

The African Group first submitted a Draft WIPO Treaty on Exceptions and Limitations for the Disabled, Educational and Research Institutions, Libraries and Archive Centers in June 2010. The original proposal took inspiration from the draft treaty submitted by Brazil, Ecuador, and Paraguay and supported by Mexico, with the addition of some revisions. The Draft Treaty was revised in June 2011. The following discussion will cover only the revised text.

It should be pointed out at the outset that the African Group text is a comprehensive text that covers each segment of exceptions and limitations to copyright that have been discussed above.

The Preamble of the Draft Treaty acknowledges the urgent need to broaden the scope of copyright exceptions and limitations for disabled persons, libraries, archives, and education and research institutions and, furthermore, the need to introduce new international rules in order to provide adequate solutions to the needs of vulnerable persons and the challenges and opportunities presented by economic, social, cultural, and technological developments. The Preamble maintains that the territorial nature of copyright and related laws can be an obstacle to cross-border exploitation of works, performances, or productions and therefore can inhibit the normal access, particularly through new technologies, by persons with disabilities to education, culture, information, and knowledge.

Article 3 sets out the beneficiaries of exceptions and limitations as follows:

1. Contracting Parties shall provide the exceptions and limitations guaranteed in this Treaty for the benefit of persons with disabilities, educational and research institutions as well as libraries and archives, in this Article referred to as Beneficiaries.
2. Contracting Parties shall extend the provisions of this Treaty to persons with any other disability who, due to that disability, need an accessible format of a type that could be made under Article 4 in order to access a

187 Draft WIPO Treaty on Exceptions and Limitations for the Disabled, Educational and Research Institutions, Libraries and Archive Centers, Twenty-Second Session of the WIPO Standing Committee on Copyright and Related Rights (SCCR), June 15–24, 2011, WIPO Doc. SCCR/22/12. See, also, Draft WIPO Treaty on Exceptions and Limitations for the Disabled, Educational and Research Institutions, Libraries and Archive Centers, Twentieth Session of the WIPO Standing Committee on Copyright and Related Rights (SCCR), June 21–24, 2010, WIPO Doc. SCCR/20/11, June 15, 2010.

copyright work to substantially the same degree as a person without a disability.

The Draft Treaty prescribes exceptions and limitations for each category of beneficiaries. For the disabled, it sets out the following limitations and exceptions to exclusive rights of the copyright owner:

> It shall be permitted without the authorization of the owner of copyright to make an accessible format of a work, supply that accessible format, or copies of that format, to persons with disabilities by any means, including by non-commercial lending or electronic communication by wire or wireless means, without the authorization of the owner of copyright, and undertake any other intermediate steps to achieve these objectives, when all of the following conditions are met:
>
> (a) the person or organization wishing to undertake any activity under this provision has lawful access to that work or a copy of that work;
> (b) the work is converted to an accessible format, which may include any means needed to navigate information in the accessible format, but does not introduce changes other than those needed to make the work accessible to persons with disabilities;
> (c) copies of the work are supplied exclusively to be used by persons with disabilities;
> (d) the activity is undertaken on a non-profit basis; and
> (e) the owner of the right is recognized as such.

The Draft Treaty prescribes that persons with disabilities shall be permitted, without the authorization of the owner of copyright, to copy a work exclusively for his or her own personal use.

According to Article 7, the same rights granted to persons with disabilities shall also be available to for-profit entities and shall be extended to permit commercial rental of copies in an accessible format, if any of the following conditions are met:

> (a) the activity is undertaken on a for-profit basis, but only to the extent that those uses fall within the normal exceptions and limitations to exclusive rights that are permitted without remuneration to the owners of copyright;
> (b) the activity is undertaken by a for-profit entity on a non-profit basis, only to extend access to works to persons with disabilities; or
> (c) the work or copy of the work that is to be made into an accessible format is not reasonably available in an identical or largely equivalent format enabling access for persons with disabilities, and the entity providing this accessible format gives notice to the owner of copyright of such use and adequate remuneration for copyright owners is available.

Contracting Parties shall ensure that there is a mechanism in place to determine the level of adequate remuneration to be paid to the owner of copyright in the absence of voluntary agreement.

Exceptions and limitations are also set out for libraries and archives for the purchase and supply of works. Cross-border uses of works and materials reproduced under an exception or limitation have been permitted for libraries and archives. They may also reproduce, communicate to the public, and make available by any means, including digital transmission, a copyrighted work or material protected by related rights that they have lawfully acquired or accessed, for the personal or private use of their users, provided that such use is compatible with fair practice as determined in national law. It shall be permitted to make limited copies of published and unpublished works, regardless of their format, to meet the needs of libraries and archives, without the authorization of the owner of copyright.

Exceptions and limitations are also provided for educational and research institutions, which are permitted, without the authorization of the right holder and without financial compensation, to make copies of published and unpublished works made legally accessible to the public, regardless of their format, for purposes of education and research.

The Draft Treaty extends exceptions and limitations to related rights. It also prescribes that Contracting Parties shall agree to provide for exceptions and limitations relating to computer programs to allow interoperability, replacement, or support.

Article 20 stipulates that Contracting Parties shall ensure that imports and exports of works meet the conditions listed in the provisions of the Treaty and shall take the necessary steps for this to be permitted without the authorization of the owner of copyright in the following terms:

(a) the export to another country of any version of a work or copies of the work that any person or organization in one country is entitled to possess or make under the provisions of this Treaty and
(b) the import of that version of a work or copies of the work by a person or organization able to act under the provisions of this Treaty into another country.

According to Article 19 of the Draft Treaty, any contractual provisions which provide exemptions from the application of the limitations and exceptions shall be null and void.

Contracting Parties shall ensure that beneficiaries of the exceptions and limitations (as defined in Article 3) have the means to enjoy the exception where technical protection measures have been applied to a work, including when necessary the right to circumvent such technical protection measures so as to make the work accessible.

Conclusion

The discussions on exceptions and limitations within the SCCR have evolved considerably over the last two years, especially since a clear work plan was adopted by the Committee to discuss a possible international instrument on exceptions and limitations for visually impaired persons/persons with print disabilities, a separate international text on exceptions and limitations for libraries and archives, and a third text on exceptions and limitations for educational and research institutions. This approach was agreed to by all Members.

With regard to the international instrument on exceptions and limitations for visually impaired persons/persons with print disabilities, several texts have been proposed and the Proposal of the Chair has incorporated and considered many of the issues discussed or proposed by the Members. The African Group is among those countries that support the adoption of a binding instrument for exceptions and limitations for persons with print disabilities and the visually impaired.[188]

Common texts have been developed at the Twenty-Third and Twenty-Fourth Sessions of the SCCR for exceptions and limitations for libraries and archives, as well as for educational and research institutions.

The African Group's Draft treaty, encompassing exceptions and limitations for disabilities, libraries, archives, and educational and research institutions, has been used in the three common drafts as an important proposal.

Finally, things are definitely moving in the right direction with the proposed text presented by the Chair of the SCCR on an International Instrument on Limitations and Exceptions for Visually Impaired Persons/Persons with Print Disabilities, which is supported and endorsed by all Member countries, including the African Group.[189] As proposed by the SCCR, the General Assembly may decide in an extraordinary session to convene a Diplomatic Conference in 2013 to adopt this instrument.

Another compiled text in this regard is that on an International Instrument on Limitations and Exceptions for Libraries and Archives, endorsed by Member States and known as the 'working document containing comments on and textual suggestions towards an appropriate international legal instrument (in whatever form) on exceptions and limitations for libraries and archives'. This document also has considered the relevant part of the African Proposal and constitutes the basis for the future text-based work on the matter. The SCCR hopes to complete a final text and submit recommendations to the WIPO General Assembly by the end of its Twenty-Eighth Session.

---

188 See, WIPO Doc. SCCR/22/18.

189 The most recent text is *Revised Working Document on an International Instrument on Limitations and Exceptions for Visually Impaired Persons/Persons with Print Disabilities*, document prepared by the WIPO Secretariat for the Twenty-Fourth Session of the WIPO Standing Committee on Copyright and Related Rights (SCCR), WIPO Doc. SCCR/24/9 PROV, July 25, 2012.

On the exceptions and limitations to copyright for educational and research institutions and persons with other disabilities, the SCCR has agreed that the document containing comments and textual suggestions compiled by the WIPO Secretariat, called 'Provisional Working Document Towards a Appropriate International Legal Instrument (in whatever form) on Limitations and Exceptions for Educational, Teaching and Research Institutions and Persons with Other Disabilities', is to be restructured properly and will constitute the basis for the future text-based work with the target to submit its recommendations to the WIPO General Assembly by the Thirtieth Session of the SCCR.

African Positions on Selected International Intellectual Property Issues

Previous sections have reviewed the contributions of the African Group in the transformation of the international IP landscape through its initiatives and its leading role in addressing IP issues relating to TK, TCEs, GRs, public health, exceptions and limitations to copyright. This section addresses a number of other IP issues debated at the international arena with a particular focus on the African countries' common positions. These are: protection of life forms; patenting of micro-organisms and non-biological and microbiological processes; the research exemption/exception; and genetically modified organisms (GMOs).

Protection of Life Forms

The African Group has shown reluctance to grant IP protection to life forms from the very commencement of discussions on the subject in various forums and intergovernmental organizations, including the WTO, WIPO, and UNEP-CBD. They took the same position in the African Model Law for the Protection of the Rights of Local Communities, Farmers and Breeders, and for the Regulation of Access to Biological Resources adopted by the African Union in 2000.[190]

Part of the Preamble of the Model Law reads that 'all forms of life are the basis for human survival, and, therefore, the patenting of life, or the exclusive appropriation of any life form or part or derivative thereof violates the fundamental human right to life'. Further, Paragraph 9 of the Model Law prescribes as follows:

> 1) Patents over life forms and biological processes are not recognized and cannot be applied for.
> 2) The collector shall, therefore, not apply for patents over life forms and biological processes under this legislation or under any other legislation

190 See, African Model Law for the Protection of the Rights of Local Communities, Farmers and Breeders, and for the Regulation of Access to Biological Resources; available at: http://www.flag-sa.org/downdocs/oaulocalfarmersrights-booklet.pdf (last accessed on November 20, 2012).

> relevant to the regulation of access and use of a biological resource, community innovation, practice, knowledge and technology, and the protection of rights therein.

In the course of the review of TRIPs Article 27.3(b), the African Group submitted a paper stating its position with regard to the protection of life forms and other biological materials. According to the African proposal of June 2003:

> Patents on life forms are unethical and the TRIPS Agreement should prohibit them, through modifying the requirement to provide for patents on micro-organisms and on non-biological and microbiological processes for the production of plants or animals. Such patents are contrary to the moral and cultural norms of many societies in Members of the WTO. They make the exception in Article 27.2 for protecting ordre public and morality, which Members that consider patents on life forms to be contrary to the fabric of their society and culture, and to be immoral, and which they would otherwise invoke, meaningless in this regard.[191]

The proposal went on to state that:

> [The] African Group maintains its reservations about patenting any life forms and the Group proposes that Article 27.3(b) be revised to prohibit patents on plants, animals, micro-organisms, essentially biological processes for the production of plants or animals, and non-biological and microbiological processes for the production of plants or animals.

On several other occasions, the African Group has reiterated the same position. According to the Group, it is not ethically correct to offer IP protection to any life form.

Patenting of Micro-organisms and Non-Biological and Microbiological Processes

As pointed out above, the African Group has consistently raised serious concerns about patents on life forms and research tools and, on the basis of these concerns, it has maintained that there should not be a possibility, within the framework of the TRIPs Agreement, of granting patents on micro-organisms or on non-biological and microbiological processes for the production of plants and animals.[192]

The Group is of the view that the distinctions drawn in TRIPs Article 27.3(b) between 'plants and animals' and 'micro-organisms' and between 'essentially biological processes' and 'non-biological and microbiological processes' for the production of plants or animals are artificial and unwarranted. It therefore takes the

191 WTO Doc. IP/C/W/404.

192 Ibid., p. 4.

position that these distinctions should be removed from the TRIPs Agreement so that the exclusion from patentability in paragraph 3(b) covers plants, animals, and micro-organisms, as well as essentially biological processes and non-biological and microbiological processes for the production of plants or animals.[193]

At the Fifth Meeting of the Conference of the Parties of the Convention on Biological Diversity, held in Nairobi, Kenya, May 15–26, 2000, with respect to technical issues related to patent protection under Article 27.3(b), the African Group:

> highlighted the incongruencies raised by the artificial distinction made between plants and animals (which may be excluded from patentability) and micro-organisms (which may not be excluded), as well as between essentially biological processes for making plants and animals (which may be excluded) and micro-biological processes (which may not be excluded).

It contended that these distinctions are spurious and challenge the basic tenets of intellectual property law.

Most African patent laws exclude all varieties of plants and animals and all essentially biological processes for the production of plants or animals from patentable subject matter.

Research Exemption/Exception

Most African countries make exceptions to patent protection with regard to scientific research, experimental use, or use for non-commercial purposes. The scope of the exemption/exception may be different in various jurisdictions, although the aim is to allow entities undertaking research to gain from prior existing knowledge which is already available in the field.

A number of countries provide a so-called research exemption/exception either in their law or through case law in the common law countries. In general, the research exemption/exception enables researchers to examine the stated effects of patented inventions and improve such patented inventions without having to fear infringing the patent. Proponents of the research exemption/exception argue that, since much research is cumulative in nature, negotiating and concluding multiple patent licenses before any actual research takes place could involve significant transaction costs.[194]

In some countries, it is explicitly stated that the exemption is applicable when research is carried out without commercial or gainful intent. In some other

---

193 Ibid.

194 *Exclusions from Patentable Subject Matter and Exceptions and Limitations to the Rights*, document prepared by the Secretariat for the Thirteenth Session of the WIPO Standing Committee on the Law of Patents (SCP), Geneva, March 23–27, 2009, WIPO Doc. SCP/13/3, February 4, 2009, p. 27.

countries, the provision explicitly prescribes that the experimental use exemption is applicable also for acts anticipating a future commercial exploitation. In yet other countries, the law is silent on the matter and the courts must decide on the scope of the exemption.[195]

In general, African countries are in favor of more extensive use of exemptions/exceptions to IP rights for scientific research or experimental use.

Genetically Modified Organisms (GMOs)

There are sharp differences of opinion about the environmental and health impacts of genetically modified (GM) crops and foods. Proponents of modern biotechnology argue that crops genetically modified to resist pests and diseases and therefore requiring less use of pesticides and herbicides are safer for the natural environment than conventional crops and are less likely to result in pesticide-related illness. Opponents focus on the potential detrimental impacts of GM crops. The development and commercialization of GM products have also raised complex social and ethical concerns. These range from fundamental opposition to the artificial manipulation of plants and animals to the argument that global justice is not being served by current applications of biotechnology.[196]

The position of the large life-science corporations such as Monsanto and Novartis is that genetic engineering can reduce or even obviate pesticide use. Monsanto's claim is that when they produce packages of herbicides and plants resistant to these herbicides, their aim is not to ensure that farmers will need to increase herbicide use. Their main interest is to ensure that farmers use their herbicides. If these are more effective than alternative products, overall herbicide use may decrease. According to the company, 'Roundup agricultural herbicides and other products are used to sustainably and effectively control weeds on the farm. Their use on Roundup Ready crops has allowed farmers to conserve fuel, reduce tillage and decrease the overall use of herbicides'.[197]

The African Union has taken some regional initiatives on the issue of GMO in the area of agriculture. According to 'An African Position on GMOs in Agriculture', a paper presented at the Conference of AU Ministers of Agriculture in Libreville, Gabon, in 2006,[198] there is a need to have one position with regard to GMOs in

---

195 Ibid., p. 28.

196 See, Mugabe, J. (2003) 'Biotechnology and Sustainable Development in Africa, Towards Regional Consensus and Common Strategy', Paper Prepared for the 1st Meeting of the African Ministerial Conference on Science and Technology, November 2003, Johannesburg, South Africa NEPAD, http://www.nepadst.org/doclibrary/pdfs/doc08_112003b.pdf (last accessed on November 20, 2012).

197 See, Monsanto website, http://www.monsanto.com, 'Products', 'Weed Control' (last accessed on November 20, 2012).

198 Conference of African Union Ministers of Agriculture, Libreville, Gabon, November 27–December 1, 2006, 'An African Position on Genetically Modified Organisms

Africa given that the two positions on the matter are both extreme. The paper goes on to state that the absence of an African consensus and strategic approaches to address these emerging biotechnology issues has allowed different interest groups to exploit uncertainty in policy-making, regardless of what may be the objective situation for Africa. Both pro- and anti-biotech advocacy groups can affect African decision-making adversely, as they portray agricultural opportunities in extremes, making it appear as if it is an 'either-or' situation.[199] According to the paper, the consideration of the following matters is required at the outset:

- In Africa the majority of farmers are small holder farmers;
- These new technologies should focus on solving African problems as identified from the African perspective and should not be imposed on Africa from elsewhere;
- The GE [genetic engineering] technologies should build on and complement local knowledge/technologies that have been used to breed crops over many years and to develop technologies suited to the local environment;
- The GE technologies should also focus on indigenous African crops such as yams, sorghum, potatoes, etc. and not only on commercial crops such as maize and cotton;
- It is imperative to conserve and protect indigenous genetic resources;
- Biotechnology is an expensive technology and should therefore focus on where there's a comparative advantage and its development should be a selective process that targets the most efficient sector;
- African governments and RECs should allocate adequate resources to this process.[200]

The AU has developed a Model Law on Biosafety which aims to provide African countries with a guideline with regard to the regulation of GMOs. Most African governments are still skeptical about GMO crops as a result of concerns about food safety, the environment, and the general public's mistrust of multinationals, which are often seen as manipulative and unscrupulous. Pro-GMO proponents say that the advantages of GMO crops include high yields, virus resistance, nutritional enhancement, herbicide resistance, extended shelf life for food products, insect resistance, and water retention capacities.[201] However, anti-GMO activists fear that GMOs have the potential to enlarge internal organs and harm consumers.

in Agriculture', http://www.africa-union.org/root/au/AUC/Departments/HRST/biosafety/DOC/African Position On GMOs.pdf (last accessed on November 20, 2012).

199 Ibid., p. 1.

200 Ibid., p. 2.

201 See, Tsiko, S. (2011), 'Africa Still Debating GMOs' Pros and Cons', *The Herald* (Zimbabwe), April 25, 2011; available at: http://allafrica.com/stories/201104260172.html, accessed February 18, 2012.

They also worry about the environmental effects of GMO crops, including the elimination of natural control mechanisms.[202]

Most African countries still have no capacity to monitor and regulate the use of and flow of GMO seed and food items. Some have not developed clear policies on GMO crops. So far, only five African countries—Burkina Faso, Egypt, Kenya, Mauritius, and South Africa—have legislation on biosafety that authorize the use of GMO crops and food. Among these, South Africa plays a leading role and has set up comprehensive mechanisms.

Finally, there is no best way of dealing with GMOs in developing countries in general and in African countries in particular. It is undeniably true that despite the controversy over GMOs, their introduction into African countries aids in the fight against food shortages. At the same time, the safety of these GMOs should still remain on the agenda. Consequently, a balanced approach is required and governments need to make informed decisions based on a number of considerations that include the science of genetic technology, the potential benefits, and the possible risks.

Conclusions on Chapter 4

The dynamism of African countries as a group at the international level has been demonstrated in this chapter through their breakthrough initiatives and proposals in the areas of TK, TCEs, GRs, IP and public health, exceptions and limitations to copyright; protection of life forms; the research exemption; and GMOs.

African countries have been eager to see the international community recognize the rights of their traditional and local communities whose knowledge has been widely misappropriated by outsiders without any consideration and by using the IP system/protection as a 'safe haven' to safeguard their use of the misappropriated knowledge. In WIPO's IGC, the African Group initiated the first document on objectives and principles for addressing this issue and took the lead by proposing text-based negotiations in the Committee. The same dynamism is perceived in the WTO, where several initiatives on TK in general and the disclosure of the country of origin of GRs or associated TK in patent applications have been proposed or endorsed by the African Group. As far as TK and TCEs are concerned, the African countries will be satisfied only if the international community adopts a treaty on the matter to protect the rights of their traditional and local communities. This goes along with the support of the African countries for the adoption of an international binding system of the disclosure of the country of origin/source of the GRs or associated TK or TCEs.

In the area of IP and public health, the African Group broke the taboo in 2001 by proposing that the WTO deal with this matter. This breakthrough initiative, influenced by the HIV/AIDS calamity that the continent was facing, opened

202 Ibid.

new windows on the way to deal with the issue of patents and public health in the context of access to medicines. This may be seen in the Doha Declaration on the TRIPs Agreement and Public Health, adopted in 2001, and subsequent Decisions of the WTO General Council. In WHO and WIPO, African countries have shown the same dynamism. The African Group played a very active role in the initiatives and actions undertaken by WHO. In the negotiation process of WHO's Global Strategy and Plan of Action, proposals from the African Regional Office shed significant light on some of the issues discussed. In WIPO, the African Group proposed that the SCP discuss the issue of patents and health. Despite the establishment of mechanisms at the international level, what is also required is to see African countries develop their research and scientific capacities in relation to public health as well as the infrastructure to enable the acquisition of new technology in this area.

Another area where the African Group has been very active is on exceptions and limitations to copyright, where the Group has proposed a comprehensive draft treaty which is considered to be an important document in the discussion of the three topics subject of international legal instruments: exceptions and limitations for visually impaired persons/persons with print disabilities; exceptions and limitations for libraries and archives; and exceptions and limitations for educational and research institutions and persons with other disabilities.

Regarding the protection of life forms, the African Group is in common agreement that no protection should be available under patents. As for GMOs, only five African countries have provided a legal framework to address them. Member countries are still divided on this subject. A balanced approach is required. Concerning the research exemption/exception, most of the African countries advocate its wide use.

Finally, this chapter has demonstrated that the world has changed and Africa is changing along with it by being an active player on the international stage, especially in regard to international IP issues.

Chapter 5
General Conclusions

In the past, Africa was considered to be a passive continent that had offered no breakthrough initiatives in the field of intellectual property. Most efforts to establish norms in IP were carried out by the developed countries, who made greater use of the system. Intellectual property was almost never considered by African countries to be a tool for development. The situation changed dramatically in the late 1990s, when African countries began to introduce important initiatives in the setting of international IP standards.

In the field of public health, the African Group's breakthrough initiative was its April 2001 proposal to the WTO's Council for TRIPs to discuss issues relating to the relationship between the patent system and access to medicines and other public health issues. At the outset of the discussions, some countries considered it unthinkable that a trade organization should deal with access to medicines or public health. However, a common response to tackle the HIV/AIDS pandemic was required at the international level. Several issues relating to, *inter alia*, the use of the compulsory license regime, exhaustion of rights and parallel imports of generic drugs, the extent to which use could be made of provisions relating to 'emergency situations', and how the so-called 'flexibilities' in the TRIPs Agreement could be employed in this regard came under discussion. Thanks to the African Group's leadership and initiatives on these matters, the debates eventually led to adoption of the Declaration on the TRIPs Agreement and Public Health on November 14, 2001, which provided much-needed clarification on the interpretation of provisions of the TRIPs Agreement relating to these issues. The final form of the Declaration was largely determined by the draft originally introduced by the African Group and supported by most other developing countries.

Other, subsequent African proposals relate to the Decision of the WTO's General Council on the implementation of Paragraph 6 of the Declaration on the TRIPs Agreement and Public Health. The challenge here was to reply to the concerns of those countries which lack manufacturing capacity to produce the needed drugs through the use of compulsory licenses. Finally, the WTO General Council decided on August 30, 2003 to waive the requirements that importing countries must pay remuneration to the rights holder and that exporting countries must produce products predominately to supply their own domestic markets.

Finally, the text for amending TRIPs, Article 31bis, has been heavily influenced by the African proposed text. Amendment of the TRIPs Agreement was considered necessary to put into place a permanent system for the use of compulsory licenses to meet public health needs. The Protocol Amending the TRIPs Agreement was adopted and is open for acceptance by WTO Members. Few African countries have so far accepted the Protocol, primarily because of the contents of its Annexes. Most of them argue that the system is burdensome and complicated. The pace of acceptance has increased recently.

WHO has taken a number of initiatives that have facilitated access to medicines by developing countries. The final report, including its recommendations, of the Commission on Intellectual Property, Innovation and Public Health, introduced new ways of resolving the issues relating to the relationship between patents and public health. The adoption in 2008 of the Global Strategy and Plan of Action on Public Health, Innovation and Intellectual Property is another tool to implement objectives intended to assist developing countries and enhance their research capacities in the pharmaceutical field. The same dynamism of the African countries, via the African Group or the Regional Office for Africa, was seen here, where they made important proposals during the debates leading up to the adoption of the Global Strategy and Plan of Action.

In addition, on the initiative of the African Group, a draft resolution on Counterfeit Medical Products has been discussed in WHO since 2008. The fight against counterfeit medical products is among the priorities of the region, and the African countries support the mechanisms put into place to carry on this task.

The number of people infected with HIV/AIDS has declined dramatically since the height of the epidemic in 1997. Although the number of infected people is still high in sub-Saharan Africa, the drop in that number has been significant in the last five years.[1] Measures taken by WHO Member States to fight against HIV/AIDS have contributed to this success, and the collaboration among international organizations has facilitated the implementation of these measures in the field.

The Global Strategy and Plan of Action adopted by the WHO World Health Assembly in May 2008 helped to strengthen the tripartite collaboration between WHO, WIPO, and WTO.

The year 2011 may be considered the turning point. The African Group again called upon the Standing Committee on the Law of Patents to deal with the relationship between patents and health by proposing a work program which was welcomed by many Member States. The US proposal submitted in the Seventeenth Session of the SCP has also contributed to the debate on health issues.

The work program proposed by both the African Group (with the joint sponsorship of the Development Agenda Group) and the United States has requested that a number of studies be undertaken. If adopted, this work program will open another window for WIPO to closely examine the relevant issues.

In the arena of TK, TCEs and GRs, the contributions of the African Group may be considered milestone initiatives. At the WTO, the issue of protection of TK and folklore first came to light in the course of the review of TRIPs Article 27.3(b), as recommended by the TRIPs Agreement itself. It later became part of the new mandate of the Council for TRIPs provided under the Doha Ministerial

1 See, UNAIDS, *World AIDS Day Report*, 2011, p. 6.

Declaration, which instructed the Council to also discuss the relationship between the TRIPs Agreement and the CBD and the protection of TK and folklore.

The African Group's position paper of June 2003 may be considered a groundbreaking initiative which gained the support of many countries and also led to deeper examination of the issues. Another important proposal backed by the African Group and which is currently on the table is the proposal to amend the TRIPs Agreement to incorporate a new Article 29*bis* containing a requirement for disclosure of the country of origin of GRs and associated TK, along with appropriate sanctions for failure of compliance. In fact, the disclosure requirement is the key issue that has dominated the discussions. Despite support for the disclosure requirement by more than 100 countries, no consensus on the issue has been achieved so far. The Draft Modality Text also endorsed by the African Group is still on the table but appears to have little chance to succeed. Ultimately, the disclosure requirement is the key to successful handling of issues of biopiracy and misappropriation of TK and TCEs/EoF. The amendment of the TRIPs Agreement by the inclusion of the proposed Article 29*bis* may be the best way to go.

Within WIPO, the African Group has played a very important role in the IGC since its establishment in 2000, taking several initiatives that have changed the shape of debates pertaining to the protection of TK, TCEs, and GRs. Its breakthrough initiative relates to the first proposal on objectives and principles, which was adopted by the IGC as the first document giving a new direction to its work. Another important initiative concerned the IGC's mandate in 2009 in its proposal on the text-based negotiations on GRs, TK, and TCEs.

Ultimately, the African Group will feel satisfied with the results of these negotiations only if an international treaty is adopted in the fields of TK, TCEs, and GRs to prevent their widespread misappropriation. In addition, in the sphere of GRs, African countries yearn for a patent system which incorporates the requirement to disclose the country of origin of GRs or associated TK or TCEs in a patent application at the filing stage.

Although African countries are generally in favor of extensive use and broad definition of the public domain, they do not feel that this applies to TK. Up until recently, it was wrongly claimed by many that TK was part of the public domain and could be considered part of a common heritage that anyone could access freely and utilize without any return to the communities that were its holders. This perception of the nature of TK continues to be supported by certain groups. In reaction to this, it is quite natural to see African countries supporting the fight against expansion of the concept of 'public domain' to include TK. The multifaceted nature of both TK and the public domain makes their relationship very complex. Nowadays, it is widely understood that TK is owned by a particular traditional community and should be considered to be that community's creation, and that its public availability should not be interpreted to mean that it forms part of the public domain. TK is protectable subject matter.

On matters pertaining to limitations and exceptions to copyright, which are currently being discussed in WIPO's Standing Committee on Copyright and

Related Rights (SCCR), the African Group has submitted a Draft Text for a WIPO Treaty on Exceptions and Limitations for the Disabled, Educational and Research Institutions, Libraries and Archive Centers. Things are definitely moving in the right direction with the proposed draft text presented by the Chair of the SCCR on an International Instrument on Limitations and Exceptions for Visually Impaired Persons/Persons with Print Disabilities, which is supported and endorsed by all Member countries, including the African Group.[2] The Committee agreed to recommend that the WIPO General Assembly, convened in extraordinary session on December 17 and 18, 2012, evaluate the text of document SCCR/25/2 and decide whether to convene a diplomatic conference in 2013 to adopt a legal instrument/treaty on appropriate exceptions and limitations for persons with visual impairment and/or print disabilities, whose exact legal nature is still unknown. Another compiled text in this regard is that on an International Instrument on Limitations and Exceptions for Libraries and Archives, endorsed by Member States and known as the 'working document containing comments on and textual suggestions towards an appropriate international legal instrument (in whatever form) on exceptions and limitations for libraries and archives'. This document includes the African Proposal and constitutes the basis for the future text-based work on the matter. The SCCR hopes to complete a final text and submit recommendations to the WIPO General Assembly by the end of its Twenty-Eighth Session. On the exceptions and limitations to copyright for educational and research institutions and persons with other disabilities, the SCCR has agreed that the document containing comments and textual suggestions compiled by the WIPO Secretariat, called 'Provisional Working Document Towards a Appropriate International Legal Instrument (in whatever form) on Limitations and Exceptions for Educational, Teaching and Research Institutions and Persons with Other Disabilities', is to be restructured properly and will constitute the basis for the future text-based work, with the target to submit its recommendations to the WIPO General Assembly by the Thirtieth Session of the SCCR.

With regard to the *selected IP matters* addressed in this book, the African Group is opposed to IP protection for life forms. This has been very clearly displayed in the text of the AU's Model Law for the Protection of the Rights of Local Communities, Farmers and Breeders, and for the Regulation of Access to Biological Resources and in the African Group's paper presented to the Council for TRIPs on the amendment of TRIPs Article 29. In addition, most African patent laws exclude any variety of animal or plant or any essentially biological process for the production of animals or plants from patent protection. Concerning the research exemption/exception, African countries are in favor of its more extensive use to promote scientific research and experimentation. As for GMOs, many African countries are reluctant to authorize their widespread use. At this time, only five African countries have legislation on biosafety that authorizes the use of GMO crops and food. Despite the controversy over GMOs, it is undeniable that

2 The most recent text is the Revised Working Document.

their introduction into African countries aids in the fight against food shortages. At the same time, the safety of these GMOs should still remain on the agenda. Consequently, a balanced approach is required and governments need to make informed decisions based on a number of considerations that include the science of genetic technology, the potential benefits and the possible risks.

At the regional level, several initiatives have been taken by the AU, ARIPO, and OAPI. Under the AU, there have been three breakthrough initiatives: adoption of the African Model Law for the Protection of the Rights of Local Communities, Farmers and Breeders, and for the Regulation of Access to Biological Resources in 2000; adoption of the African Model Law on Biosafety; and the proposed establishment of a Pan-African Intellectual Property Organization (PAIPO). The Model Law has been implemented by a few African countries and has inspired a number of countries to adopt a hybrid system of protection as provided thereunder. More importantly, the Model Law enabled African countries to speak with one voice during the negotiations that led to the adoption of the Nagoya Protocol. The Ministerial Conference of Science and Technology adopted in mid-November 2012 in Brazzaville the Final Draft Statute establishing PAIPO. PAIPO will become operational once the final draft is approved by the Heads of States in the Assembly of AU Member States. Its role and relationship with the ARIPO and OAPI is yet to be further clarified.

All the African countries examined in this book, namely Botswana, Burundi, Egypt, Ghana, Kenya, Mauritius, Morocco, South Africa, and Tunisia have modern IP laws that are in full compliance with international standards. The remaining issue, however, is how to use IP as a tool for development in these countries and elsewhere.

Finally, the dynamism of the African Group at the international level must be echoed at the national level if any fundamental change is to be expected. Africa is no longer an observer but a dynamic actor on the international scene. African countries must 'Africanize' IP to take advantage of their huge intangible and tangible assets that the rest of the world is jealously contemplating. The best way to do so would be for the African countries to adopt a comprehensive, coherent, and consistent regional policy on IP in which the interdisciplinary dimensions of IP are stressed.

The world has changed and Africa is changing along with it by being an active player on the international stage, especially in regard to international IP issues.

Bibliography

Books, Journal Articles, and Chapters in Books

Bramley, C., Biénabe, E and Kirsten, J (2007), 'The Economics of Geographical Indications: Towards a Conceptual Framework for Geographical Indication Research in Developing Countries', Contributed Paper for the International Roundtable on the Economics of Intellectual Property Rights, WIPO, Geneva, November 26–27.

Kongolo, T. (1999), 'Does the Congo's Copyright and Neighboring Rights Law Conflict with the TRIPs Agreement?', *The Journal of World Intellectual Property* 2:2, 311–327.

Kongolo, T. (1999b), 'Trademarks and Geographical Indications within the Frameworks of the African Intellectual Property Organization Agreement and the TRIPs Agreement', *Journal of World Intellectual Property* 2:5, 833–844.

Kongolo, T. (1999c), 'The African Patent Systems and TRIPs', *Patent World* 117, 17–20.

Kongolo, T. (2000), 'The New OAPI Agreement As Revised in February 1999', *The Journal of World Intellectual Property* 3:5, 717–735.

Kongolo, T. (2000b), 'The African Intellectual Property Organizations—The Necessity of Adopting One Uniform System for All Africa', *The Journal of World Intellectual Property* 3:2, 265–288.

Kongolo, T. (2001), 'Public Interest *versus* the Pharmaceutical Industry's Monopoly in South Africa', *The Journal of World Intellectual Property* 4:5, 609–627.

Kongolo, T. (2001b), 'Towards a More Balanced Coexistence of Traditional Knowledge and Pharmaceuticals Protection in Africa', *Journal of World Trade* 35:2, 349–361.

Kongolo, T. (2002), 'Are Well-Known Marks Well Known in African Countries?', *Journal of World Intellectual Property* 5:2, 273–289.

Kongolo, T. (2002b), 'Biodiversity and African Countries', *European Intellectual Property Review (EIPR)* 24:12, 579–584.

Kongolo, T. (2002c), 'Morocco's Patent System and Its International Connection', *IDEA: The Journal of Law and Technology* 42:1, 181–204.

Kongolo, T. (2002d), 'Towards a New Fashion of Protecting Pharmaceutical Patents in Africa', *International Industrial Property Review and Copyright Law (IIC)* 33, 185–211.

Kongolo, T. (2002e), 'WTO DOHA Ministerial Declaration and Intellectual Property: African Perspectives', *African Yearbook of International Law* 9, 185–211.

Kongolo, T. (2003), 'Computer Programs Protection in Africa', *International Journal of Technology Transfer and Commercialisation* 2:2, 139–149.

Kongolo, T. (2003b), 'TRIPS, The Doha Declaration and Public Health', *The Journal of World Intellectual Property* 6:2, 373–378.

Kongolo, T. (2004), 'Compulsory Licence Issues in African Arab Countries', *The Journal of World Intellectual Property* 7:2, 185–199.

Kongolo, T. (2004b), 'Panorama of the Most Controversial IP Issues in Developing Countries', *European Intellectual Property Review (EIPR)* 26:6, 258–262.

Kongolo, T. (2006), 'Intellectual Property and Public Health—Unpleasant Marriage?', *The Geneva Post Quarterly: The Journal of World Affairs* 1:1, 185–208.

Kongolo, T. (2006b), 'The International Intellectual Property System(s) and African Countries: Issues, Challenges and New Expectations', *African Yearbook of International Law* 12:2, 191–205.

Kongolo, T. (2008), *Unsettled International Intellectual Property Issues* (New York/The Hague: Kluwer Law International).

Kongolo, T. (2011), 'Any New Developments with Regard to the GI Issues Debated under WTO?', *European Intellectual Property Review (EIPR)* 33:2, 83–90.

Kongolo, T. (2011b), 'IP and Misappropriation of the Public Domain', *European Intellectual Property Review* 33:12, 780–794.

Kongolo, T. (2012), 'Towards an International Legal Instrument on Exceptions and Limitations for Visually Impaired Persons/Persons with Print Disabilities', *European Intellectual Property Review* 34:12, 823–833.

Mugabe, J. (2003) 'Biotechnology and Sustainable Development in Africa, Towards Regional Consensus and Common Strategy', Paper Prepared for the 1st Meeting of the African Ministerial Conference on Science and Technology, November 2003, Johannesburg, South Africa NEPAD; available at: http://www.nepadst.org/doclibrary/pdfs/doc08_112003b.pdf (last accessed on November 20, 2012).

Tsiko, S. (2011), 'Africa Still Debating GMOs' Pros and Cons', *The Herald* (Zimbabwe), April 25, 2011; available at: http://allafrica.com/stories/201104260172.html (last accessed on February 18, 2012).

WHO, *Public Health, Innovation and Intellectual Property: Report of the Commission on Intellectual Property Rights, Innovation and Public Health*, WHO, Geneva, 2006.

Treaties, Conventions, Laws, and Associated Documents

African Model Law for the Protection of the Rights of Local Communities, Farmers and Breeders, and for the Regulation of Access to Biological Resources; available at: http://www.flag-sa.org/downdocs/oaulocalfarmersrights-booklet.pdf (last accessed on November 20, 2012).

The Agreement on the Creation of the ARIPO, adopted on December 9, 1976, amended by the Administrative Council of ARIPO on December 10, 1982, December 12, 1986, and November 27, 1996 and by the Council of Ministers on August 13, 2004.

The Banjul Protocol on Marks, as amended by the Administrative Council on November 28, 1997, May 26, 1998, and November 26, 1999 and by the Council of Ministers on August 13, 2004.

Egypt, Ministry of Agriculture and Land Reclamation, Agricultural Research Center, Agricultural Genetic Engineering Research Institute (Ageri), Biosafety Regulations and Guidelines, January 1994.

International Convention for the Protection of Performers, Producers of Phonograms and Broadcasting Organizations, done at Rome, October 26, 1961; available at: http://www.wipo.int/treaties/en/ip/rome/trtdocs_wo024.html (last accessed on December 7, 2011).

Joint Recommendation Concerning Provisions on the Protection of Marks, and Other Industrial Property Rights in Signs, on the Internet, Adopted by the Assembly of the Paris Union for the Protection of Industrial Property and the General Assembly of the World Intellectual Property Organization (WIPO) at the Thirty-Sixth Series of Meetings of the Assemblies of the Member States of WIPO, September 24 to October 3, 2001; available at: http://www.wipo.int/about-ip/en/development_iplaw/pub845.htm (last accessed on February 15, 2012).

Joint Recommendation Concerning Provisions on the Protection of Well-Known Marks, adopted by the Assembly of the Paris Union for the Protection of Industrial Property and the General Assembly of the World Intellectual Property Organization (WIPO) at the Thirty-Fourth Series of Meetings of the Assemblies of the Member States of WIPO, September 20 to 29, 1999, WIPO, Geneva, 2000; available at: http://www.wipo.int/about-ip/en/development_iplaw/pdf/pub833.pdf (last accessed on December 3, 2011).

Kenya, National Policy on Traditional Knowledge, Genetic Resources and Traditional Cultural Expressions, 2009, available at: http://www.wipo.int/wipolex/en/details.jsp?id=11300 (last accessed on November 27, 2012).

Lisbon Agreement for the Protection of Appellations of Origin and their International Registration, done October 31, 1958, as revised at Stockholm on July 14, 1967, and as amended on September 28, 1979 (Lisbon Agreement), Article 2; available at: http://www.wipo.int/lisbon/en/legal_texts/lisbon_agreement.html#P22_1099 (last accessed on December 6, 2011).

Mauritius, GMOs Act, 2004, *Government Gazette of Mauritius*, No. 40, April 30, 2004.

Paris Convention for the Protection of Industrial Property, of March 20, 1883, as revised at Brussels on December 14, 1900, at Washington on June 2, 1911, at The Hague on November 6, 1925, at London on June 2, 1934, at Lisbon on October 31, 1958, and at Stockholm on July 14, 1967, and as amended on September 28, 1979; available at: http://www.wipo.int/treaties/en/ip/paris/trtdocs_wo020.html (last accessed on November 20, 2012).

The Protocol on Patents and Industrial Designs, as amended by the Administrative Council of the ARIPO on December 11, 1987, April 27, 1994, November 28, 1997, May 26, 1998, November 26, 1999, November 30, 2001, November 21, 2003, and November 24, 2006.

Regulations for Implementing the Banjul Protocol, adopted by the Administrative Council of the ARIPO at Kariba, Zimbabwe on November 24, 1995 and amended by the Council on November 28, 1997, May 26, 1998, and November 26, 1999 and as amended by the Council of Ministers on August 13, 2004.

Regulations for Implementing the Protocol on Patents and Industrial Designs within the Framework of the ARIPO, entered into force April 25, 1984, and amended by the Administrative Council of the ARIPO on April 27, 1994, November 27, 1998, November 24, 2000, November 21, 2003, and November 24, 2006.

South African GMO Act, Act No. 15 of 1997, *UPOV Gazette*, No. 93, June 2002; as revised by the GMO Amendment of 2006 and promulgated by the President on April 11, 2007, *Government Gazette*, April 17, 2007.

Official Documents

'Access to Medicines for HIV/AIDS and other Pandemics', Proposal from a group of developed countries, WTO Doc. IP/C/W/313, October 4, 2001.

African Group Proposal on the Protection of Traditional Knowledge, Traditional Cultural Expressions and Genetic Resources, document submitted by the African Group to the Intergovernmental Committee on Intellectual Property and Genetic Resources, Traditional Knowledge and Folklore, Thirteenth Session, Geneva, October 13–17, 2008, WIPO Doc. WIPO/GRTKF/IC/13/9.

African Group Submission on Document WIPO/GRTKF/IC/13/9, document prepared by the WIPO Secretariat for the Intergovernmental Committee on Intellectual Property and Genetic Resources, Traditional Knowledge and Folklore, Fourteenth Session, Geneva, June 29 to July 3, 2009, WIPO Doc. WIPO/GRTKF/IC/14/9.

African Union, Fifth Ordinary Session of the African Ministerial Conference on Science and Technology (Amcost V), November 12 to 15, 2012, Brazzaville, Congo, Final Draft Statute of the Pan-African Intellectual Property Organization (PAIPO), AU/STRC/522, November 2012.

Article 27.3(b), Relationship between the TRIPS Agreement and the CBD, and the Protection of Traditional Knowledge and Folklore, Joint Communication from the African Group, WTO Doc. IP/C/W/404.

Article 27.3(b), Relationship between the TRIPS Agreement and the CBD, and the Protection of Traditional Knowledge and Folklore, Communication from

Switzerland, WTO Docs. IP/C/W/433, IP/C/W/423, IP/C/W/400/Rev.1, IP/C/M/49.

Article 27.3(b), Relationship between the TRIPS Agreement and the CBD, and the Protection of Traditional Knowledge and Folklore, Communication from the United States, WTO Docs. IP/C/W/257, April 2, 2001, and IP/C/W/434, November 26, 2004.

Assembly of the African Union, Eighth Ordinary Session, January 29–30, 2007, Addis Ababa, Ethiopia, 'Decisions and Declarations', African Union Doc. No. Assembly/AU/Dec. 134–164 (VII) and Assembly/AU/Decl.1–61 (VIII), Decision 138 (VII).

The Case for a Treaty on Exceptions and Limitations for Libraries and Archives: Background Paper by IFLA, ICA, EIFL and INNOVARTE, document presented by Brazil, Twenty-Third Session of the WIPO Standing Committee on Copyright and Related Rights (SCCR), Geneva, November 21–25, 28, and 29 and December 2, 2011, WIPO Doc. SCCR 23/3, November 18, 2011.

Communication from Kenya on Behalf of the African Group, WTO Doc. WT/GC/W/302, August 6, 1999.

Review of the Provisions of Article 27.3(b) – Communication from Kenya on Behalf of the African Group, WTO Doc. IP/C/W/163, November 8, 1999.

Communication from the European Communities and their Member States, WTO Doc. IP/C/W/280, June 12, 2001.

Consensus Document on an International Instrument on Limitations and Exceptions for Persons with Print Disabilities, Presented by Argentina, Australia, Brazil, Chile, Ecuador, Mexico, Paraguay, and the United States of America, Twenty-Second Session of the WIPO Standing Committee on Copyright and Related Rights (SCCR), June 15–24, 2011, WIPO Doc. SCCR/22/15.

Conclusions of the Twenty-First Session of the SCCR, Geneva, November 8–12, 2010.

Conclusions of the Twenty-Third Session of the WIPO Standing Committee on Copyright and Related Rights (SCCR), Geneva, November 21–25, 28, and 29 and December 2, 2011.

Conference of African Union Ministers of Agriculture, Libreville, Gabon, November 27–December 1, 2006, 'An African Position on Genetically Modified Organisms in Agriculture'; available at http://www.africa-union.org/root/au/AUC/Departments/HRST/biosafety/DOC/African Position on GMOs.pdf (last accessed on November 20, 2012).

Decision of the WTO General Council of August 30, 2003, WTO Doc. WT/L/540.

Decision of the WTO General Council of November 30, 2011, WTO Doc. WT/L/829, December 5, 2011.

Declaration on the TRIPS Agreement and Public Health, adopted on November 14, 2001, WTO Doc. WT/MIN(01)/DEC/2, November 20, 2001.

Doha Ministerial Declaration, adopted on November 14, 2001,WTO Doc. WT/MIN(01)/DEC/1, November 20, 2001.

Draft Articles and Thematic Clusters on Limitations and Exceptions to Copyright for the Benefit of Educational, Teaching and Research Institutions, document proposed by Brazil, at the Twenty-Fourth Session of the WIPO Standing Committee on Copyright and Related Rights, July 16–25, 2012, WIPO Doc. SCCR/24/7, July 16, 2012; available at: http://www.wipo.int/edocs/mdocs/copyright/en/sccr_24/sccr_24_7.pdf (last accessed on July 31, 2012).

Draft Articles on The Protection of Traditional Knowledge Prepared at IWG 2, document prepared by the WIPO Secretariat for the Second Intersessional Working Group of the Intergovernmental Committee on Intellectual Property and Genetic Resources, Traditional Knowledge and Folklore, Geneva, February 21–25, 2011, WIPO Doc. WIPO/GRTKF/IWG/2/3.

Draft Articles on The Protection of Traditional Knowledge Prepared at IWG 2, document prepared by the WIPO Secretariat for the Eighteenth Session of the Intergovernmental Committee on Intellectual Property and Genetic Resources, Traditional Knowledge and Folklore, Geneva, May 9–13, 2011, WIPO Doc. WIPO/GRTKF/IC/18/7.

Draft Consensus Instrument Proposal by the Delegation of the United States of America, Twentieth Session of the WIPO Standing Committee on Copyright and Related Rights (SCCR), Geneva, June 21–24, 2010, WIPO Doc. SCCR/20/10, June 10, 2010.

Draft Decision to Enhance Mutual Supportiveness between the TRIPS Agreement and the Convention on Biological Diversity, WTO Doc. TN/C/W/59, April 19, 2011.

Draft Joint Recommendation concerning the Improved Access to Works Protected by Copyright for Persons with a Print Disability, Proposal by the Delegation of the European Union, Geneva, Twenty-First Session of the WIPO Standing Committee on Copyright and Related Rights (SCCR), Geneva, June 21–24, 2010, WIPO Doc. SCCR/20/12, June 17, 2010.

Draft Ministerial Declaration on the TRIPs Agreement and Public Health, Proposal by the African Group [and Others], WTO Doc. IP/C/W/312, WT/GC/W/450, October 4, 2001.

Draft Regional Policy and Legal Framework for Plant Variety Protection, ARIPO Council of Ministers, Thirteenth Session, Accra, Ghana, December 1–2, 2011.

Draft Report of the Intergovernmental Committee on Intellectual Property and Genetic Resources, Traditional Knowledge and Folklore, Nineteenth Session, Geneva, July 18–22, 2011, WIPO Doc. WIPO/GRTKF/IC/19/12/Prov. 2.

Draft Report of the Intergovernmental Committee on Intellectual Property and Genetic Resources, Traditional Knowledge and Folklore, Twenty-Second Session, Geneva, July 9–13, 2012, WIPO Doc. WIPO/GRTKF/IC/22/6/Prov. 2 of November 5, 2012.

Draft WIPO Treaty on Exceptions and Limitations for the Disabled, Educational and Research Institutions, Libraries and Archive Centers, Twentieth Session of the WIPO Standing Committee on Copyright and Related Rights (SCCR), June 21–24, 2010, WIPO Doc. SCCR/20/11, June 15, 2010.

Draft WIPO Treaty on Exceptions and Limitations for the Disabled, Educational and Research Institutions, Libraries and Archive Centers, Twenty-Second Session of the WIPO Standing Committee on Copyright and Related Rights (SCCR), June 15–24, 2011, WIPO Doc. SCCR/22/12.

Exclusions from Patentable Subject Matter and Exceptions and Limitations to the Rights, document prepared by the Secretariat for the Thirteenth Session of the WIPO Standing Committee on the Law of Patents (SCP), Geneva, March 23–27, 2009, WIPO Doc. SCP/13/3, February 4, 2009.

Extraordinary Conference of the African Ministers of Council on Science and Technology (AMCOST), November 20–24, 2006, Cairo, Egypt, 'Establishing a Pan-African Intellectual Property Organization (PAIPO)—A Concept Paper', African Union Doc. No. EXT/AU/EXP/ST/8(II).

Extraordinary Conference of the African Ministers of Council on Science and Technology (AMCOST), November 20–24, 2006, Cairo, Egypt, 'Report of the Meeting of Experts', African Union Doc. No. EXT/AU/EXP/ST/Rpt.(II).

A Gap Analysis Report on The African Model Law on the Protection of the Rights of Local Communities, Farmers and Breeders, and for the Regulation of Access to Biological Resources, Commissioned by the Department of Human Resources, Science and Technology of the African Union Commission, February 2012.

Limitations and Exceptions regarding Education, document proposed by the Delegations of Ecuador, Peru and Uruguay at the Twenty-Fourth Session of the WIPO Standing Committee on Copyright and Related Rights, July 16–25, 2012, WIPO Doc. SCCR/24/6, July 16, 2012.

Matters Concerning Intellectual Property and Genetic Resources, Traditional Knowledge and Folklore, WIPO Doc. WO/GA/26/6, August 25, 2000.

Matters Concerning the Intergovernmental Committee on Intellectual Property and Genetic Resources, Traditional Knowledge and Folklore, Agenda Item 28, Decision of the WIPO General Assembly, Thirty-Eighth (Nineteenth Ordinary) Session, September 22 to October 1, 2009, WIPO Doc. WIPO/GRTKF/IC/15/REF-DECISION 28.

Matters Concerning the Intergovernmental Committee on Intellectual Property and Genetic Resources, Traditional Knowledge and Folklore (IGC), document prepared by the WIPO Secretariat for the WIPO General Assembly, Fortieth (Twentieth Ordinary) Session, Geneva, September 26 to October 5, 2011, WIPO Doc. WO/GA/40/7.

Matters Concerning the Intergovernmental Committee on Intellectual Property and Genetic Resources, Traditional Knowledge and Folklore (IGC), WIPO General Assembly, Decision, Forty-First (Twenty-First Extraordinary) Session, Geneva, October 1-9, 2012.

Ministerial Decisions of the Fourth Ordinary Session of the African Ministerial Conference on Science and Technology (AMCOST IV), March 10, 2010, Cairo, Egypt, African Union Doc. No. AU/MIN/ST/DEC (IV).

Objectives and Principles for Exceptions and Limitations for Libraries and Archives, document presented by the United States of America, Twenty-Third

Session of the WIPO Standing Committee on Copyright and Related Rights (SCCR), Geneva, November 21–25, 28, and 29 and December 2, 2011, WIPO Doc. SCCR/23/4, November 22, 2011.

The Position of the African Group, paper presented by the African Group to the Intergovernmental Committee on Intellectual Property and Genetic Resources, Traditional Knowledge and Folklore, Third Session, Geneva, June 13–21, 2002, WIPO Doc. WIPO/GRTKF/IC/3/15.

Proposal by Brazil, Chile, Nicaragua and Uruguay for Work Related to Exceptions and Limitations, Sixteenth Session of the WIPO Standing Committee on Copyright and Related Rights (SCCR), Geneva, March 10–12, 2008, WIPO Doc. SCCR/16/2, July 17, 2008.

Proposal by Brazil, Ecuador and Paraguay, relating to Limitations and Exceptions, Treaty proposed by the World Blind Union (WBU), Eighteenth Session of the WIPO Standing Committee on Copyright and Related Rights (SCCR), Geneva, May 25–29, 2009, WIPO Doc. SCCR/18/5, May 25, 2009.

Proposal by Chile on the Analysis of Exceptions and Limitations, Thirteenth Session of the WIPO Standing Committee on Copyright and Related Rights (SCCR), Geneva, November 21–23, 2005, SCCR/13/5, November 22, 2005.

Proposal by Chile on the Subject 'Exceptions and Limitations to Copyright and Related Rights', Twelfth Session of the WIPO Standing Committee on Copyright and Related Rights (SCCR), Geneva, November 17–19, 2004, document prepared by the Secretariat, SCCR/12/3, November 4, 2004.

Proposal of the African Group on Genetic Resources and Future Work, document prepared by the WIPO Secretariat for the Intergovernmental Committee on Intellectual Property and Genetic Resources, Traditional Knowledge and Folklore, Seventeenth Session, Geneva, December 6–10, 2010, WIPO Doc. WIPO/GRTKF/IC/17/10.

Proposal of the African Group on the Mandate of the Intergovernmental Committee, document prepared by the WIPO Secretariat for the Intergovernmental Committee on Intellectual Property and Genetic Resources, Traditional Knowledge and Folklore, Fourteenth Session, Geneva, June 29 to July 3, 2009, WIPO Doc. WIPO/GRTKF/IC/14/8 Rev.

Proposal on an International Instrument on Limitations and Exceptions for Persons with Print Disabilities, document prepared by the Chair, Twenty-Second Session of the WIPO Standing Committee on Copyright and Related Rights (SCCR), June 15–24 2011, WIPO Doc. SCCR/22/16, November 4, 2011.

Proposal on Limitations and Exceptions for Libraries and Archives, Document Presented by Brazil, Ecuador and Uruguay, Twenty-Third Session of the WIPO Standing Committee on Copyright and Related Rights (SCCR), Geneva, November 21–25, 28, and 29 and December 2, 2011, WIPO Doc. SCCR/23/5, November 22, 2011.

The Protection of Traditional Cultural Expressions/Expressions of Folklore: Overview of Policy Objectives and Core Principles, document prepared by the WIPO Secretariat for the Intergovernmental Committee on Intellectual Property and Genetic Resources, Traditional Knowledge and Folklore, Seventh Session, Geneva, November 1–5, 2004, WIPO Doc. WIPO/GRTKF/IC/7/3.

The Protection of Traditional Cultural Expressions/Expressions of Folklore: Revised Objectives and Principles, document prepared by the WIPO Secretariat for the Intergovernmental Committee on Intellectual Property and Genetic Resources, Traditional Knowledge and Folklore, Seventeenth Session, Geneva, December 6–10, 2010, WIPO Doc. WIPO/GRTKF/IC/17/4 Prov.

Protection of Traditional Knowledge: Overview of Policy Objectives and Core Principles, document prepared by the WIPO Secretariat for the Intergovernmental Committee on Intellectual Property and Genetic Resources, Traditional Knowledge and Folklore, Seventh Session, Geneva, November 1–5, 2004, WIPO Doc. WIPO/GRTKF/IC/7/5.

The Protection of Traditional Knowledge: Revised Objectives and Principles, document prepared by the WIPO Secretariat for WIPO/GRTKF/IC/16/5 Prov.

Provisional Working Document Containing Comments on and Textual Suggestions Towards an Appropriate International Legal Instrument (in whatever form) on Limitations and Exceptions for Educational, Teaching and Research Institutions and Persons with other Disabilities, produced by the WIPO Secretariat (Working document (Rev. 5)), July 25, 2012.

Provisional Working Document Containing Comments on and Textual Suggestions Towards an Appropriate International Legal Instrument (in whatever form) on Exceptions and Limitations for Libraries and Archives, document prepared by the Secretariat, Twenty-Third Session of the WIPO Standing Committee on Copyright and Related Rights (SCCR), Geneva, November 21–25, 28, and 29 and December 2, 2011, WIPO Doc. SCCR 23/8, May 25, 2012; available at: http://www.wipo.int/edocs/mdocs/mdocs/en/sccr_23/sccr_23_8_prov.pdf (last accessed on July 31, 2012).

Recent Intellectual Property Developments in the Africa Region and Proposals for the Harmonization of ARIPO and OAPI Systems, ARIPO Council of Ministers, Thirteenth Session, Accra, Ghana, December 1–2, 2011, ARIPO Doc. No. ARIPO/AC/XIII/13, October 31, 2011.

Report adopted by the WIPO Standing Committee on the Law of Patents (SCCR), WIPO Doc. SCCR 22/18, December 9, 2011.

Report from His Excellency Ambassador Philip Richard Owade on Key Issues Pending from the 2010–2011 Biennium, WIPO Docs. WIPO/GRTKF/IC/20/INF/4, WIPO/GRTKF/IC/21/INF/4, WIPO/GRTKF/IC/22/INF/4.

Report of the Intergovernmental Committee on Intellectual Property and Genetic Resources, Traditional Knowledge and Folklore, First Session, Geneva, April 30 to May 3, 2001, WIPO Doc. WIPO/GRTKF/IC/1/13.

Report of the Intergovernmental Committee on Intellectual Property and Genetic Resources, Traditional Knowledge and Folklore, Fifth Session, Geneva, July 7–15, 2003, WIPO Doc. WIPO/GRTKF/IC/5/15.

Report of the Intergovernmental Committee on Intellectual Property and Genetic Resources, Traditional Knowledge and Folklore, Sixth Session, Geneva, March 15–19, 2004, WIPO Doc. WIPO/GRTKF/IC/6/14.

Report of the Meeting of the Group of Technical and Legal Experts on Traditional Knowledge Associated with Genetic Resources in the Context of the International Regime on Access and Benefit-Sharing, Hyderabad, India, June 16–19, 2009, UNEP Doc. UNEP/CBD/WG-ABS/8/2, p. 21; available at: http://www.abs-alliance.org/version02/files/ABS%20WG-8/abswg-08-02-en.pdf (last accessed on November 20, 2012).

Report of the Regional Consultation on Public Health, Innovation and Intellectual Property, WHO Regional Office for Africa, September 3–5, 2007, Brazzaville, Congo.

Report of the Situation of Counterfeit Medicines based on Data Collection Tool, WHO Regions for Africa and Eastern Mediterranean, 2010, WHO Doc. WHO/ACM/3.

Report of the WIPO General Assembly, Twenty-Sixth (Twelfth Extraordinary) Session, Geneva, September 25 to October 3, 2000, WIPO Doc. WO/GA/26/10.

Report of the WIPO General Assembly, Thirtieth (Sixteenth Ordinary) Session, Geneva, September 22 to October 1, 2003, WIPO Doc. WO/GA/30/8.

Report of the WIPO General Assembly, Fortieth (Twentieth Ordinary) Session, Geneva, September 26 to October 5, 2011, WIPO Doc. WO/GA/40/19.

Report on the Work of the Standing Committee on Copyright and Related Rights, July 26, 2011, Fortieth (Twentieth Ordinary) Session, Geneva, September 26 to October 5, 2011, WIPO Doc. WO/GA/40/6.

Report on the Work of the Standing Committee on Copyright and Related Rights, August 13, 2012, Forty-First (Twenty-First Extraordinary) Session, Geneva, October 1 to 9, 2012, WIPO Doc. WO/GA/41/17.

Reproduction of Document WIPO/GRTKF/IC/9/5 'The Protection of Traditional Knowledge: Revised Objectives and Principles', document prepared by the WIPO Secretariat for the Intergovernmental Committee on Intellectual Property and Genetic Resources, Traditional Knowledge and Folklore, Eleventh Session, Geneva, July 3–12, 2007, WIPO Doc. WIPO/GRTKF/IC/11/5(c).

Revised Working Document on an International Instrument on Limitations and Exceptions for Visually Impaired Persons/Persons with Print Disabilities, Twenty-Fourth Session of the WIPO Standing Committee on Copyright and Related Rights (SCCR), adopted by the Committee, WIPO Doc. SCCR/24/9, October 19, 2012.

Submission by The African Group: Objectives, Principles and Elements of an International Instrument, or Instruments, on Intellectual Property in Relation to Genetic Resources and on the Protection of Traditional Knowledge and Folklore, document submitted by the African Group to the Intergovernmental Committee on Intellectual Property and Genetic Resources, Traditional

Knowledge and Folklore, Sixth Session, Geneva, March 15–19, 2004, WIPO Doc. WIPO/GRTKF/IC/6/12.

Submission by the African Group and other Developing Countries, WTO Doc. IP/C/W/296, June 29, 2001.

Survey on Existing Forms of Intellectual Property Protection for Traditional Knowledge – Preliminary Analysis and Conclusions, document prepared by the WIPO Secretariat for the Intergovernmental Committee on Intellectual Property and Genetic Resources, Traditional Knowledge and Folklore, Second Session, Geneva, December 10–14, 2001, WIPO Doc. WIPO/GRTKF/IC/2/9.

'Taking Forward the Review of Article 27.3(b) of the TRIPs Agreement', WTO Doc. IP/C/W/404, June 26, 2003.

WHO, Executive Board, EB124/16, Public Health, Innovation and Intellectual Property: Global Strategy and Plan of Action, Report by the Secretariat, 124th Session, November 20, 2008.

WHO Resolution WHA59.24, 'Public Health, Innovation, Essential Health Research and Intellectual Property Rights: Towards a Global Strategy and Plan of Action', The Fifty-Ninth World Health Assembly, May 27, 2006.

WHO Resolution WHA61.21 on Global Strategy and Plan of Action on Public Health, Innovation and Intellectual Property, The Sixty-First World Health Assembly, Geneva, May 19–24, 2008.

WIPO, Report of the Standing Committee on the Law of Patents, Fifth Session, Geneva, May 14–19, 2001, WIPO Doc. SCP/5/6, para. 51.

WIPO, Standing Committee on the Law of Patents, Patents and Health: Comments Received from Members and Observers of the Standing Committee on the Law of Patents (SCP), Seventeenth Session, Geneva, December 5–9, 2011.

WIPO, Standing Committee on the Law of Patents, Patents and Health: Proposal by the Delegation of the United States of America, Seventeenth Session, Geneva, December 5–9, 2011.

WIPO, Standing Committee on the Law of Patents, Proposal Submitted by the Delegation of South Africa on behalf of the African Group and the Development Agenda Group, Sixteenth Session, Geneva, May 16–20, 2011.

WIPO, Standing Committee on the Law of Patents, WIPO Activities on Patents and Health, Seventeenth Session, Geneva, December 5–9, 2011.

WIPO Doc. WIPO/GRTKF/IC/11/4C.

Working Document on an International Instrument on Limitations and Exceptions for Visually Impaired Persons/Persons with Print Disabilities, WIPO Doc. SCCR/22/16, as revised.

Working Document on an International Instrument on Limitations and Exceptions for Visually Impaired Persons/Persons with Print Disabilities, Twenty-Third Session of the WIPO Standing Committee on Copyright and Related Rights (SCCR), adopted by the Committee, WIPO Doc. SCCR/23/7, December 16, 2011.

WTO, Council for TRIPs, Minutes of the Meeting of April 21–22, 1999, WTO Doc. IP/C/M/23, July 2, 1999.
WTO, Council for TRIPs, Minutes of the Meeting of October 20–21, 1999, WTO Doc. IP/C/M/25, December 22, 1999.
WTO, Council for TRIPs, Minutes of the Meeting of June 8–9, 2009, WTO Doc. IP/C/M/60, September 28, 2009.
WTO, Council for TRIPs, Review of the Provisions of Article 27.3(b) – Communication from Mauritius on Behalf of the African Group, WTO Doc. IP/C/W/206, September 20, 2000.
WTO Doc. IP/C/M/36, July 18, 2002,
WTO Doc. IP/C/M/37, October 11, 2002.
WTO Doc. IP/C/M/40.
WTO Doc. IP/C/W/339, March 4, 2002.
WTO Doc. IP/C/W/351, June 24, 2002.
WTO Doc. IP/C/W/352, June 20, 2002.
WTO Doc. IP/C/W/354, June 24, 2002.
WTO Doc. IP/C/W/355, June 24, 2002.
WTO Doc. IP/C/W/358, July 9, 2002.
WTO Doc. IP/C/W/363, July 11, 2002.
WTO Doc. IP/C/W/405, August 28, 2003.
WTO Doc. IP/C/W/437, December 10, 2004.
WTO Doc. IP/C/W/437/Rev.1, March 23, 2005.
WTO Doc. IP/C/W/440, March 1, 2005.
WTO Doc. TN/C/W/52, July 19, 2008.
WTO Doc. WT/1/641, December 8, 2005.
WTO Doc. WT/GC/M/82, November 13, 2003.
WTO Docs. WT/GC/W/564/Rev.2; TN/C/W/41/Rev.2; IP/C/W/474, July 5, 2006.
WTO Docs. WT/GC/W/566, TN/C/W/42, IP/C/W/473, June 14, 2006.

Legal Cases

Pharmaceutical Company Lawsuit against the Government of South Africa, Case number: 4183/98 of February 18, 1998, reprinted at: http://www.cptech.org/ip/health/sa/pharmasuit.html (last accessed on November 30, 2012).

Internet-Based Resources

'About WHO' on the WHO website at: http://www.who.int/about/en (last accessed on January 31, 2012).
'Concern Rises Over Proposed Pan-African IP Organisation', *IP Watch*, August 30, 2007, available at: http://www.ip-watch.org/weblog/2007/08/30/concern-

arises-over-proposed-pan-african-ip-organisation/ (last accessed on January 10, 2012).

British Library submission to the UKIPO on: 'Taking Forward The Gowers Review of Intellectual Property: Proposed Changes to Copyright Exceptions', available at: http://pressandpolicy.bl.uk/imagelibrary/downloadMedia.ashx?MediaDetailsID=130 (last accessed on February 21, 2012).

'The Global Strategy and Plan of Action on Public Health, Innovation and Intellectual Property' on the WHO website at: http://www.who.int/phi/implementation/phi_globstat_action/en/index.html (last accessed on January 31, 2012).

Monsanto website, http://www.monsanto.com, 'Products', 'Weed Control' (last accessed on November 20, 2012).

OAU, Heads of State and Government, African Summit on HIV/AIDS, Tuberculosis and Other Related Infectious Diseases, held at Abuja, Nigeria on April 26–27, 2001, 'The Abuja Declaration on HIV/AIDS, Tuberculosis and Other Related Infectious Diseases', available at: http://www.uneca.org/adf2000/Abuja%20Declaration.htm (last accessed on November 20, 2012).

'Public Health, Innovation and Intellectual Property' on the WHO website at: http://www.who.int/phi/about/en (last accessed on January 31, 2012).

UNAIDS, *World AIDS Day Report*, 2011, available at: http://www.unaids.org/en/media/unaids/contentassets/documents/unaidspublication/2011/JC2216_WorldAIDSday_report_2011_en.pdf (last accessed on January 31, 2012).

'WHO-WIPO-WTO Holding Technical Symposium on Access to Medicines in July 2010', available at: http://www.wto.org/english/news_e/news10_e/trip_21jun10_e.htm (last accessed on January 31, 2012).

'WHO, WIPO, WTO to Hold 2nd Technical Symposium on Patents, Access to Medicines', available at: http://www.wto.org/english/news_e/news11_e/trip_21jan11_e.htm (last accessed on January 31, 2012).

Index